TOKYO GHOUL :re

東京喰種

4

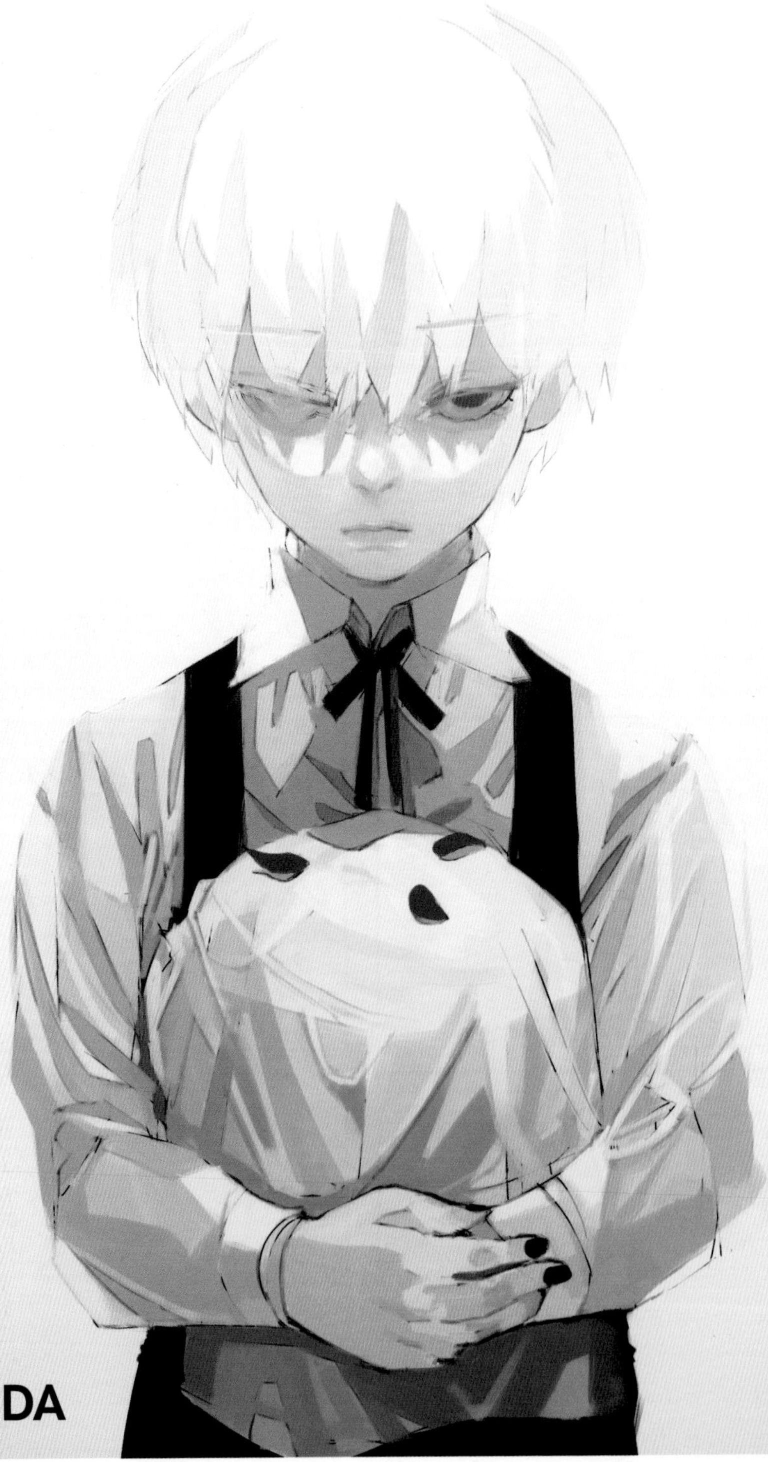

SUI ISHIDA

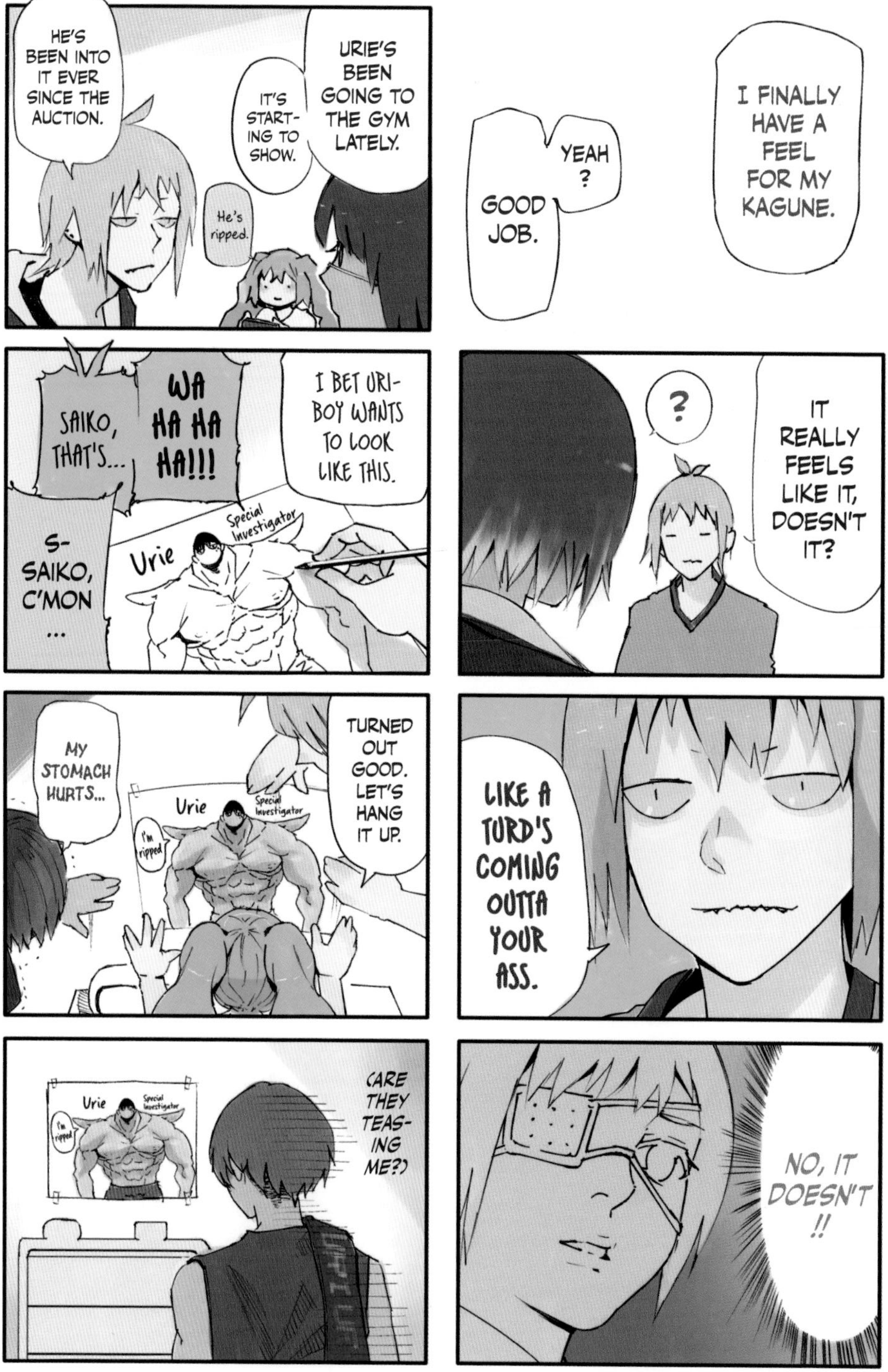
I FINALLY HAVE A FEEL FOR MY KAGUNE.
YEAH?
GOOD JOB.
URIE'S BEEN GOING TO THE GYM LATELY.
IT'S STARTING TO SHOW.
HE'S BEEN INTO IT EVER SINCE THE AUCTION.
He's ripped.
?
IT REALLY FEELS LIKE IT, DOESN'T IT?
I BET URI-BOY WANTS TO LOOK LIKE THIS.
WA HA HA HA!!!
SAIKO, THAT'S...
Special Investigator
Urie
S-SAIKO, C'MON...
LIKE A TURD'S COMING OUTTA YOUR ASS.
TURNED OUT GOOD. LET'S HANG IT UP.
Special Investigator
Urie
I'm ripped
MY STOMACH HURTS...
NO, IT DOESN'T!!
(ARE THEY TEASING ME?)
Urie
Special Investigator
I'm ripped

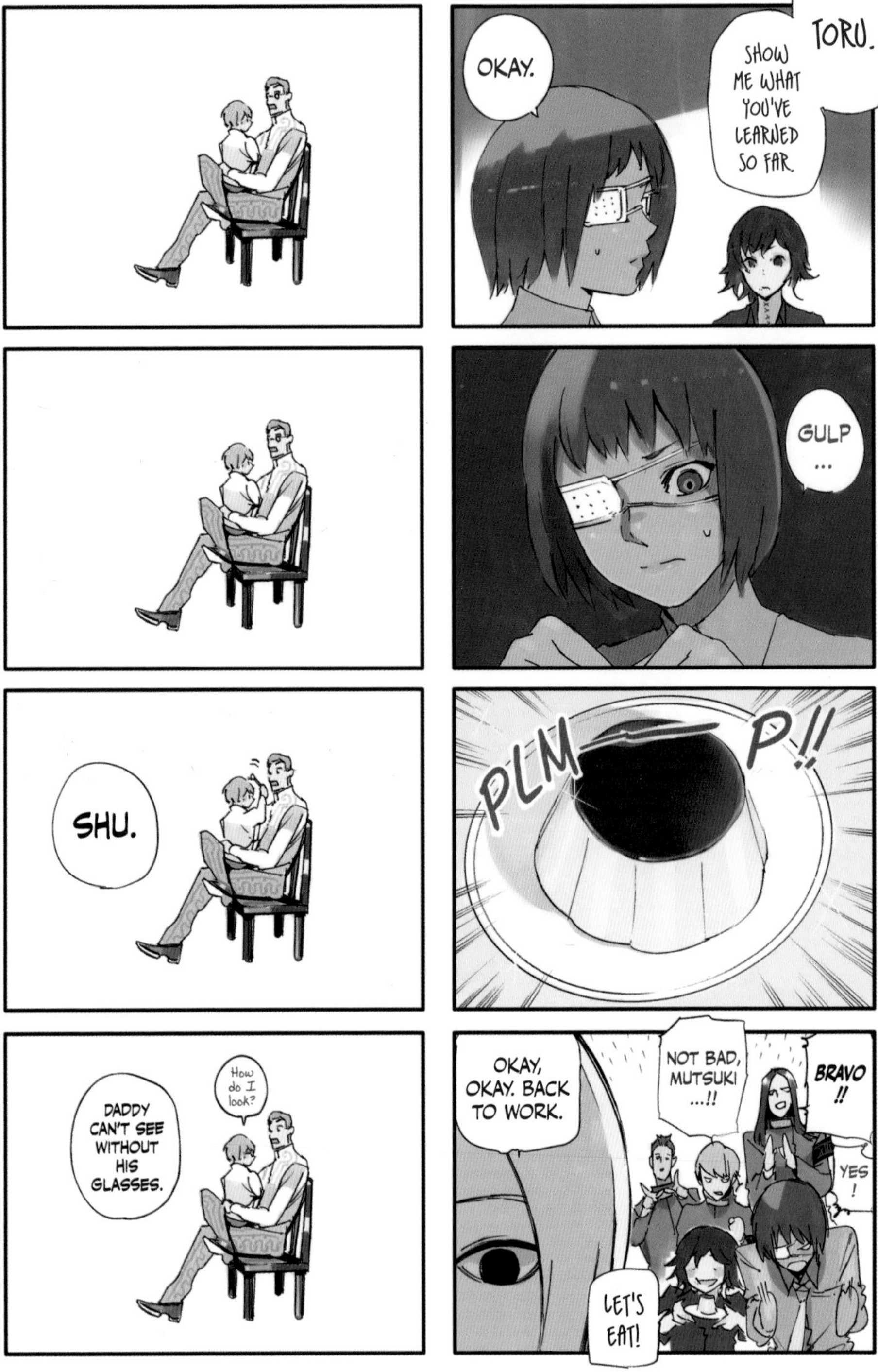
TORU.
SHOW ME WHAT YOU'VE LEARNED SO FAR.
OKAY.
GULP ...
PLM— P!!
SHU.
BRAVO !!
YES !
NOT BAD, MUTSUKI ...!!
OKAY, OKAY. BACK TO WORK.
LET'S EAT!
How do I look?
DADDY CAN'T SEE WITHOUT HIS GLASSES.

TOKYO GHOUL:re 4 C★O★N★T★E★N★T★S

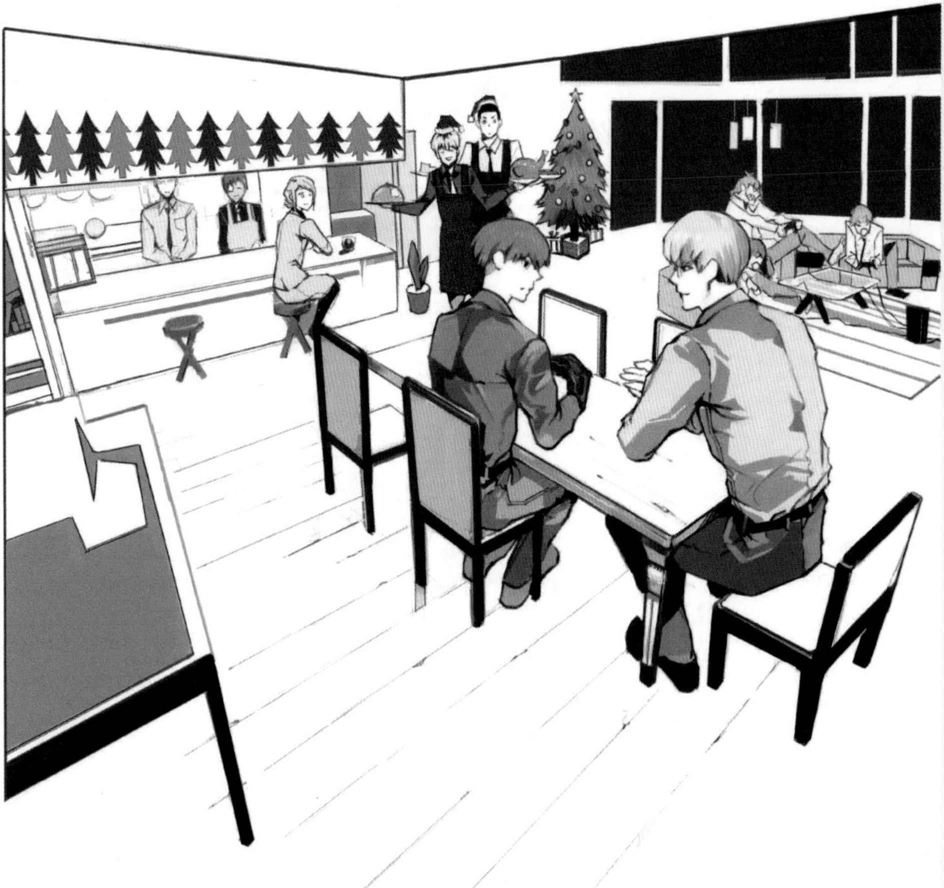

CCG Ghoul Investigators

Tokyo Ghoul :re

The CCG is the only organization in the world that investigates and solves Ghoul-related crimes. Founded by the Washu Family, the CCG developed and evolved Quinques, a type of weapon derived from Ghouls' Kagune. Quinx, an advanced, next-generation technology is currently under development, where humans are implanted with Quinque.

Mado Squad

Qs (Quinx)
- Investigators implanted with Quinque. They all live together
- in a house called the **Chateau** with Investigator Sasaki.

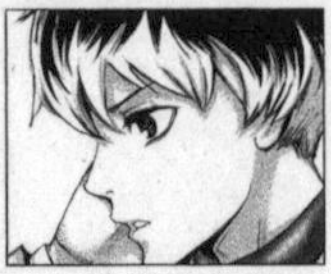

Haise Sasaki
佐々木琲世
Rank 1 Investigator
Mentor to the Quinx Squad. Despite being half-Ghoul, he is passionate about guiding the Quinxes. He has no memory of his past. And whose voice sometimes echoes in his head...?!

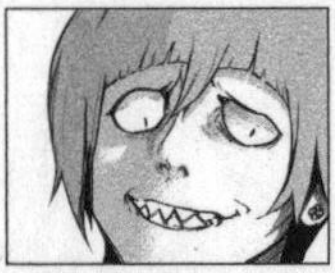

Ginshi Shirazu
不知吟士
Rank 3 Investigator
Current squad leader of the Quinx Squad. Agreed to the Quinx procedure for mainly financial reasons. Despite his thuggish appearance, he has a very caring side. Eradicated the Nutcracker, a Rate ≥S Ghoul.

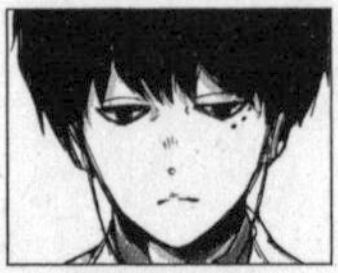

Kuki Urie
瓜江久生
Rank 2 Investigator
Former squad leader of the Quinx Squad. The most talented fighter in the squad. His father, a special investigator, was killed by a Ghoul. Urie seeks to avenge his death. On his own authority he recently underwent the Frame Release procedure, with unknown results.

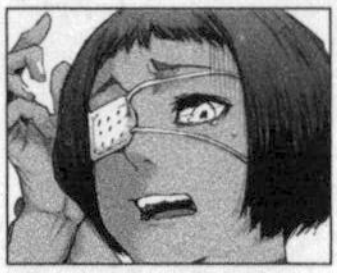

Toru Mutsuki
六月 透
Rank 3 Investigator
Both his parents were killed by a Ghoul and he decided to become a Ghoul investigator. Assigned female at birth, he decided to transition after undergoing the Quinx procedure. Skilled with knives.

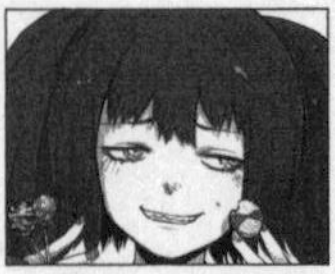

Saiko Yonebayashi
米林才子
Rank 3 Investigator
Little aptitude as an investigator, but was by far the most suitable candidate for the Quinx procedure. Very bad at time management. A sucker for games and snacks.

Hirako Squad

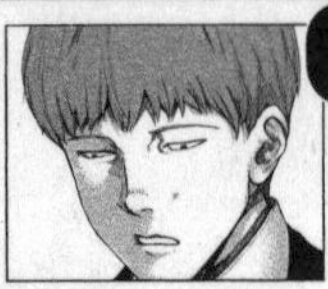

Take Hirako
平子 丈
Senior Investigator
In pursuit of the Orochi. A reticent investigator.

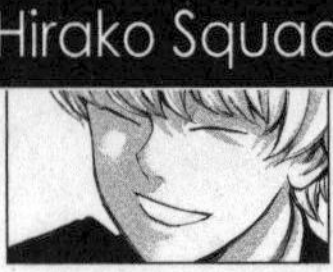

Kuramoto Ito
伊東倉元
Rank 1 Investigator
Member of the Hirako Squad. Has a cheerful disposition.

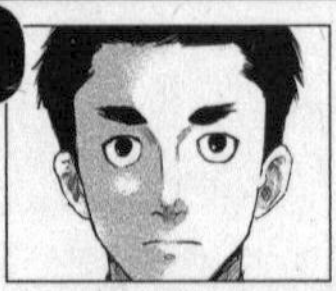

Takeomi Kuroiwa
黒磐武臣
Rank 1 Investigator
The son of Special Investigator Iwao Kuroiwa. Has a strong sense of justice and has restrained Ghouls with his bare hands.

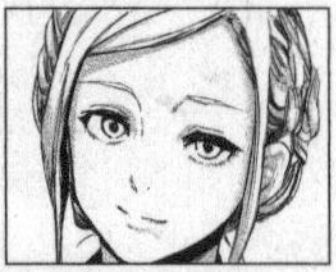

Akira Mado
真戸 暁
Senior Investigator
Mentors Haise. Takes after her father. Determined to eradicate Ghouls. Investigating the Aogiri Tree.

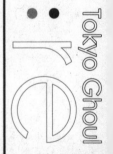

:re Tokyo Ghoul

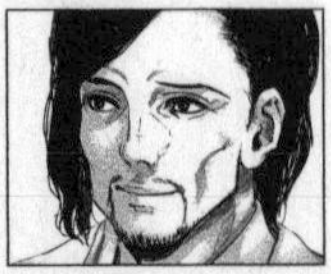

Yoshitoki Washu
和修吉時
CCG Bureau Chief
Supervisor of the Quinx Project. A member of the CCG's founding family, but he still has an approachable side.

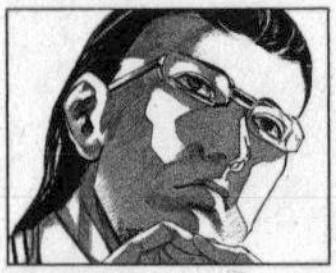

Matsuri Washu
和修 政
Assistant Special Investigator
Yoshitoki's son. A Washu supremacist. He is skeptical of Quinxes. Commanded the succesful Operation Auction Sweep.

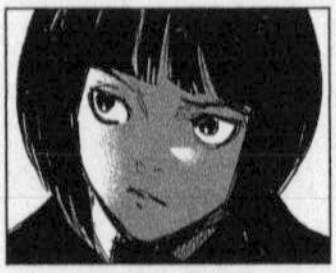

Kori Ui
宇井 郡
Special Investigator
Unknown

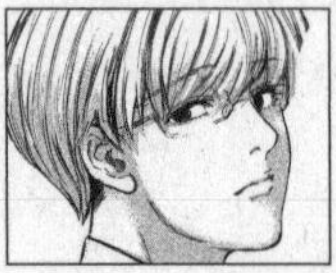

Kisho Arima
有馬貴将
Special Investigator
An undefeated investigator respected by many at the CCG.

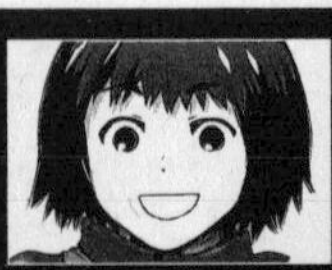

Chie Hori
掘 ちえ
A freelance photographer selling information. What's her connection to the Tsukiyama family...?

Tokyo Ghoul :re

● Ghouls

They appear human, but have a unique predation organ called Kagune and can only survive by feeding on human flesh. They are the nemesis of humanity. Besides human flesh, the only other thing they can ingest is coffee. Ghouls can only be wounded by Kagune or a Quinque made from a Kagune. One of the most prominent Ghoul factions is the Aogiri Tree, a hostile organization that is increasing its strength.

Rosewald Family Faction

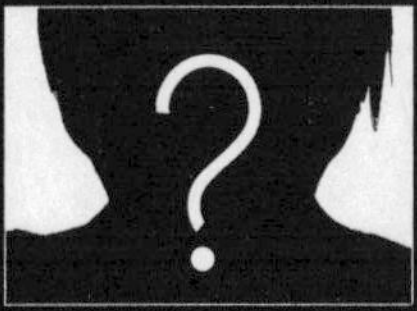
?

● Shu Tsukiyama
月山 習

Unknown

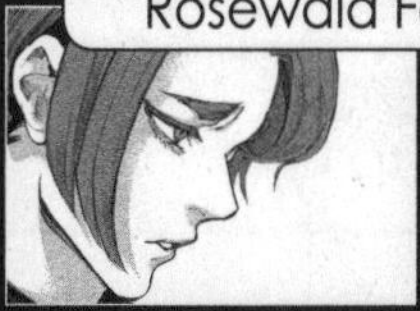

● Kanae von Rosewald
カナエ=フォン・ロゼヴァルト

Tsukiyama family retainer. Procures gourmet meals for Shu Tsukiyama.

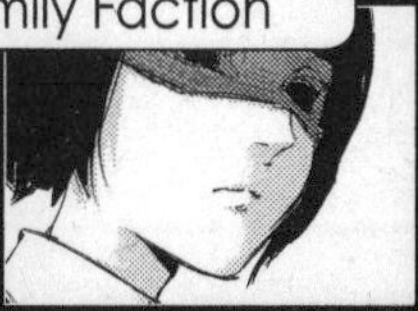

● Matsumae
松前

Tsukiyama family retainer. Wields a detachable Kagune.

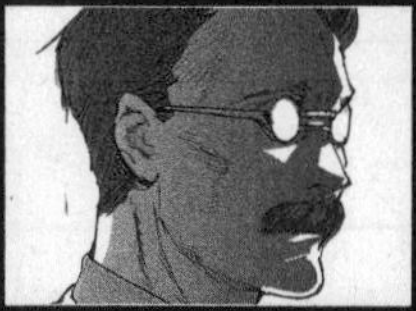

● Mirumo Tsukiyama
月山観母

Unknown

Aogiri Tree

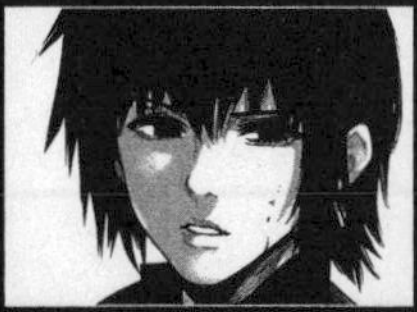

● Ayato
アヤト

A leading member of the Aogiri Tree. A Rate SS Ghoul known as the Rabbit.

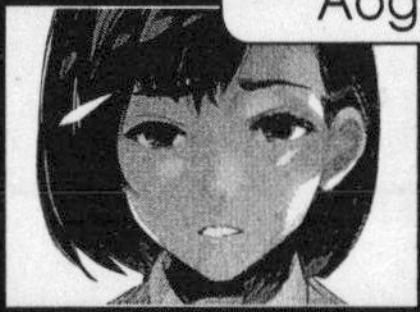

● Hinami Fueguchi
フエグチヒナミ

Member of the Aogiri Tree. Captured by Haise Sasaki during Operation Auction Sweep and sent to Cochlea.

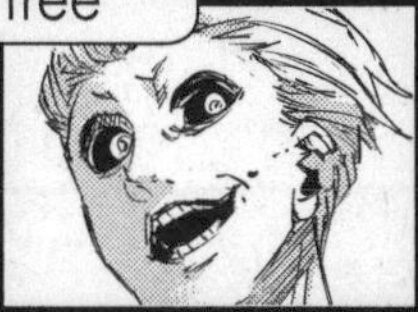

● Naki
ナキ

Member of the Aogiri Tree. Rate S. Frequently flips out of control.

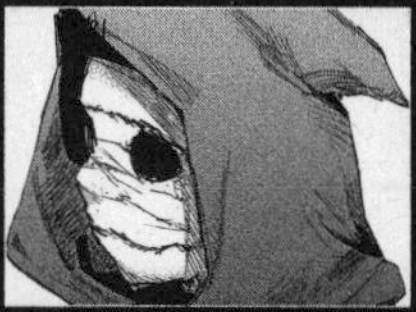

● Eto
エト

Member of the Aogiri Tree.

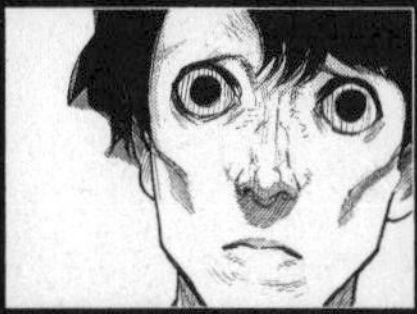

● The Torso (Karao Saeki)
トルソー(冴木空男)

Rate A Ghoul. Abused his position as a taxi driver to prey on women with scars. Obsessed with Toru Mutsuki.

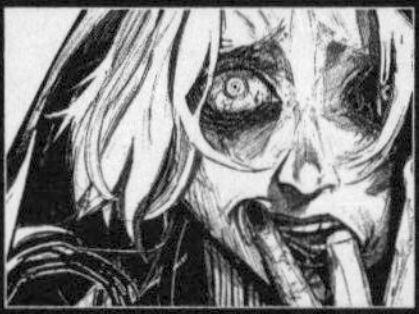

● The Owl
オウル

The current incarnation of Ghoul Investigator Seido Takizawa after Professor Kano implanted him with a Kakuho. Overwhelmingly powerful.

Café:re

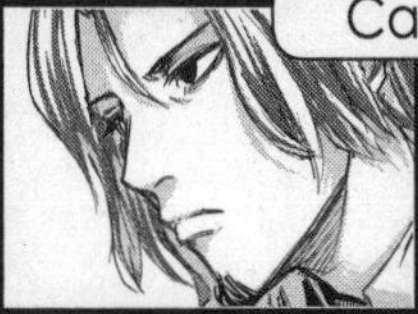

Unknown

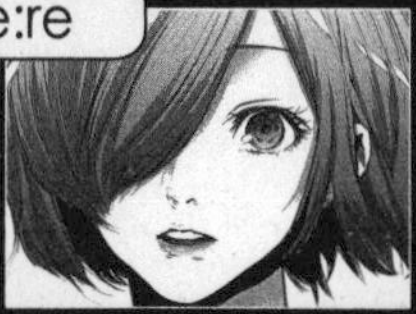

Unknown

So far in :re

T ● K Y ● G H ● U L

The Quinx Project was implemented to develop investigators to surpass Kisho Arima in order to combat the growing strength of Ghoul organizations. Some in the CCG view these unusual investigator who fight using Ghoul abilities with suspicion. Their mentor, Haise Sasaki, leads the four motley investigators during Operation Auction Sweep. Thanks to the Qs, Suzuya Squad and all the other investigators who take part, the operation is a success. And now...?!

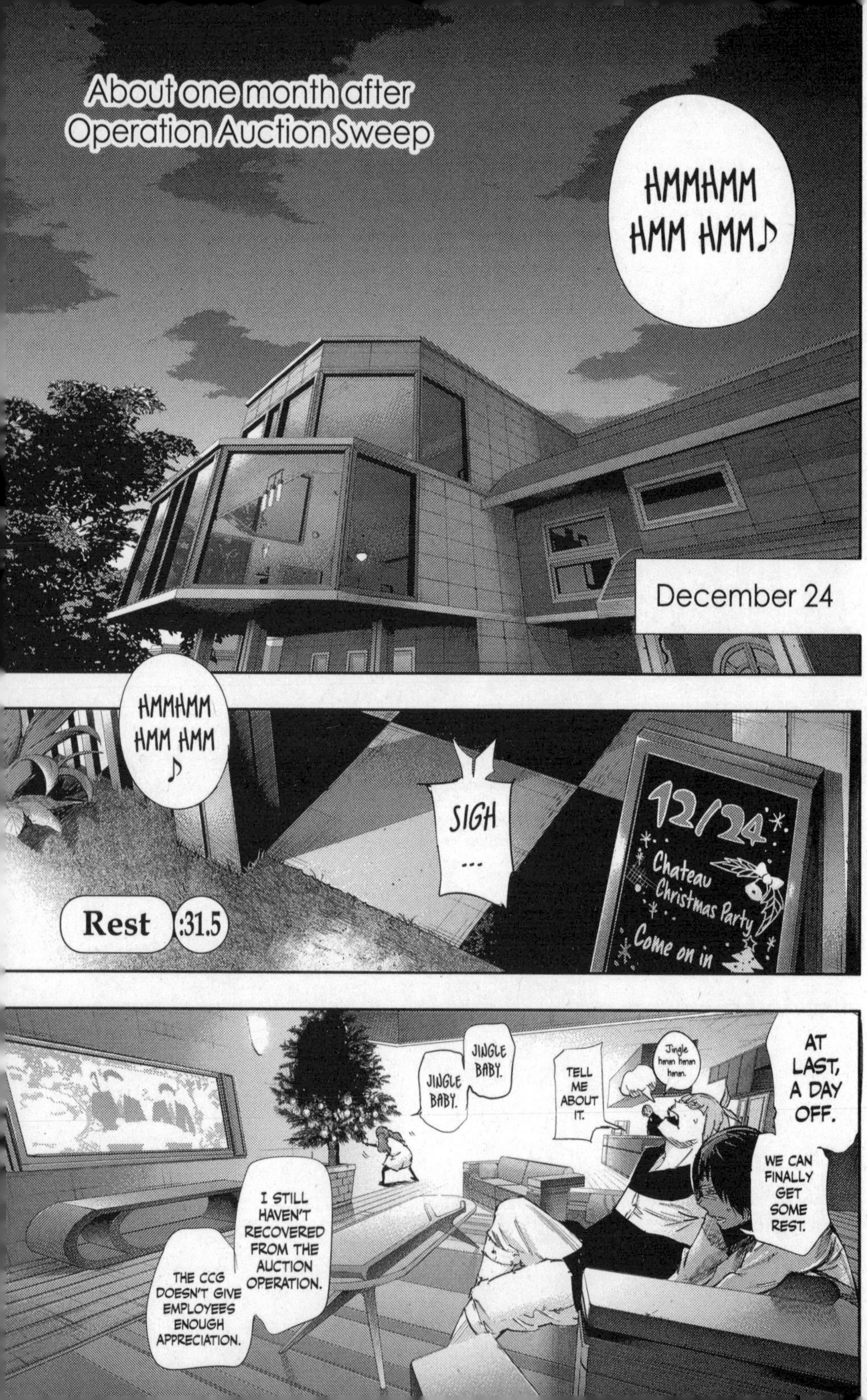
About one month after Operation Auction Sweep
HMMHMM HMM HMM♪
December 24
12/24 Chateau Christmas Party Come on in
SIGH ...
HMMHMM HMM HMM ♪
Rest :31.5
AT LAST, A DAY OFF.
Jingle hmm hmm hmm.
TELL ME ABOUT IT.
WE CAN FINALLY GET SOME REST.
JINGLE BABY.
JINGLE BABY.
I STILL HAVEN'T RECOVERED FROM THE AUCTION OPERATION.
THE CCG DOESN'T GIVE EMPLOYEES ENOUGH APPRECIATION.

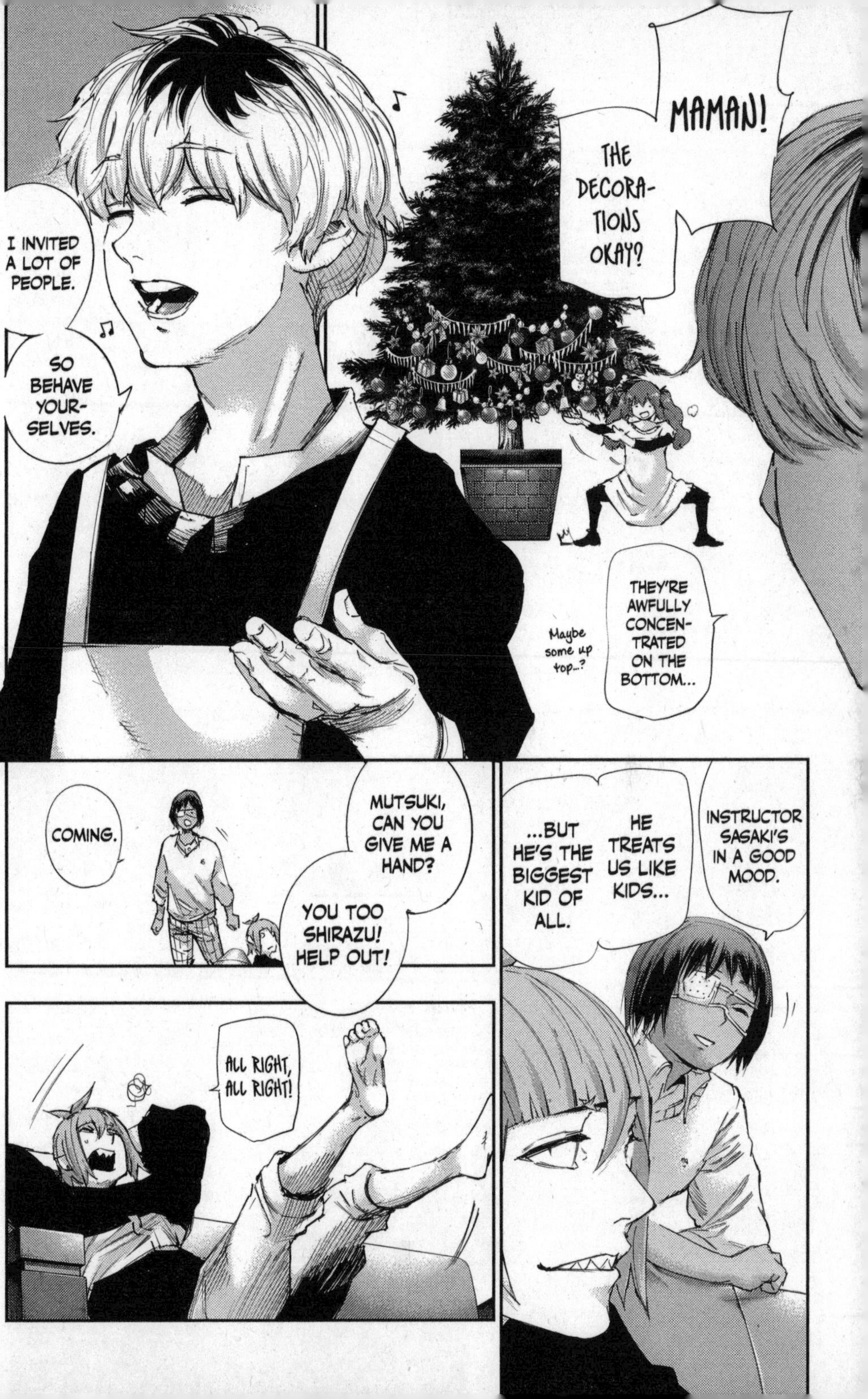
MAMAN!
THE DECORA-TIONS OKAY?
THEY'RE AWFULLY CONCEN-TRATED ON THE BOTTOM...
Maybe some up top...?
I INVITED A LOT OF PEOPLE.
SO BEHAVE YOUR-SELVES.
INSTRUCTOR SASAKI'S IN A GOOD MOOD.
HE TREATS US LIKE KIDS...
...BUT HE'S THE BIGGEST KID OF ALL.
MUTSUKI, CAN YOU GIVE ME A HAND?
COMING.
YOU TOO SHIRAZU! HELP OUT!
ALL RIGHT, ALL RIGHT!

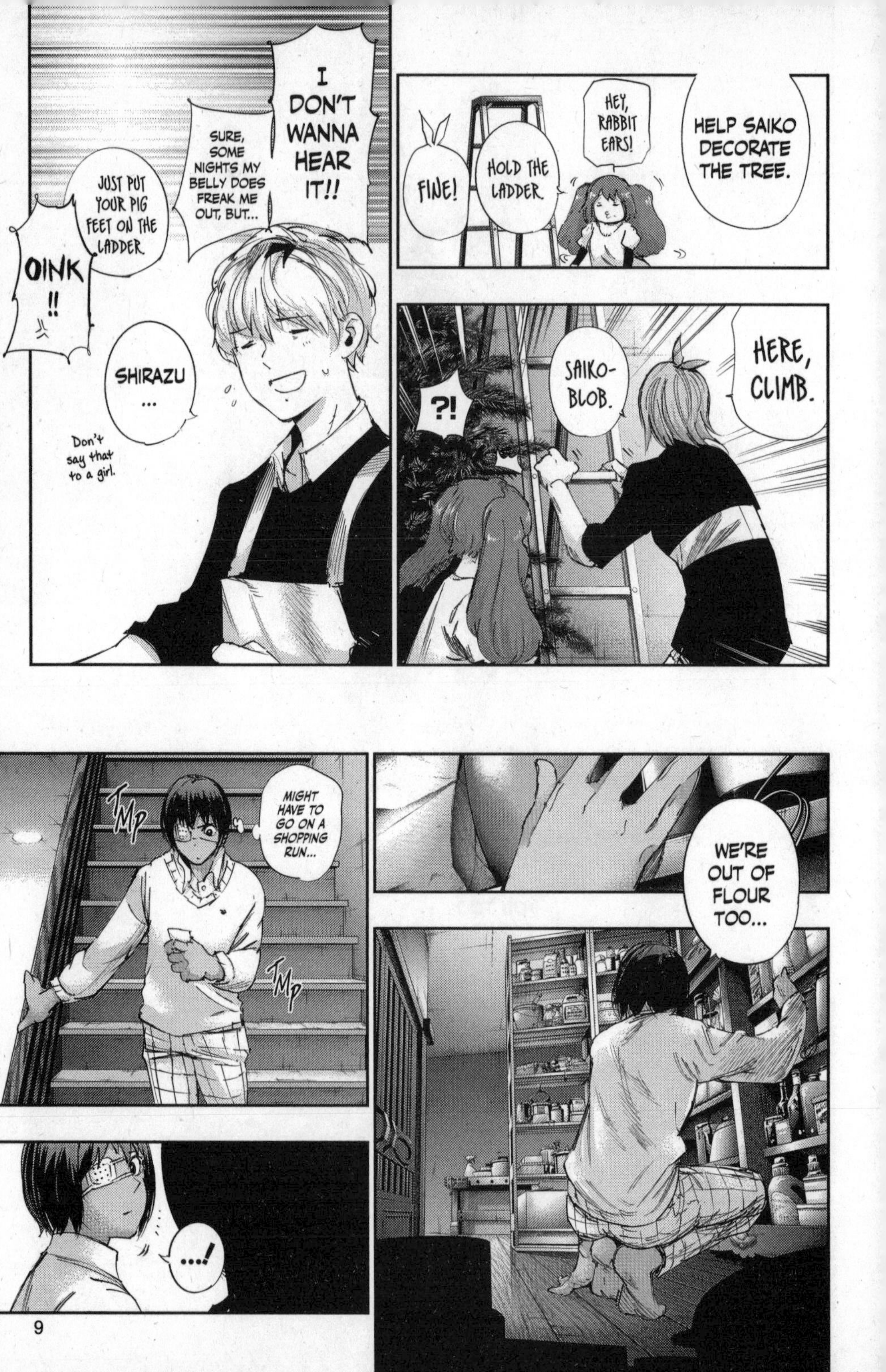
HELP SAIKO DECORATE THE TREE.
HEY, RABBIT EARS!
HOLD THE LADDER.
FINE!
HERE, CLIMB.
SAIKO-BLOB.
?!
I DON'T WANNA HEAR IT!!
SURE, SOME NIGHTS MY BELLY DOES FREAK ME OUT, BUT...
JUST PUT YOUR PIG FEET ON THE LADDER.
OINK!!
SHIRAZU...
Don't say that to a girl.
WE'RE OUT OF FLOUR TOO...
TMP
MIGHT HAVE TO GO ON A SHOPPING RUN...
TMP
...!

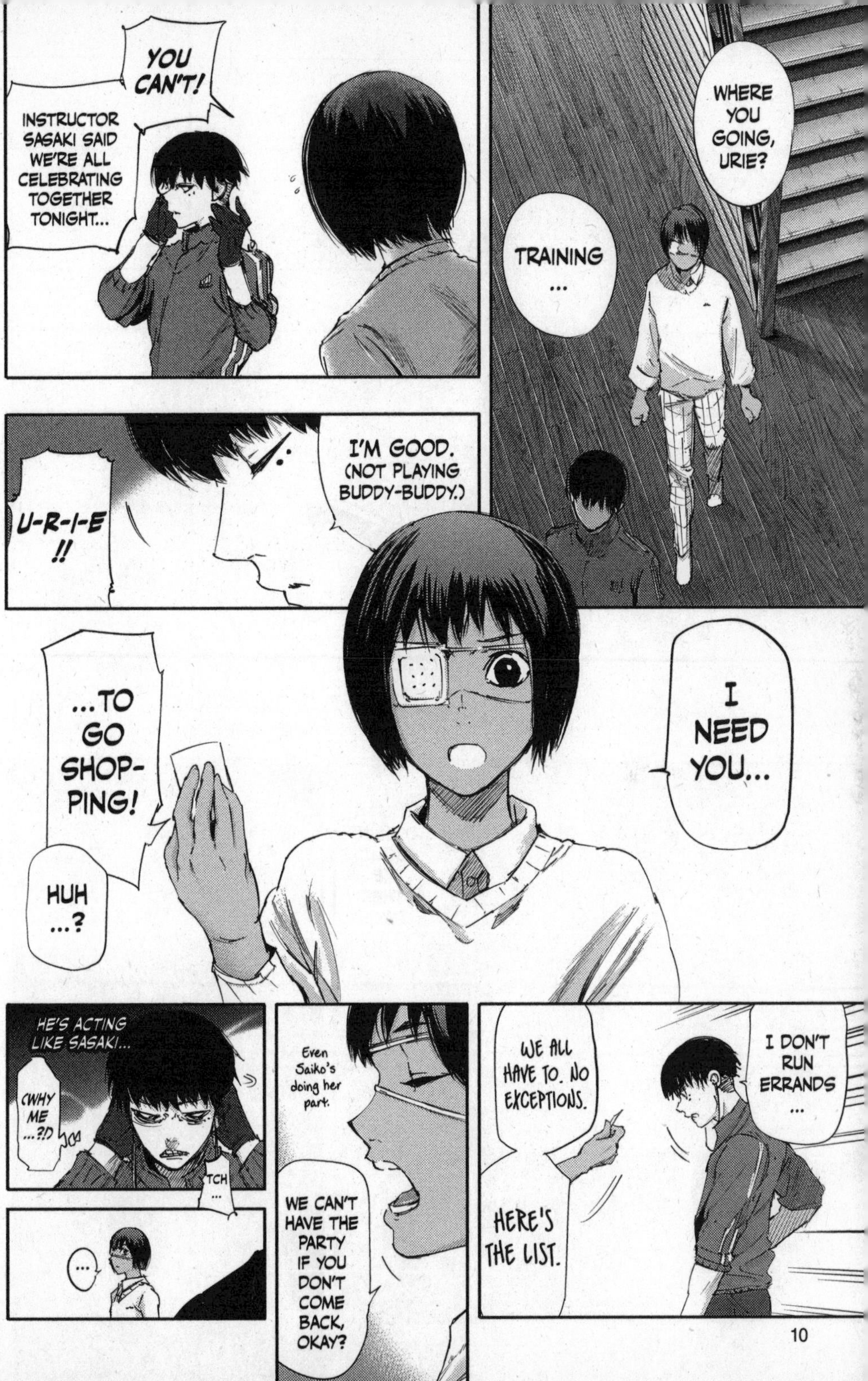
WHERE YOU GOING, URIE?
TRAINING ...
YOU CAN'T!
INSTRUCTOR SASAKI SAID WE'RE ALL CELEBRATING TOGETHER TONIGHT...
I'M GOOD. (NOT PLAYING BUDDY-BUDDY.)
U-R-I-E !!
I NEED YOU...
...TO GO SHOP-PING!
HUH ...?
I DON'T RUN ERRANDS ...
WE ALL HAVE TO. NO EXCEPTIONS.
HERE'S THE LIST.
Even Saiko's doing her part.
WE CAN'T HAVE THE PARTY IF YOU DON'T COME BACK, OKAY?
HE'S ACTING LIKE SASAKI...
(WHY ME ...?!)
TCH ...
...

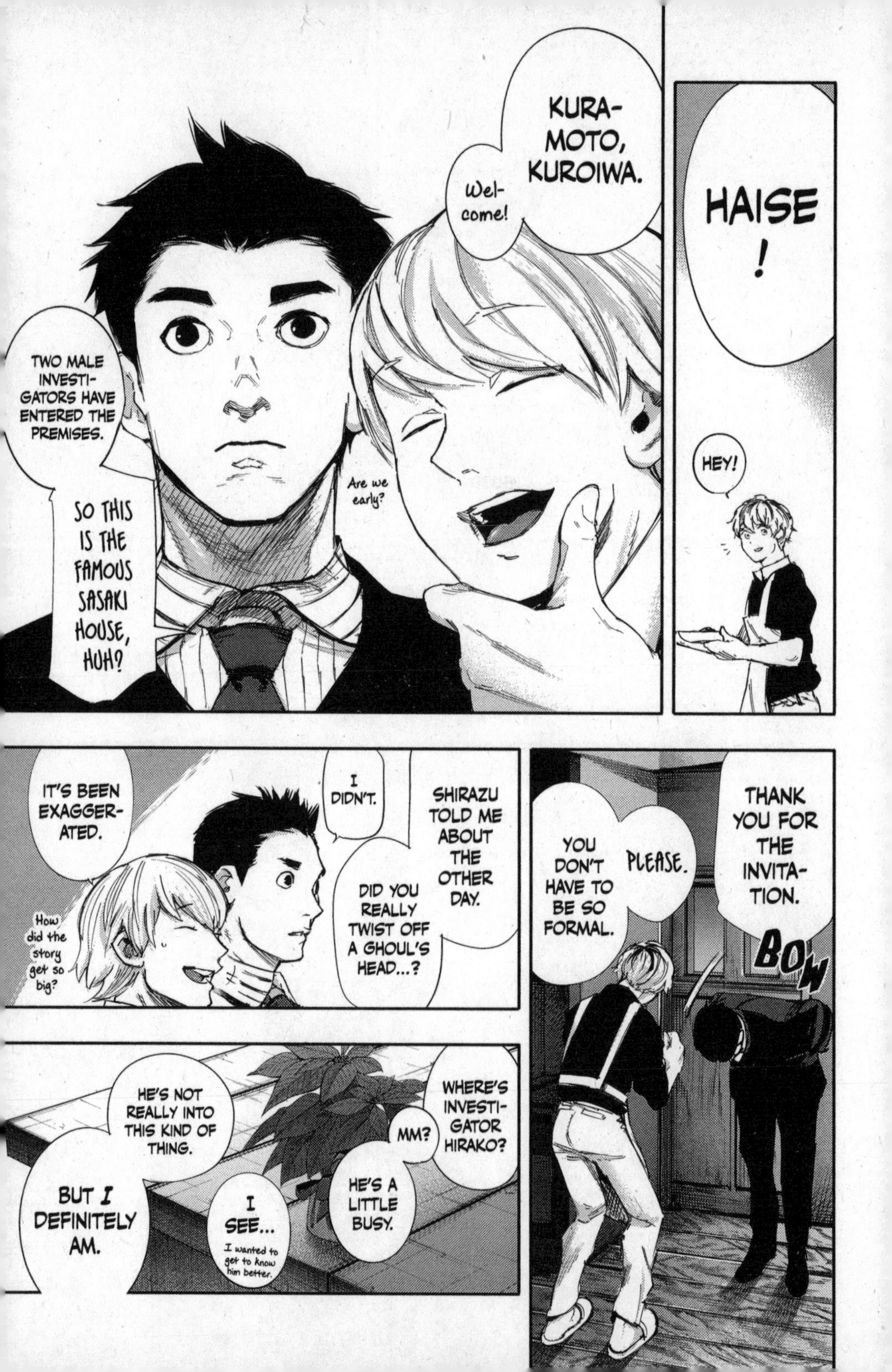
HAISE !
HEY!
KURA-MOTO, KUROIWA.
Wel-come!
Are we early?
TWO MALE INVESTI-GATORS HAVE ENTERED THE PREMISES.
SO THIS IS THE FAMOUS SASAKI HOUSE, HUH?
THANK YOU FOR THE INVITA-TION.
BOW
PLEASE.
YOU DON'T HAVE TO BE SO FORMAL.
SHIRAZU TOLD ME ABOUT THE OTHER DAY.
DID YOU REALLY TWIST OFF A GHOUL'S HEAD...?
I DIDN'T.
IT'S BEEN EXAGGER-ATED.
How did the story get so big?
WHERE'S INVESTI-GATOR HIRAKO?
MM?
HE'S A LITTLE BUSY.
I SEE...
I wanted to get to know him better.
HE'S NOT REALLY INTO THIS KIND OF THING.
BUT I DEFINITELY AM.

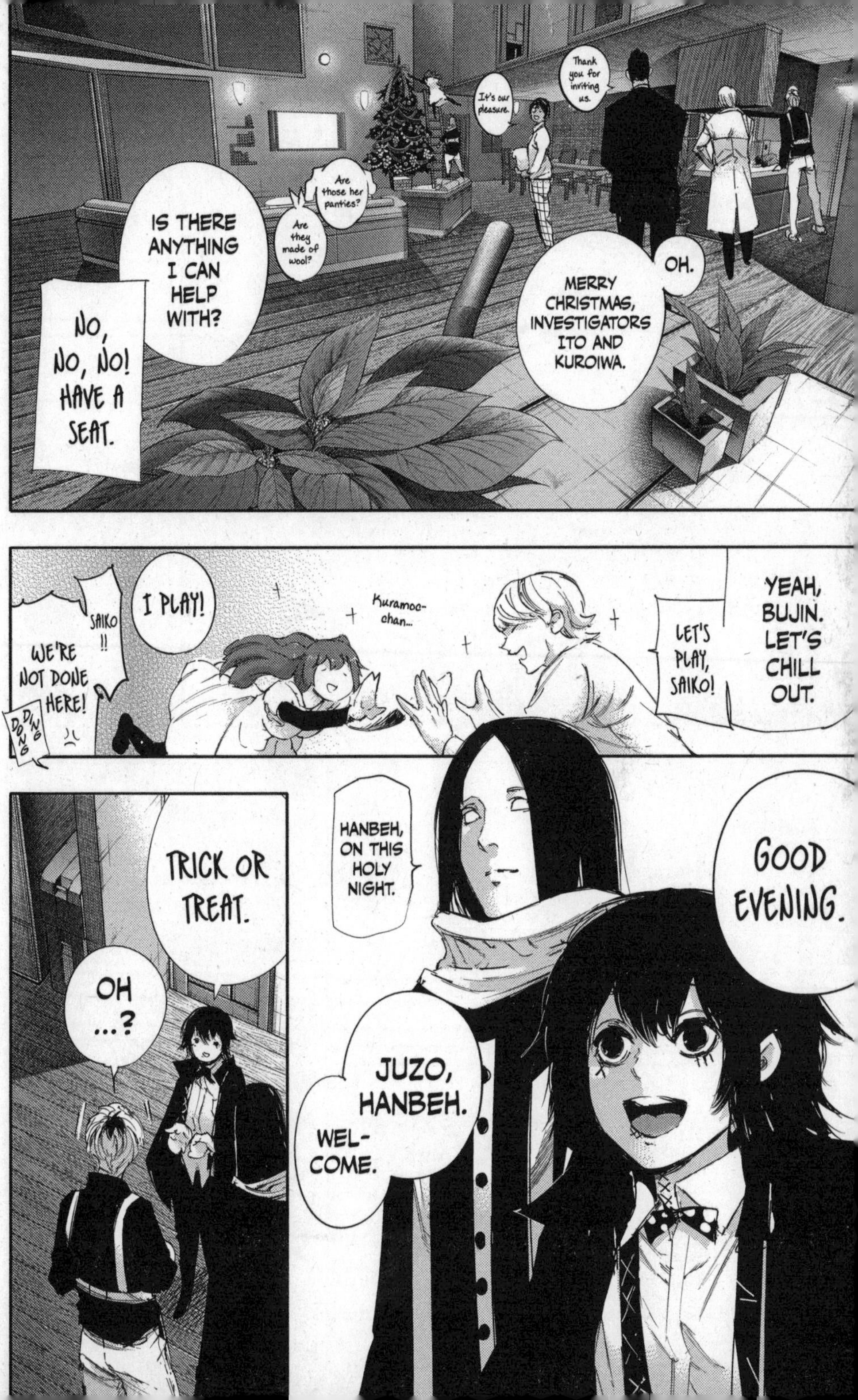
Thank you for inviting us.
It's our pleasure.
OH.
MERRY CHRISTMAS, INVESTIGATORS ITO AND KUROIWA.
Are those her panties?
Are they made of wool?
IS THERE ANYTHING I CAN HELP WITH?
NO, NO, NO! HAVE A SEAT.
YEAH, BUJIN. LET'S CHILL OUT.
LET'S PLAY, SAIKO!
Kuramoe-chan...
I PLAY!
SAIKO!!
WE'RE NOT DONE HERE!
DING DONG
GOOD EVENING.
HANBEH, ON THIS HOLY NIGHT.
JUZO, HANBEH.
WEL-COME.
TRICK OR TREAT.
OH ...?

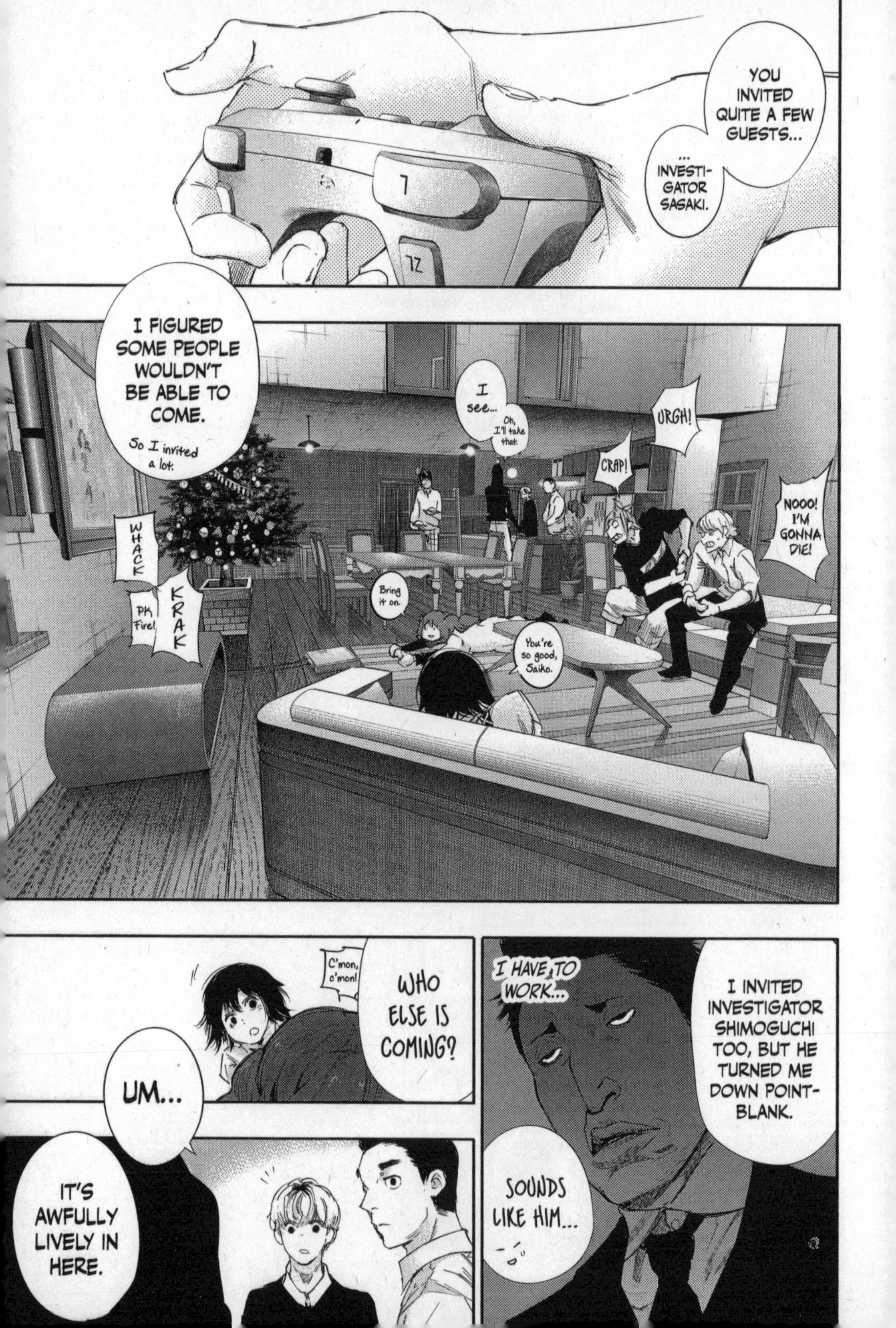
YOU INVITED QUITE A FEW GUESTS...
... INVESTIGATOR SASAKI.
I FIGURED SOME PEOPLE WOULDN'T BE ABLE TO COME.
So I invited a lot.
I see...
Oh, I'll take that.
URGH!
NOOO! I'M GONNA DIE!
CRAP!
WHACK
Bring it on.
KRAK
PK Fire!
You're so good, Saiko.
I INVITED INVESTIGATOR SHIMOGUCHI TOO, BUT HE TURNED ME DOWN POINT-BLANK.
I HAVE TO WORK...
SOUNDS LIKE HIM...
WHO ELSE IS COMING?
C'mon, c'mon!
UM...
IT'S AWFULLY LIVELY IN HERE.

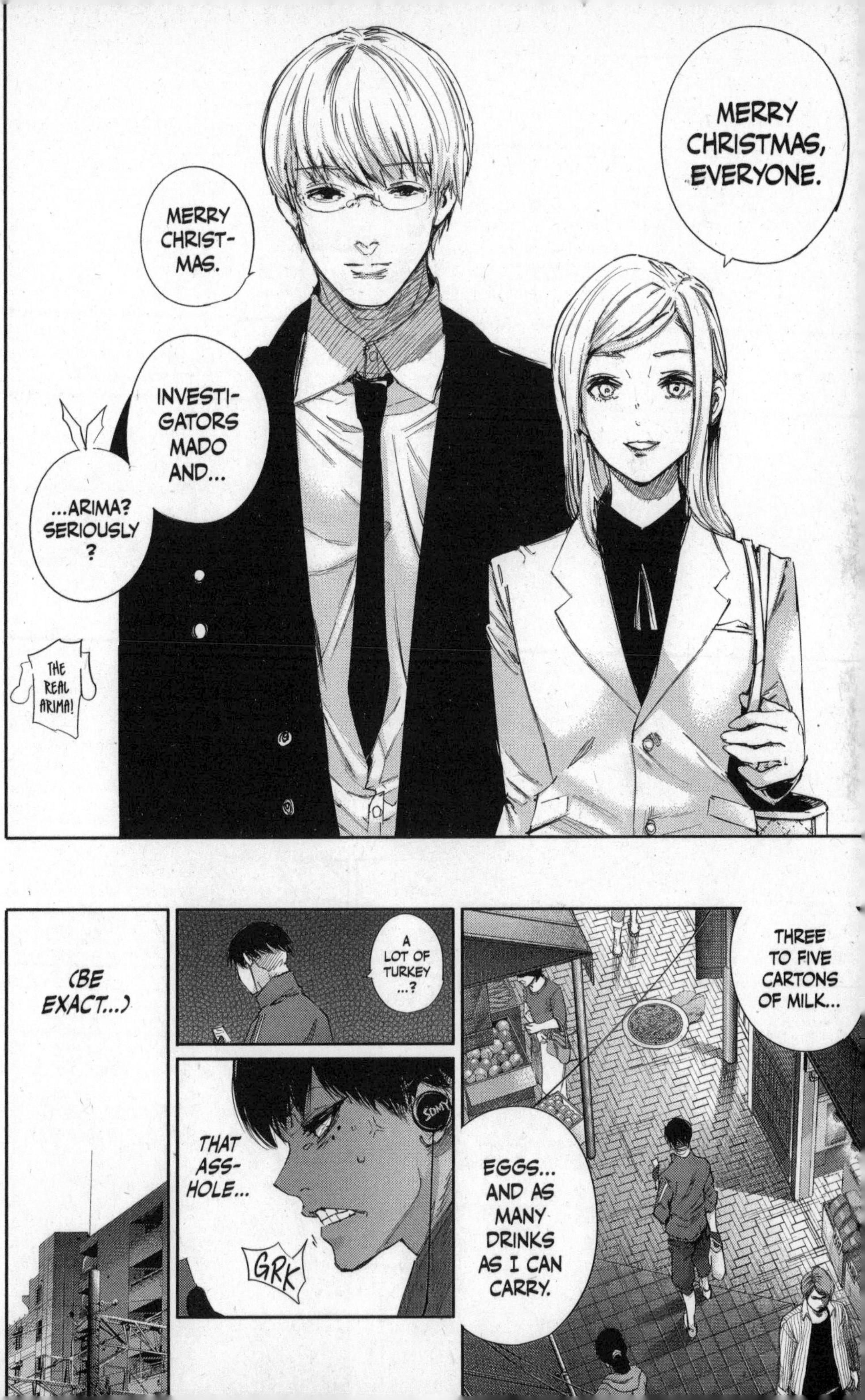
MERRY CHRISTMAS, EVERYONE.
MERRY CHRIST-MAS.
INVESTI-GATORS MADO AND...
...ARIMA? SERIOUSLY?
THE REAL ARIMA!
THREE TO FIVE CARTONS OF MILK...
EGGS... AND AS MANY DRINKS AS I CAN CARRY.
A LOT OF TURKEY ...?
THAT ASS-HOLE...
GRK
(BE EXACT...)

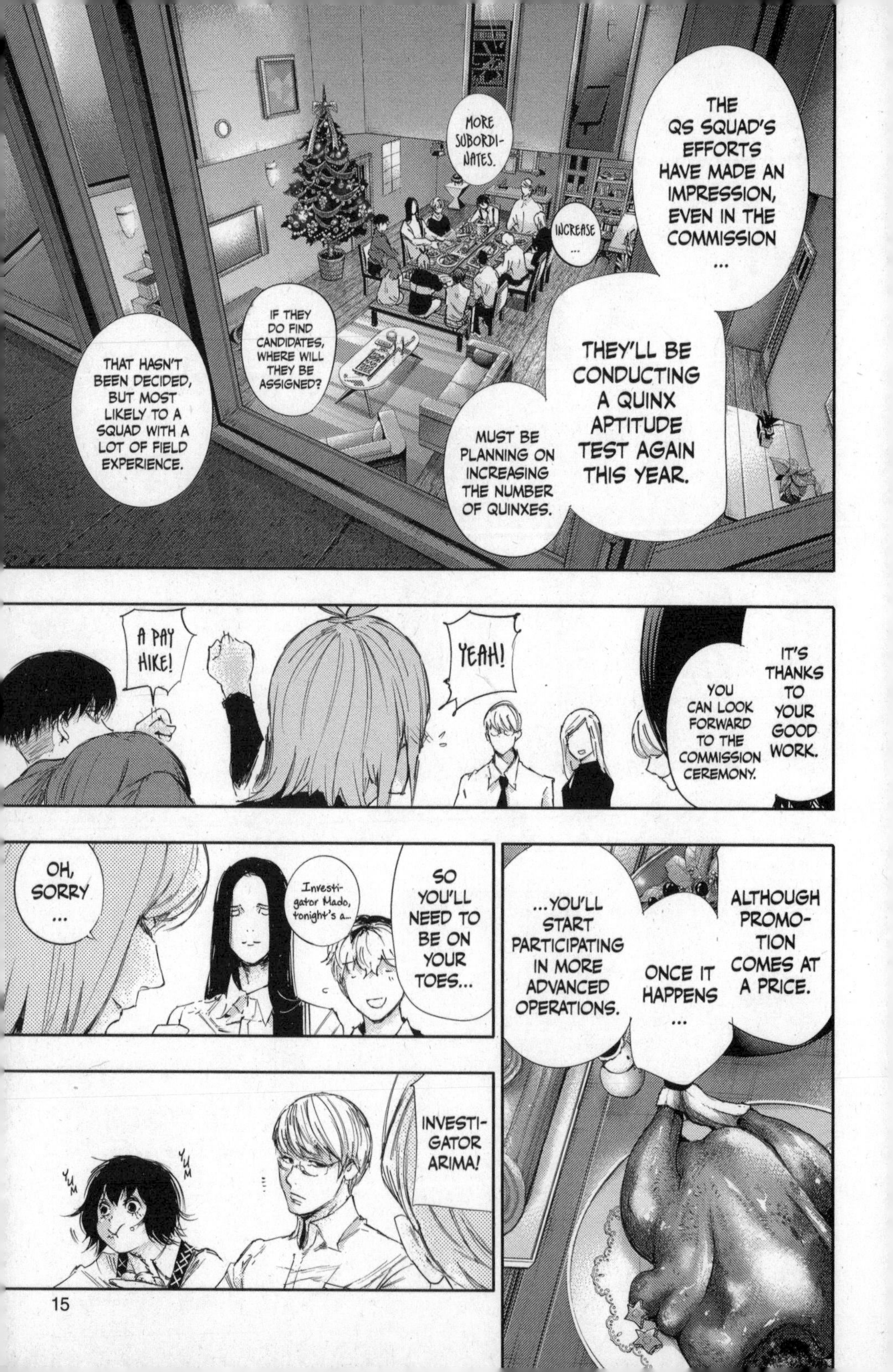
THE QS SQUAD'S EFFORTS HAVE MADE AN IMPRESSION, EVEN IN THE COMMISSION ...
INCREASE ...
MORE SUBORDINATES.
THEY'LL BE CONDUCTING A QUINX APTITUDE TEST AGAIN THIS YEAR.
MUST BE PLANNING ON INCREASING THE NUMBER OF QUINXES.
IF THEY DO FIND CANDIDATES, WHERE WILL THEY BE ASSIGNED?
THAT HASN'T BEEN DECIDED, BUT MOST LIKELY TO A SQUAD WITH A LOT OF FIELD EXPERIENCE.
IT'S THANKS TO YOUR GOOD WORK.
YOU CAN LOOK FORWARD TO THE COMMISSION CEREMONY.
YEAH!
A PAY HIKE!
ALTHOUGH PROMOTION COMES AT A PRICE.
ONCE IT HAPPENS ...
...YOU'LL START PARTICIPATING IN MORE ADVANCED OPERATIONS.
SO YOU'LL NEED TO BE ON YOUR TOES...
Investigator Mado, tonight's a...
OH, SORRY ...
INVESTIGATOR ARIMA!
YUM
YUM

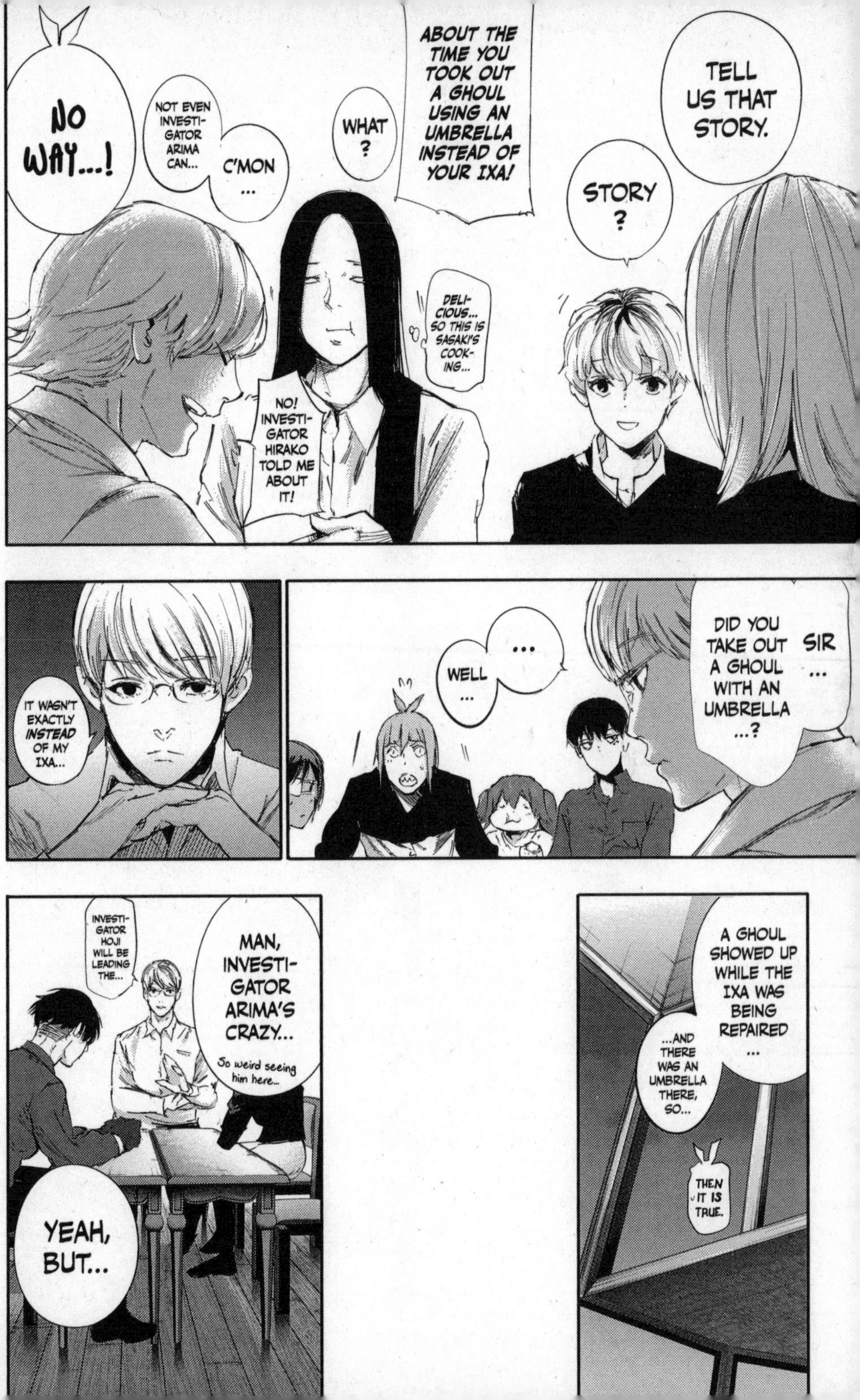
TELL US THAT STORY.
STORY?
ABOUT THE TIME YOU TOOK OUT A GHOUL USING AN UMBRELLA INSTEAD OF YOUR IXA!
WHAT?
DELICIOUS... SO THIS IS SASAKI'S COOKING...
C'MON...
NOT EVEN INVESTIGATOR ARIMA CAN...
NO WAY...!
NO! INVESTIGATOR HIRAKO TOLD ME ABOUT IT!
SIR...
DID YOU TAKE OUT A GHOUL WITH AN UMBRELLA...?
...
WELL...
IT WASN'T EXACTLY *INSTEAD* OF MY IXA...
A GHOUL SHOWED UP WHILE THE IXA WAS BEING REPAIRED...
...AND THERE WAS AN UMBRELLA THERE, SO...
THEN IT IS TRUE.
MAN, INVESTIGATOR ARIMA'S CRAZY...
INVESTIGATOR HOJI WILL BE LEADING THE...
So weird seeing him here...
YEAH, BUT...

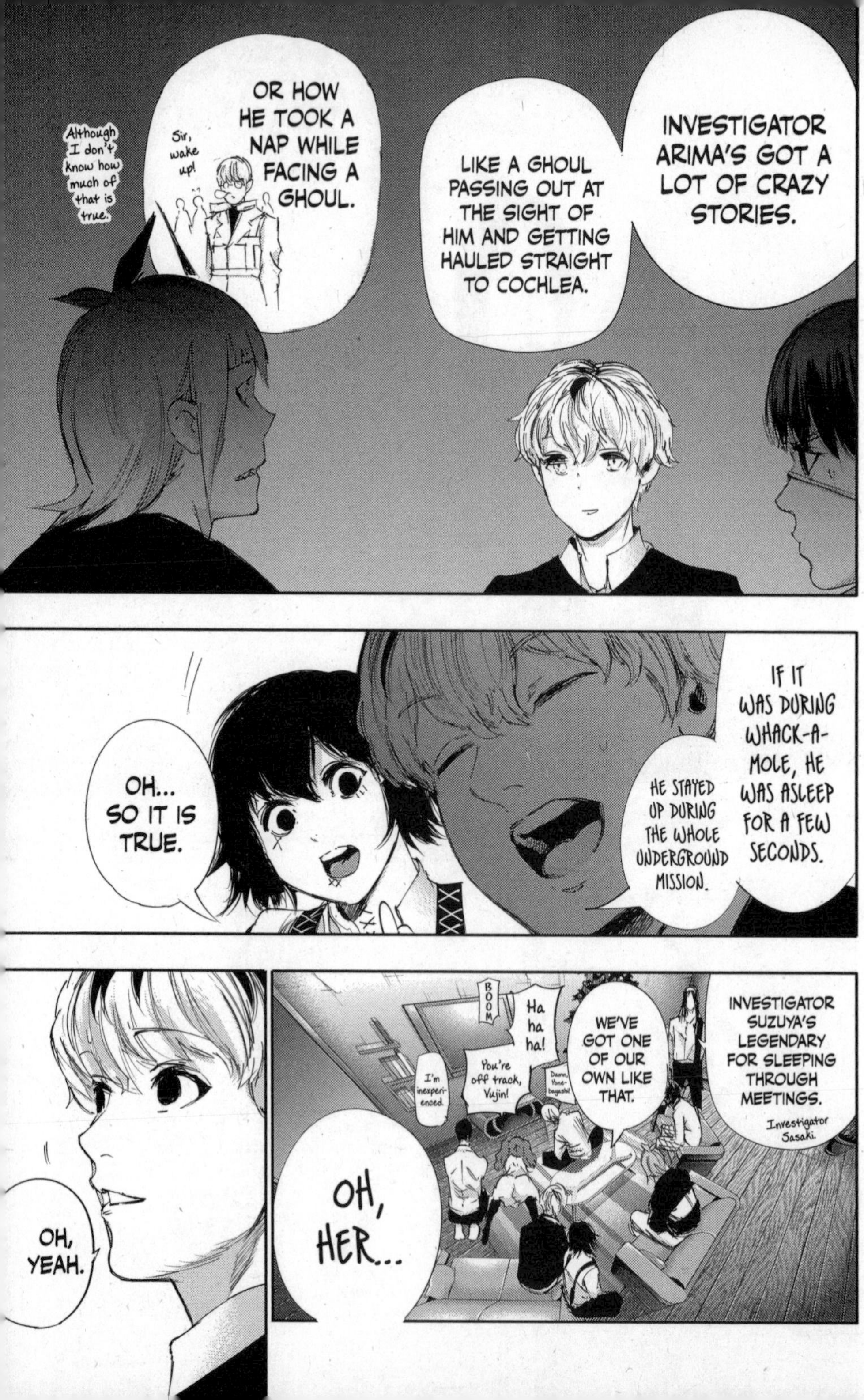
INVESTIGATOR ARIMA'S GOT A LOT OF CRAZY STORIES.
LIKE A GHOUL PASSING OUT AT THE SIGHT OF HIM AND GETTING HAULED STRAIGHT TO COCHLEA.
OR HOW HE TOOK A NAP WHILE FACING A GHOUL.
Sir, wake up!
Although I don't know how much of that is true.
IF IT WAS DURING WHACK-A-MOLE, HE WAS ASLEEP FOR A FEW SECONDS.
HE STAYED UP DURING THE WHOLE UNDERGROUND MISSION.
OH... SO IT IS TRUE.
INVESTIGATOR SUZUYA'S LEGENDARY FOR SLEEPING THROUGH MEETINGS.
Investigator Sasaki.
WE'VE GOT ONE OF OUR OWN LIKE THAT.
Ha ha ha!
BOOM
Damn, Yonebayashi!
You're off track, Vujin!
I'm inexperienced.
OH, HER...
OH, YEAH.

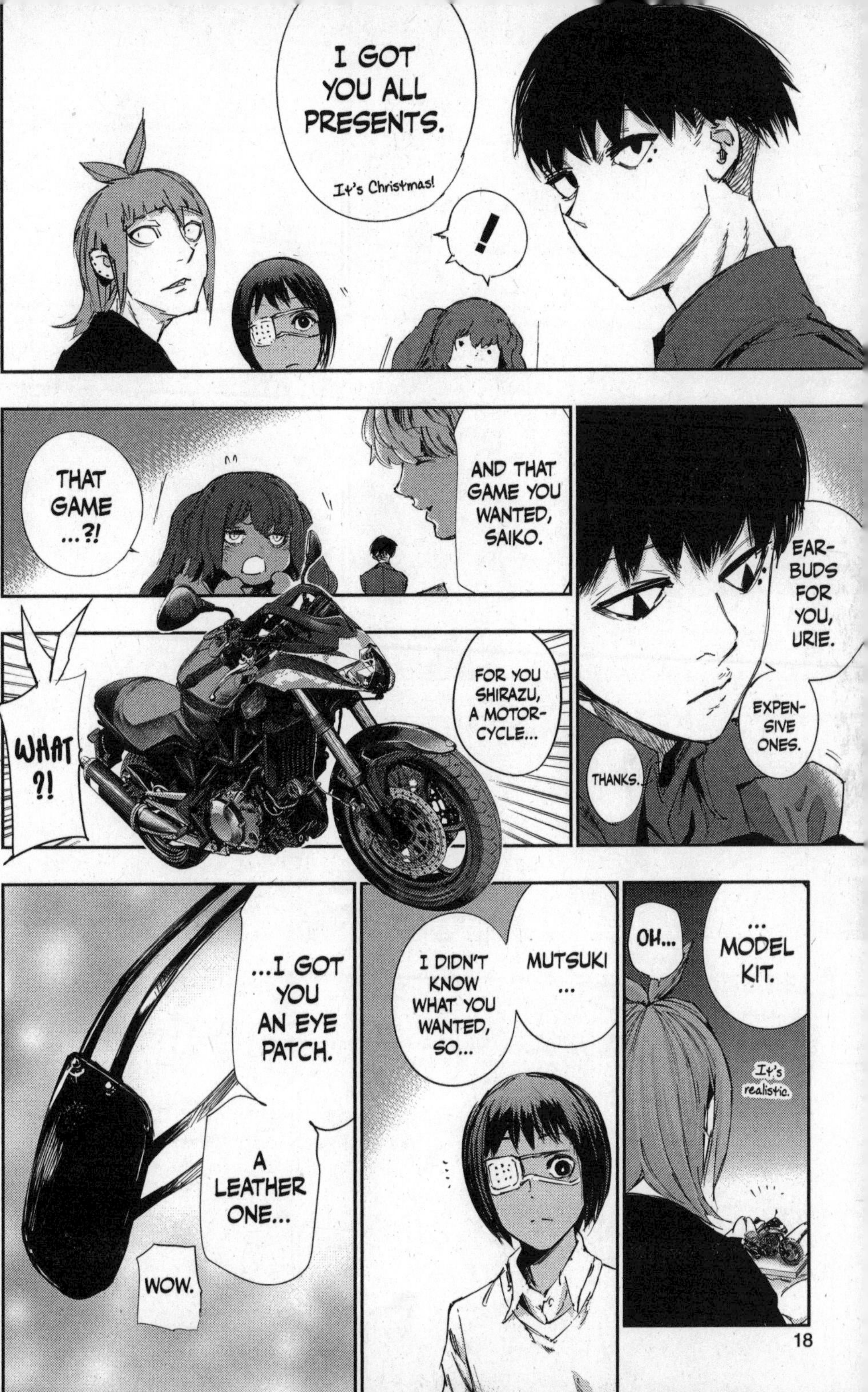
I GOT YOU ALL PRESENTS.
It's Christmas!
!
EAR-BUDS FOR YOU, URIE.
EXPEN-SIVE ONES.
THANKS.
AND THAT GAME YOU WANTED, SAIKO.
THAT GAME ...?!
FOR YOU SHIRAZU, A MOTOR-CYCLE...
WHAT ?!
... MODEL KIT.
OH...
It's realistic.
MUTSUKI ...
I DIDN'T KNOW WHAT YOU WANTED, SO...
...I GOT YOU AN EYE PATCH.
A LEATHER ONE...
WOW.

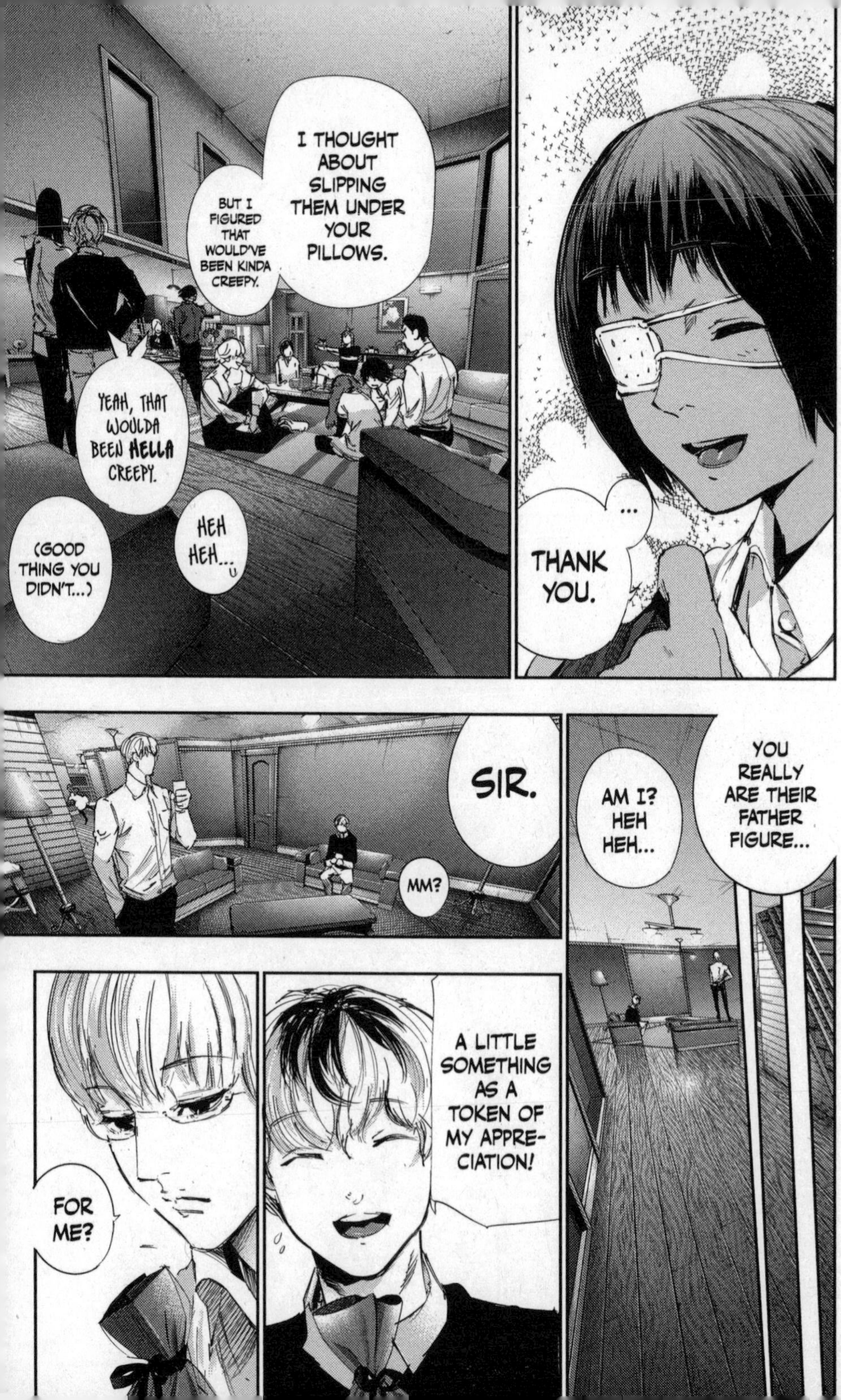
...
THANK YOU.
I THOUGHT ABOUT SLIPPING THEM UNDER YOUR PILLOWS.
BUT I FIGURED THAT WOULD'VE BEEN KINDA CREEPY.
YEAH, THAT WOULDA BEEN HELLA CREEPY.
HEH HEH...
(GOOD THING YOU DIDN'T...)
YOU REALLY ARE THEIR FATHER FIGURE...
AM I? HEH HEH...
SIR.
MM?
A LITTLE SOMETHING AS A TOKEN OF MY APPRE-CIATION!
FOR ME?

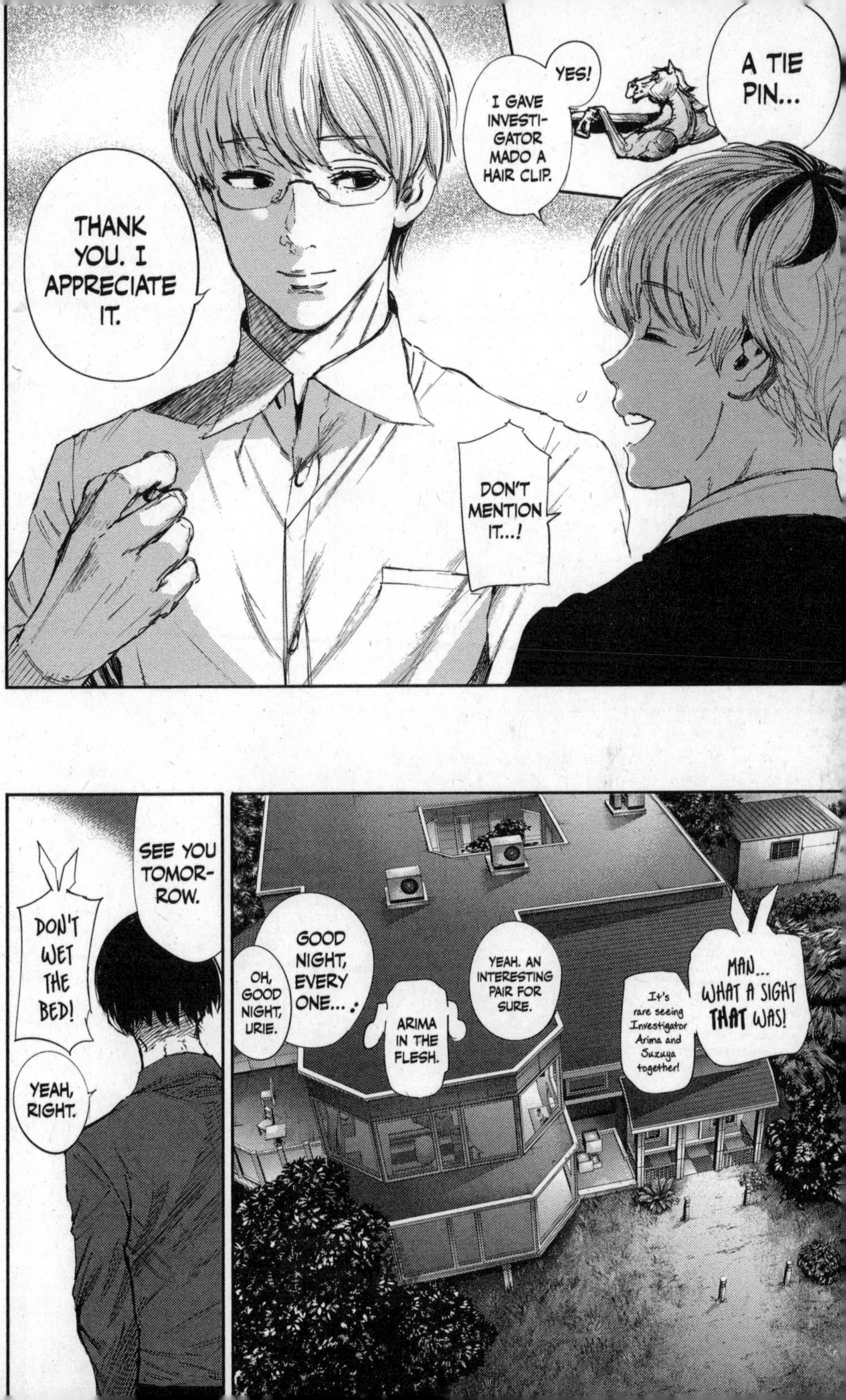
A TIE PIN...
YES! I GAVE INVESTIGATOR MADO A HAIR CLIP.
THANK YOU. I APPRECIATE IT.
DON'T MENTION IT...!
MAN... WHAT A SIGHT THAT WAS!
It's rare seeing Investigator Arima and Suzuya together!
YEAH. AN INTERESTING PAIR FOR SURE.
ARIMA IN THE FLESH.
GOOD NIGHT, EVERY ONE...
OH, GOOD NIGHT, URIE.
SEE YOU TOMORROW.
DON'T WET THE BED!
YEAH, RIGHT.

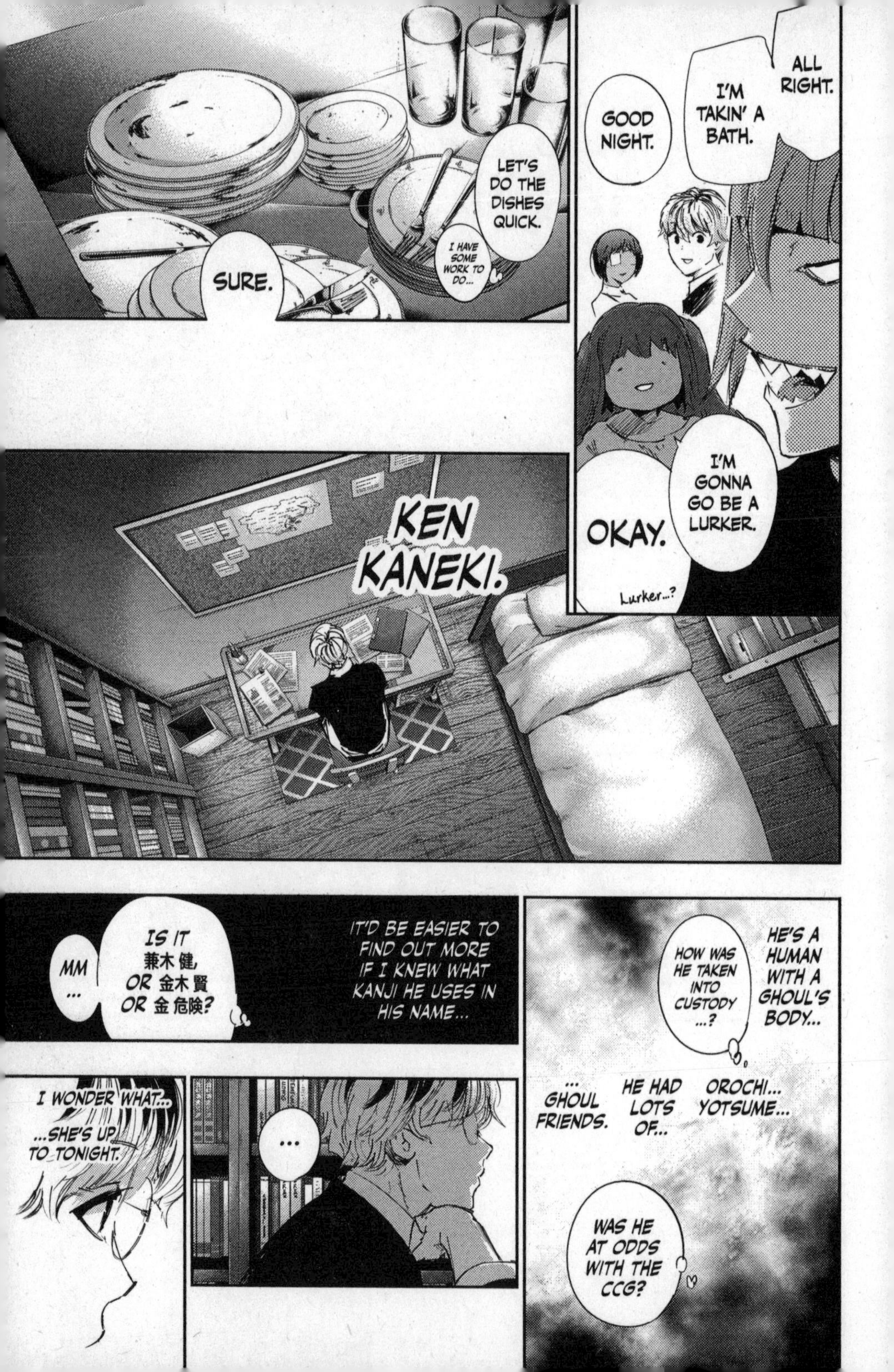
ALL RIGHT.
I'M TAKIN' A BATH.
GOOD NIGHT.
I'M GONNA GO BE A LURKER.
OKAY.
Lurker...?
LET'S DO THE DISHES QUICK.
I HAVE SOME WORK TO DO...
SURE.
KEN KANEKI.
HE'S A HUMAN WITH A GHOUL'S BODY...
HOW WAS HE TAKEN INTO CUSTODY ...?
OROCHI... YOTSUME...
HE HAD LOTS OF...
...GHOUL FRIENDS.
WAS HE AT ODDS WITH THE CCG?
IT'D BE EASIER TO FIND OUT MORE IF I KNEW WHAT KANJI HE USES IN HIS NAME...
IS IT 兼木健, OR 金木賢 OR 金危険?
MM ...
...
I WONDER WHAT...
...SHE'S UP TO TONIGHT.

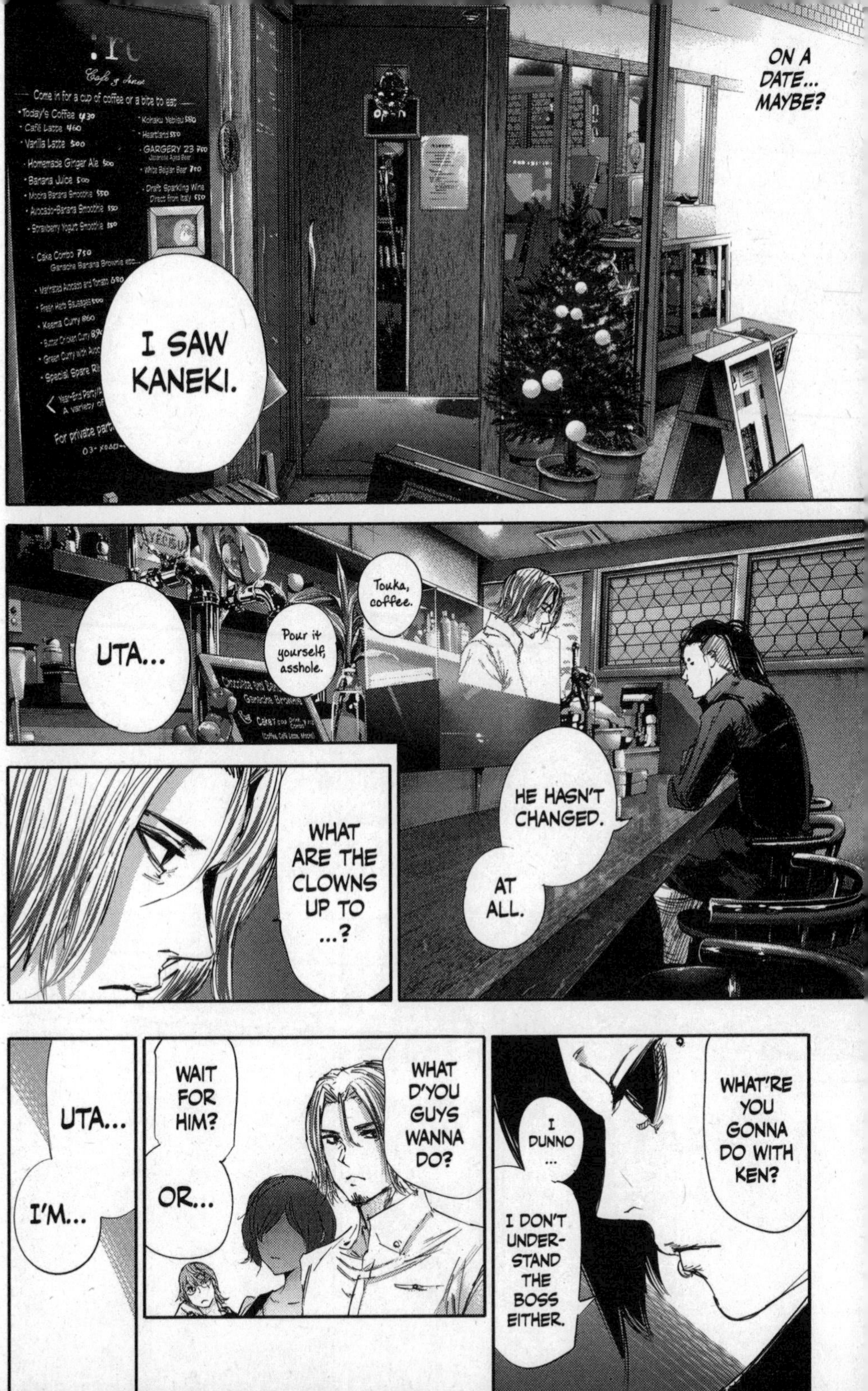
ON A DATE... MAYBE?
Come in for a cup of coffee or a bite to eat
Today's Coffee 430
Café Latte 460
Vanilla Latte 500
Homemade Ginger Ale 500
Banana Juice 500
Cake Combo 750
Keema Curry 860
I SAW KANEKI.
Touka, coffee.
Pour it yourself, asshole.
UTA...
HE HASN'T CHANGED.
AT ALL.
WHAT ARE THE CLOWNS UP TO ...?
WHAT'RE YOU GONNA DO WITH KEN?
I DUNNO ...
I DON'T UNDER-STAND THE BOSS EITHER.
WHAT D'YOU GUYS WANNA DO?
WAIT FOR HIM?
OR...
UTA...
I'M...

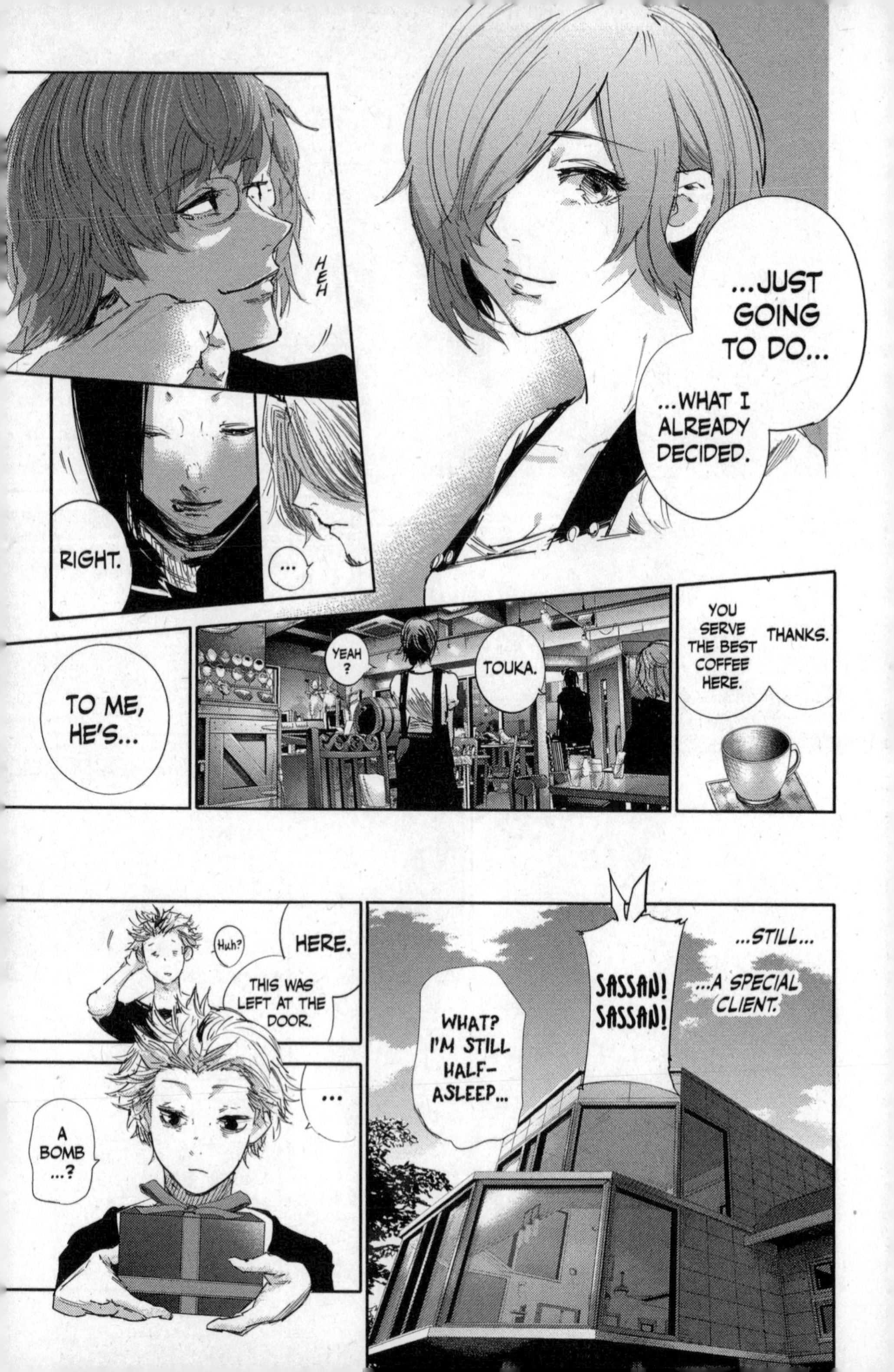
...JUST GOING TO DO...
...WHAT I ALREADY DECIDED.
HEH
...
RIGHT.
YOU SERVE THE BEST COFFEE HERE.
THANKS.
TOUKA.
YEAH?
TO ME, HE'S...
...STILL...
...A SPECIAL CLIENT.
SASSAN! SASSAN!
WHAT? I'M STILL HALF-ASLEEP...
HERE.
Huh?
THIS WAS LEFT AT THE DOOR.
...
A BOMB...?

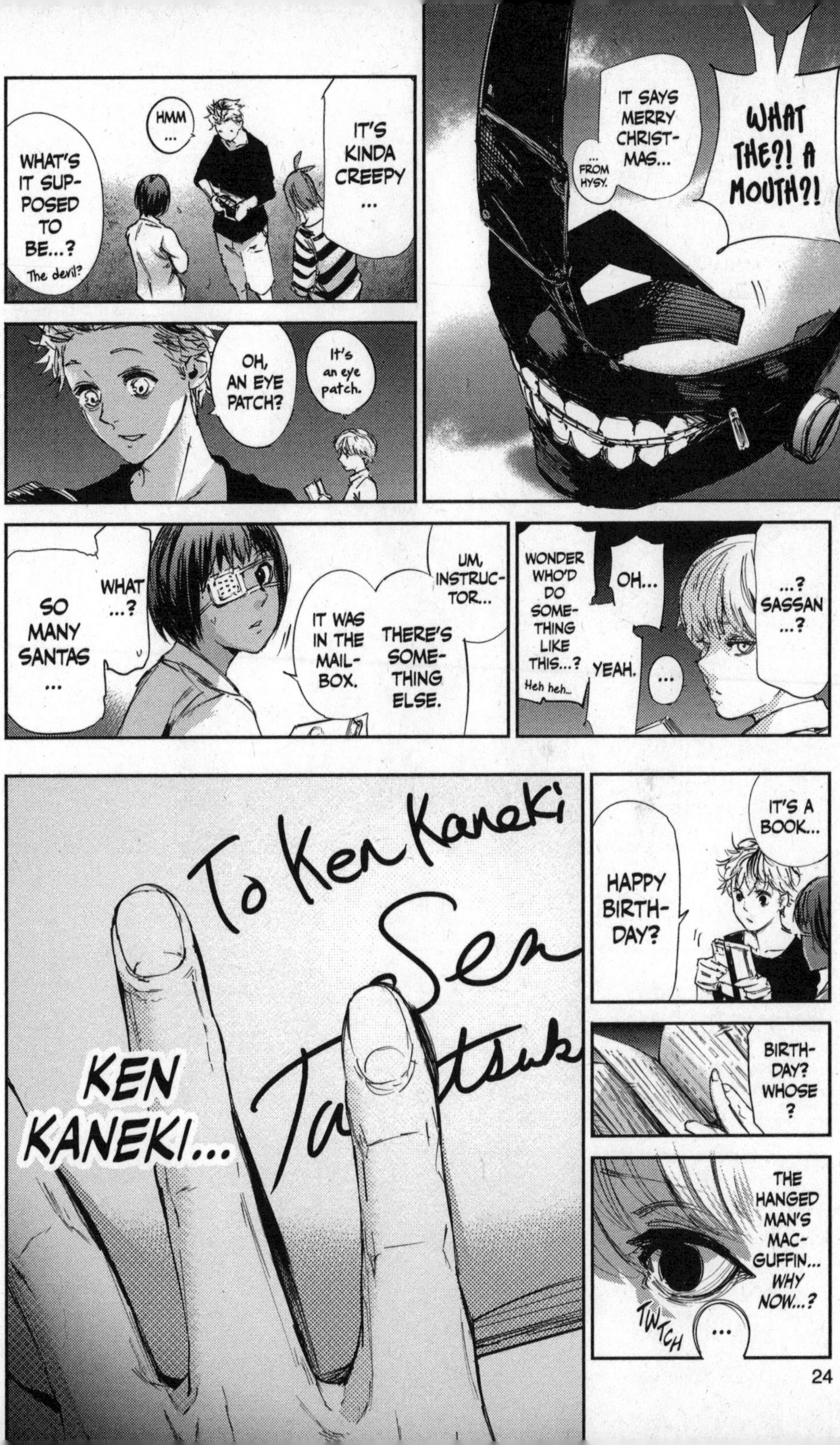
WHAT THE?! A MOUTH?!
IT SAYS MERRY CHRIST-MAS...
... FROM HYSY.
IT'S KINDA CREEPY ...
HMM ...
WHAT'S IT SUP-POSED TO BE...?
The devil?
It's an eye patch.
OH, AN EYE PATCH?
...? SASSAN ...?
...
OH...
YEAH.
WONDER WHO'D DO SOME-THING LIKE THIS...?
Heh heh...
UM, INSTRUCTOR...
THERE'S SOME-THING ELSE.
IT WAS IN THE MAIL-BOX.
WHAT ...?
SO MANY SANTAS ...
IT'S A BOOK...
HAPPY BIRTH-DAY?
BIRTH-DAY? WHOSE ?
THE HANGED MAN'S MAC-GUFFIN... WHY NOW...?
TWITCH
...
To Ken Kaneki
Sen
KEN KANEKI...

Investigator Ito invited me to the Chateau where Investigator Sasaki and the Quinx Squad live.

The Chateau is a three-story Western-style house. It has a training facility on the first floor, a conference room and a living room on the second floor, and the bedrooms on the third floor.

The second floor also has a guest room. The third floor has empty bedrooms, most likely in case their squad grows. It is a rather spacious structure.

I was taken to the second-floor living room. I asked if I could help, but Investigator Sasaki was thoughtful and told me to just relax.

I appreciated his kind gesture, but I could not just sit and wait while Investigator Sasaki prepared for the evening. So I assisted him where I could.

However, Investigator Sasaki is an efficient and quick cook. There was no room for me. Perhaps I only got in his way.

Investigators Arima and Mado also arrived and chatted with Urie when he returned from shopping. I wonder what they were talking about.

Knowing how dedicated Urie is to his work, he must have been asking them about their past experiences and how they prepare for investigations.

Later, we all had dinner. Investigator Sasaki's cooking was delicious.

The meal included a range of dishes, from rustic fare to the more adventurous foods we young investigators prefer. Yonebayashi's appetite was something to behold.

I imagined Investigator Sasaki preparing all their meals while working a case. My respect for him grew even stronger.

When we were done with dinner, I played some video games at Yonebayashi's urging.

The rule of the game was to circle the track a specified number of times. We each had to choose a racer and compete against each other.

By using items available along the way, it was possible to impede the other racers. The game not only required driving skills, but also knowing when and where to deploy those items.

Yonebayashi and Shirazu were skilled, as expected. Lacking in experience, my score was dismal.

Investigator Ito seemed to be well versed in this kind of activity. He put up a good fight against those two. However, he could not beat Yonebayashi.

Yonebayashi dominated from beginning to end. I have known her since her days in the Academy, but I was surprised to see a new talent of hers.

We excused ourselves at around 9:00 p.m., due to work the next day.

Investigator Ito smiled on his way back home. He seemed to have enjoyed the evening.

With a busy father, I never had the opportunity to gather around a table at this time of year. So I enjoyed the evening as well.

I would once again like to thank Investigator Ito for the invitation and Investigator Sasaki for his hospitality.

I will cherish this evening and devote myself to the duties as an investigator.

-Takeomi Kuroiwa

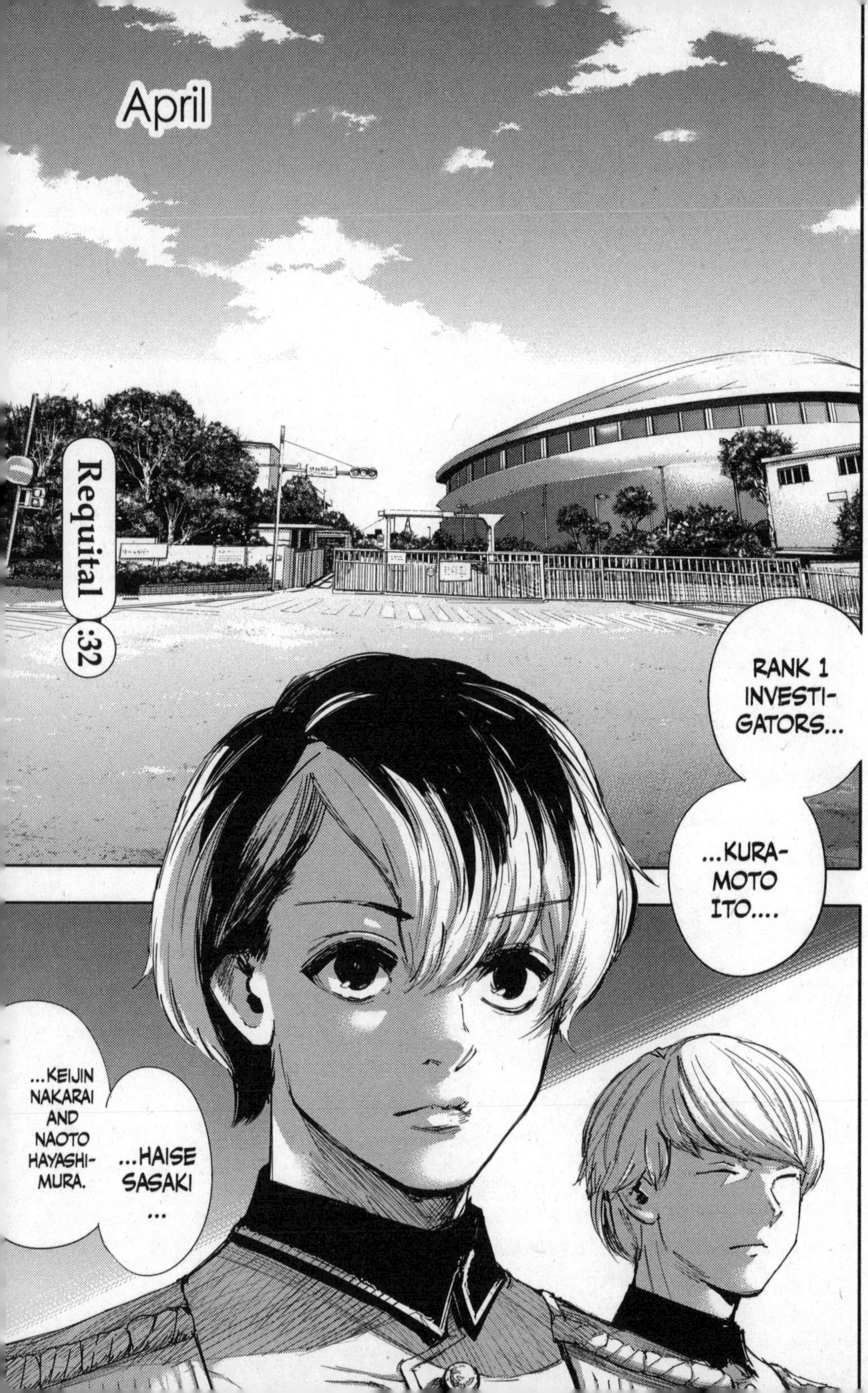
April
Requital :32
RANK 1 INVESTIGATORS...
...KURAMOTO ITO....
...HAISE SASAKI ...
...KEIJIN NAKARAI AND NAOTO HAYASHIMURA.

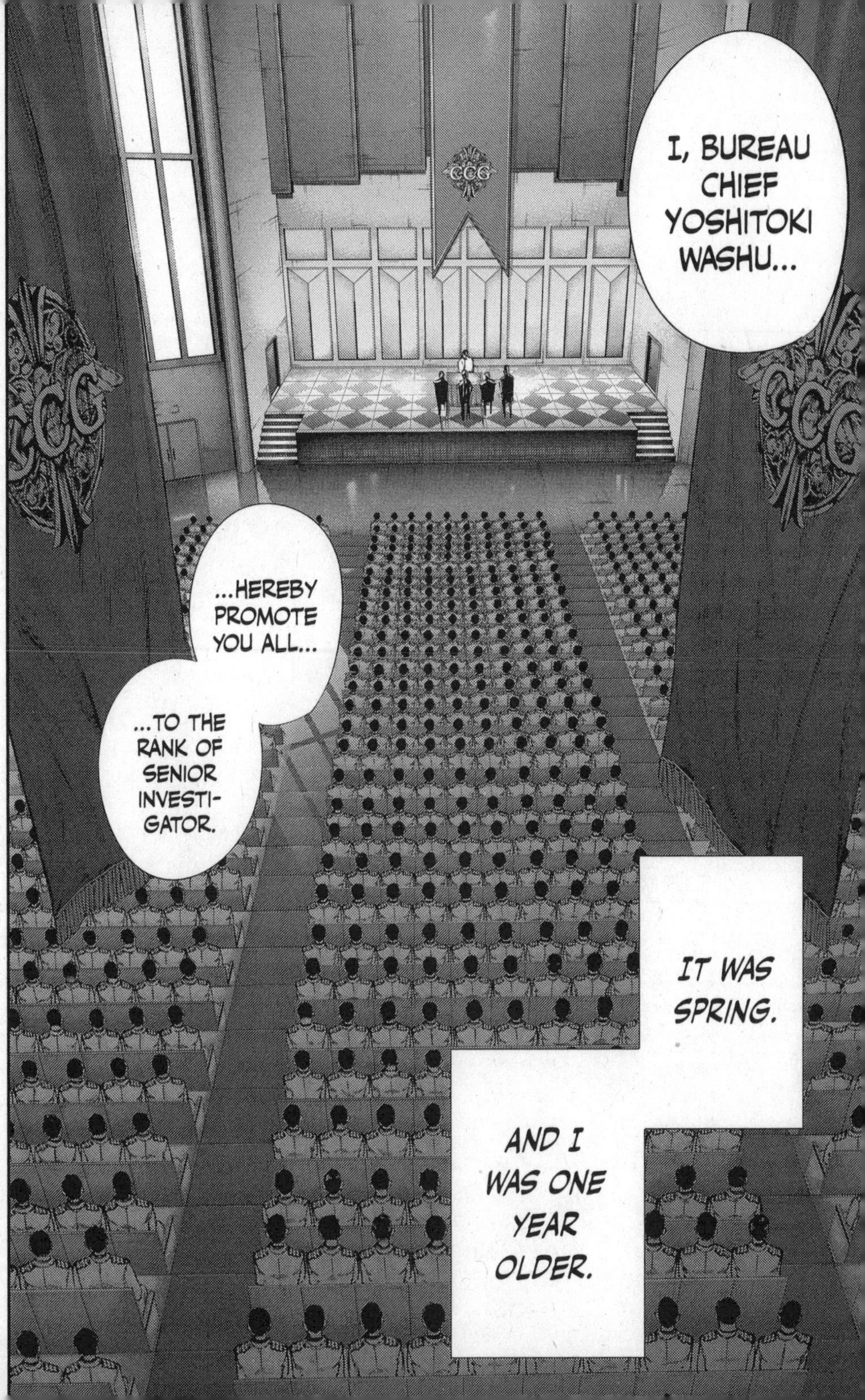
CCG
I, BUREAU CHIEF YOSHITOKI WASHU...
...HEREBY PROMOTE YOU ALL...
...TO THE RANK OF SENIOR INVESTI-GATOR.
IT WAS SPRING.
AND I WAS ONE YEAR OLDER.

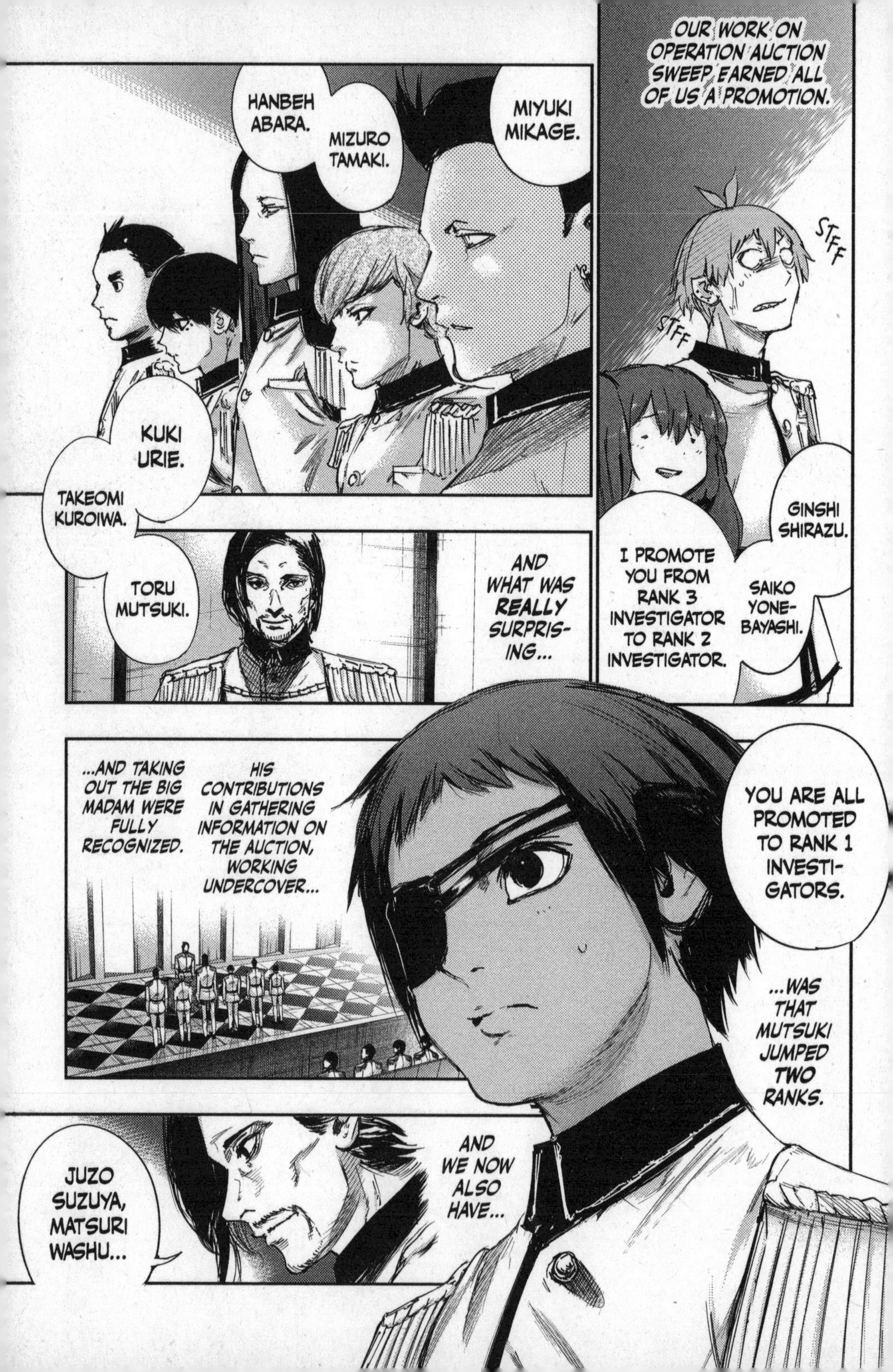
OUR WORK ON OPERATION AUCTION SWEEP EARNED ALL OF US A PROMOTION.
STFF
STFF
GINSHI SHIRAZU.
SAIKO YONE-BAYASHI.
I PROMOTE YOU FROM RANK 3 INVESTIGATOR TO RANK 2 INVESTIGATOR.
MIYUKI MIKAGE.
MIZURO TAMAKI.
HANBEH ABARA.
KUKI URIE.
TAKEOMI KUROIWA.
AND WHAT WAS REALLY SURPRIS-ING...
TORU MUTSUKI.
YOU ARE ALL PROMOTED TO RANK 1 INVESTI-GATORS.
...WAS THAT MUTSUKI JUMPED TWO RANKS.
HIS CONTRIBUTIONS IN GATHERING INFORMATION ON THE AUCTION, WORKING UNDERCOVER...
...AND TAKING OUT THE BIG MADAM WERE FULLY RECOGNIZED.
AND WE NOW ALSO HAVE...
JUZO SUZUYA, MATSURI WASHU...

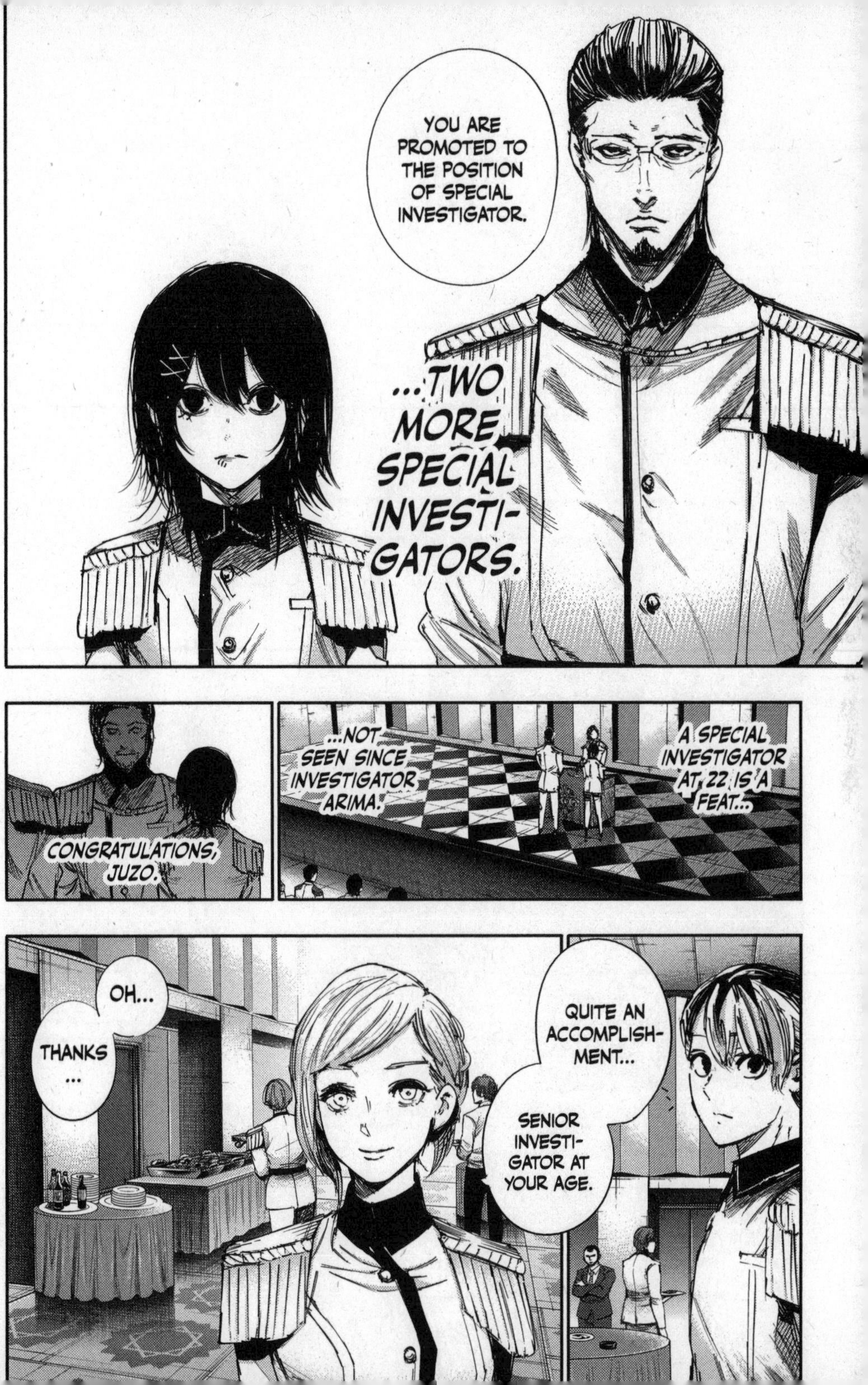
YOU ARE PROMOTED TO THE POSITION OF SPECIAL INVESTIGATOR.
...TWO MORE SPECIAL INVESTI-GATORS.
A SPECIAL INVESTIGATOR AT 22 IS A FEAT...
...NOT SEEN SINCE INVESTIGATOR ARIMA.
CONGRATULATIONS, JUZO.
QUITE AN ACCOMPLISH-MENT...
SENIOR INVESTI-GATOR AT YOUR AGE.
OH...
THANKS ...

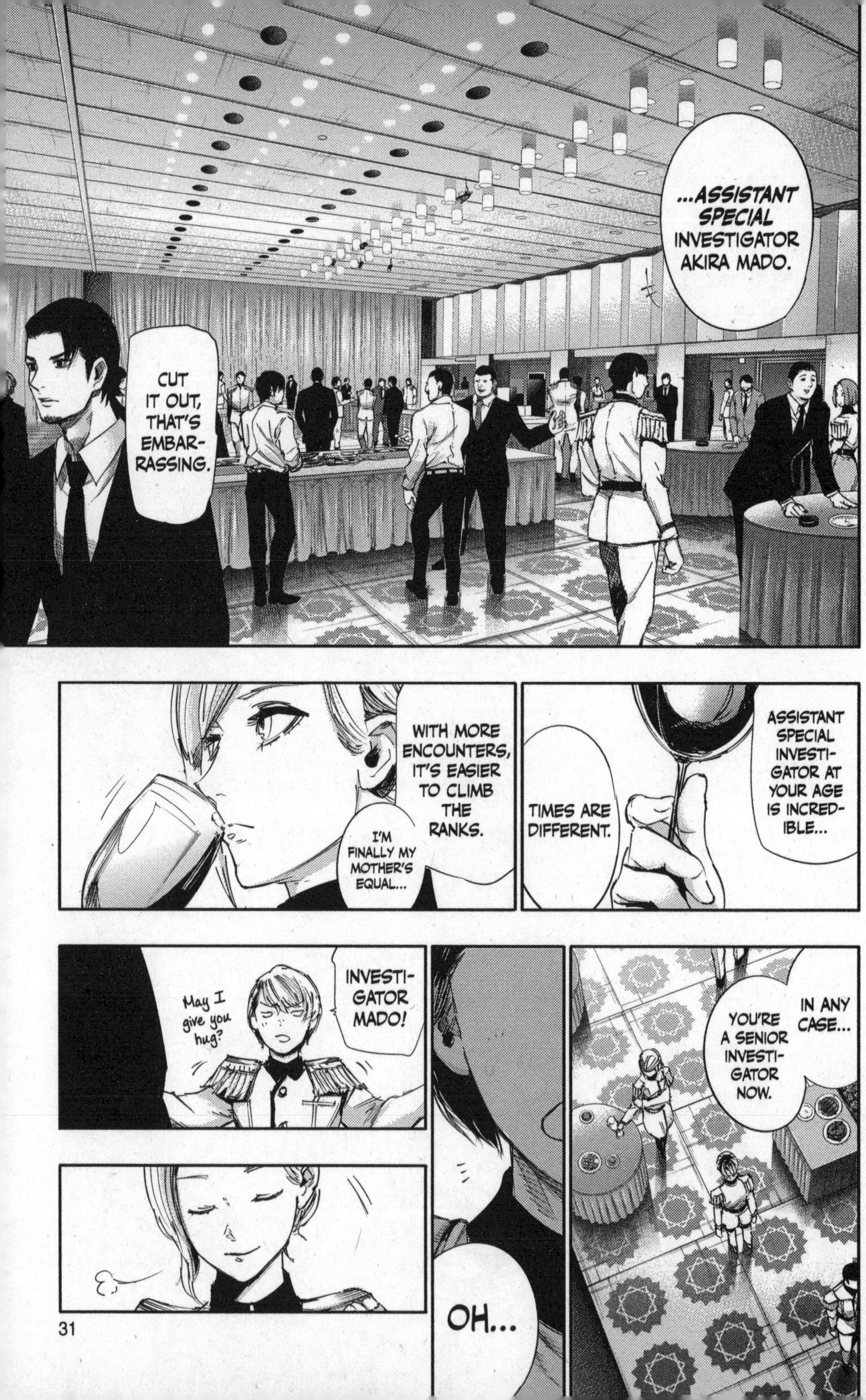
...ASSISTANT SPECIAL INVESTIGATOR AKIRA MADO.
CUT IT OUT, THAT'S EMBARRASSING.
ASSISTANT SPECIAL INVESTIGATOR AT YOUR AGE IS INCREDIBLE...
TIMES ARE DIFFERENT.
WITH MORE ENCOUNTERS, IT'S EASIER TO CLIMB THE RANKS.
I'M FINALLY MY MOTHER'S EQUAL...
IN ANY CASE...
YOU'RE A SENIOR INVESTIGATOR NOW.
OH...
INVESTIGATOR MADO!
May I give you hug?

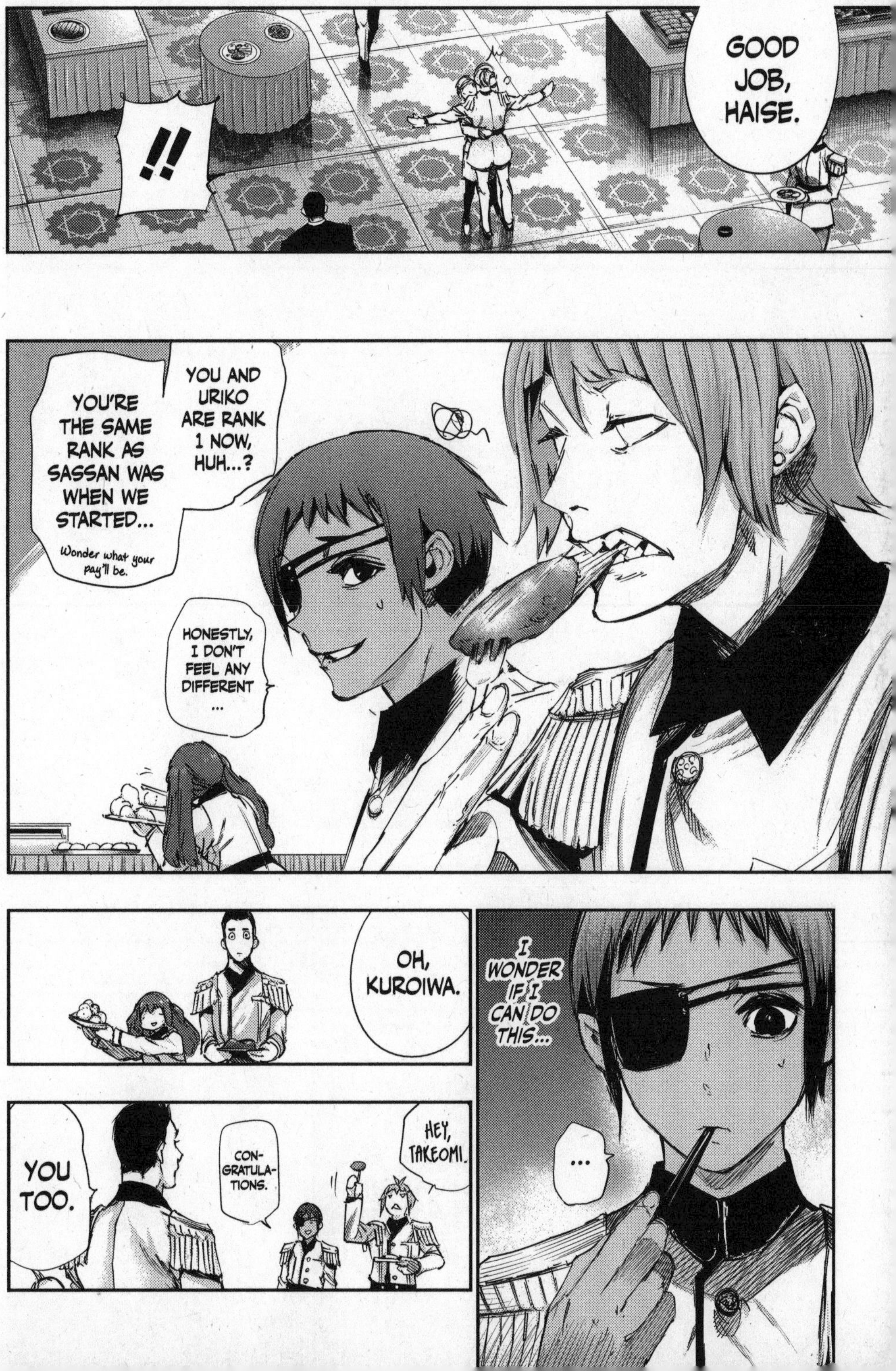
GOOD JOB, HAISE.
!!
YOU AND URIKO ARE RANK 1 NOW, HUH...?
YOU'RE THE SAME RANK AS SASSAN WAS WHEN WE STARTED...
Wonder what your pay'll be.
HONESTLY, I DON'T FEEL ANY DIFFERENT ...
I WONDER IF I CAN DO THIS...
...
OH, KUROIWA.
HEY, TAKEOMI.
CON-GRATULA-TIONS.
YOU TOO.

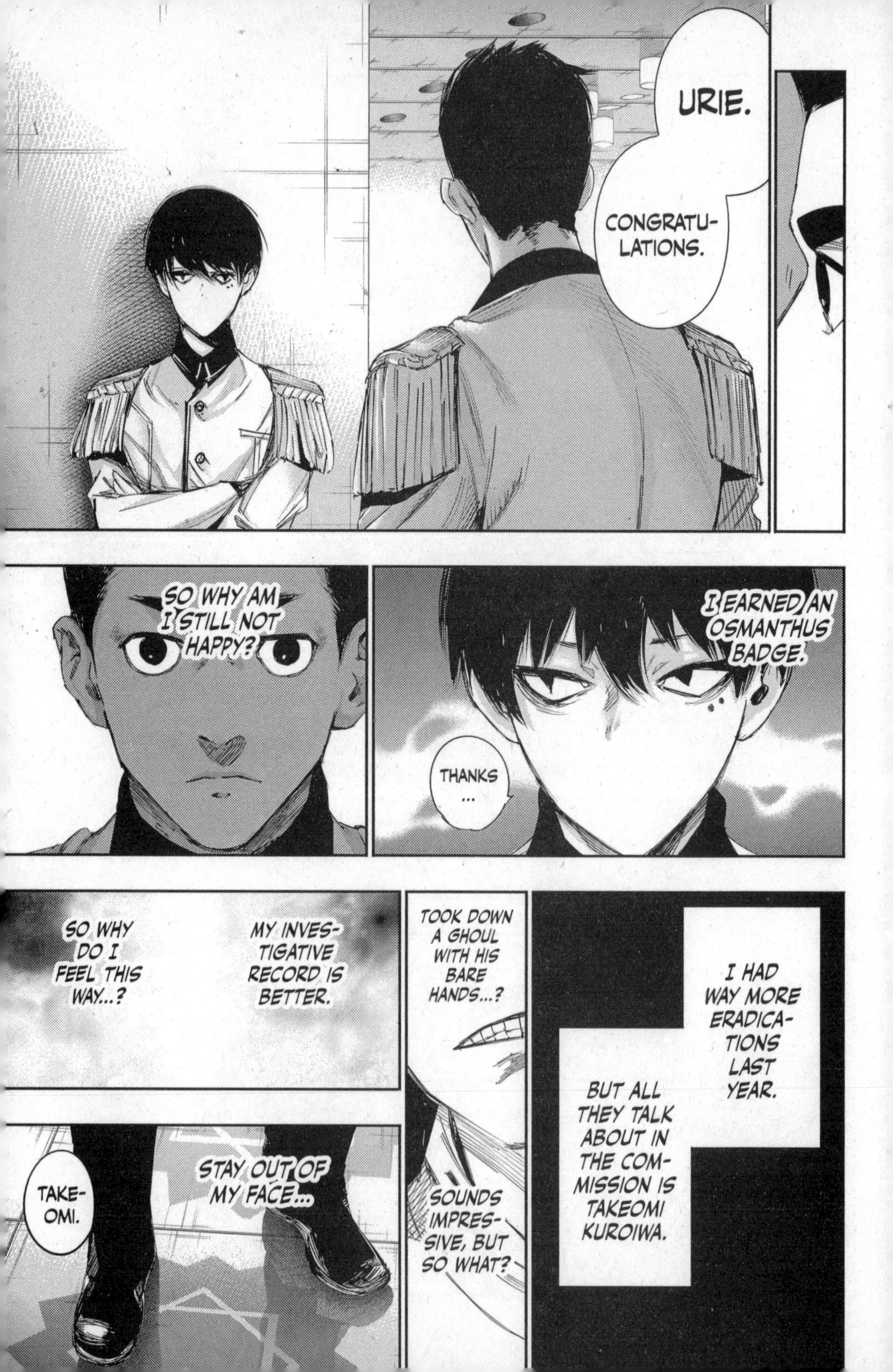
URIE.
CONGRATULATIONS.
I EARNED AN OSMANTHUS BADGE.
THANKS...
SO WHY AM I STILL NOT HAPPY?
I HAD WAY MORE ERADICATIONS LAST YEAR.
BUT ALL THEY TALK ABOUT IN THE COMMISSION IS TAKEOMI KUROIWA.
TOOK DOWN A GHOUL WITH HIS BARE HANDS...?
SOUNDS IMPRESSIVE, BUT SO WHAT?
MY INVESTIGATIVE RECORD IS BETTER.
SO WHY DO I FEEL THIS WAY...?
STAY OUT OF MY FACE...
TAKEOMI.

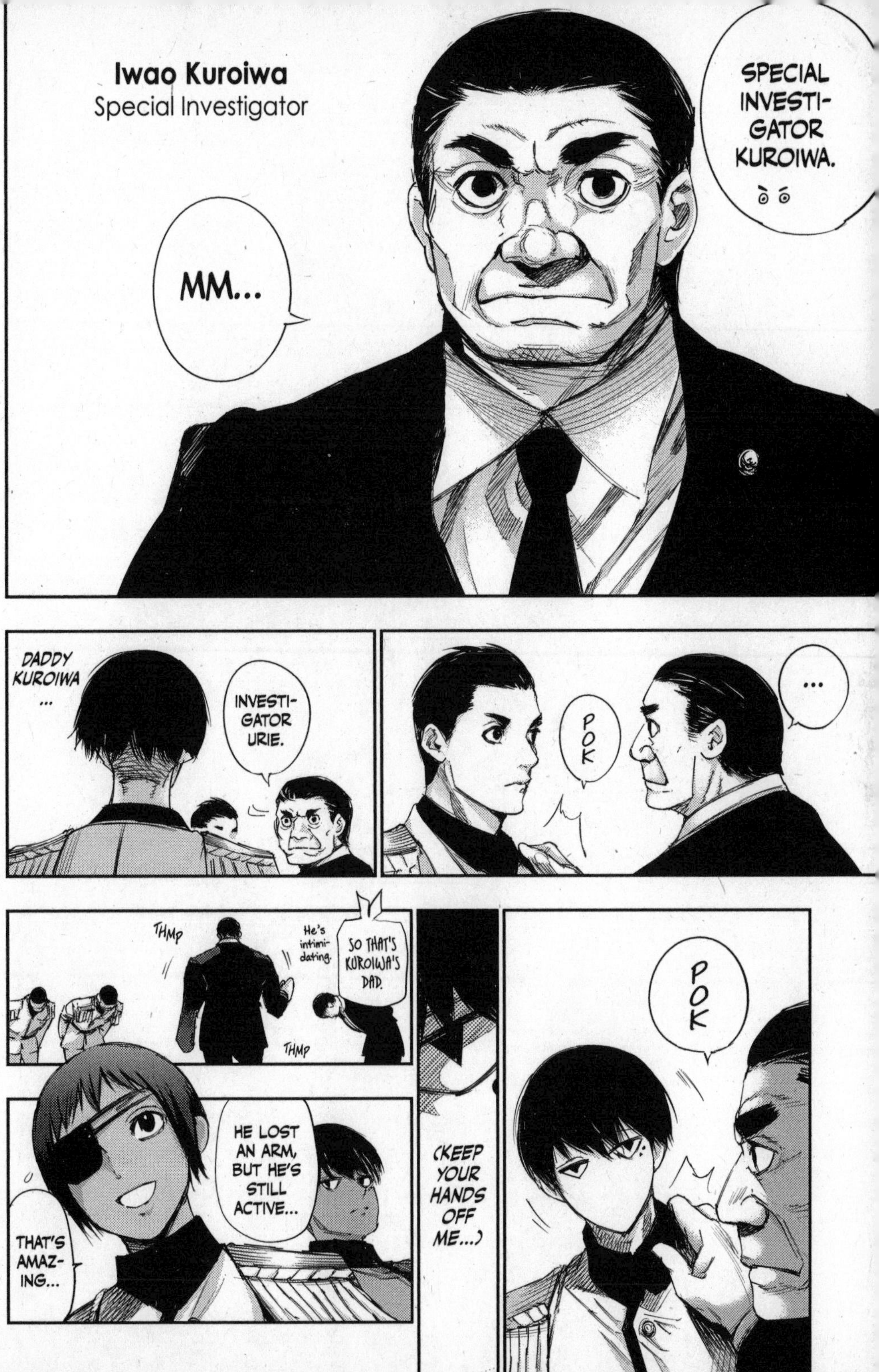
SPECIAL INVESTIGATOR KUROIWA.
Iwao Kuroiwa
Special Investigator
MM...
...
POK
INVESTIGATOR URIE.
DADDY KUROIWA ...
POK
(KEEP YOUR HANDS OFF ME...)
SO THAT'S KUROIWA'S DAD.
He's intimidating.
THMP
THMP
HE LOST AN ARM, BUT HE'S STILL ACTIVE...
THAT'S AMAZING...

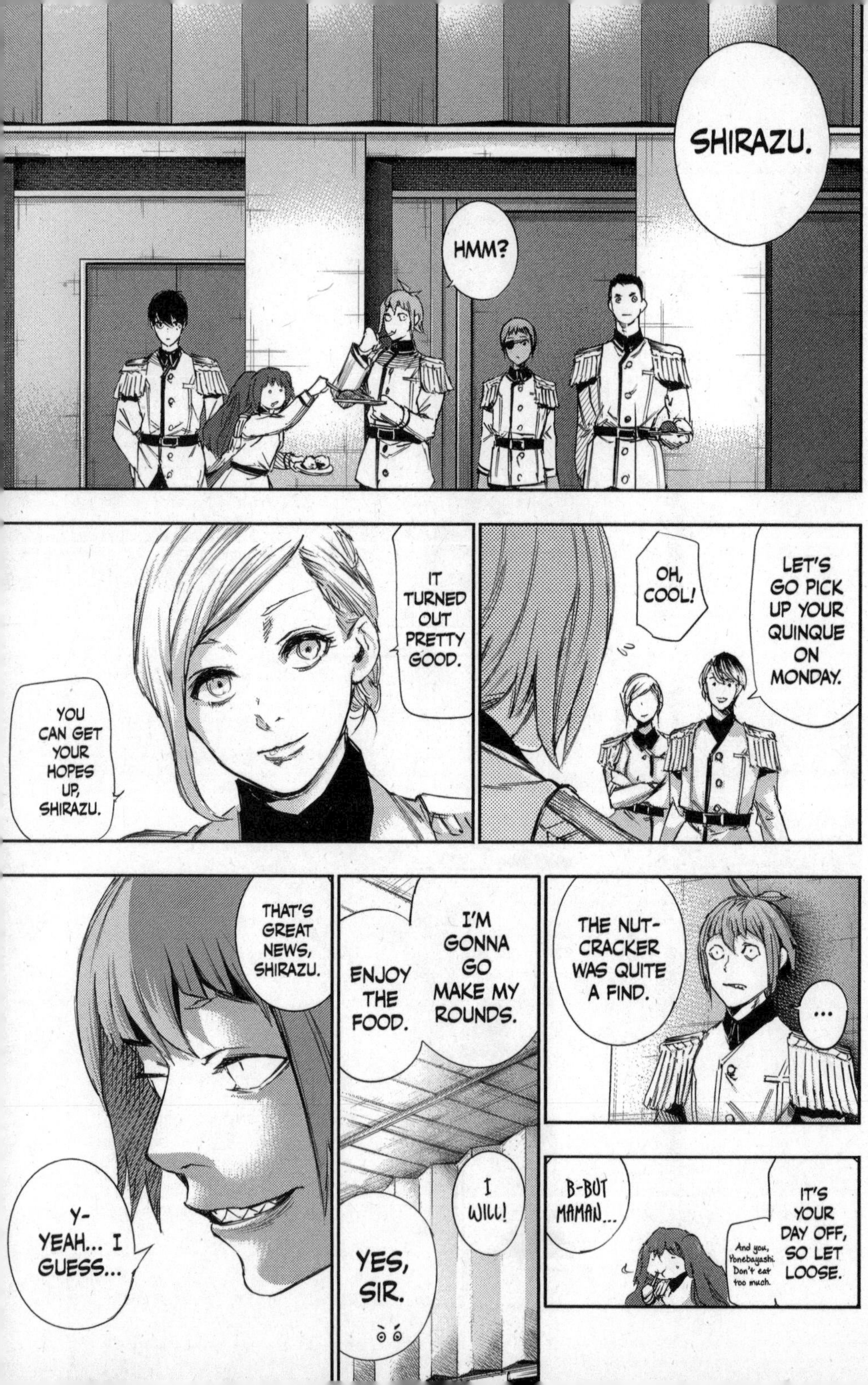
SHIRAZU.
HMM?
LET'S GO PICK UP YOUR QUINQUE ON MONDAY.
OH, COOL!
IT TURNED OUT PRETTY GOOD.
YOU CAN GET YOUR HOPES UP, SHIRAZU.
THE NUT-CRACKER WAS QUITE A FIND.
...
IT'S YOUR DAY OFF, SO LET LOOSE.
And you, Yonebayashi. Don't eat too much.
B-BUT MAMAN...
I'M GONNA GO MAKE MY ROUNDS.
ENJOY THE FOOD.
I WILL!
YES, SIR.
THAT'S GREAT NEWS, SHIRAZU.
Y-YEAH... I GUESS...

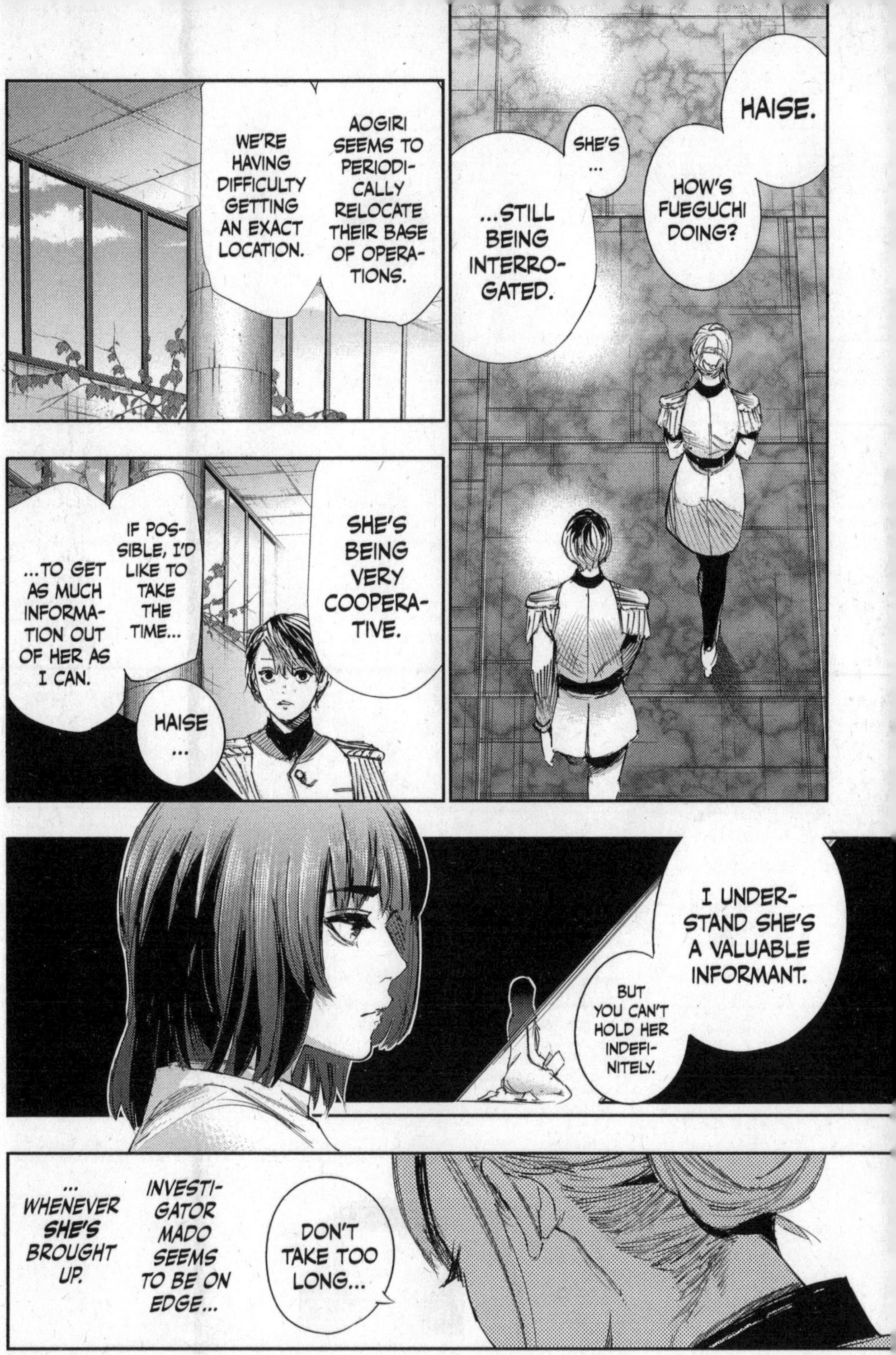
HAISE.
HOW'S FUEGUCHI DOING?
SHE'S ...
...STILL BEING INTERROGATED.
AOGIRI SEEMS TO PERIODICALLY RELOCATE THEIR BASE OF OPERATIONS.
WE'RE HAVING DIFFICULTY GETTING AN EXACT LOCATION.
SHE'S BEING VERY COOPERATIVE.
IF POSSIBLE, I'D LIKE TO TAKE THE TIME...
...TO GET AS MUCH INFORMATION OUT OF HER AS I CAN.
HAISE ...
I UNDERSTAND SHE'S A VALUABLE INFORMANT.
BUT YOU CAN'T HOLD HER INDEFINITELY.
DON'T TAKE TOO LONG...
INVESTIGATOR MADO SEEMS TO BE ON EDGE...
... WHENEVER SHE'S BROUGHT UP.

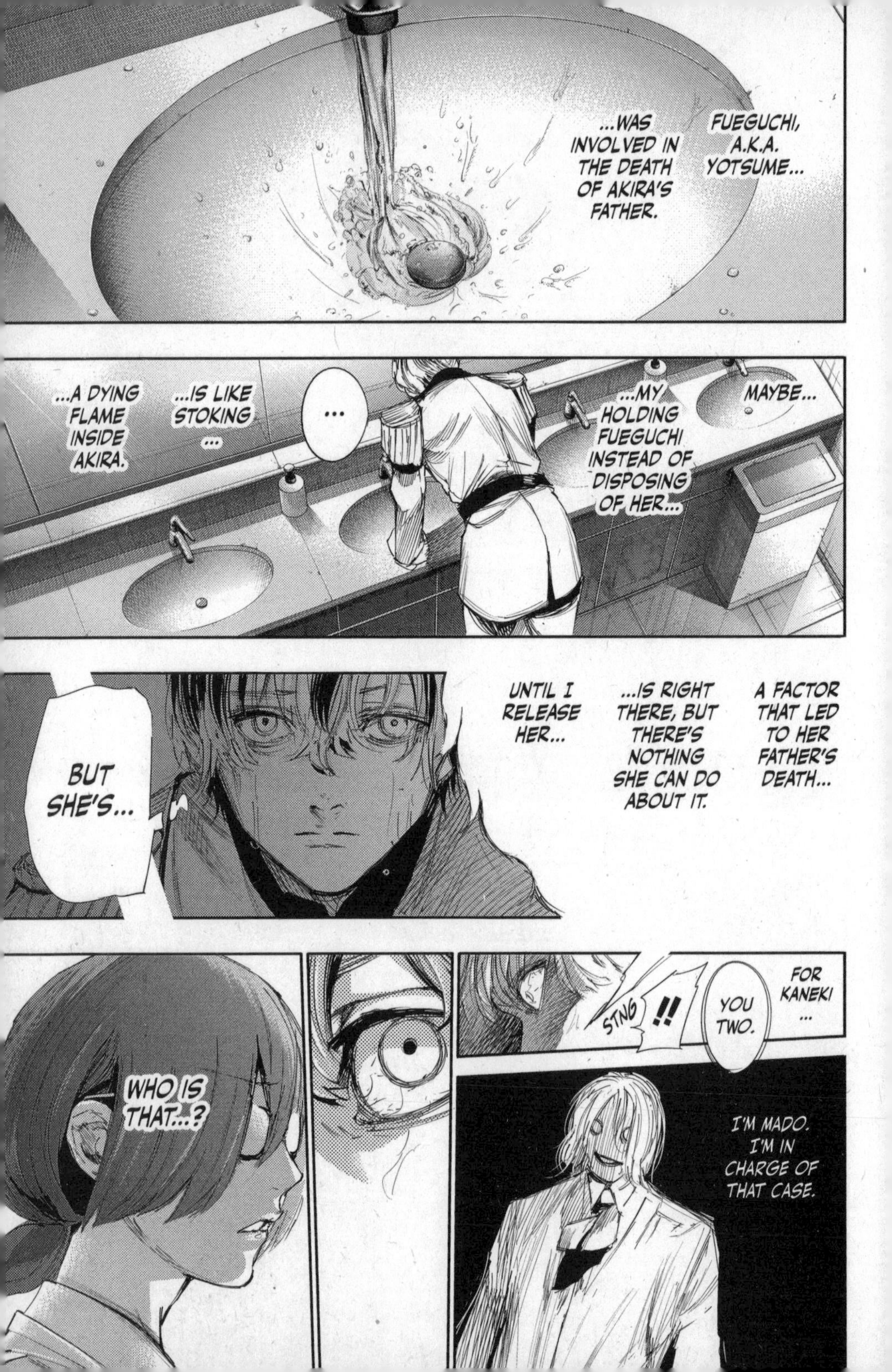
FUEGUCHI, A.K.A. YOTSUME...
...WAS INVOLVED IN THE DEATH OF AKIRA'S FATHER.
MAYBE...
...MY HOLDING FUEGUCHI INSTEAD OF DISPOSING OF HER...
...
...IS LIKE STOKING ...
...A DYING FLAME INSIDE AKIRA.
A FACTOR THAT LED TO HER FATHER'S DEATH...
...IS RIGHT THERE, BUT THERE'S NOTHING SHE CAN DO ABOUT IT.
UNTIL I RELEASE HER...
BUT SHE'S...
FOR KANEKI ...
YOU TWO.
STNG
!!
I'M MADO. I'M IN CHARGE OF THAT CASE.
WHO IS THAT...?

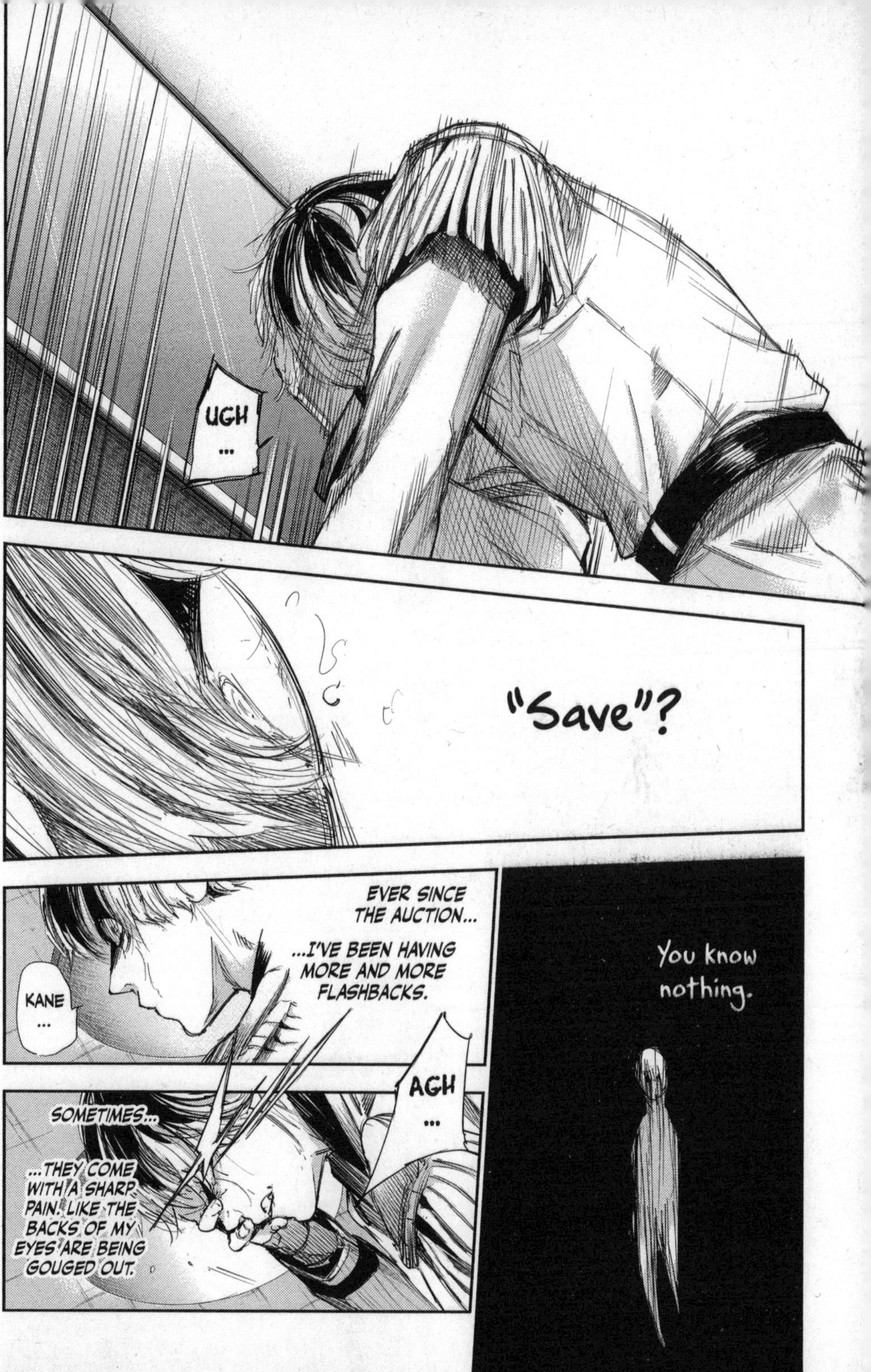
UGH...
"Save"?
You know nothing.
EVER SINCE THE AUCTION...
...I'VE BEEN HAVING MORE AND MORE FLASHBACKS.
KANE...
AGH...
SOMETIMES...
...THEY COME WITH A SHARP PAIN. LIKE THE BACKS OF MY EYES ARE BEING GOUGED OUT.

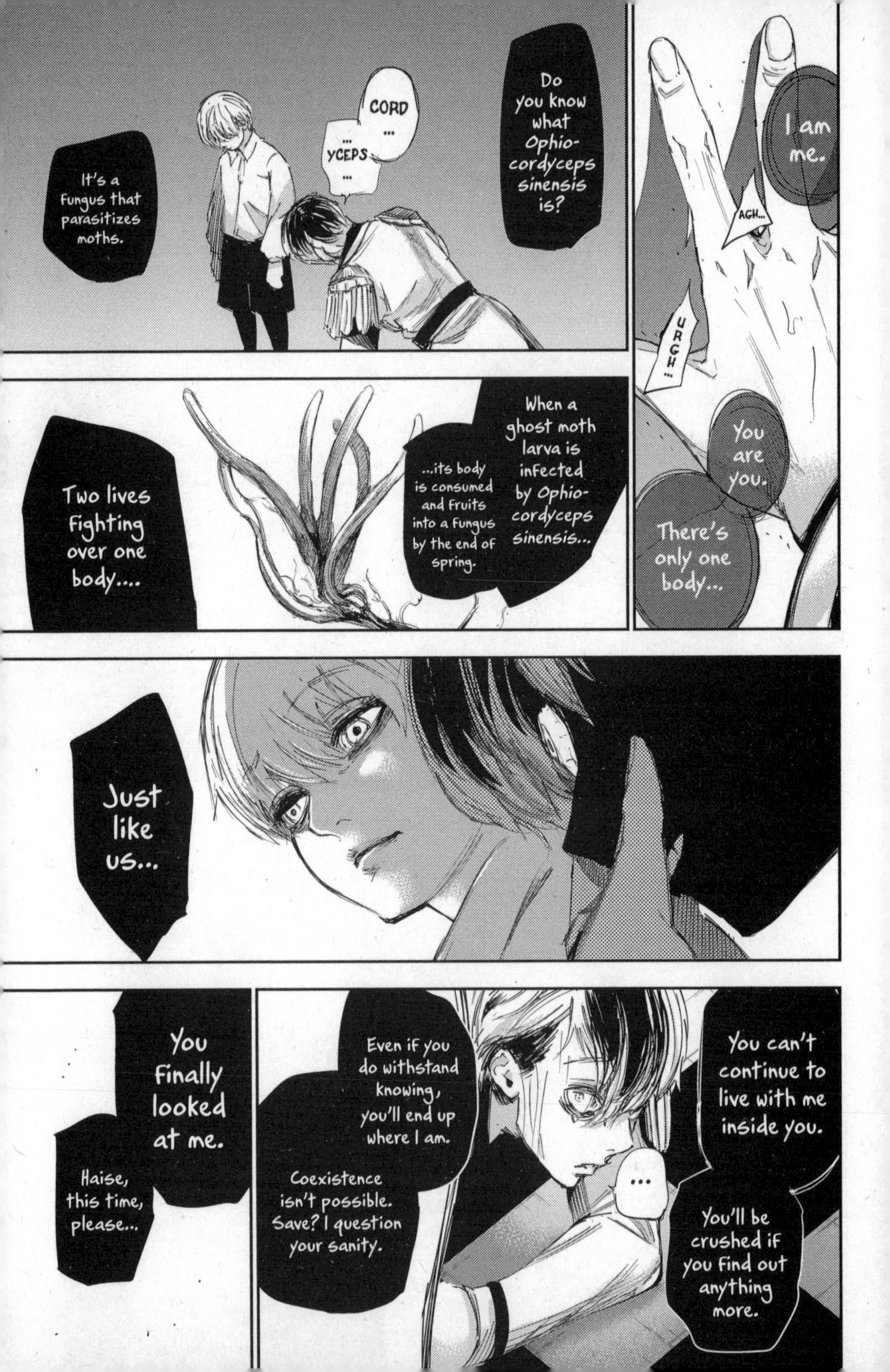
I am me.
AGH...
URGH...
You are you.
There's only one body...
Do you know what Ophio-cordyceps sinensis is?
CORD...
...YCEPS...
It's a fungus that parasitizes moths.
When a ghost moth larva is infected by Ophio-cordyceps sinensis...
...its body is consumed and fruits into a fungus by the end of spring.
Two lives fighting over one body....
Just like us...
You can't continue to live with me inside you.
Even if you do withstand knowing, you'll end up where I am.
...
You'll be crushed if you find out anything more.
Coexistence isn't possible. Save? I question your sanity.
You finally looked at me.
Haise, this time, please...

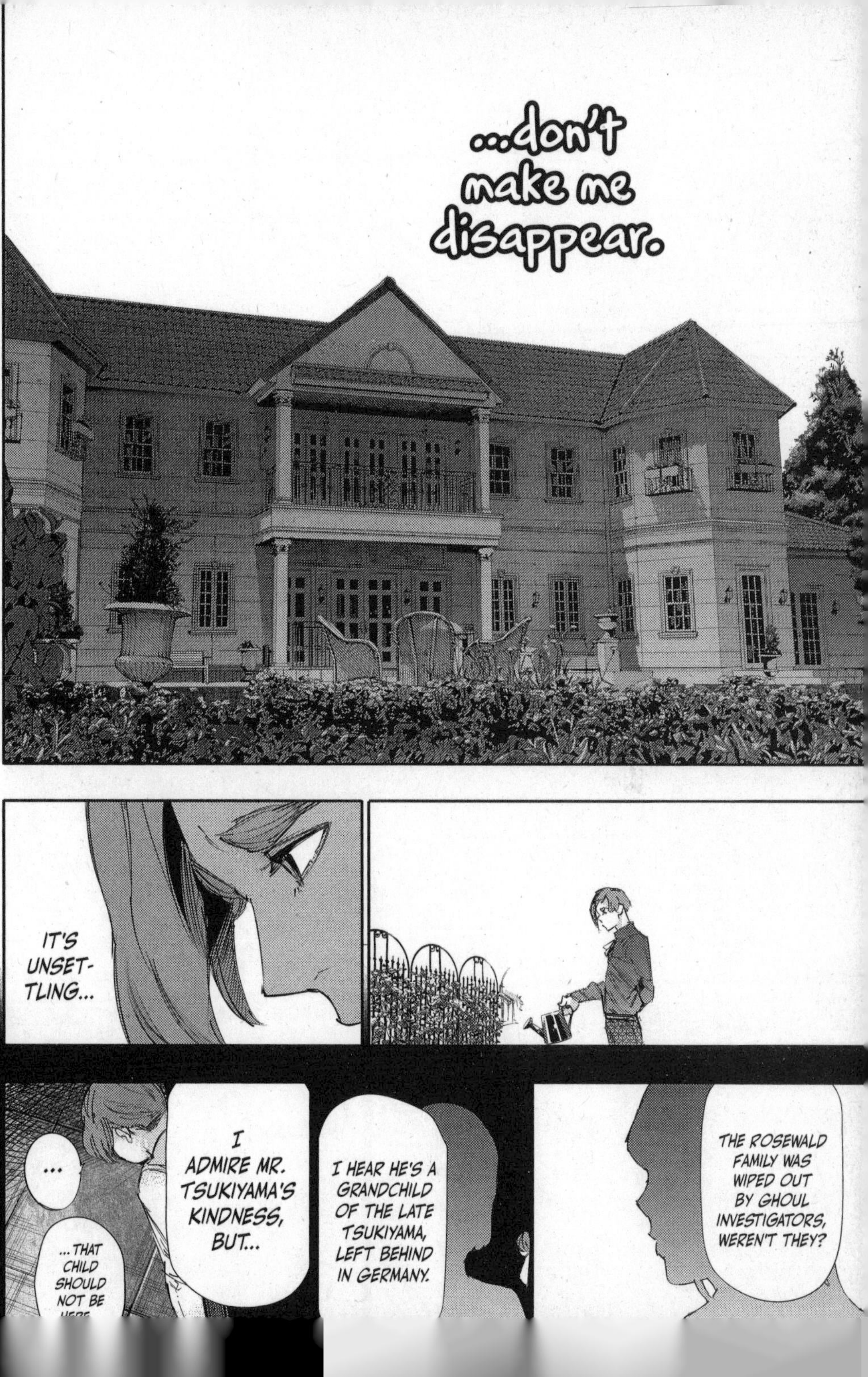
...don't make me disappear.
IT'S UNSET-TLING...
THE ROSEWALD FAMILY WAS WIPED OUT BY GHOUL INVESTIGATORS, WEREN'T THEY?
I HEAR HE'S A GRANDCHILD OF THE LATE TSUKIYAMA, LEFT BEHIND IN GERMANY.
I ADMIRE MR. TSUKIYAMA'S KINDNESS, BUT...
...
...THAT CHILD SHOULD NOT BE

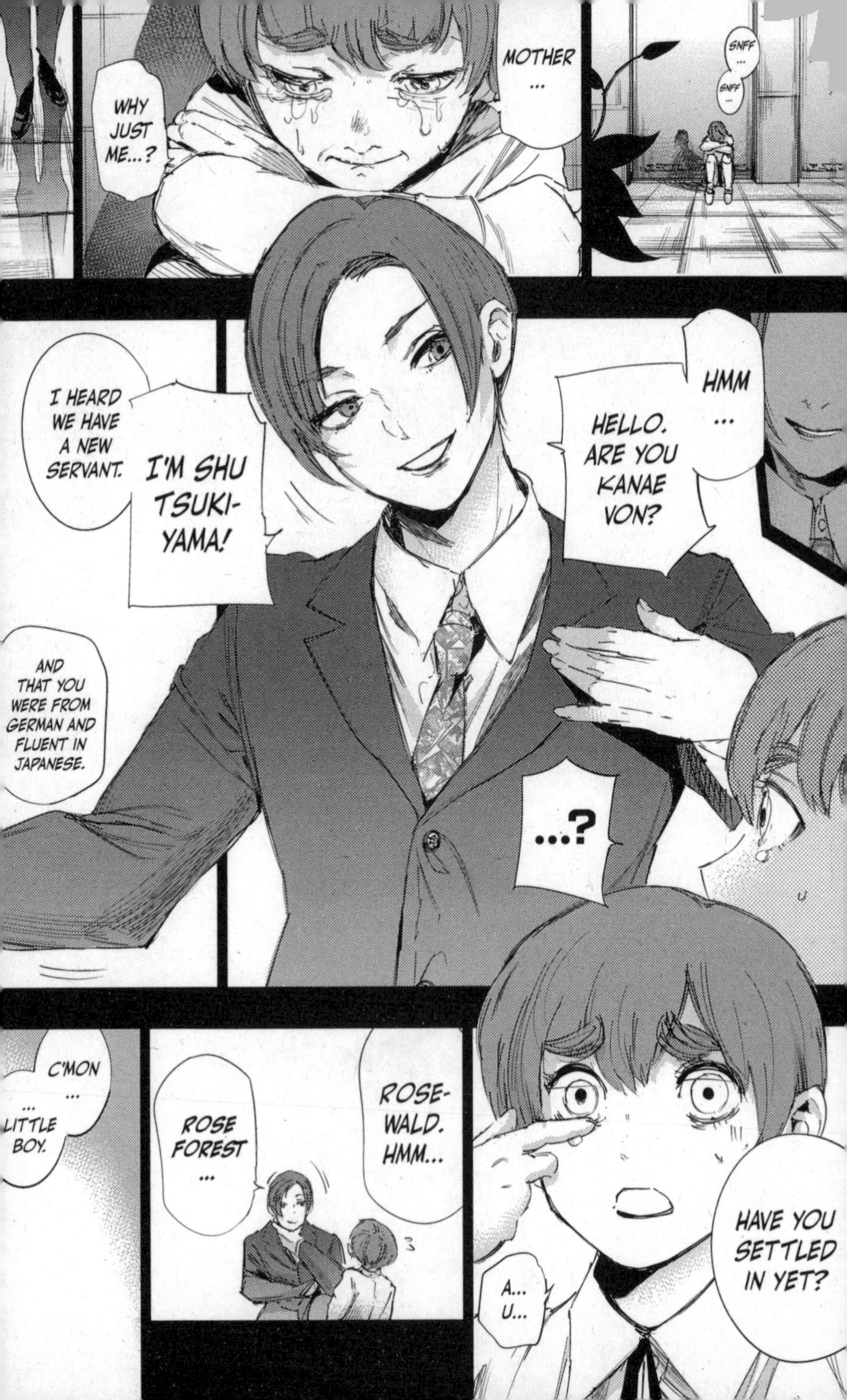
SNFF...
SNFF...
MOTHER...
WHY JUST ME...?
HMM...
HELLO. ARE YOU KANAE VON?
I'M SHU TSUKI-YAMA!
I HEARD WE HAVE A NEW SERVANT.
AND THAT YOU WERE FROM GERMAN AND FLUENT IN JAPANESE.
...?
HAVE YOU SETTLED IN YET?
A... U...
ROSE-WALD. HMM...
ROSE FOREST...
C'MON... LITTLE BOY.

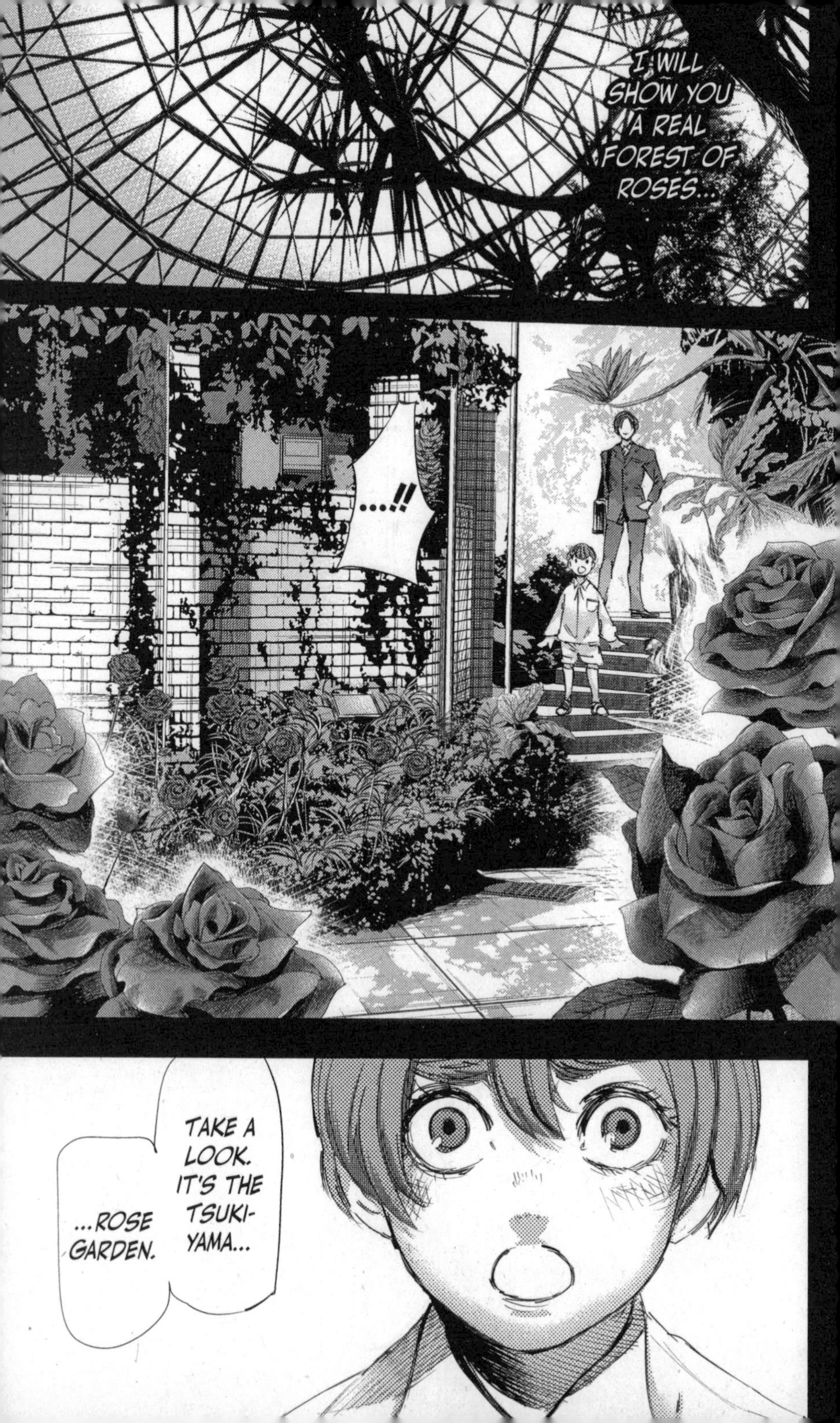
I WILL SHOW YOU A REAL FOREST OF ROSES...
...!!
TAKE A LOOK. IT'S THE TSUKI-YAMA...
...ROSE GARDEN.

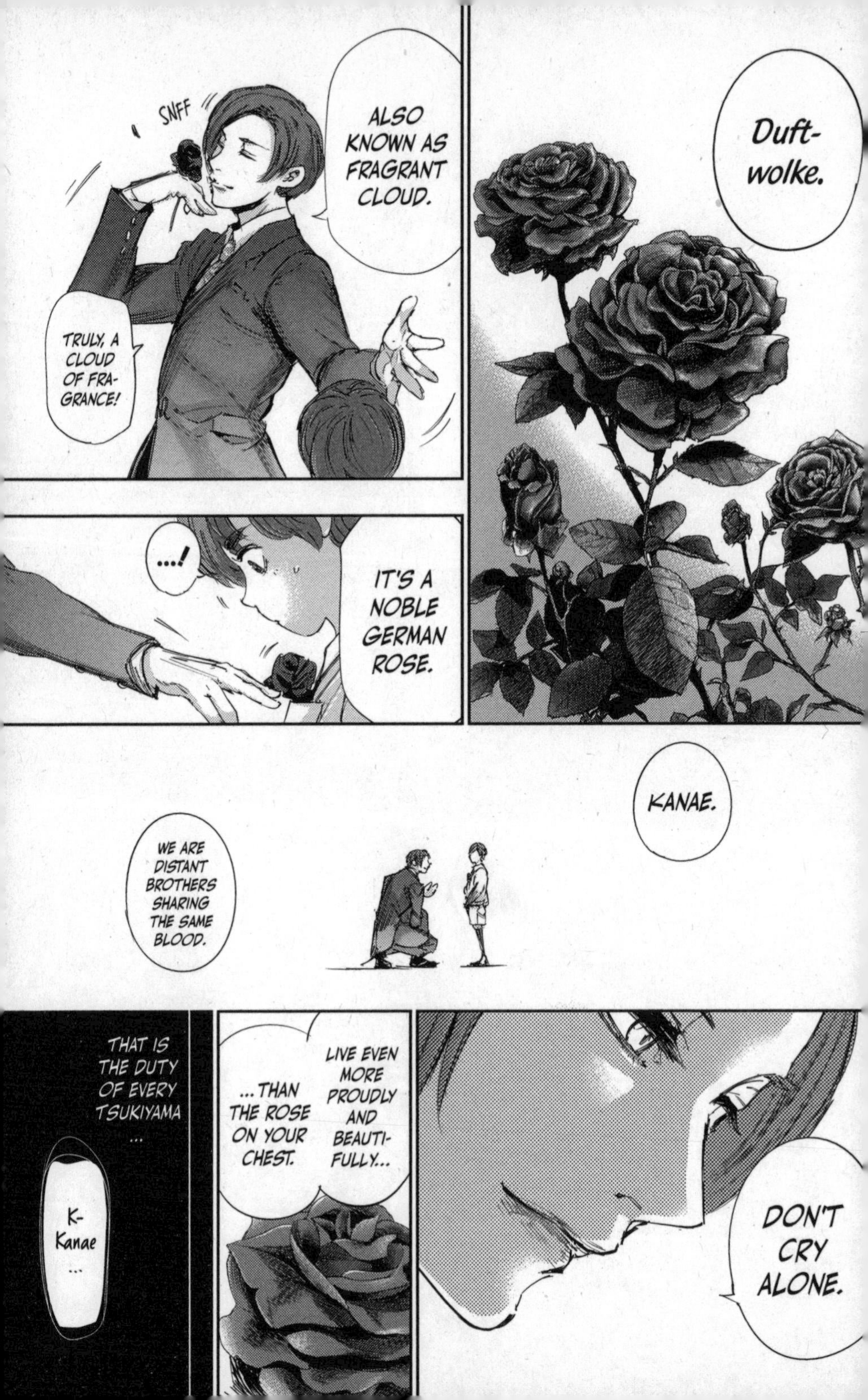
Duft-wolke.
ALSO KNOWN AS FRAGRANT CLOUD.
SNFF
TRULY, A CLOUD OF FRA-GRANCE!
IT'S A NOBLE GERMAN ROSE.
...!
KANAE.
WE ARE DISTANT BROTHERS SHARING THE SAME BLOOD.
DON'T CRY ALONE.
LIVE EVEN MORE PROUDLY AND BEAUTI-FULLY...
...THAN THE ROSE ON YOUR CHEST.
THAT IS THE DUTY OF EVERY TSUKIYAMA ...
K-Kanae ...

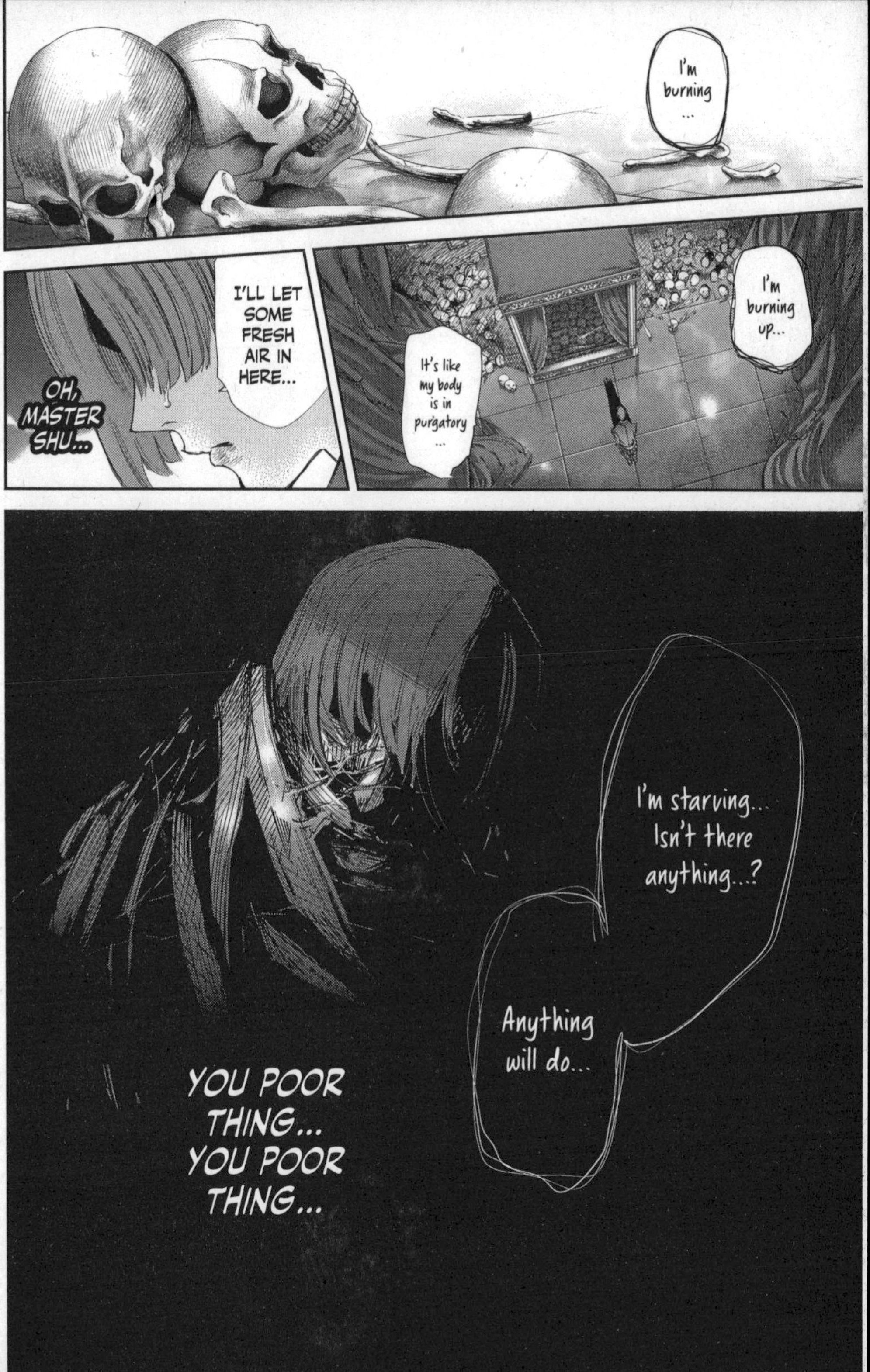
I'm burning ...
I'm burning up...
It's like my body is in purgatory ...
I'LL LET SOME FRESH AIR IN HERE...
OH, MASTER SHU...
I'm starving... Isn't there anything...?
Anything will do...
YOU POOR THING... YOU POOR THING...

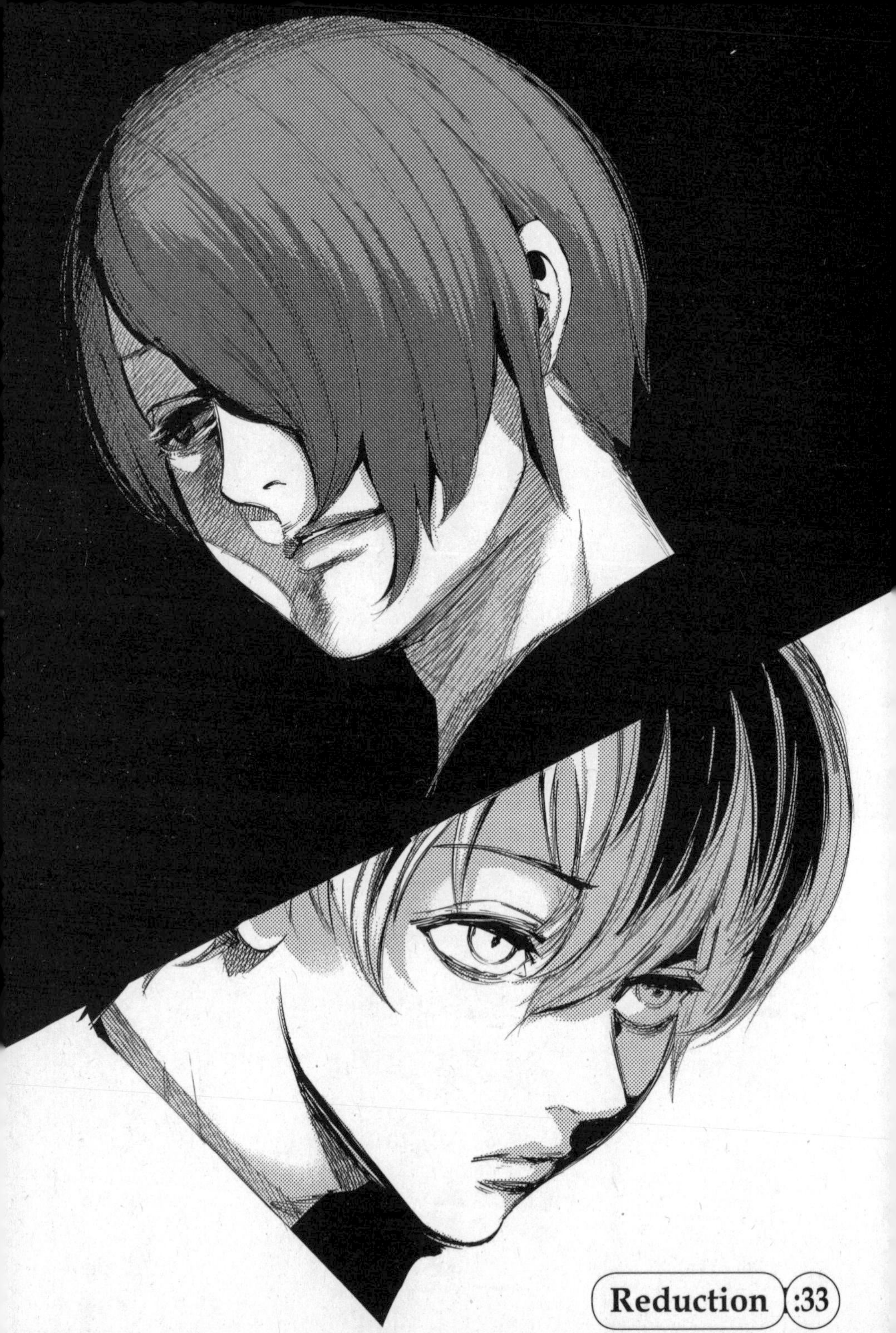

Reduction :33

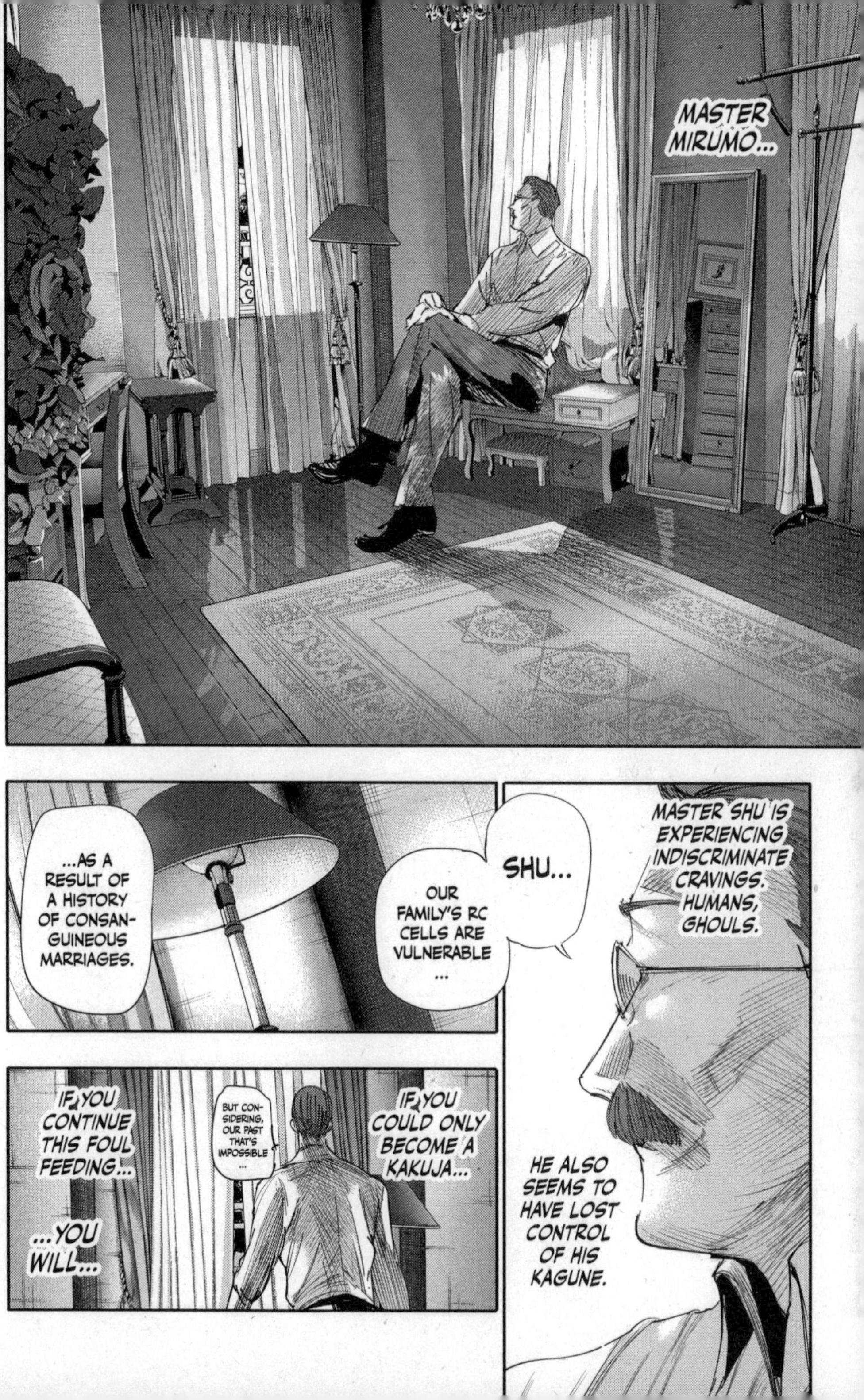
MASTER MIRUMO...
MASTER SHU IS EXPERIENCING INDISCRIMINATE CRAVINGS. HUMANS, GHOULS.
HE ALSO SEEMS TO HAVE LOST CONTROL OF HIS KAGUNE.
SHU...
OUR FAMILY'S RC CELLS ARE VULNERABLE...
...AS A RESULT OF A HISTORY OF CONSAN-GUINEOUS MARRIAGES.
IF YOU COULD ONLY BECOME A KAKUJA...
BUT CON-SIDERING, OUR PAST THAT'S IMPOSSIBLE...
IF YOU CONTINUE THIS FOUL FEEDING...
...YOU WILL...

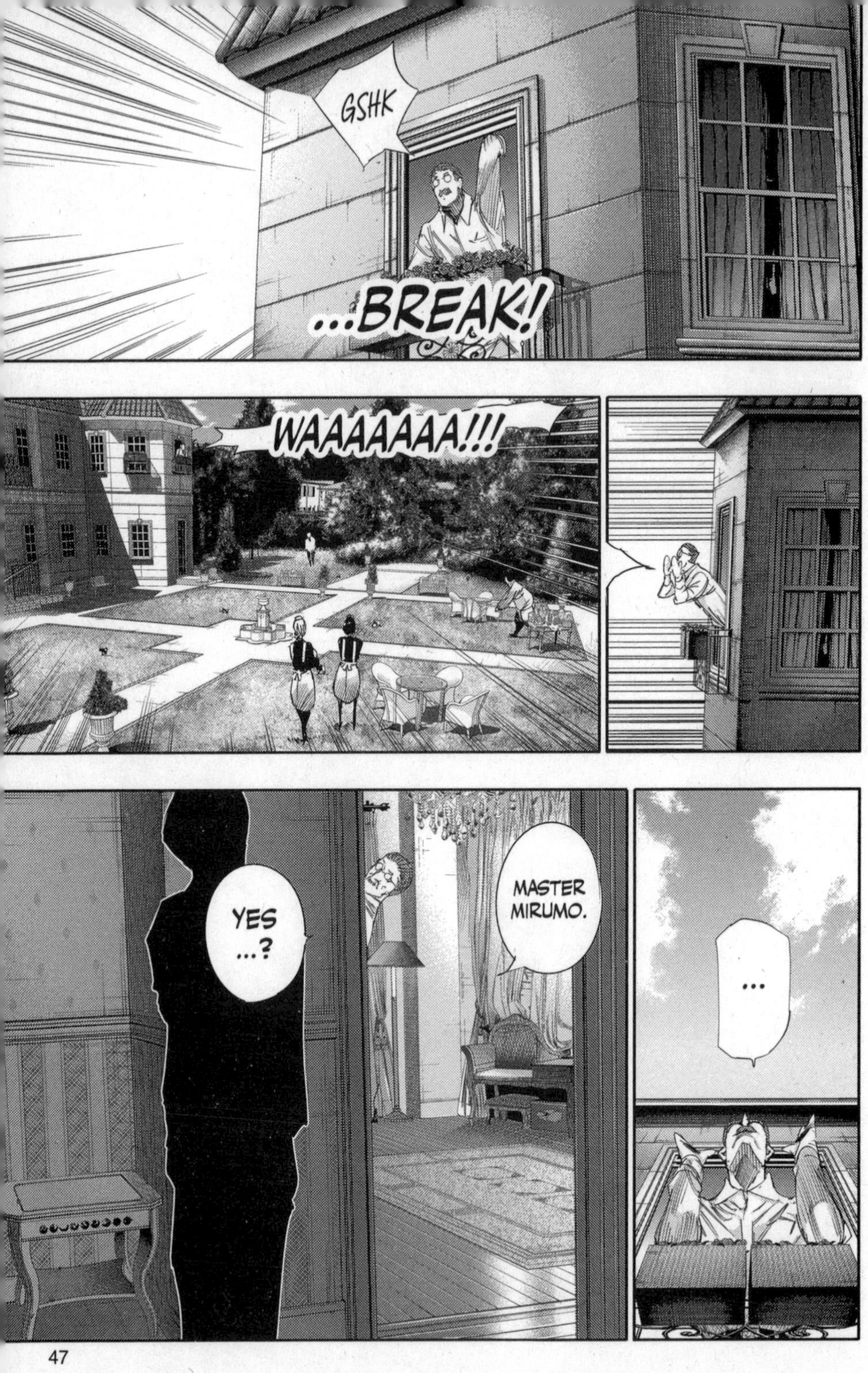
GSHK
...BREAK!
WAAAAAAA!!!
...
MASTER MIRUMO.
YES ...?

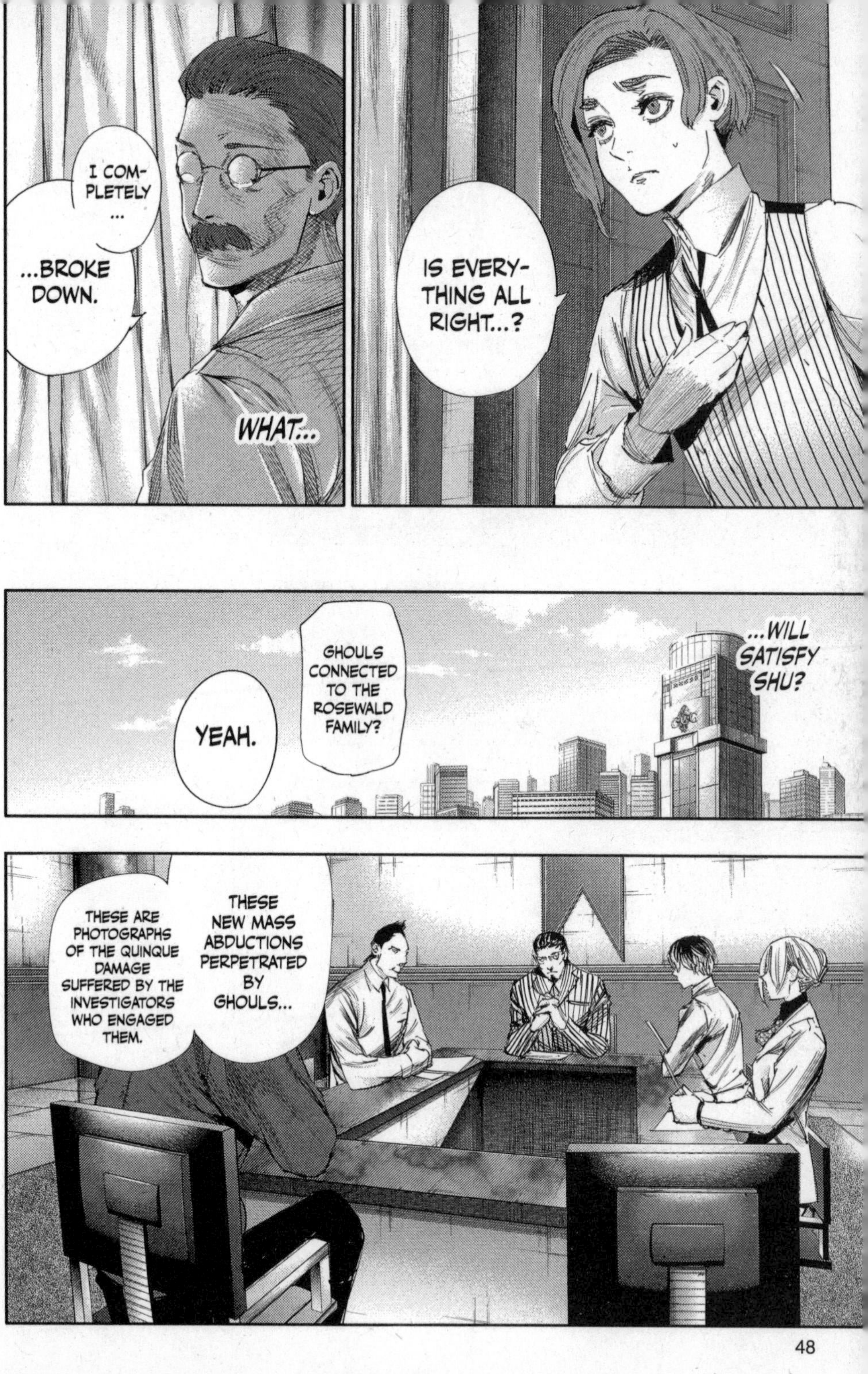
IS EVERY-THING ALL RIGHT...?
I COM-PLETELY ...
...BROKE DOWN.
WHAT...
...WILL SATISFY SHU?
GHOULS CONNECTED TO THE ROSEWALD FAMILY?
YEAH.
THESE NEW MASS ABDUCTIONS PERPETRATED BY GHOULS...
THESE ARE PHOTOGRAPHS OF THE QUINQUE DAMAGE SUFFERED BY THE INVESTIGATORS WHO ENGAGED THEM.

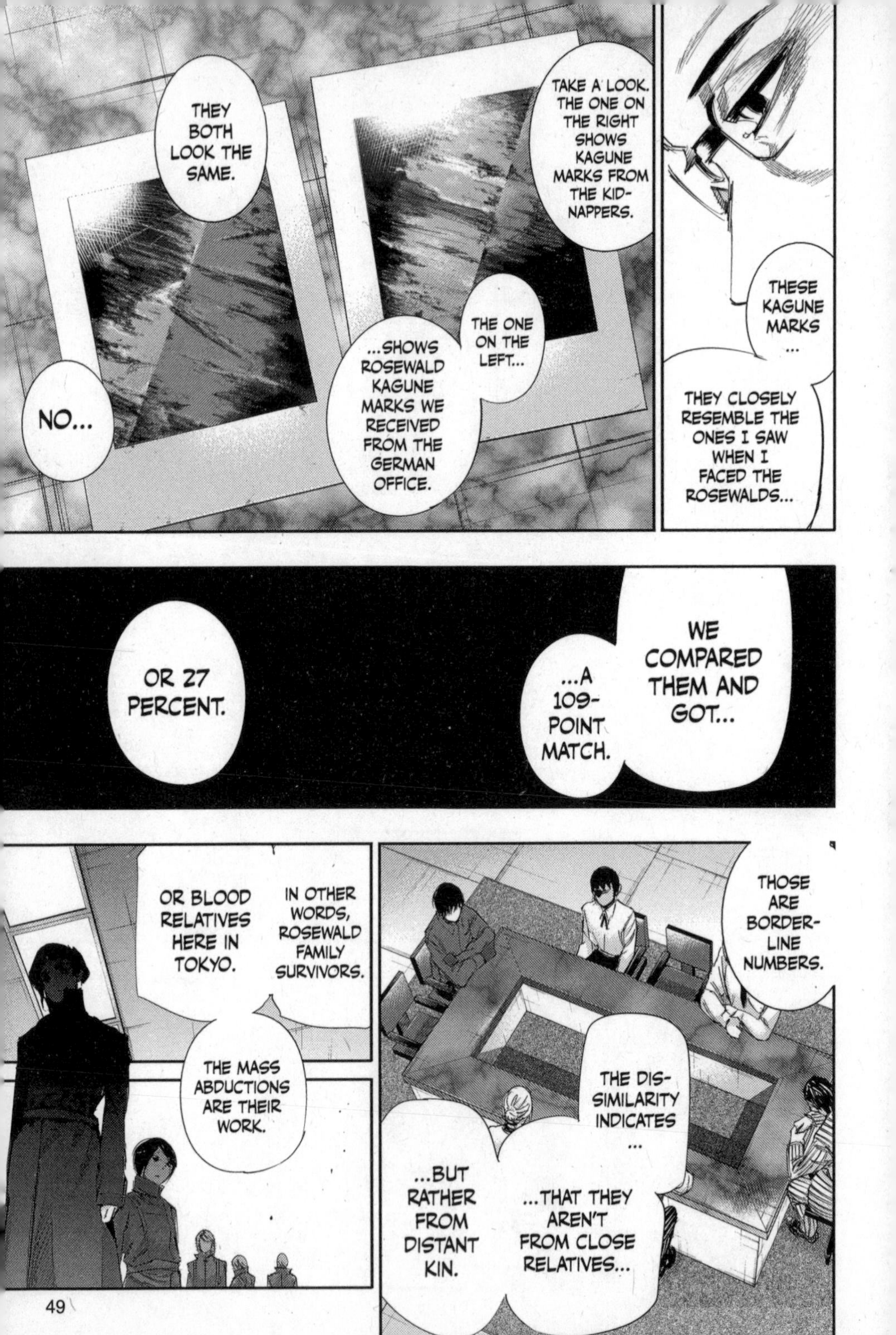
THESE KAGUNE MARKS ...
THEY CLOSELY RESEMBLE THE ONES I SAW WHEN I FACED THE ROSEWALDS...
TAKE A LOOK. THE ONE ON THE RIGHT SHOWS KAGUNE MARKS FROM THE KID-NAPPERS.
THE ONE ON THE LEFT...
...SHOWS ROSEWALD KAGUNE MARKS WE RECEIVED FROM THE GERMAN OFFICE.
THEY BOTH LOOK THE SAME.
NO...
WE COMPARED THEM AND GOT...
...A 109-POINT MATCH.
OR 27 PERCENT.
THOSE ARE BORDER-LINE NUMBERS.
THE DIS-SIMILARITY INDICATES ...
...THAT THEY AREN'T FROM CLOSE RELATIVES...
...BUT RATHER FROM DISTANT KIN.
IN OTHER WORDS, ROSEWALD FAMILY SURVIVORS.
OR BLOOD RELATIVES HERE IN TOKYO.
THE MASS ABDUCTIONS ARE THEIR WORK.

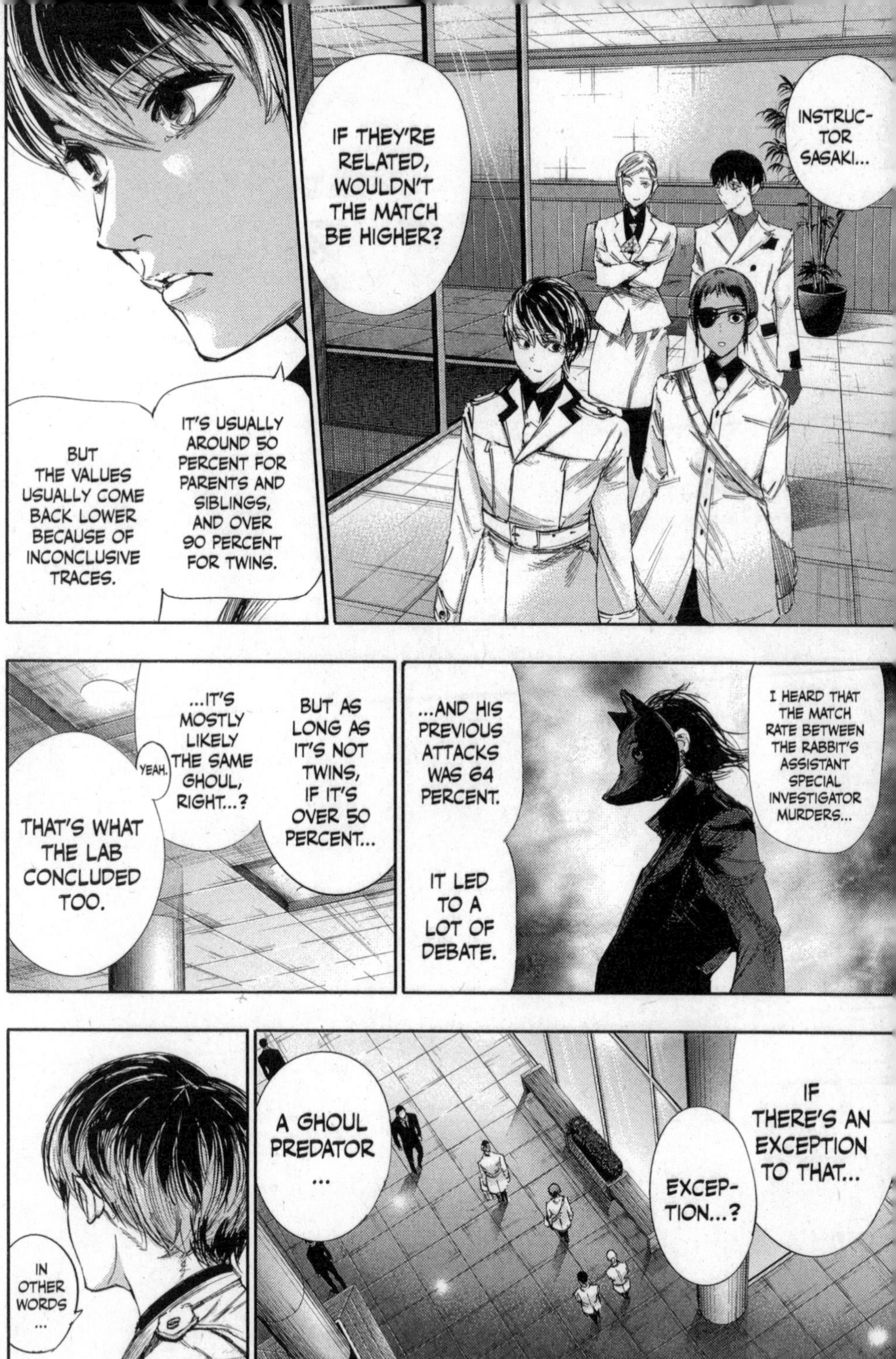
INSTRUCTOR SASAKI...
IF THEY'RE RELATED, WOULDN'T THE MATCH BE HIGHER?
IT'S USUALLY AROUND 50 PERCENT FOR PARENTS AND SIBLINGS, AND OVER 90 PERCENT FOR TWINS.
BUT THE VALUES USUALLY COME BACK LOWER BECAUSE OF INCONCLUSIVE TRACES.
I HEARD THAT THE MATCH RATE BETWEEN THE RABBIT'S ASSISTANT SPECIAL INVESTIGATOR MURDERS...
...AND HIS PREVIOUS ATTACKS WAS 64 PERCENT.
IT LED TO A LOT OF DEBATE.
BUT AS LONG AS IT'S NOT TWINS, IF IT'S OVER 50 PERCENT...
...IT'S MOSTLY LIKELY THE SAME GHOUL, RIGHT...?
YEAH.
THAT'S WHAT THE LAB CONCLUDED TOO.
IF THERE'S AN EXCEPTION TO THAT...
EXCEPTION...?
A GHOUL PREDATOR...
IN OTHER WORDS...

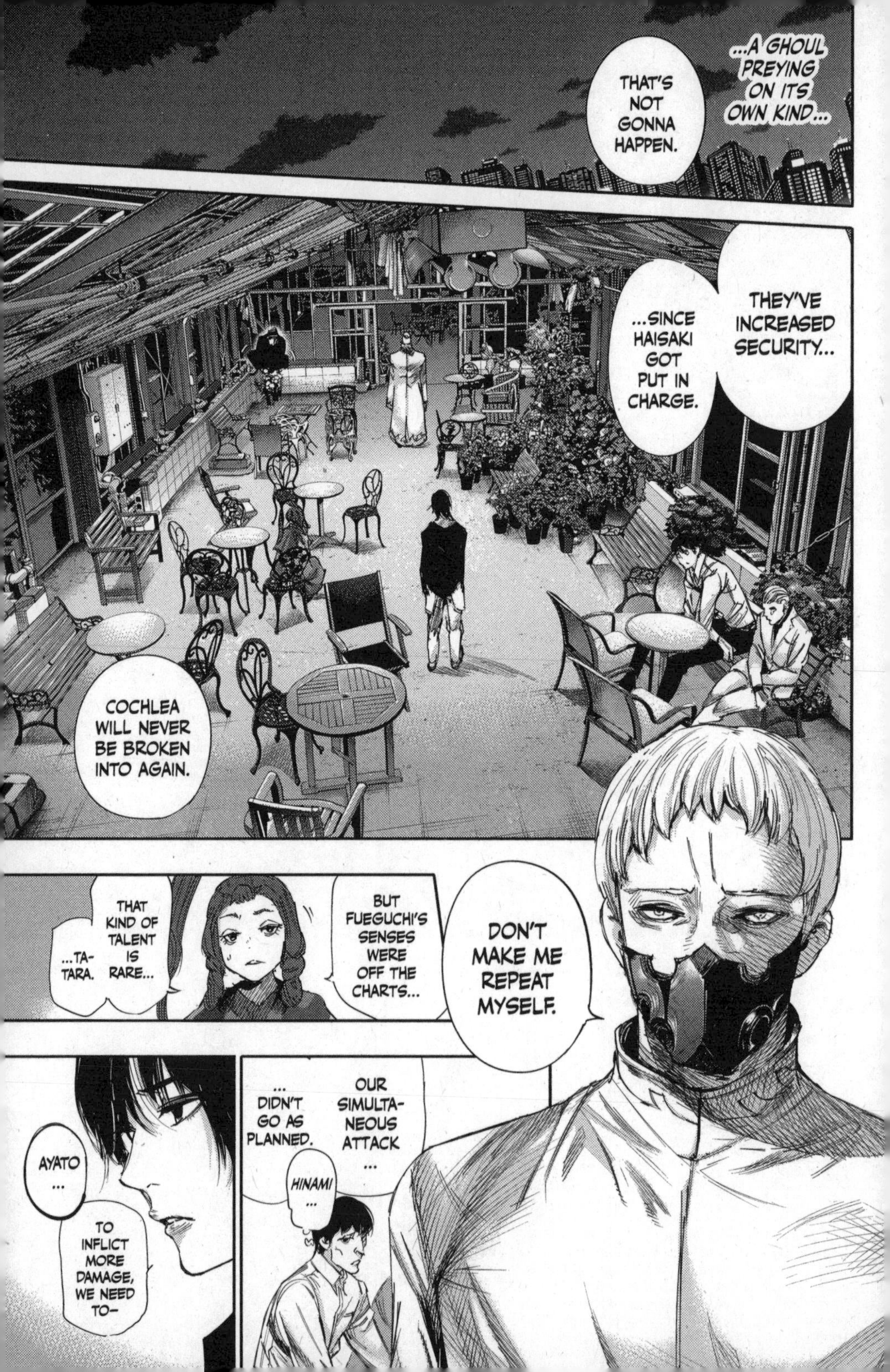
...A GHOUL PREYING ON ITS OWN KIND...
THAT'S NOT GONNA HAPPEN.
THEY'VE INCREASED SECURITY...
...SINCE HAISAKI GOT PUT IN CHARGE.
COCHLEA WILL NEVER BE BROKEN INTO AGAIN.
DON'T MAKE ME REPEAT MYSELF.
BUT FUEGUCHI'S SENSES WERE OFF THE CHARTS...
THAT KIND OF TALENT IS RARE...
...TA-TARA.
OUR SIMULTA-NEOUS ATTACK ...
... DIDN'T GO AS PLANNED.
HINAMI ...
AYATO ...
TO INFLICT MORE DAMAGE, WE NEED TO–

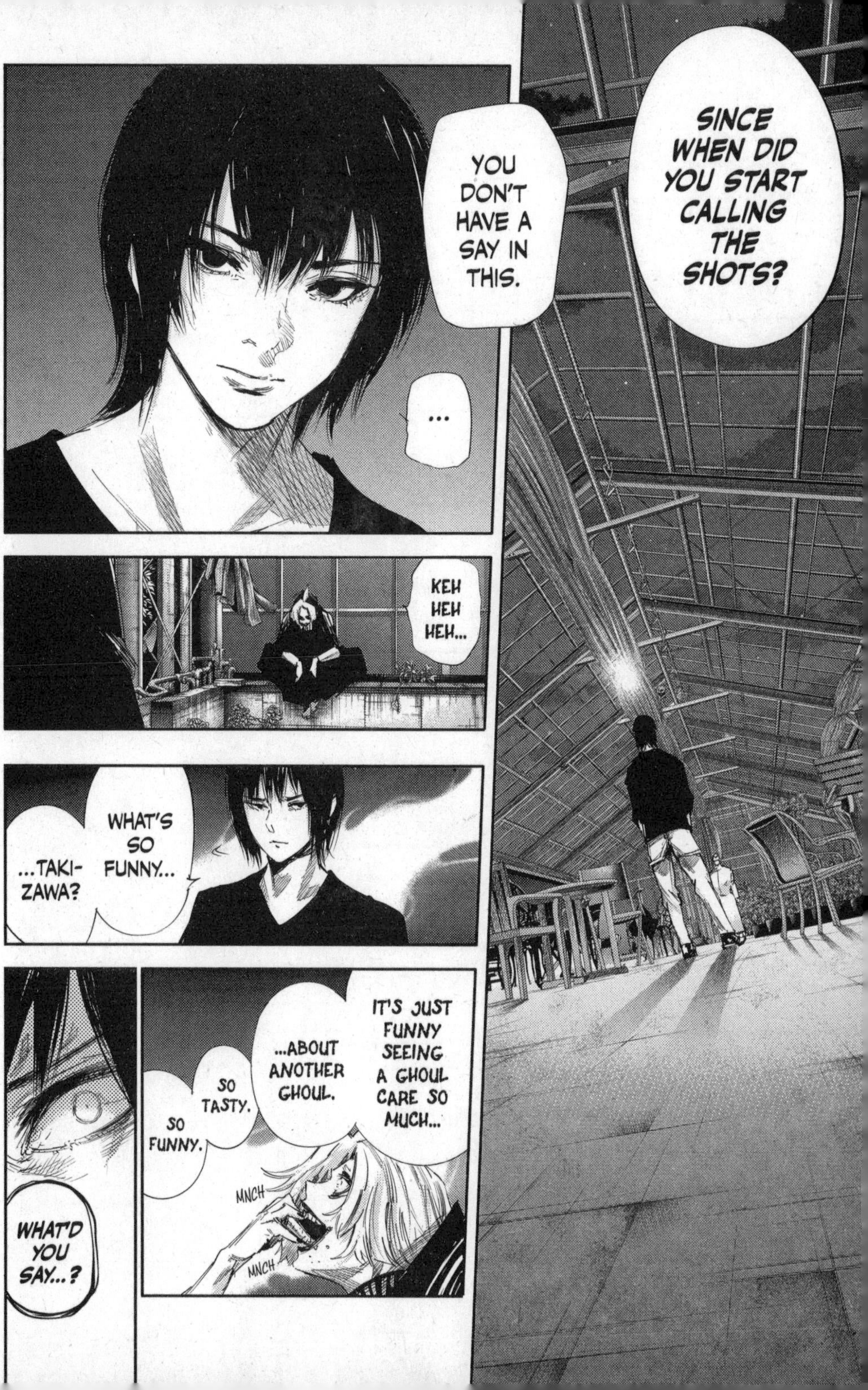
SINCE WHEN DID YOU START CALLING THE SHOTS?
YOU DON'T HAVE A SAY IN THIS.
...
KEH HEH HEH...
WHAT'S SO FUNNY...
...TAKI-ZAWA?
IT'S JUST FUNNY SEEING A GHOUL CARE SO MUCH...
...ABOUT ANOTHER GHOUL.
SO TASTY.
SO FUNNY.
MNCH
MNCH
WHAT'D YOU SAY...?

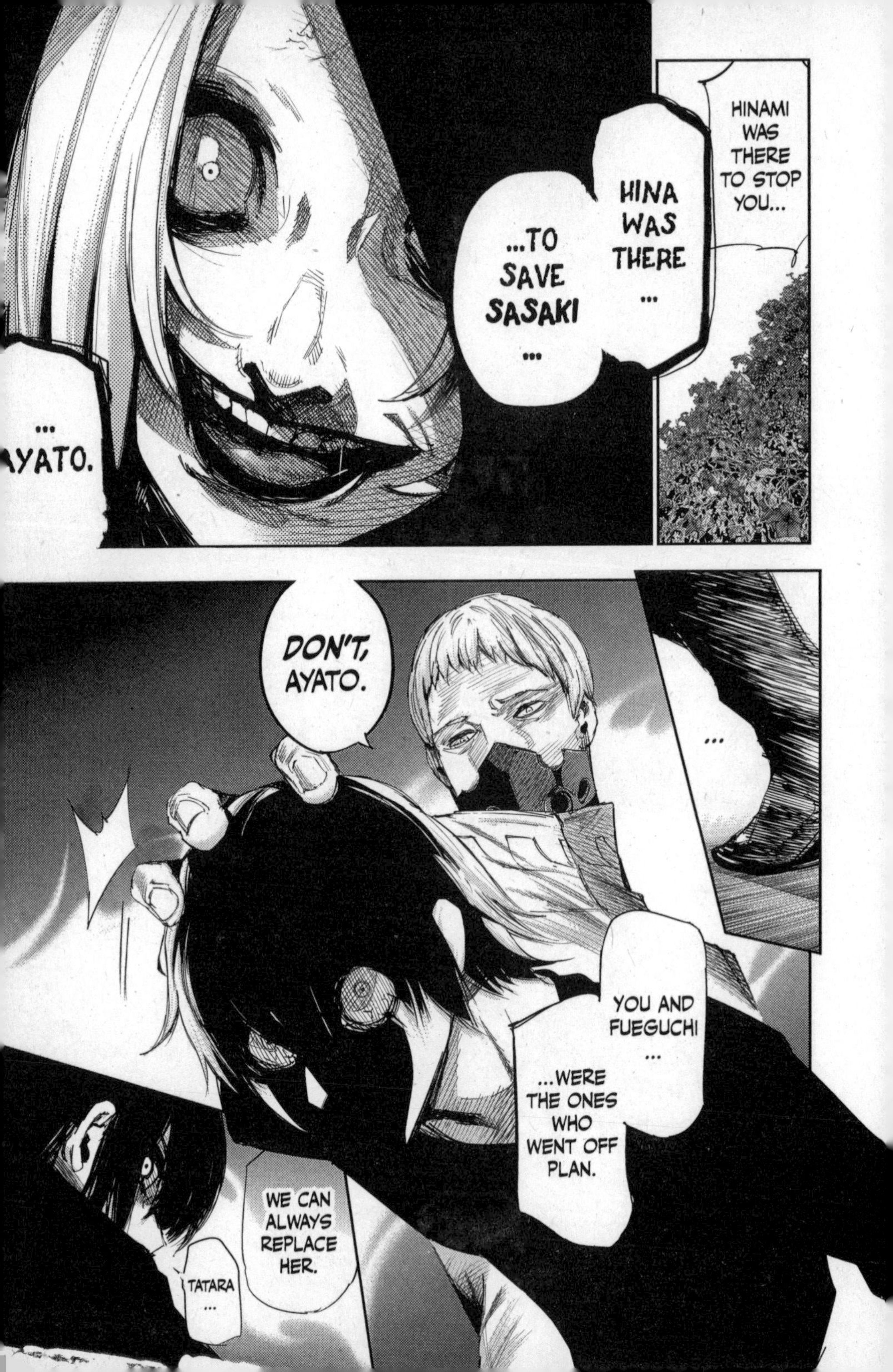
HINAMI WAS THERE TO STOP YOU...
HINA WAS THERE...
...TO SAVE SASAKI...
...AYATO.
...
DON'T, AYATO.
YOU AND FUEGUCHI...
...WERE THE ONES WHO WENT OFF PLAN.
WE CAN ALWAYS REPLACE HER.
TATARA...

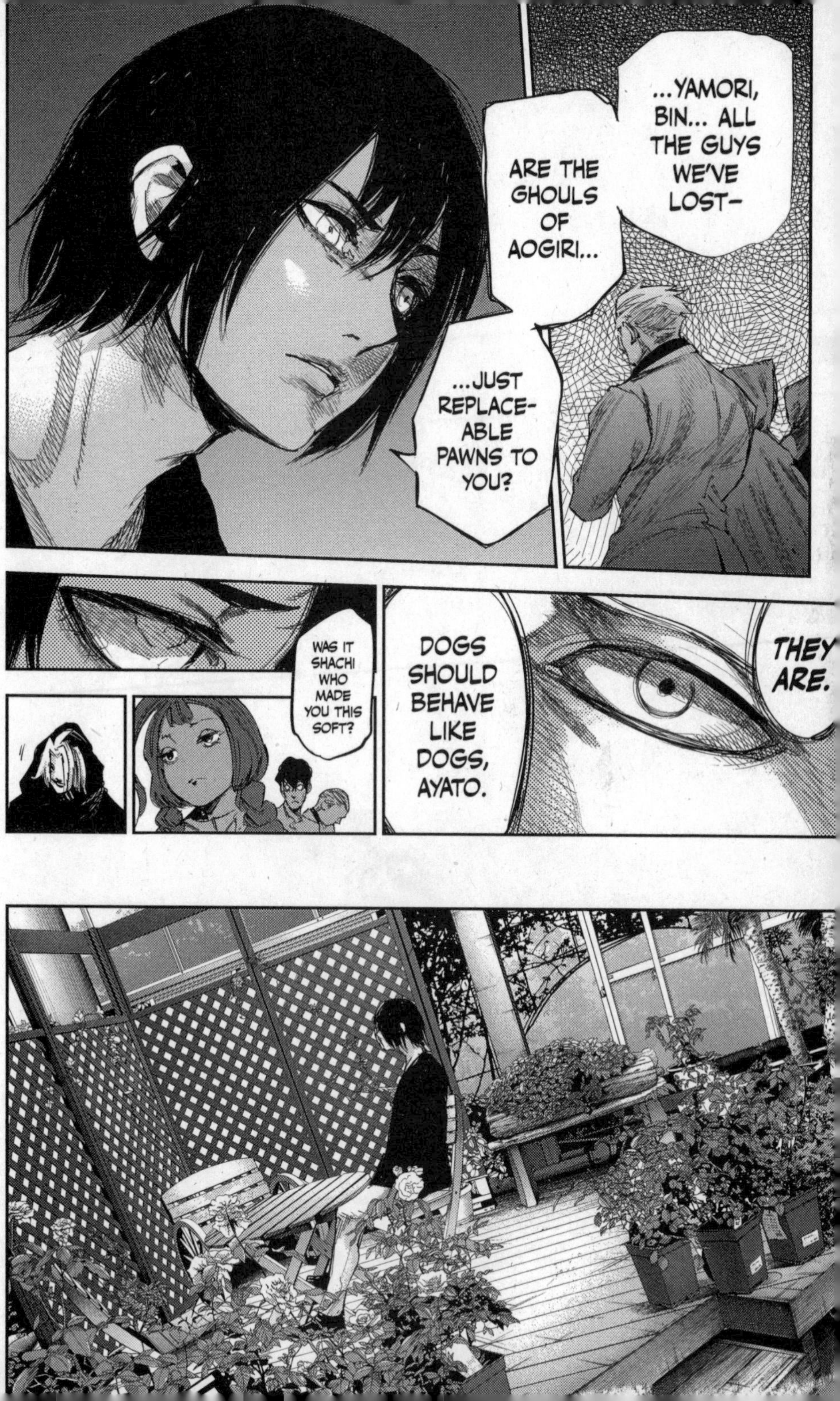
...YAMORI, BIN... ALL THE GUYS WE'VE LOST-
ARE THE GHOULS OF AOGIRI...
...JUST REPLACE-ABLE PAWNS TO YOU?
THEY ARE.
DOGS SHOULD BEHAVE LIKE DOGS, AYATO.
WAS IT SHACHI WHO MADE YOU THIS SOFT?

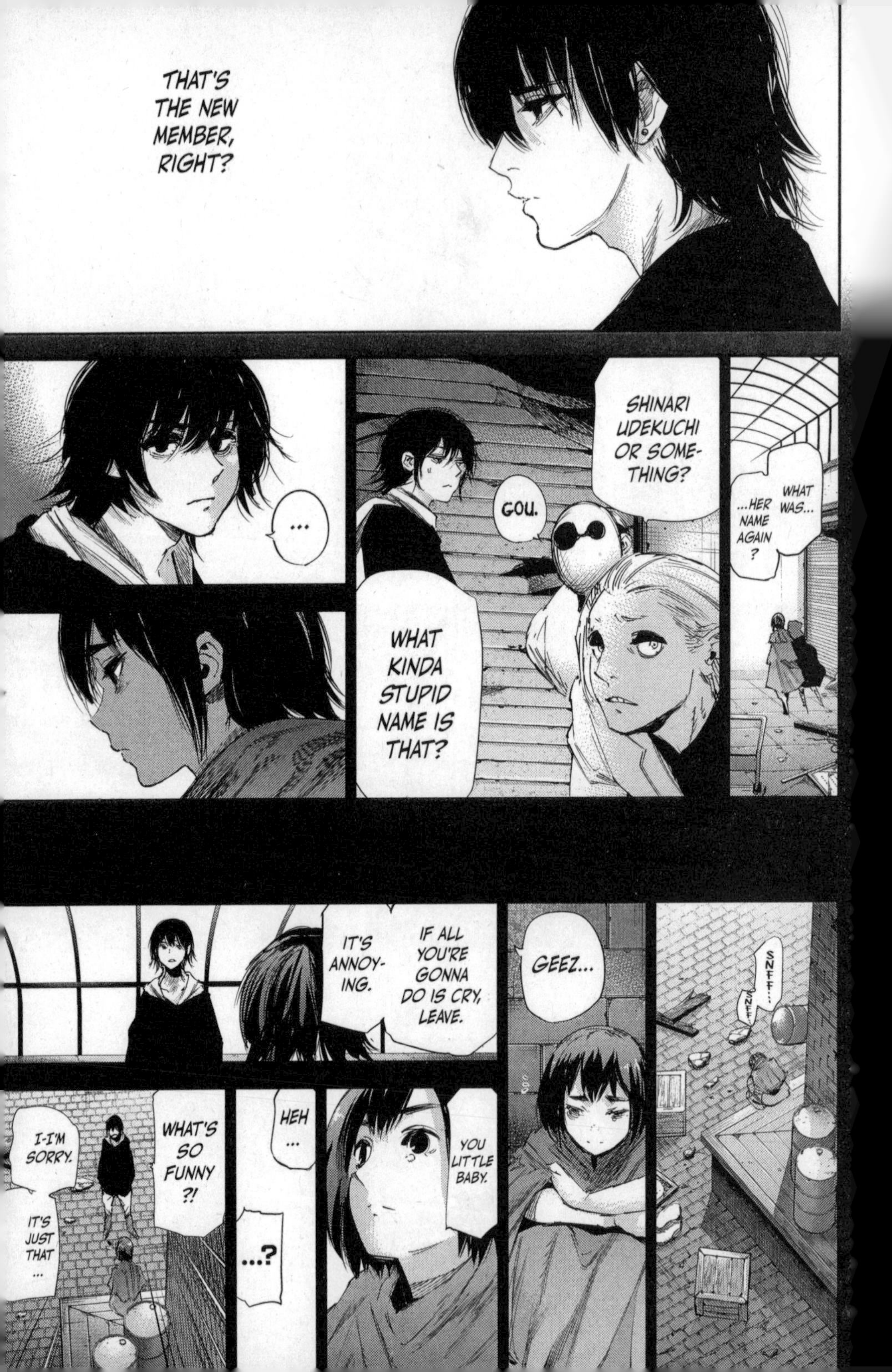
THAT'S THE NEW MEMBER, RIGHT?
WHAT WAS... ...HER NAME AGAIN?
SHINARI UDEKUCHI OR SOME-THING?
GOU.
WHAT KINDA STUPID NAME IS THAT?
...
SNFF... SNFF...
GEEZ...
IF ALL YOU'RE GONNA DO IS CRY, LEAVE.
IT'S ANNOY-ING.
YOU LITTLE BABY.
HEH...
...?
WHAT'S SO FUNNY?!
I-I'M SORRY.
IT'S JUST THAT...

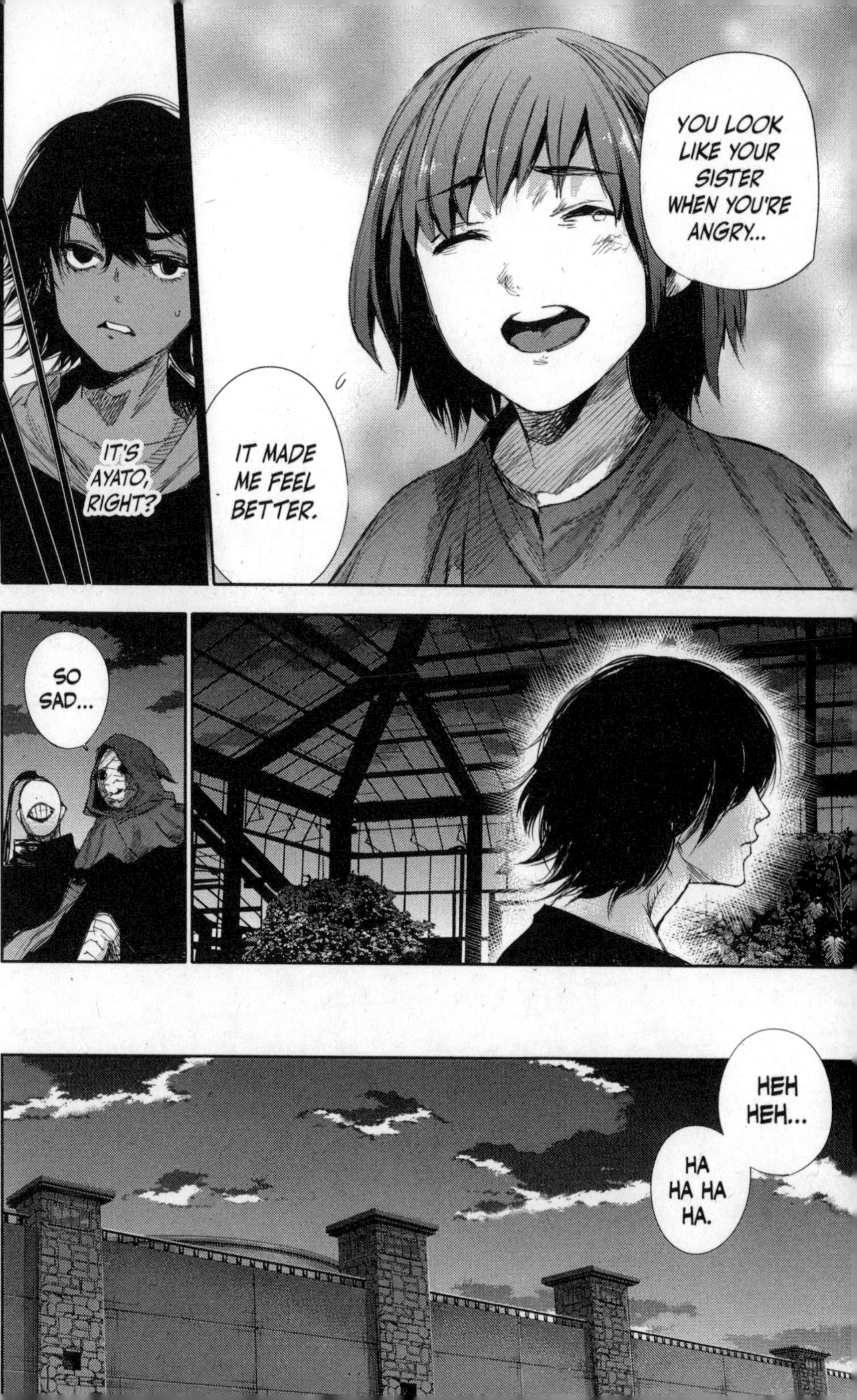
YOU LOOK LIKE YOUR SISTER WHEN YOU'RE ANGRY...
IT MADE ME FEEL BETTER.
IT'S AYATO, RIGHT?
SO SAD...
HEH HEH...
HA HA HA HA.

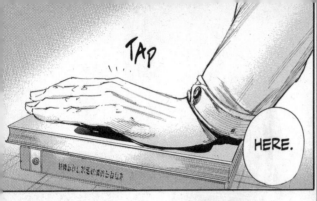

TAP

HERE.

MISS FUEGUCHI.

HI...

I'M NOT ALLOWED TO BRING TOO MANY. IT'S THE RULE.

THANKS... I APPRECIATE IT...

...KEN.

...

CAN WE START YOUR STATEMENT?

SURE...

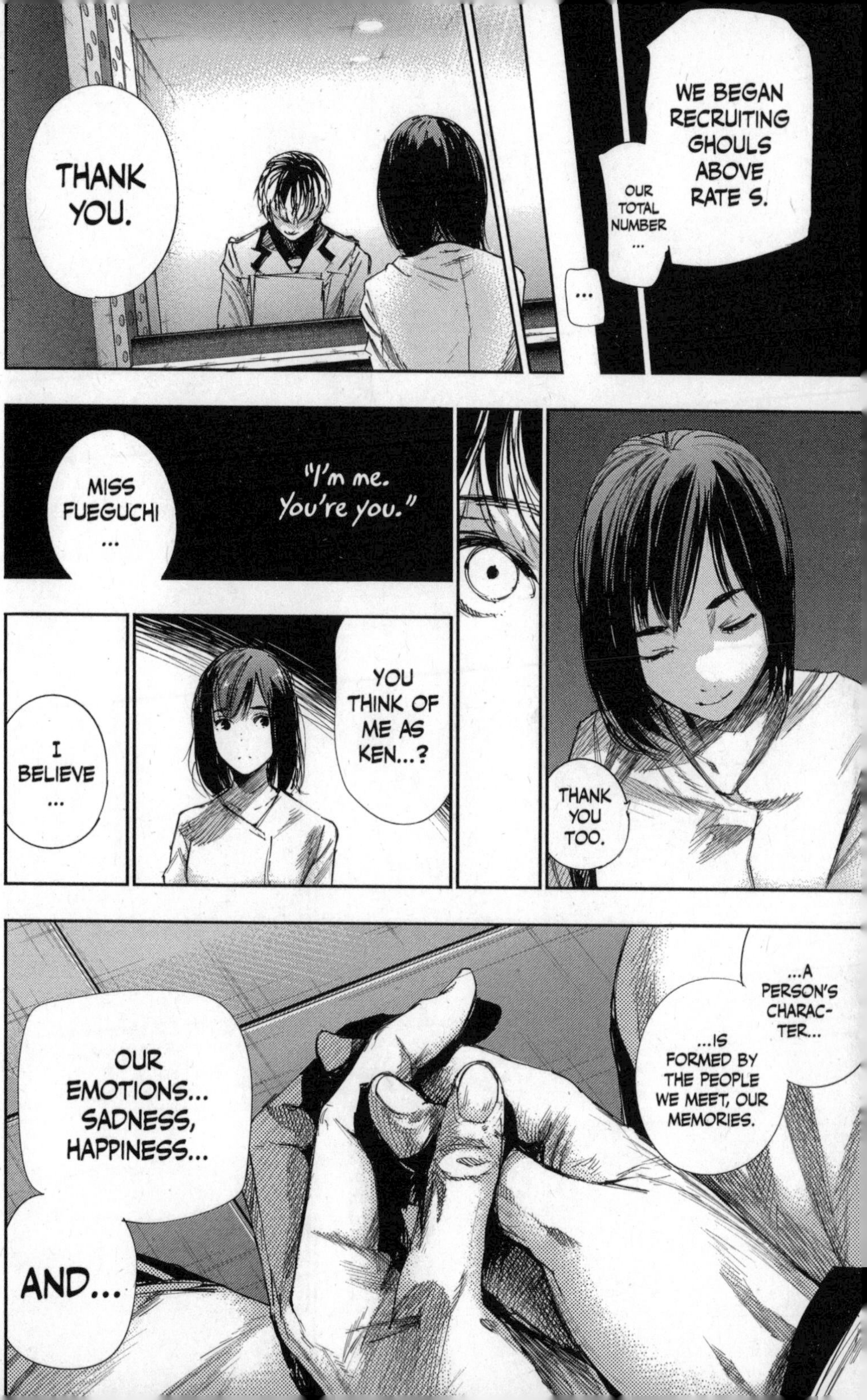
WE BEGAN RECRUITING GHOULS ABOVE RATE S.
OUR TOTAL NUMBER ...
...
THANK YOU.
THANK YOU TOO.
MISS FUEGUCHI ...
"I'm me. You're you."
YOU THINK OF ME AS KEN...?
I BELIEVE ...
...A PERSON'S CHARAC-TER...
...IS FORMED BY THE PEOPLE WE MEET, OUR MEMORIES.
OUR EMOTIONS... SADNESS, HAPPINESS...
AND...

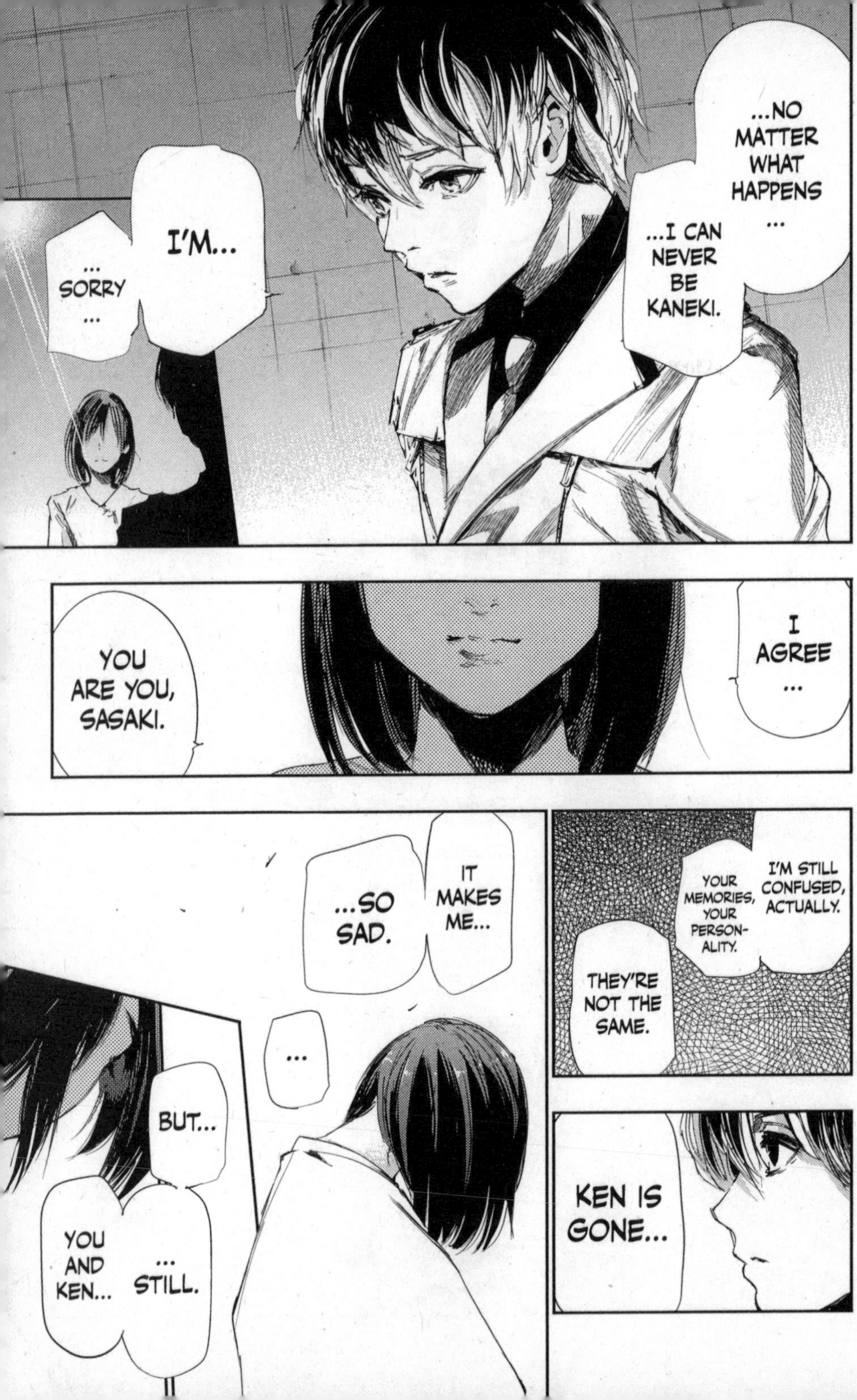
...NO MATTER WHAT HAPPENS ...
...I CAN NEVER BE KANEKI.
I'M...
... SORRY ...
I AGREE ...
YOU ARE YOU, SASAKI.
I'M STILL CONFUSED, ACTUALLY.
YOUR MEMORIES, YOUR PERSONALITY.
THEY'RE NOT THE SAME.
KEN IS GONE...
IT MAKES ME...
...SO SAD.
...
BUT...
YOU AND KEN...
... STILL.

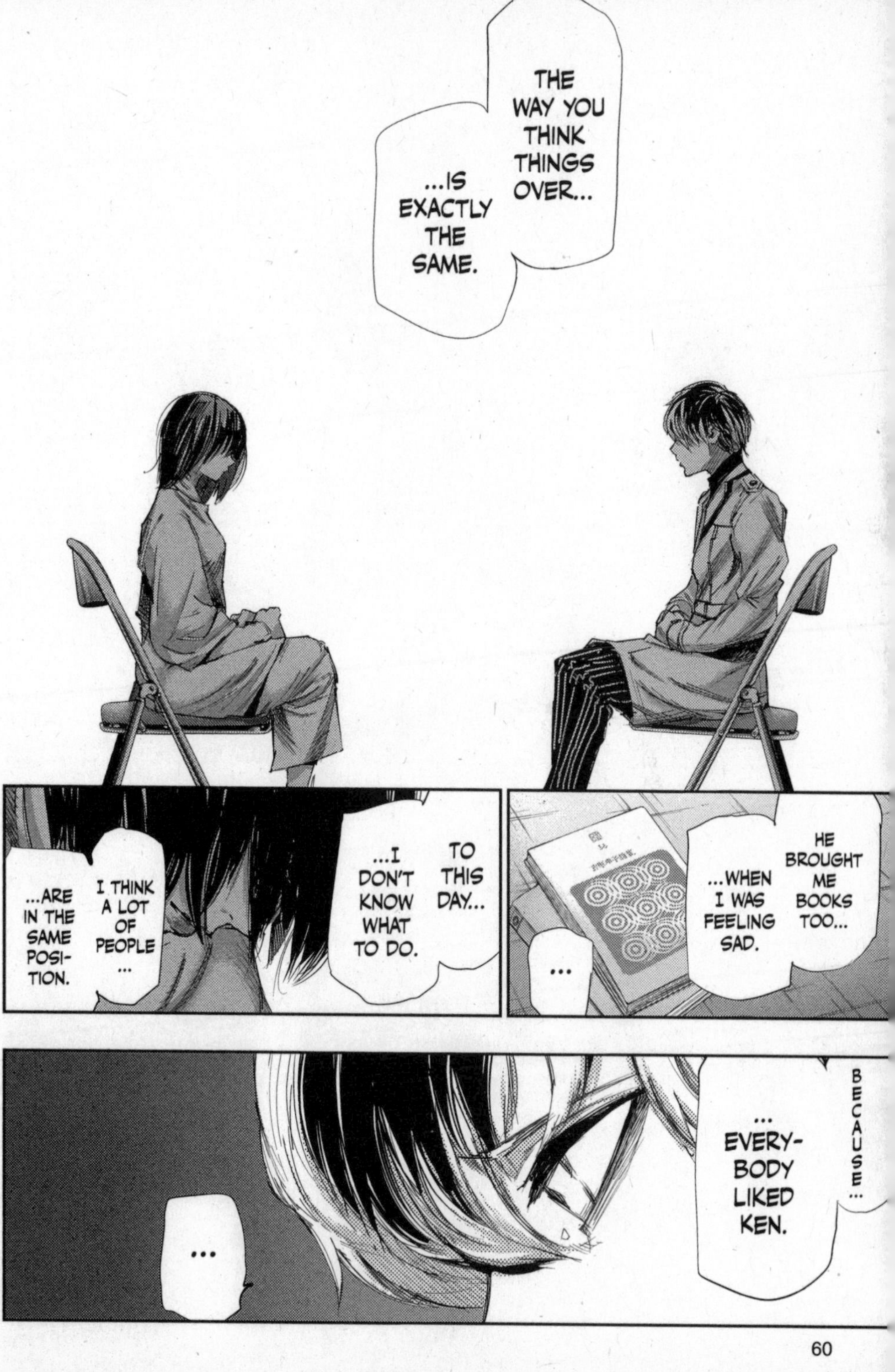
THE WAY YOU THINK THINGS OVER...
...IS EXACTLY THE SAME.
HE BROUGHT ME BOOKS TOO...
...WHEN I WAS FEELING SAD.
...
TO THIS DAY...
...I DON'T KNOW WHAT TO DO.
I THINK A LOT OF PEOPLE...
...ARE IN THE SAME POSITION.
BECAUSE...
...EVERYBODY LIKED KEN.
...

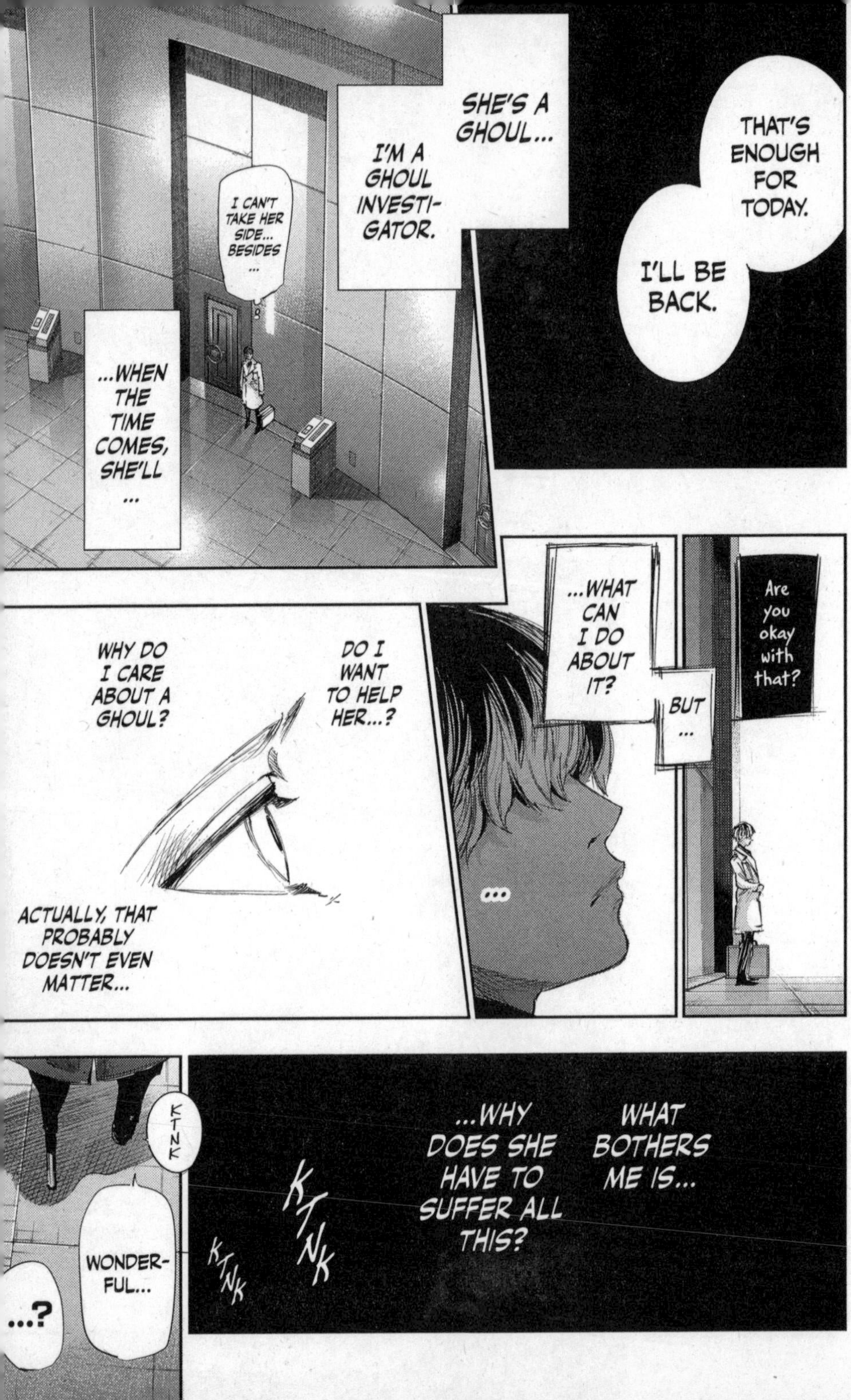
THAT'S ENOUGH FOR TODAY.
I'LL BE BACK.
SHE'S A GHOUL...
I'M A GHOUL INVESTI-GATOR.
I CAN'T TAKE HER SIDE... BESIDES ...
...WHEN THE TIME COMES, SHE'LL ...
Are you okay with that?
...WHAT CAN I DO ABOUT IT?
BUT ...
...
DO I WANT TO HELP HER...?
WHY DO I CARE ABOUT A GHOUL?
ACTUALLY, THAT PROBABLY DOESN'T EVEN MATTER...
WHAT BOTHERS ME IS...
...WHY DOES SHE HAVE TO SUFFER ALL THIS?
KTNK
KTNK
KTNK
WONDER-FUL...
...?

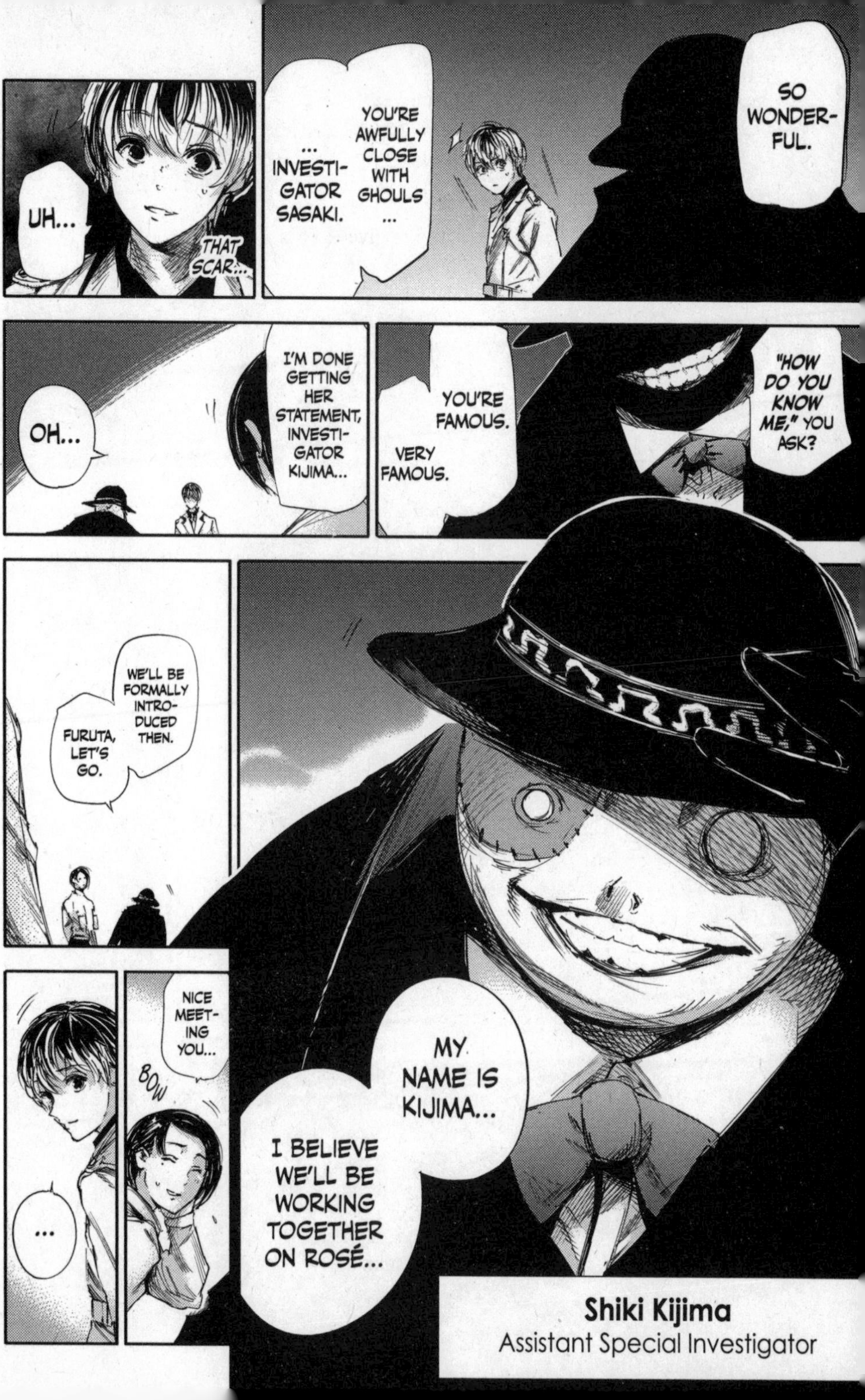
SO WONDERFUL.
YOU'RE AWFULLY CLOSE WITH GHOULS...
...INVESTIGATOR SASAKI.
THAT SCAR...
UH...
"HOW DO YOU KNOW ME," YOU ASK?
YOU'RE FAMOUS.
VERY FAMOUS.
I'M DONE GETTING HER STATEMENT, INVESTIGATOR KIJIMA...
OH...
MY NAME IS KIJIMA...
I BELIEVE WE'LL BE WORKING TOGETHER ON ROSÉ...
Shiki Kijima
Assistant Special Investigator
WE'LL BE FORMALLY INTRODUCED THEN.
FURUTA, LET'S GO.
NICE MEETING YOU...
BOW
...

Cochlea isn't the way I was told it would be.
It actually feels like the rights of Ghouls are respected here.
Maybe it's a lot easier than living in the outside world.

I have to wear restraints, but we get to exercise in the
courtyard sometimes. I'm surprised that we're given meals
too, even though it's not very often.

(The other detainees call it "stew." The fact that we can eat
it must mean it's— I wonder if they ever offer us bodies.)

Ken visited me today.

He brought a collection of poems. You can lose your memory, but you never
forget what you like, I guess.

Ken... Investigator Sasaki isn't sure about being called Ken. It's not that he
hates being called it, necessarily. He's just trying to figure out why I would.
That is so Ken.

I don't think everything's changed.

People change. That goes for me too.

I wonder what Touka would say if she met him. Would she
smack him like she used to? Or would she have nothing to say?

What would she say to me? Would she be angry? I kind of wish
she would be. I want her to yell at me like I'm a child. I know
it's selfish, but I still want to be treated like a kid by her.

After Anteiku closed down, maybe it would've
been better if I'd gone with her.

But we all got separated. Banjo couldn't stay with
us either. All I was left with was a piece of paper.

To this day I think, "If only I hadn't met
Takatsuki."

A lot happened. Both good and bad. I learned and
lost a lot.

...

I want to see Touka. Yomo, Nishio. Banjo,
Tsukiyama... Ken...

I want to see everybody from Anteiku too.

That feeling hits me out of nowhere and it makes
me think of Mom and Dad.

When I get that feeling, it becomes overwhelming
and I can't think.

I'll probably spend the rest of my life here.

Maybe it's a punishment. The price I have to pay
for trying to be strong to save somebody.

I wanted to know how you felt, Ken.

When I found out you went to save Anteiku by
yourself, I couldn't just sit and do nothing.

I'm glad it's you, Ken. Even if you're taking my
statement as a Ghoul investigator.

I hope you are the last person I speak to.

I'm scared. Scared of the day they'll dispose of me.

When I'm alone and reflect too much, I feel like I'll lose my
mind. I get so scared. If I'm not reading or looking at words,
I feel like I might die.

I'm scared.

Great Form :34

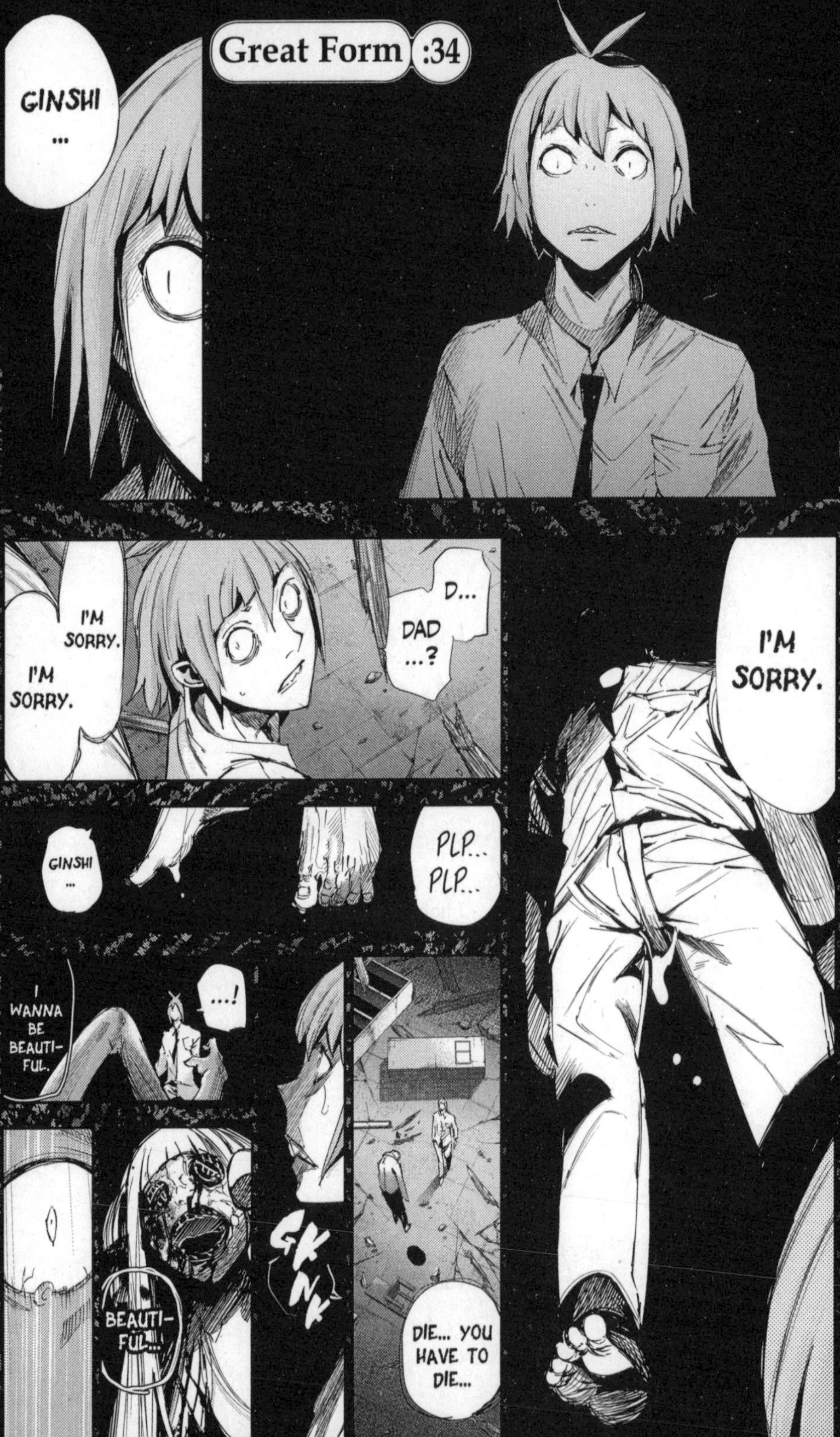
GINSHI ...
I'M SORRY.
D... DAD ...?
I'M SORRY. I'M SORRY.
PLP... PLP...
GINSHI ...
DIE... YOU HAVE TO DIE...
GKNK
...!
I WANNA BE BEAUTIFUL.
BEAUTIFUL...!

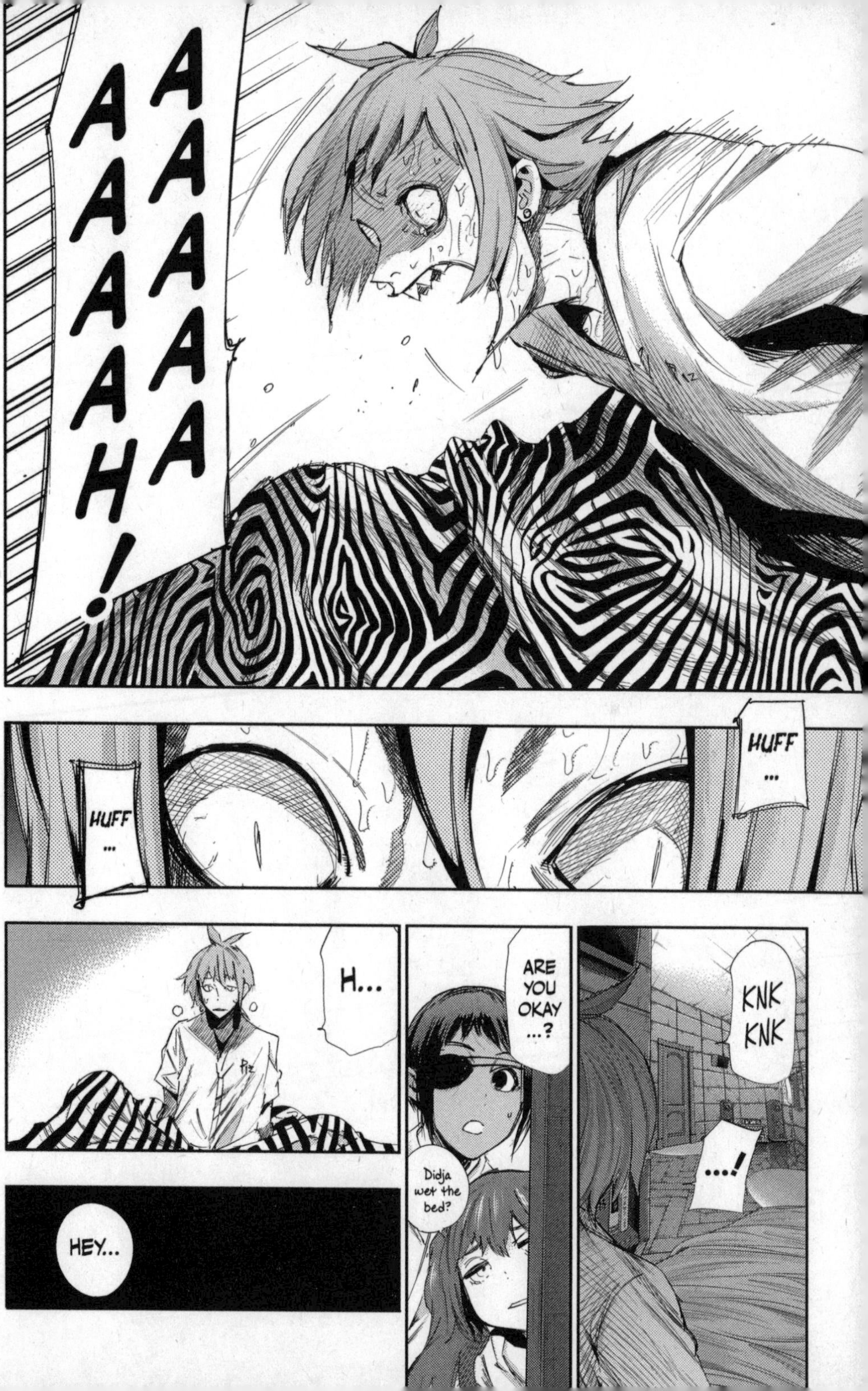
AAAAAAAAAAAAH!
HUFF...
HUFF...
KNK KNK
...!
ARE YOU OKAY...?
Didja wet the bed?
H...
HEY...

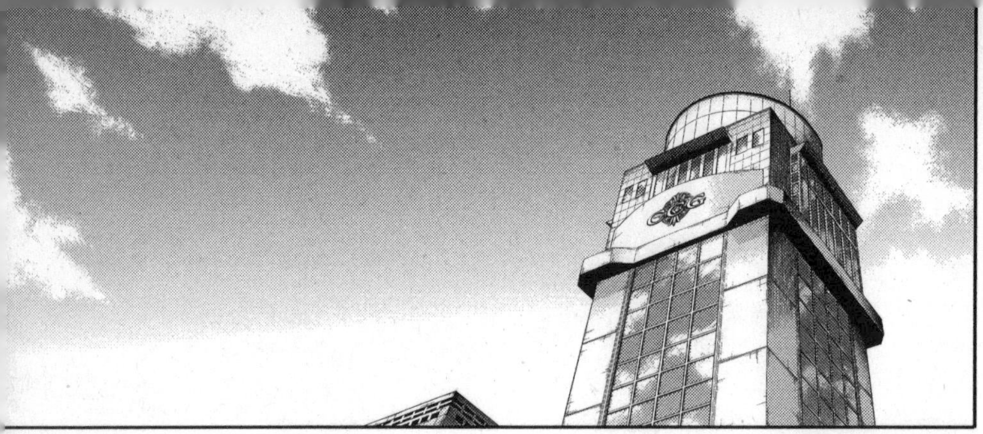

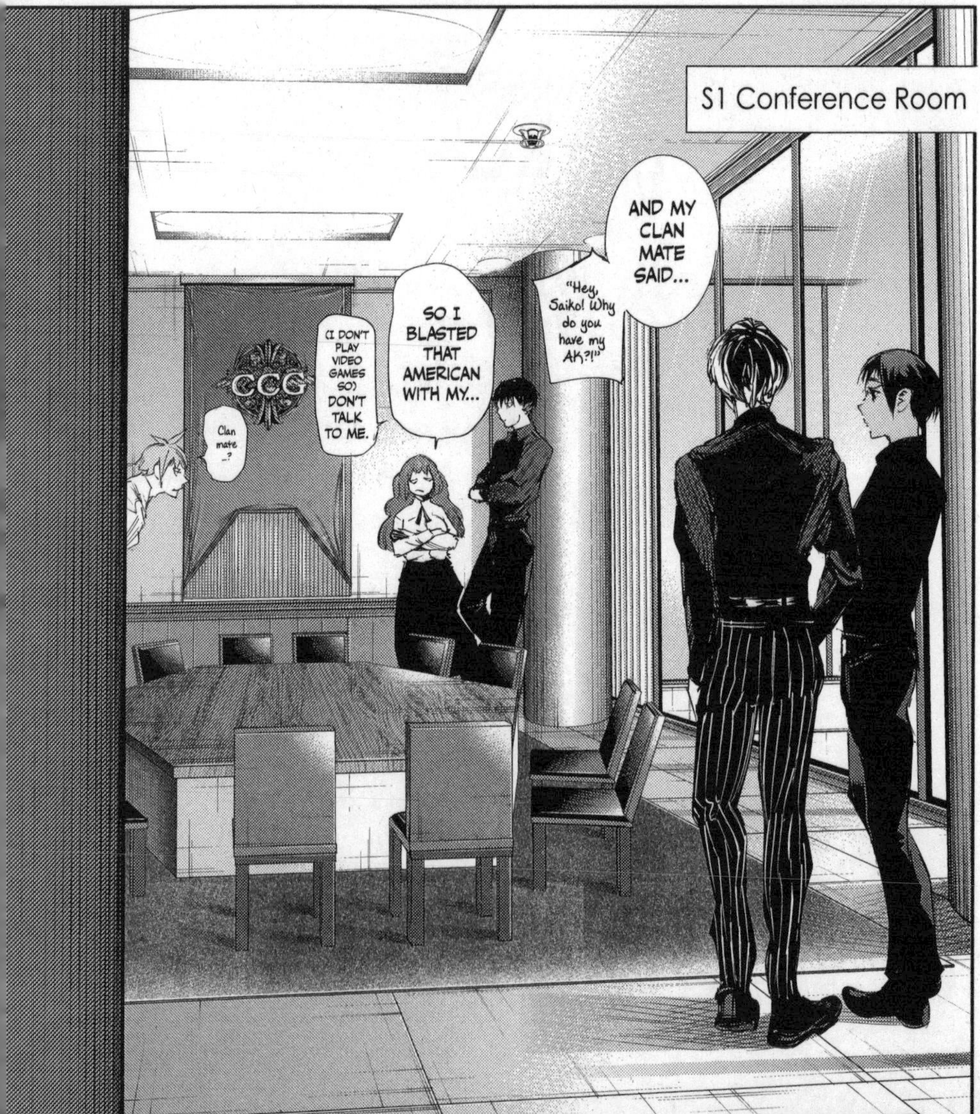
S1 Conference Room
AND MY CLAN MATE SAID...
"Hey, Saiko! Why do you have my AK?!"
SO I BLASTED THAT AMERICAN WITH MY...
(I DON'T PLAY VIDEO GAMES SO) DON'T TALK TO ME.
Clan mate...?

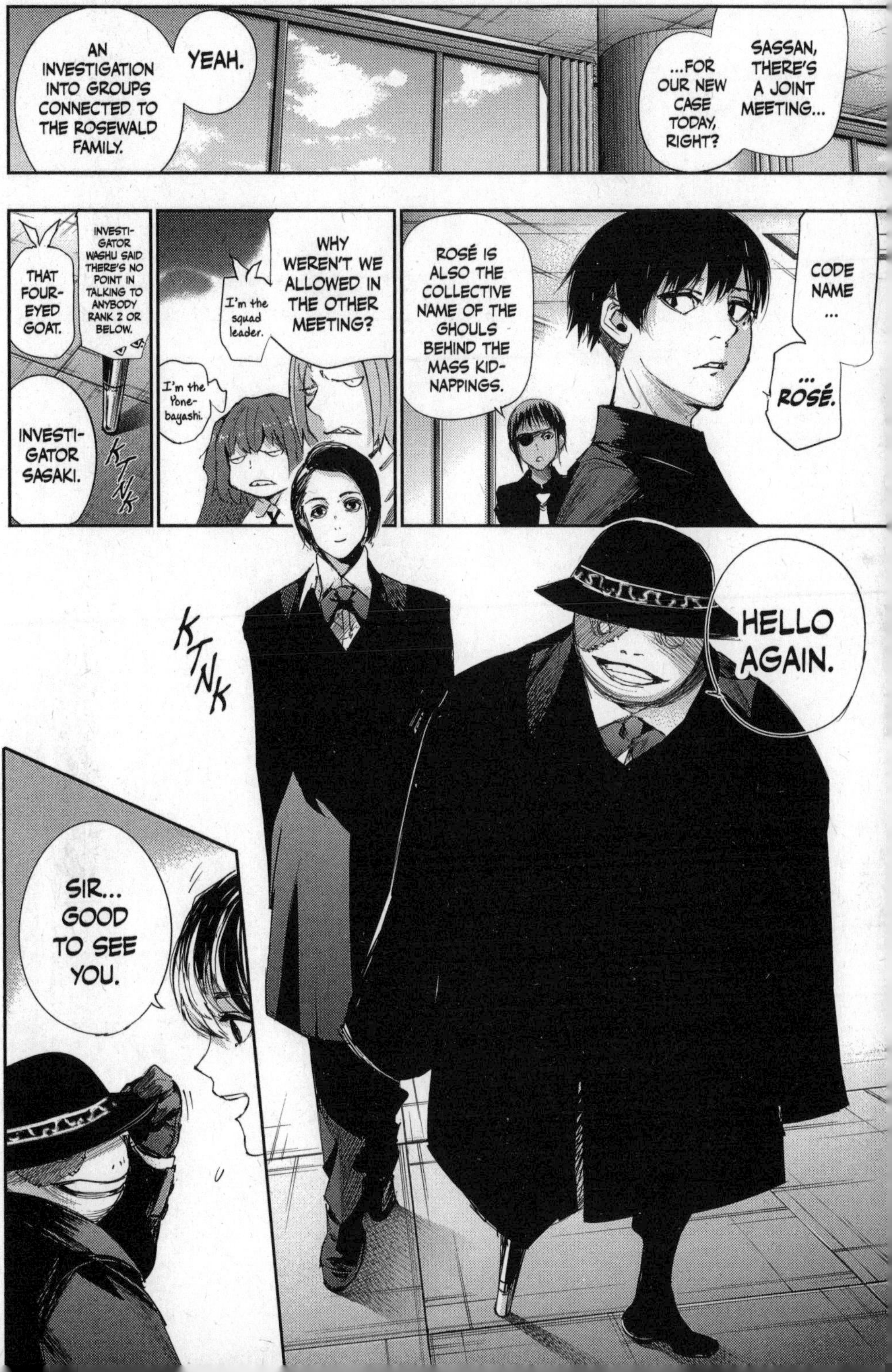
SASSAN, THERE'S A JOINT MEETING...
...FOR OUR NEW CASE TODAY, RIGHT?
YEAH.
AN INVESTIGATION INTO GROUPS CONNECTED TO THE ROSEWALD FAMILY.
CODE NAME ...
... ROSÉ.
ROSÉ IS ALSO THE COLLECTIVE NAME OF THE GHOULS BEHIND THE MASS KID-NAPPINGS.
WHY WEREN'T WE ALLOWED IN THE OTHER MEETING?
I'm the squad leader.
I'm the Yone-bayashi.
INVESTI-GATOR WASHU SAID THERE'S NO POINT IN TALKING TO ANYBODY RANK 2 OR BELOW.
THAT FOUR-EYED GOAT.
KTNK
INVESTI-GATOR SASAKI.
HELLO AGAIN.
KTNK
SIR... GOOD TO SEE YOU.

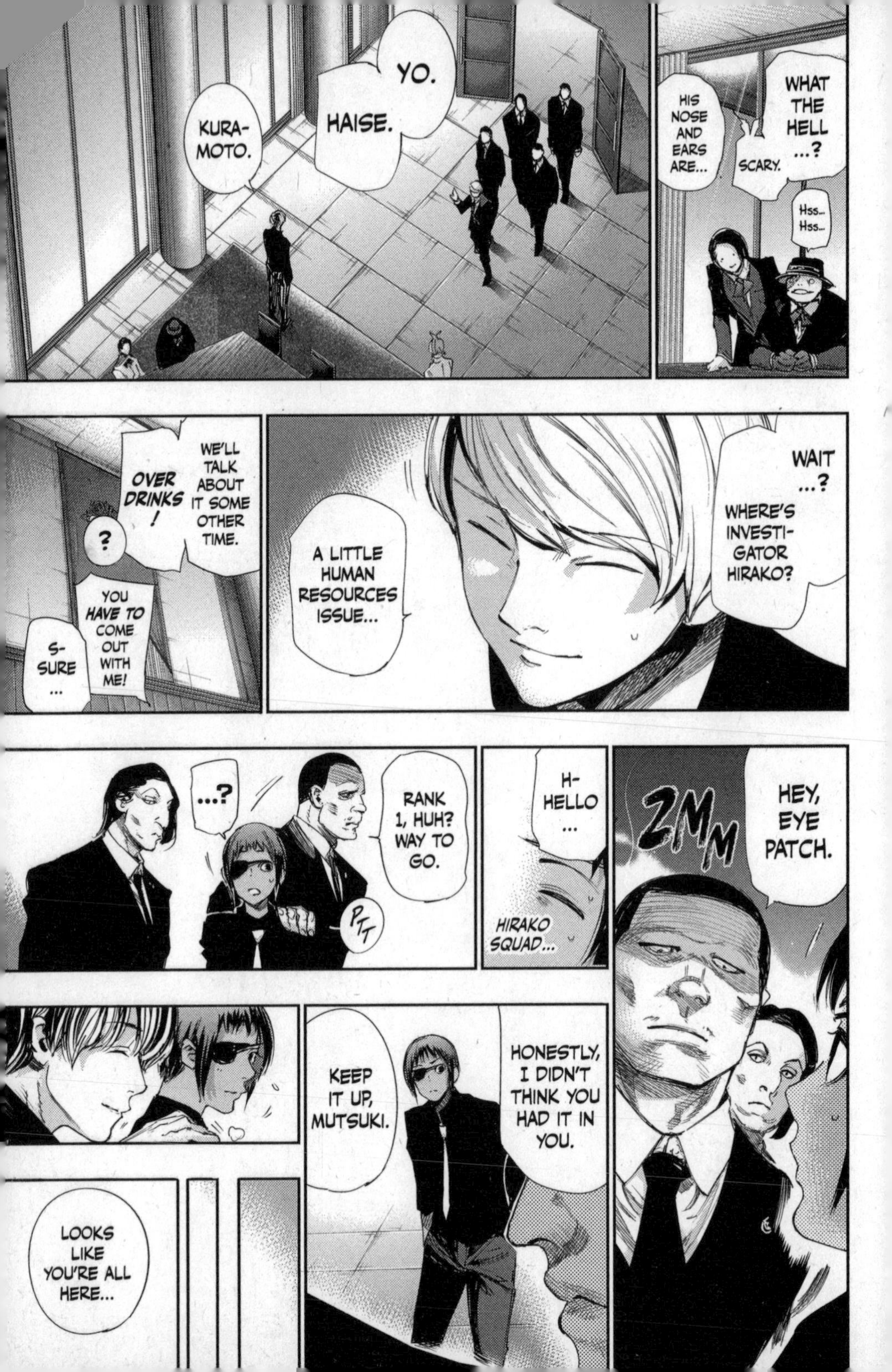
WHAT THE HELL ...?
HIS NOSE AND EARS ARE...
SCARY.
Hss... Hss...
YO.
HAISE.
KURA-MOTO.
WAIT ...?
WHERE'S INVESTI-GATOR HIRAKO?
A LITTLE HUMAN RESOURCES ISSUE...
WE'LL TALK ABOUT IT SOME OTHER TIME.
OVER DRINKS!
?
YOU HAVE TO COME OUT WITH ME!
S-SURE ...
ZMM
HEY, EYE PATCH.
H-HELLO ...
HIRAKO SQUAD...
RANK 1, HUH? WAY TO GO.
...?
PTT
HONESTLY, I DIDN'T THINK YOU HAD IT IN YOU.
KEEP IT UP, MUTSUKI.
LOOKS LIKE YOU'RE ALL HERE...

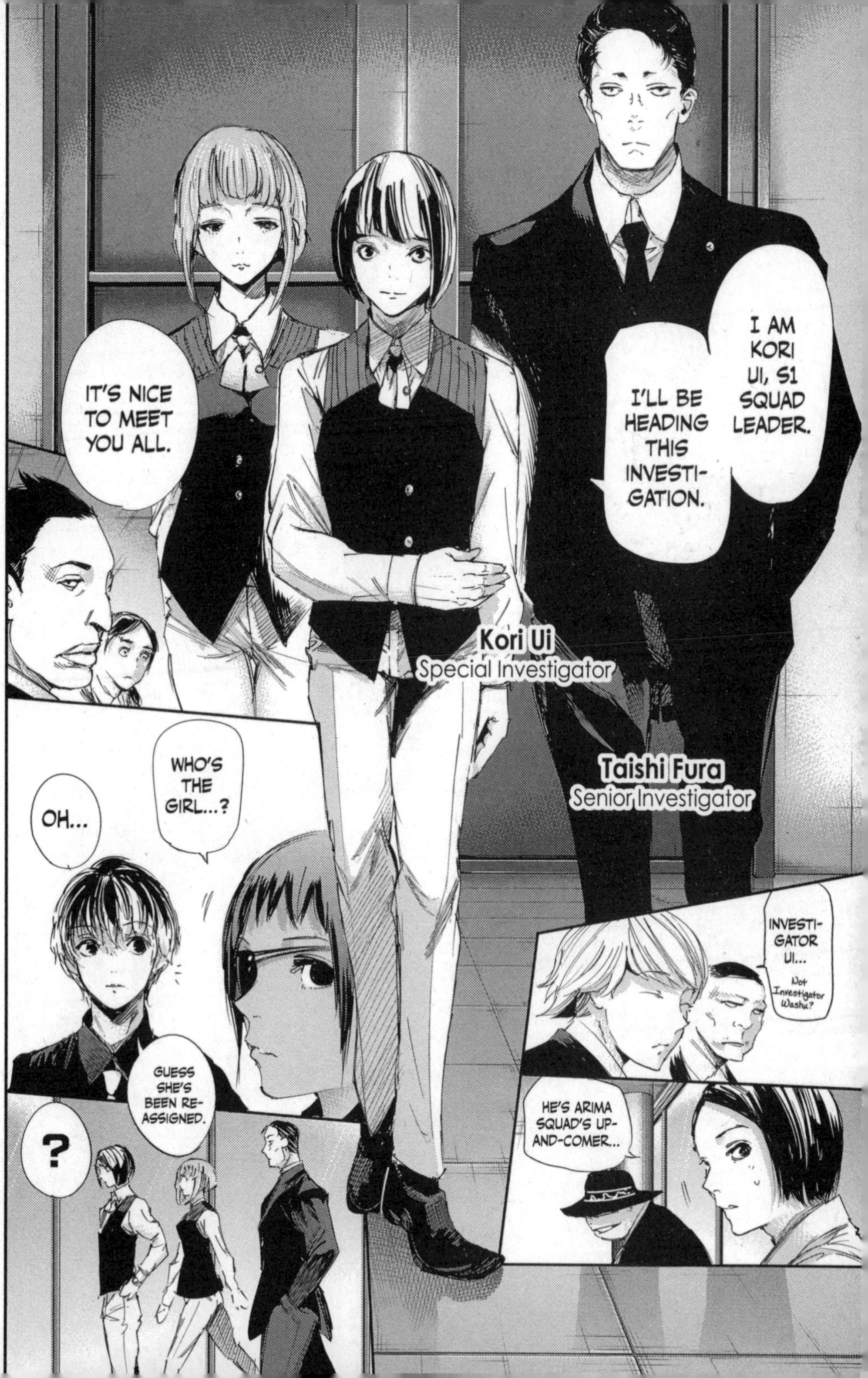
I AM KORI UI, S1 SQUAD LEADER.
I'LL BE HEADING THIS INVESTIGATION.
IT'S NICE TO MEET YOU ALL.
Kori Ui
Special Investigator
Taishi Fura
Senior Investigator
INVESTIGATOR UI...
Not Investigator Washu?
HE'S ARIMA SQUAD'S UP-AND-COMER...
WHO'S THE GIRL...?
OH...
GUESS SHE'S BEEN REASSIGNED.
?

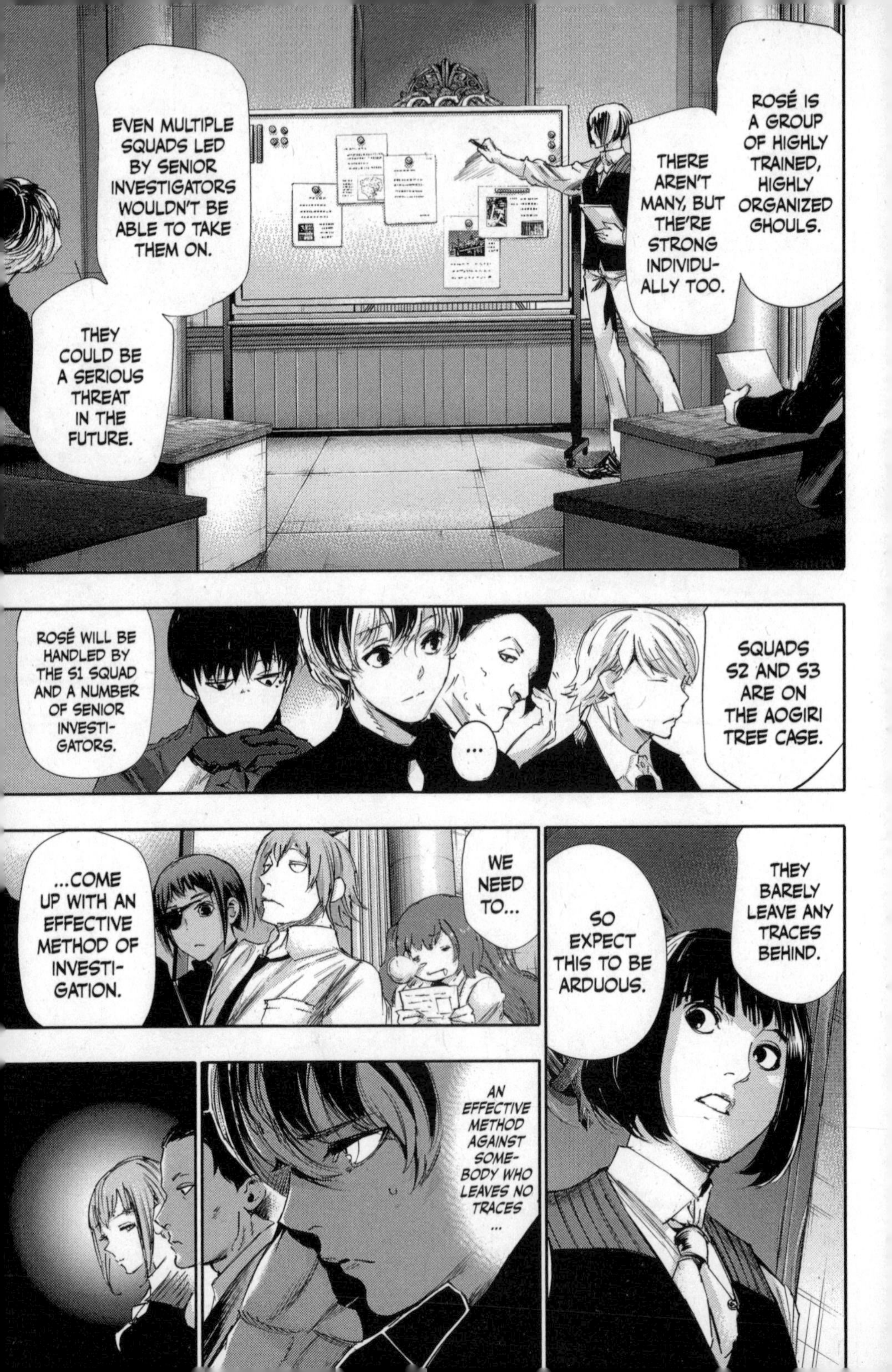
ROSÉ IS A GROUP OF HIGHLY TRAINED, HIGHLY ORGANIZED GHOULS.
THERE AREN'T MANY, BUT THE'RE STRONG INDIVIDUALLY TOO.
EVEN MULTIPLE SQUADS LED BY SENIOR INVESTIGATORS WOULDN'T BE ABLE TO TAKE THEM ON.
THEY COULD BE A SERIOUS THREAT IN THE FUTURE.
SQUADS S2 AND S3 ARE ON THE AOGIRI TREE CASE.
...
ROSÉ WILL BE HANDLED BY THE S1 SQUAD AND A NUMBER OF SENIOR INVESTIGATORS.
THEY BARELY LEAVE ANY TRACES BEHIND.
SO EXPECT THIS TO BE ARDUOUS.
WE NEED TO...
...COME UP WITH AN EFFECTIVE METHOD OF INVESTIGATION.
AN EFFECTIVE METHOD AGAINST SOMEBODY WHO LEAVES NO TRACES...

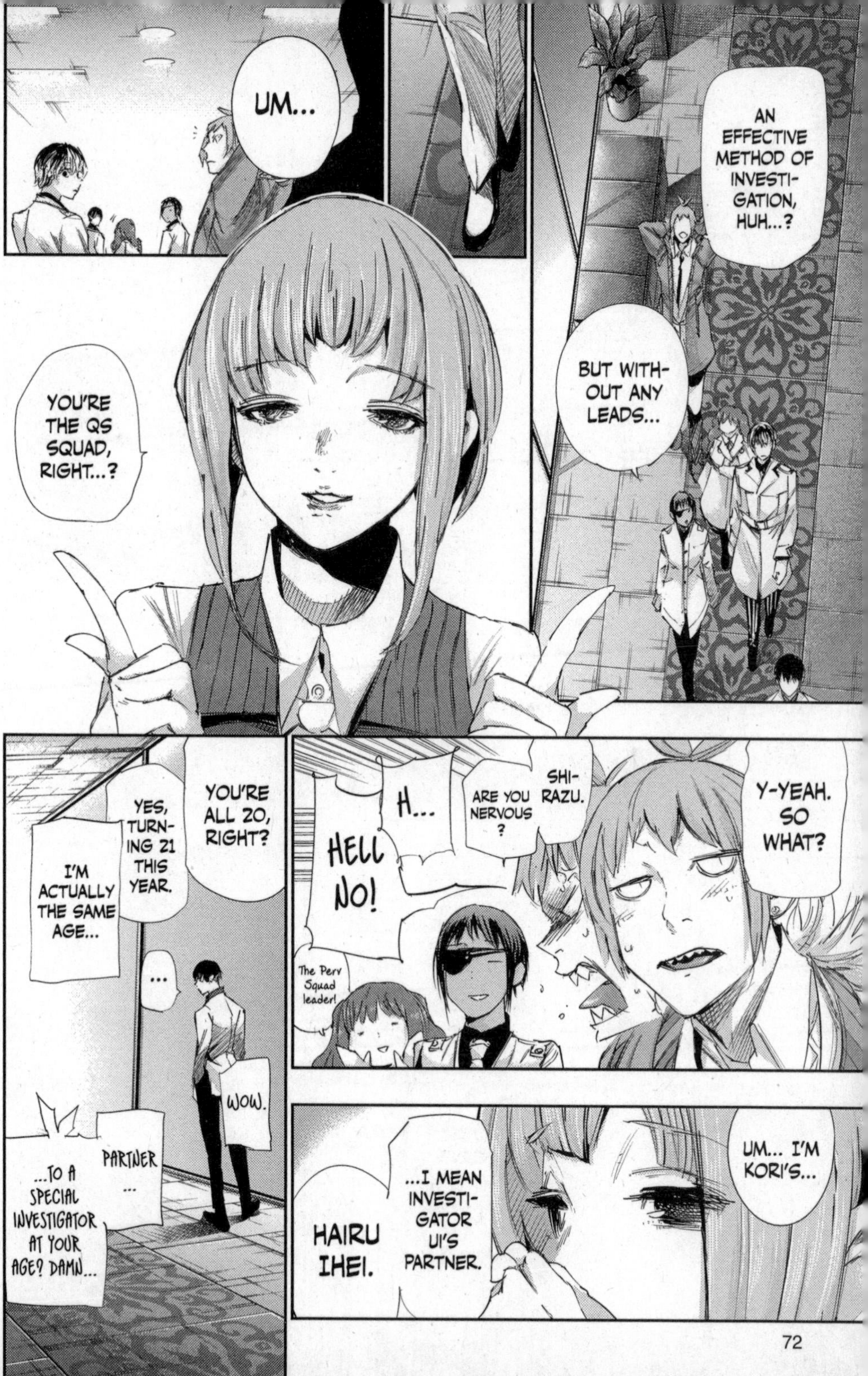
AN EFFECTIVE METHOD OF INVESTI-GATION, HUH...?
BUT WITH-OUT ANY LEADS...
UM...
YOU'RE THE QS SQUAD, RIGHT...?
Y-YEAH. SO WHAT?
SHI-RAZU.
ARE YOU NERVOUS?
H...
HELL NO!
The Perv Squad leader!
UM... I'M KORI'S...
...I MEAN INVESTI-GATOR UI'S PARTNER.
HAIRU IHEI.
YOU'RE ALL 20, RIGHT?
YES, TURNING 21 THIS YEAR.
I'M ACTUALLY THE SAME AGE...
...
WOW.
PARTNER...
...TO A SPECIAL INVESTIGATOR AT YOUR AGE? DAMN...

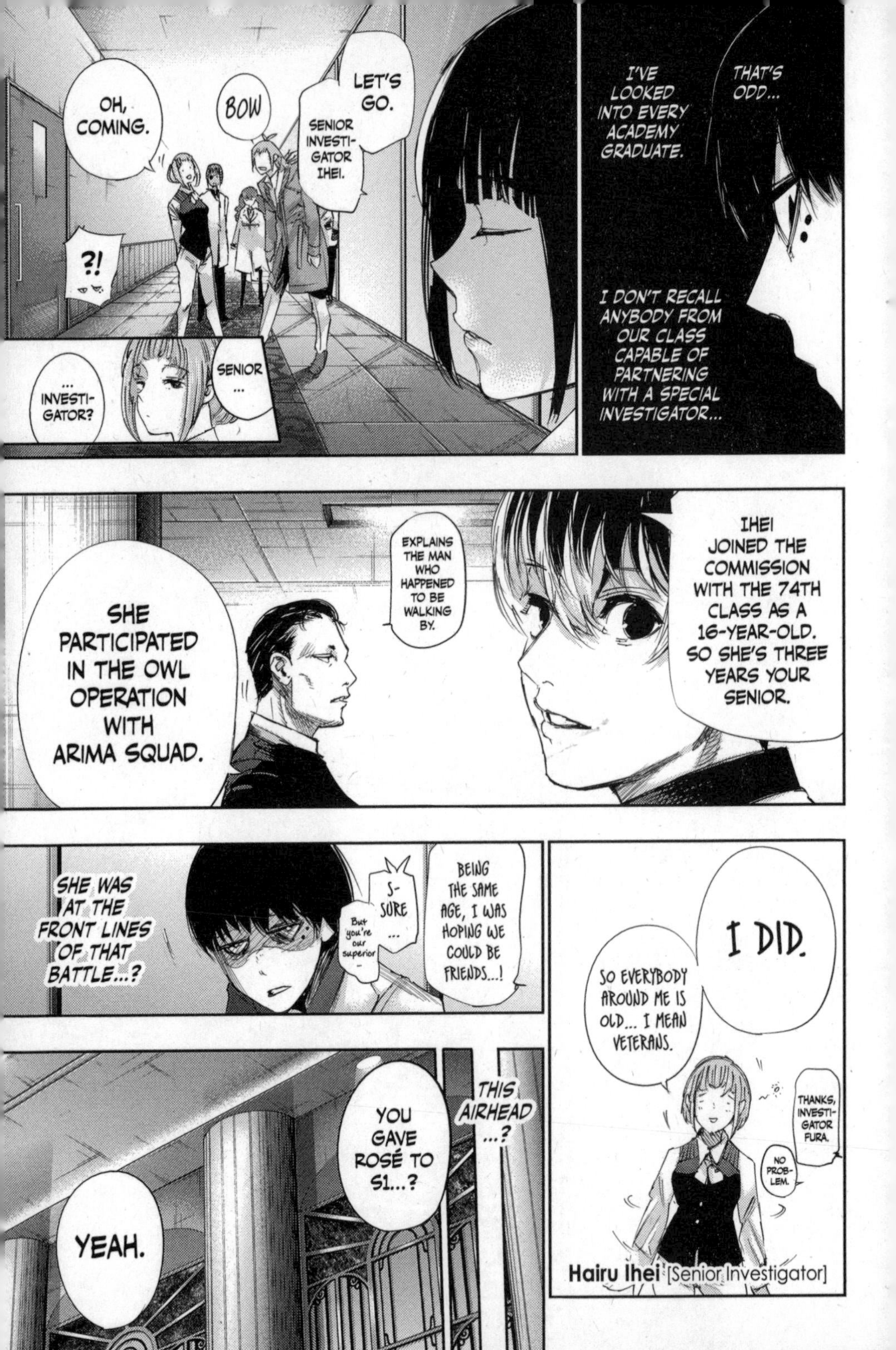
THAT'S ODD...
I'VE LOOKED INTO EVERY ACADEMY GRADUATE.
I DON'T RECALL ANYBODY FROM OUR CLASS CAPABLE OF PARTNERING WITH A SPECIAL INVESTIGATOR...
LET'S GO.
SENIOR INVESTIGATOR IHEI.
BOW
OH, COMING.
?!
SENIOR...
...INVESTIGATOR?
IHEI JOINED THE COMMISSION WITH THE 74TH CLASS AS A 16-YEAR-OLD. SO SHE'S THREE YEARS YOUR SENIOR.
EXPLAINS THE MAN WHO HAPPENED TO BE WALKING BY.
SHE PARTICIPATED IN THE OWL OPERATION WITH ARIMA SQUAD.
I DID.
SO EVERYBODY AROUND ME IS OLD... I MEAN VETERANS.
THANKS, INVESTIGATOR FURA.
NO PROBLEM.
Hairu Ihei [Senior Investigator]
BEING THE SAME AGE, I WAS HOPING WE COULD BE FRIENDS...!
S-SURE...
But you're our superior...
SHE WAS AT THE FRONT LINES OF THAT BATTLE...?
THIS AIRHEAD...?
YOU GAVE ROSÉ TO S1...?
YEAH.

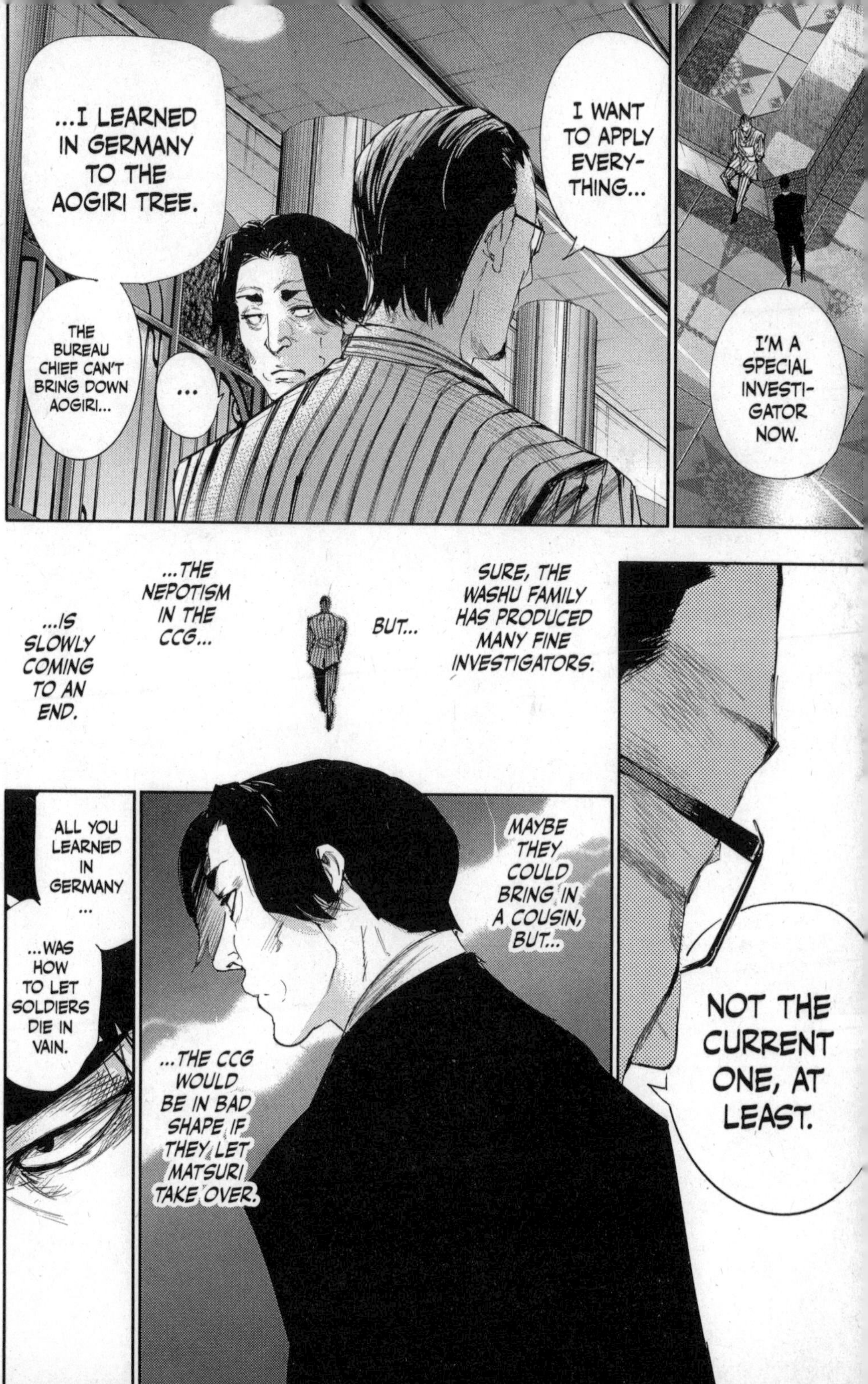
I'M A SPECIAL INVESTIGATOR NOW.
I WANT TO APPLY EVERYTHING...
...I LEARNED IN GERMANY TO THE AOGIRI TREE.
...
THE BUREAU CHIEF CAN'T BRING DOWN AOGIRI...
NOT THE CURRENT ONE, AT LEAST.
SURE, THE WASHU FAMILY HAS PRODUCED MANY FINE INVESTIGATORS.
BUT...
...THE NEPOTISM IN THE CCG...
...IS SLOWLY COMING TO AN END.
MAYBE THEY COULD BRING IN A COUSIN, BUT...
...THE CCG WOULD BE IN BAD SHAPE IF THEY LET MATSURI TAKE OVER.
ALL YOU LEARNED IN GERMANY...
...WAS HOW TO LET SOLDIERS DIE IN VAIN.

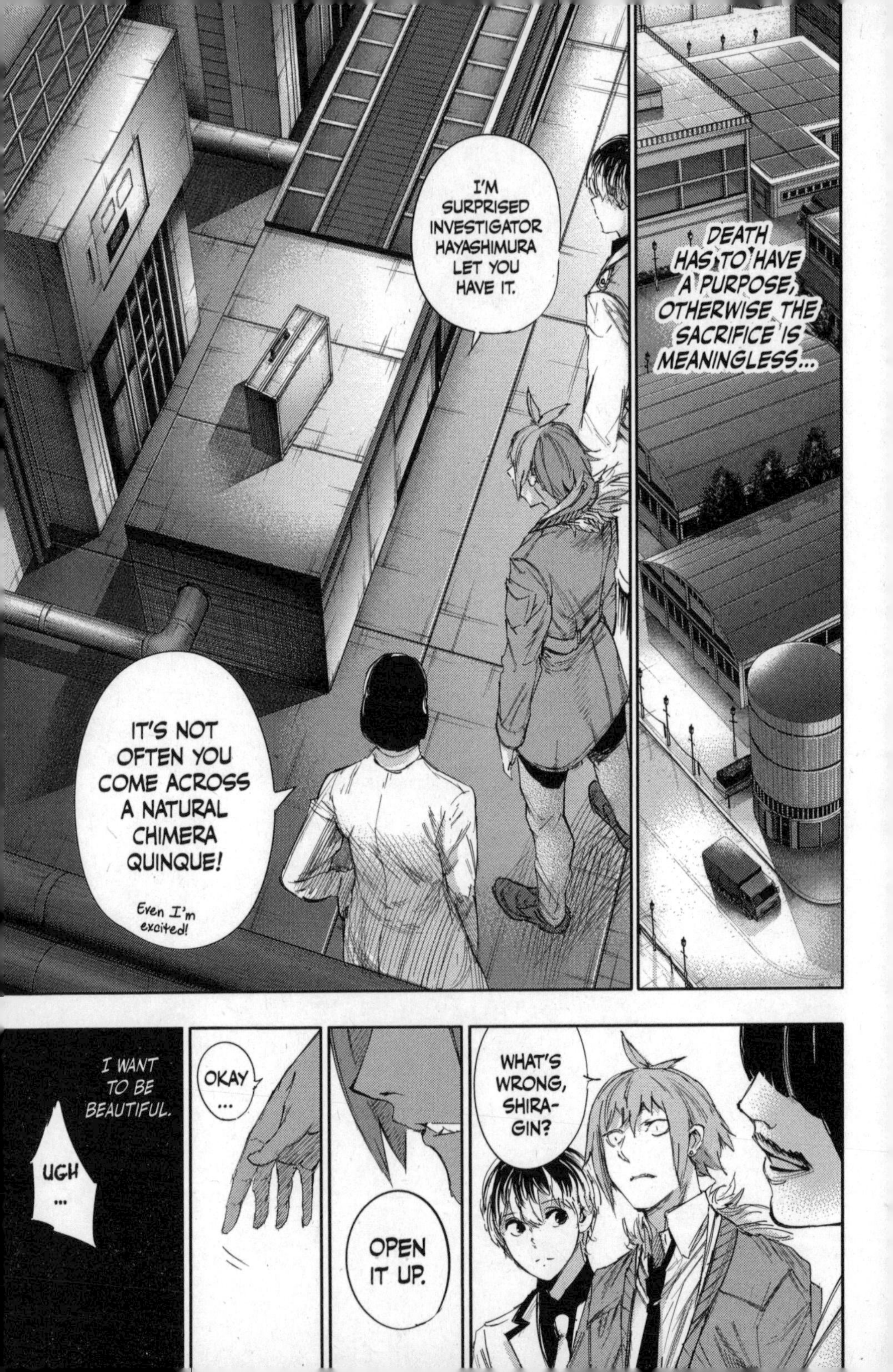
DEATH HAS TO HAVE A PURPOSE, OTHERWISE THE SACRIFICE IS MEANINGLESS...
I'M SURPRISED INVESTIGATOR HAYASHIMURA LET YOU HAVE IT.
IT'S NOT OFTEN YOU COME ACROSS A NATURAL CHIMERA QUINQUE!
Even I'm excited!
WHAT'S WRONG, SHIRAGIN?
OPEN IT UP.
OKAY ...
I WANT TO BE BEAUTIFUL.
UGH ...

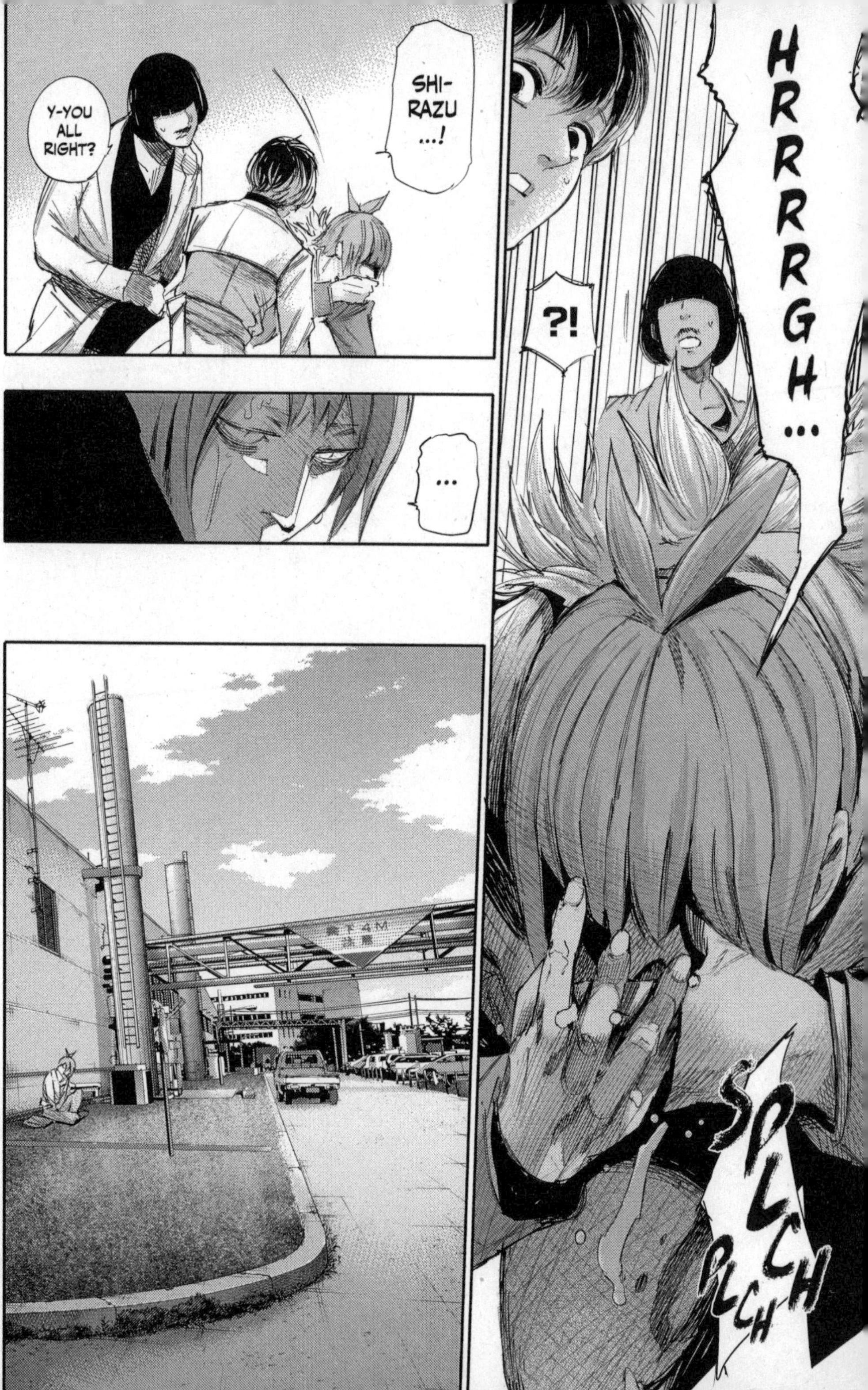
HRRRRGH...
?!
SPLCH
PLCH
SHI-RAZU...!
Y-YOU ALL RIGHT?
...

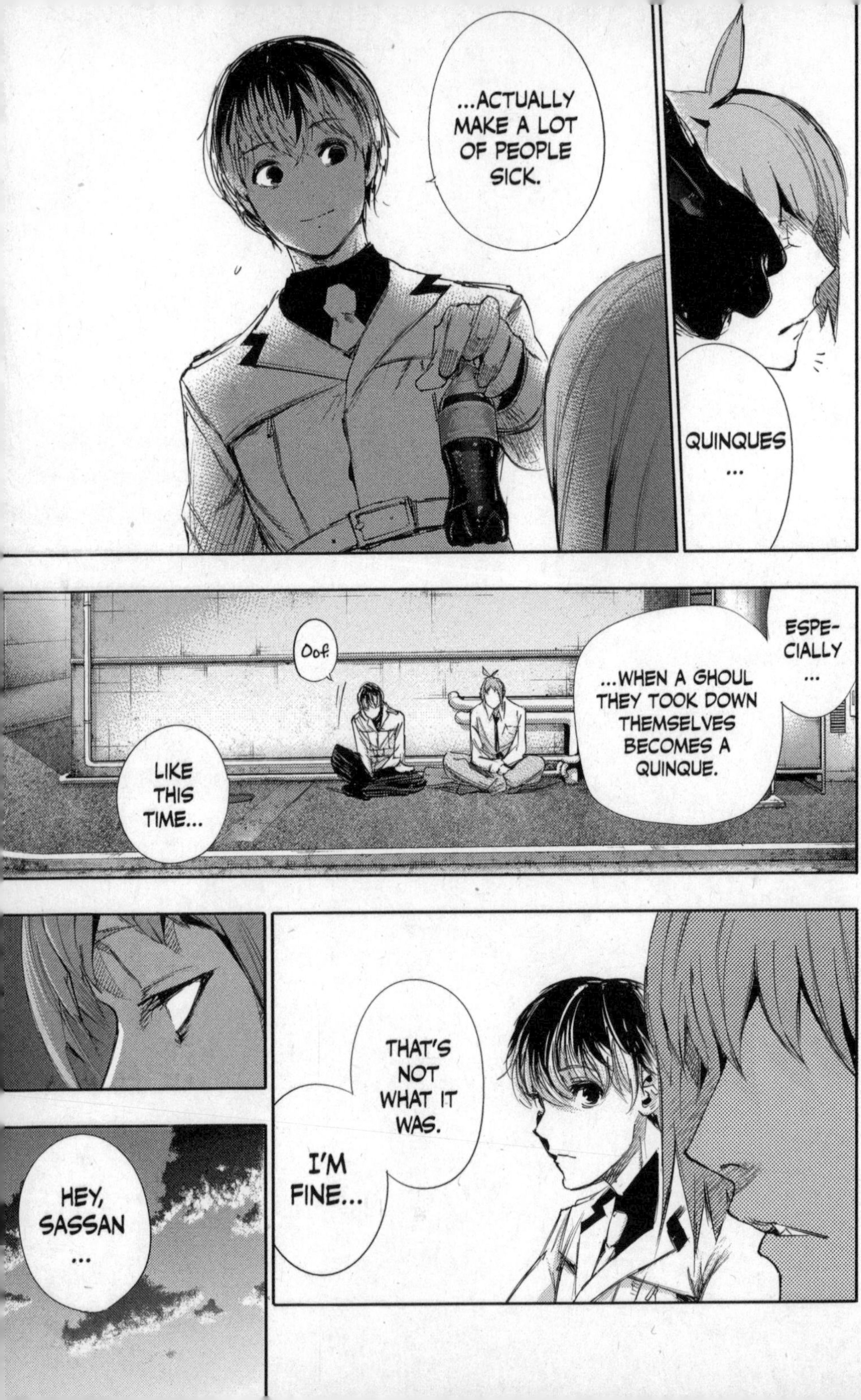
QUINQUES ...
...ACTUALLY MAKE A LOT OF PEOPLE SICK.
ESPE-CIALLY ...
...WHEN A GHOUL THEY TOOK DOWN THEMSELVES BECOMES A QUINQUE.
Oof.
LIKE THIS TIME...
THAT'S NOT WHAT IT WAS.
I'M FINE...
HEY, SASSAN ...

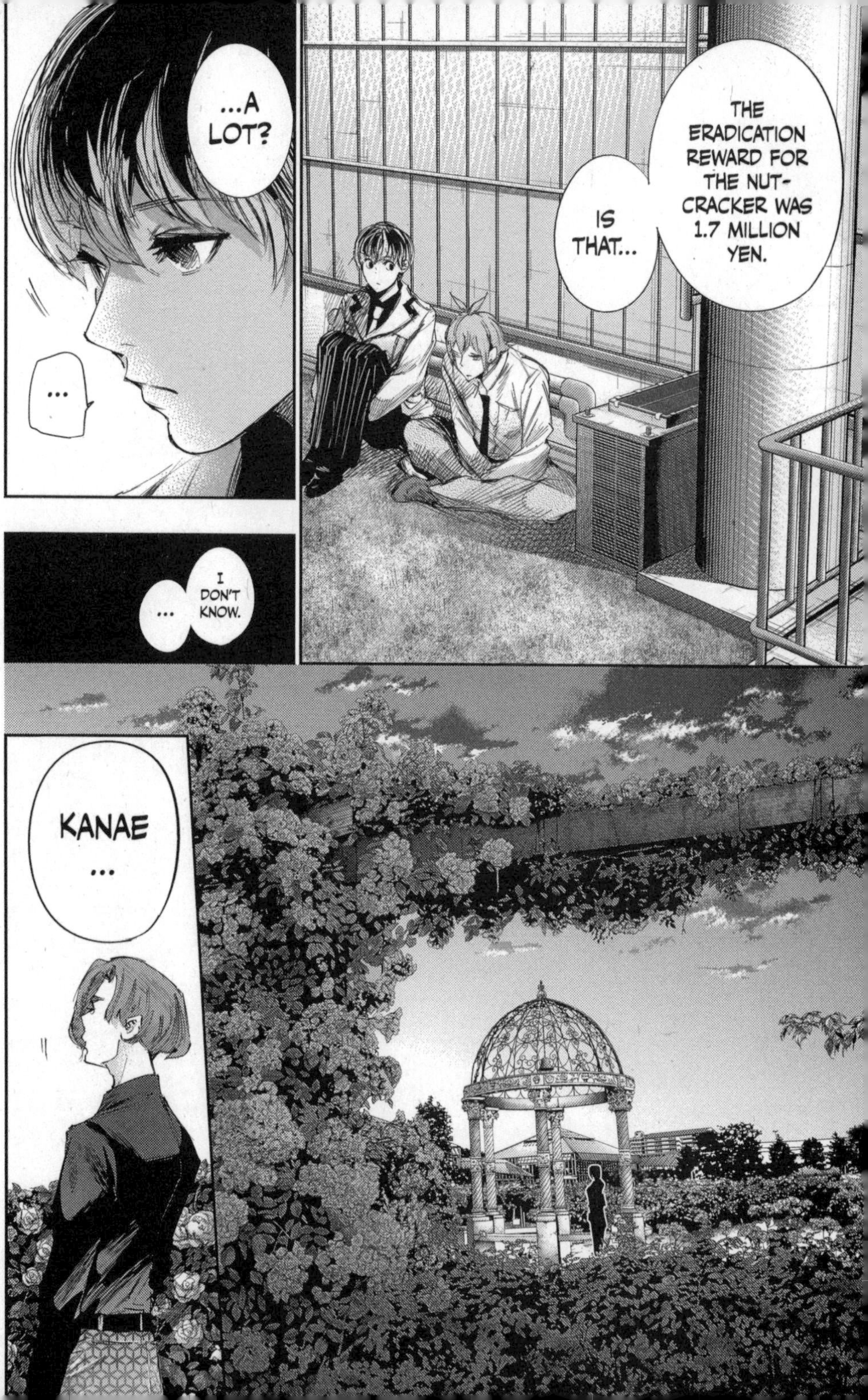
THE ERADICATION REWARD FOR THE NUT-CRACKER WAS 1.7 MILLION YEN.
IS THAT...
...A LOT?
...
...
I DON'T KNOW.
KANAE ...

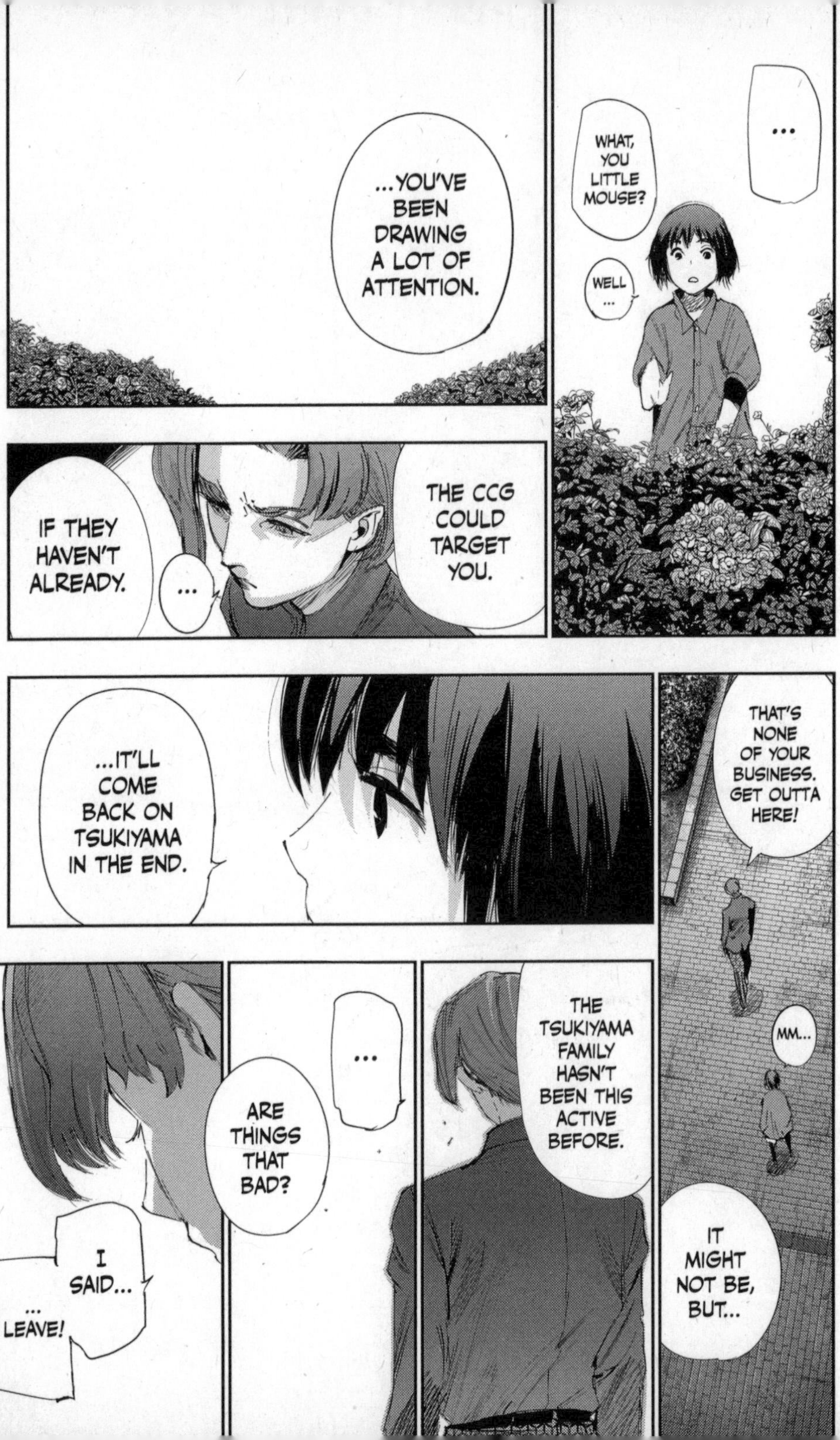
...
WHAT, YOU LITTLE MOUSE?
WELL ...
...YOU'VE BEEN DRAWING A LOT OF ATTENTION.
THE CCG COULD TARGET YOU.
...
IF THEY HAVEN'T ALREADY.
THAT'S NONE OF YOUR BUSINESS. GET OUTTA HERE!
MM...
IT MIGHT NOT BE, BUT...
...IT'LL COME BACK ON TSUKIYAMA IN THE END.
THE TSUKIYAMA FAMILY HASN'T BEEN THIS ACTIVE BEFORE.
...
ARE THINGS THAT BAD?
I SAID...
...LEAVE!

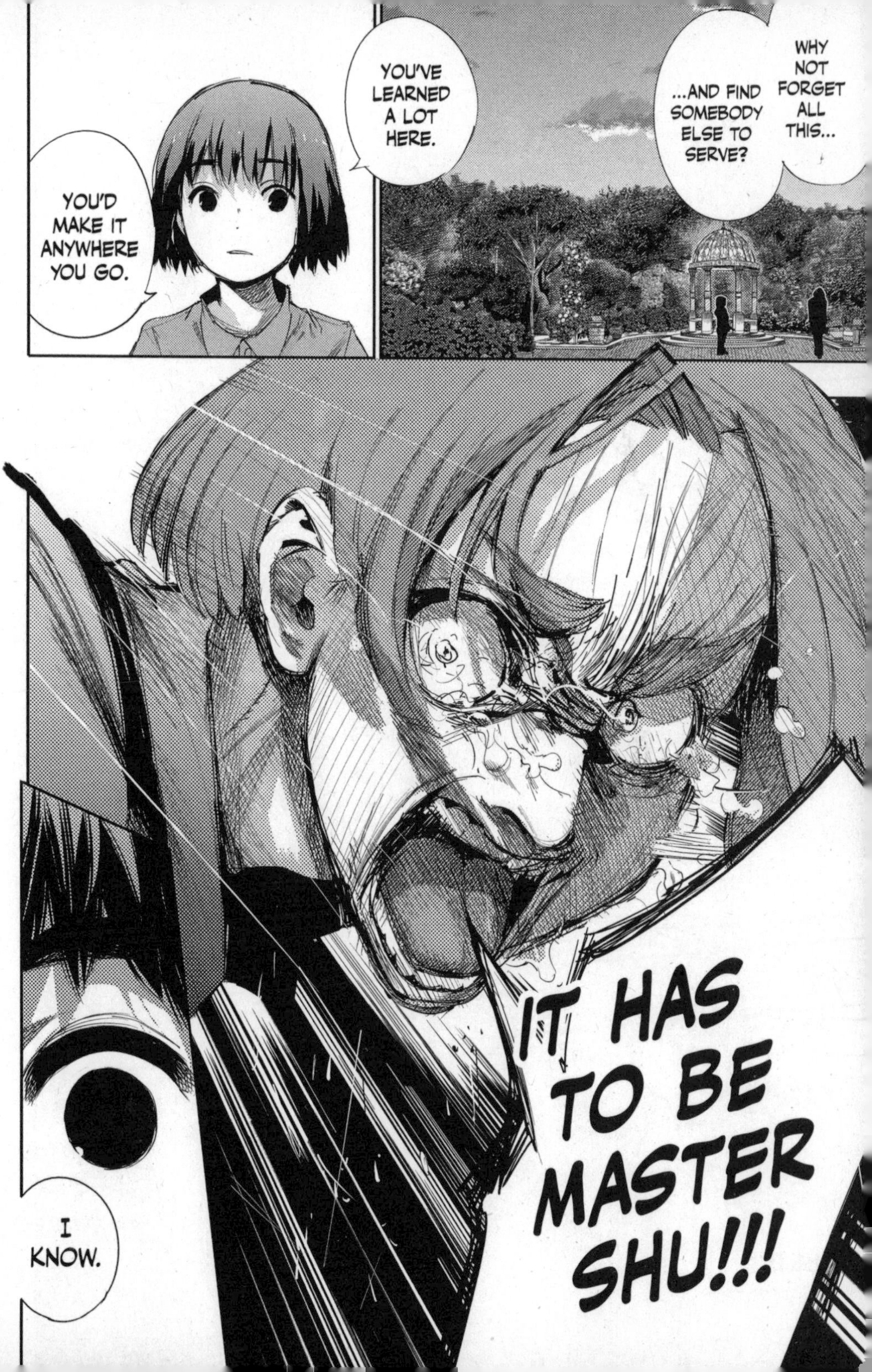
WHY NOT FORGET ALL THIS...
...AND FIND SOMEBODY ELSE TO SERVE?
YOU'VE LEARNED A LOT HERE.
YOU'D MAKE IT ANYWHERE YOU GO.
IT HAS TO BE MASTER SHU!!!
I KNOW.

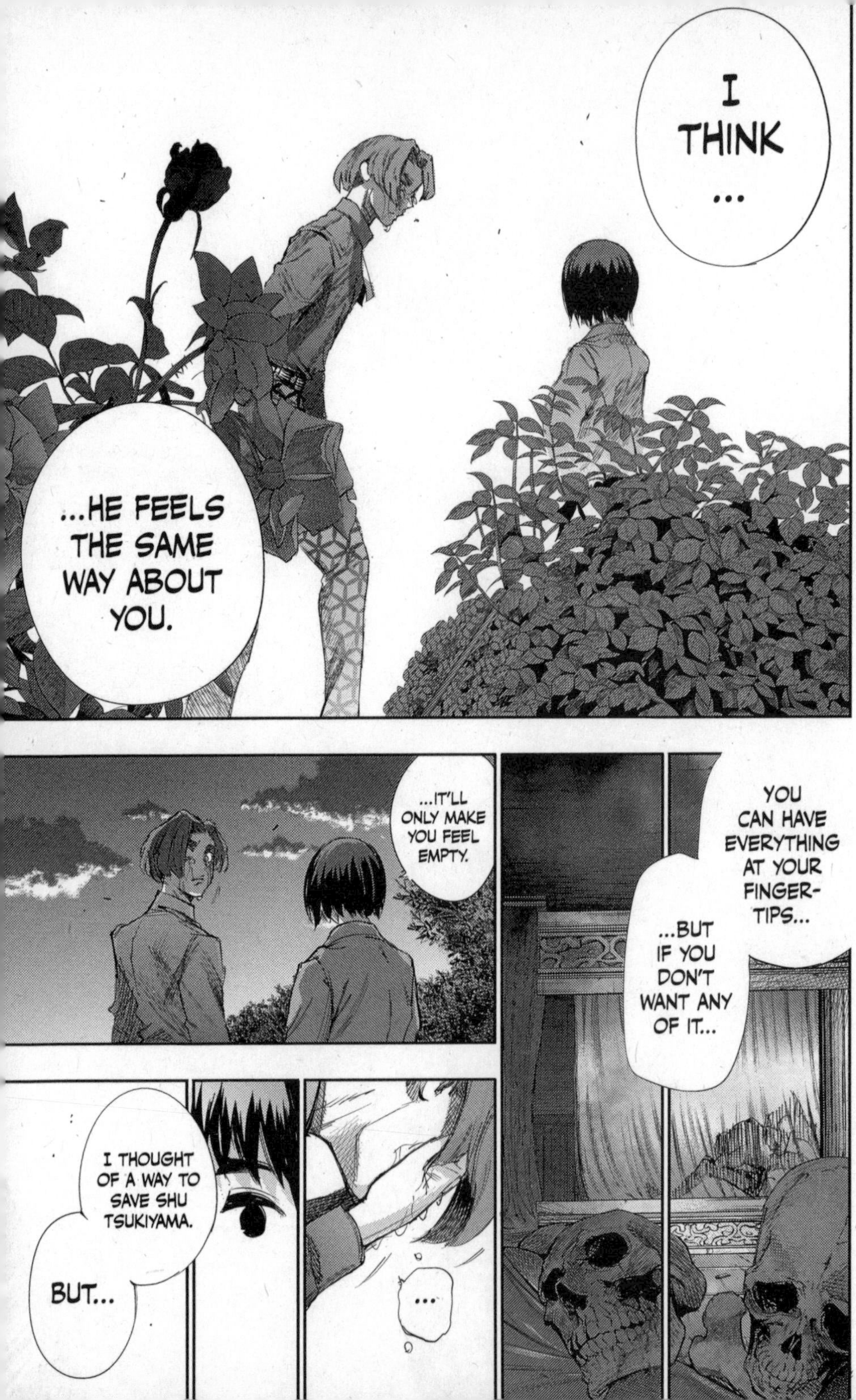
I THINK...
...HE FEELS THE SAME WAY ABOUT YOU.
YOU CAN HAVE EVERYTHING AT YOUR FINGER-TIPS...
...BUT IF YOU DON'T WANT ANY OF IT...
...IT'LL ONLY MAKE YOU FEEL EMPTY.
...
I THOUGHT OF A WAY TO SAVE SHU TSUKIYAMA.
BUT...

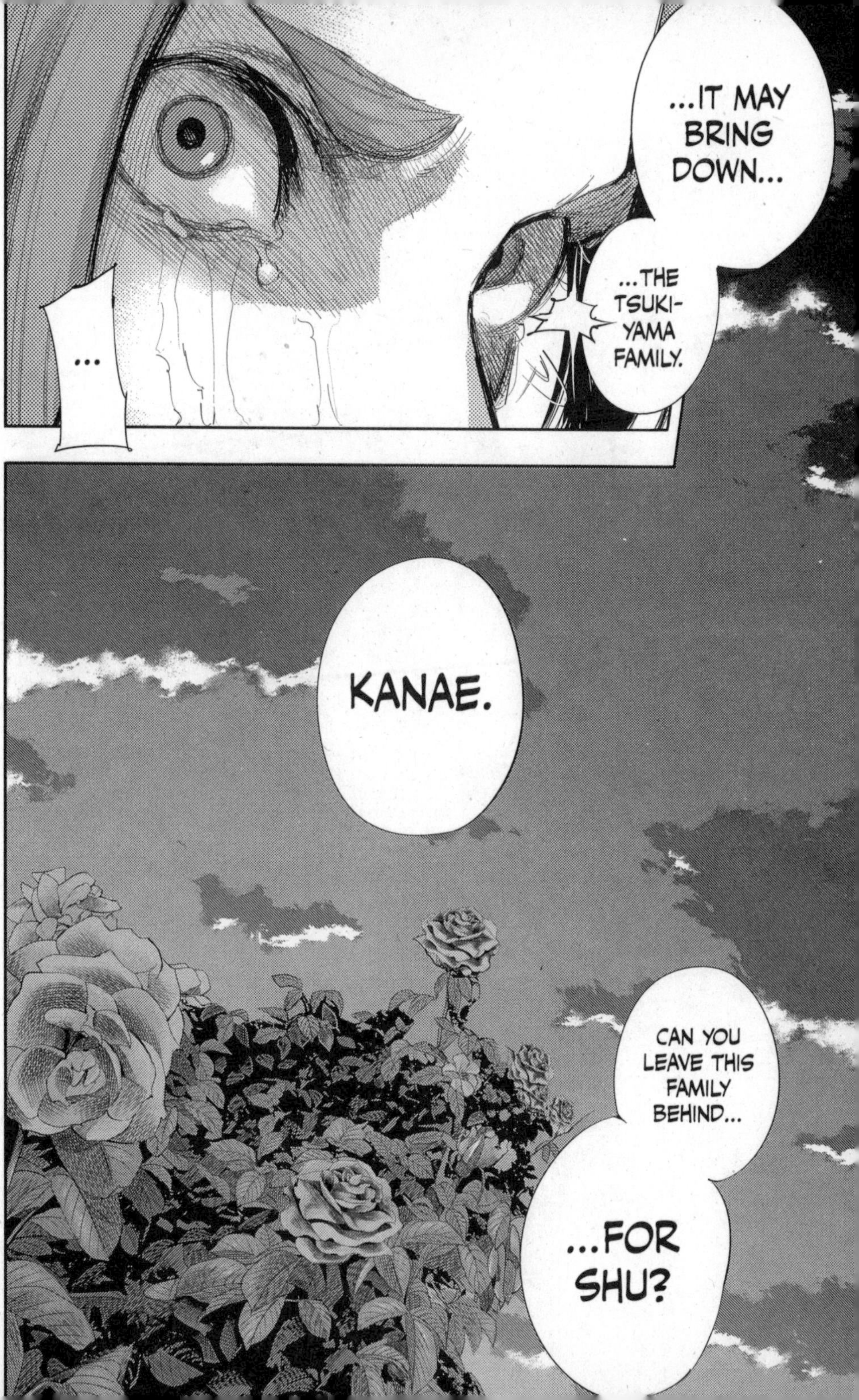
...IT MAY BRING DOWN...
...THE TSUKI-YAMA FAMILY.
...
KANAE.
CAN YOU LEAVE THIS FAMILY BEHIND...
...FOR SHU?

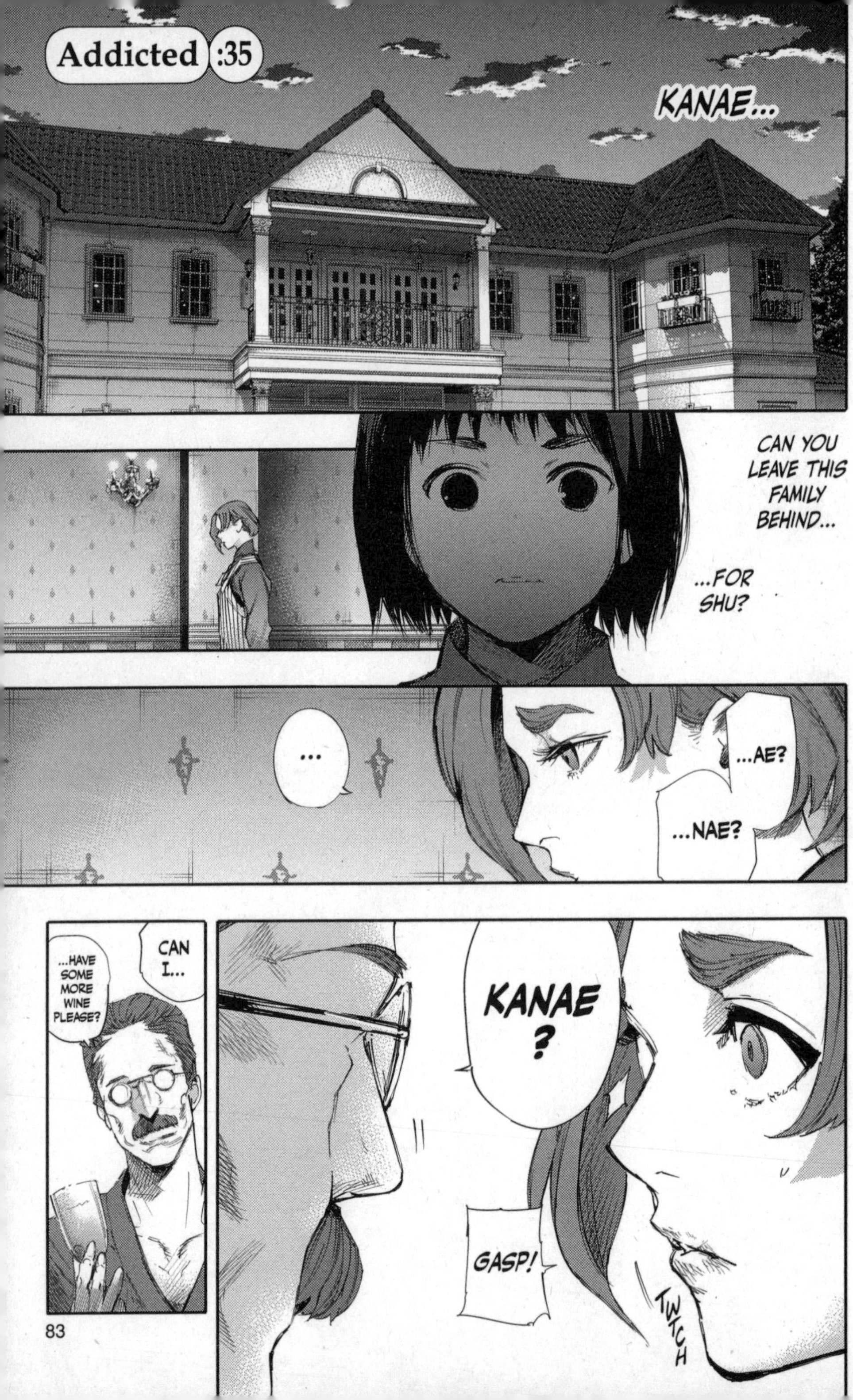
Addicted :35
KANAE...
CAN YOU LEAVE THIS FAMILY BEHIND...
...FOR SHU?
...AE?
...NAE?
...
KANAE ?
GASP!
TWITCH
CAN I...
...HAVE SOME MORE WINE PLEASE?

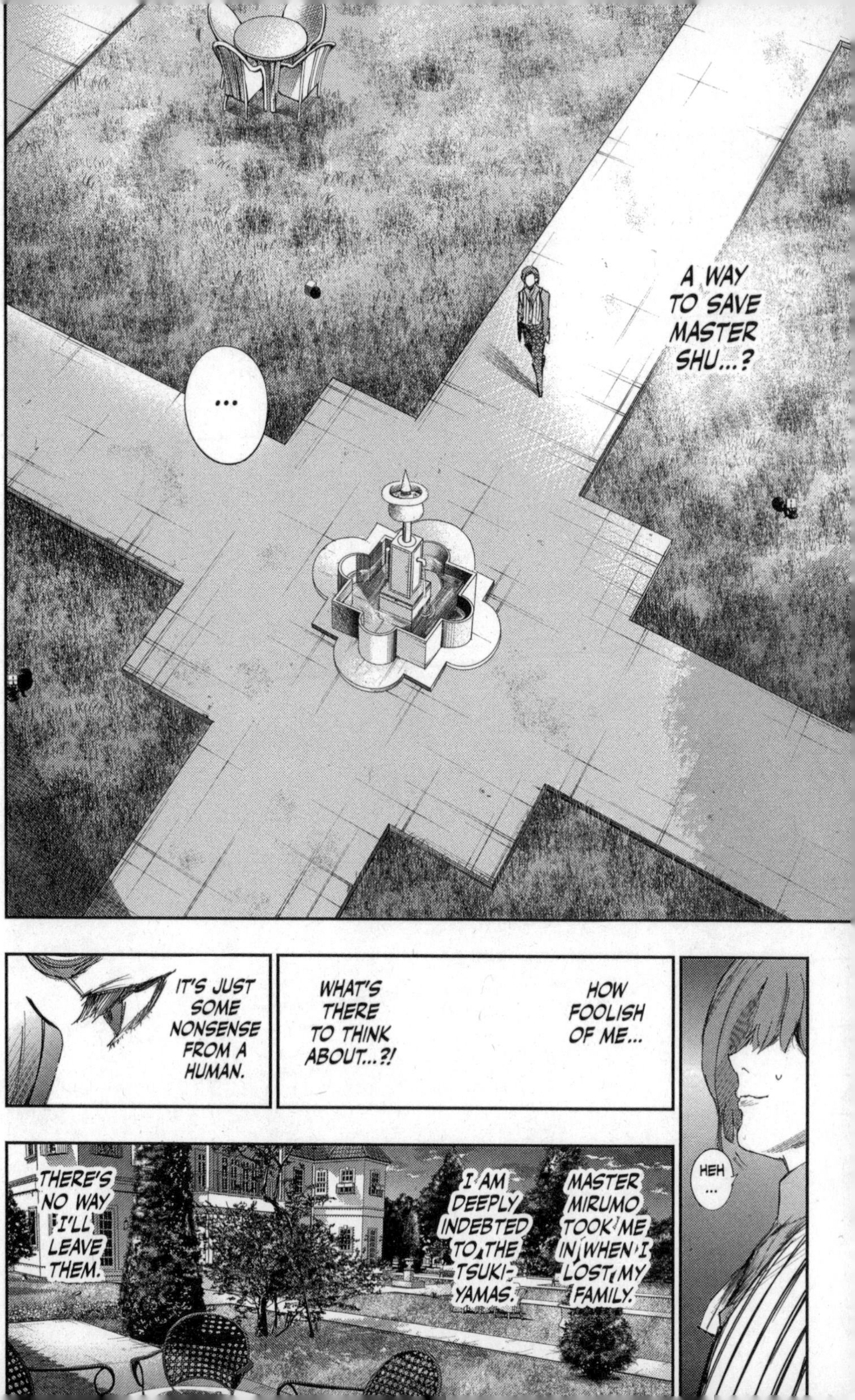
A WAY TO SAVE MASTER SHU...?
...
HEH ...
HOW FOOLISH OF ME...
WHAT'S THERE TO THINK ABOUT...?!
IT'S JUST SOME NONSENSE FROM A HUMAN.
MASTER MIRUMO TOOK ME IN WHEN I LOST MY FAMILY.
I AM DEEPLY INDEBTED TO THE TSUKI-YAMAS.
THERE'S NO WAY I'LL LEAVE THEM.

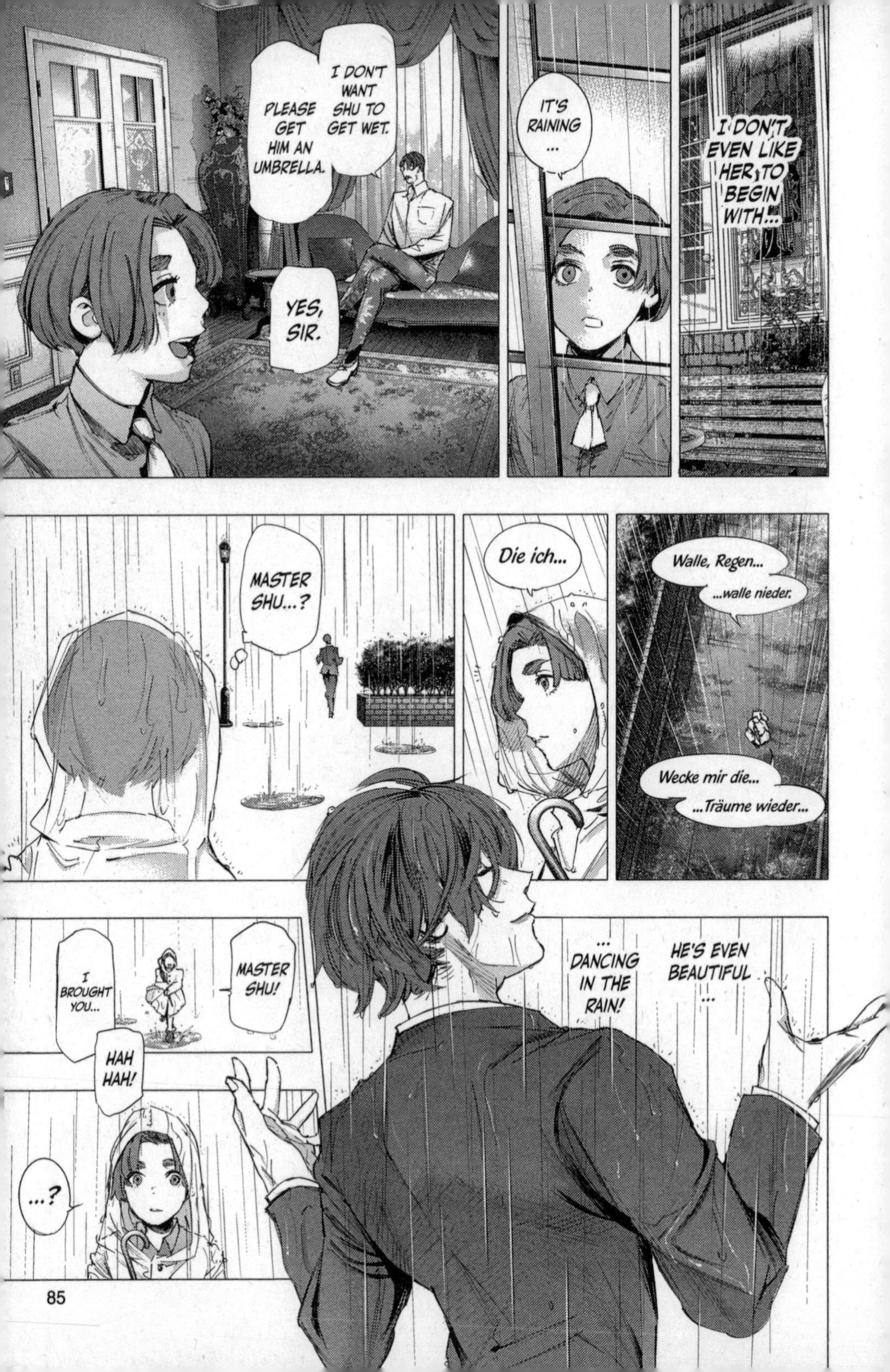

I DON'T EVEN LIKE HER TO BEGIN WITH...
IT'S RAINING ...
I DON'T WANT SHU TO GET WET.
PLEASE GET HIM AN UMBRELLA.
YES, SIR.
Walle, Regen... ...walle nieder.
Wecke mir die... ...Träume wieder...
Die ich...
MASTER SHU...?
HE'S EVEN BEAUTIFUL ...
... DANCING IN THE RAIN!
MASTER SHU!
I BROUGHT YOU...
HAH HAH!
...?

THE RAIN FEELS NICE, HORI.

IT DOES.

SO WHAT'S THE MATTER?!

CAPTURE ME AS THE RAIN TRICKLES DOWN ON ME!

WHAT?!

HUH? THAT'S OKAY.

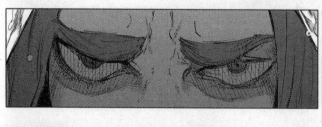

IT'S NOT OFTEN YOU GET TO SEE ME WET LIKE THIS...!

SQW

OKAY.

HA HA HA! YOU ARE A FUNNY GIRL!

VERY UNIQUE!

I THINK YOU'RE BEING THE FUNNY ONE.

MASTER SHU HAS A VERY BIG HEART...

HE MAY EVEN OFFER HIS BENEVOLENCE...

...TO A LOWLY HUMAN AT TIMES.

BUT...

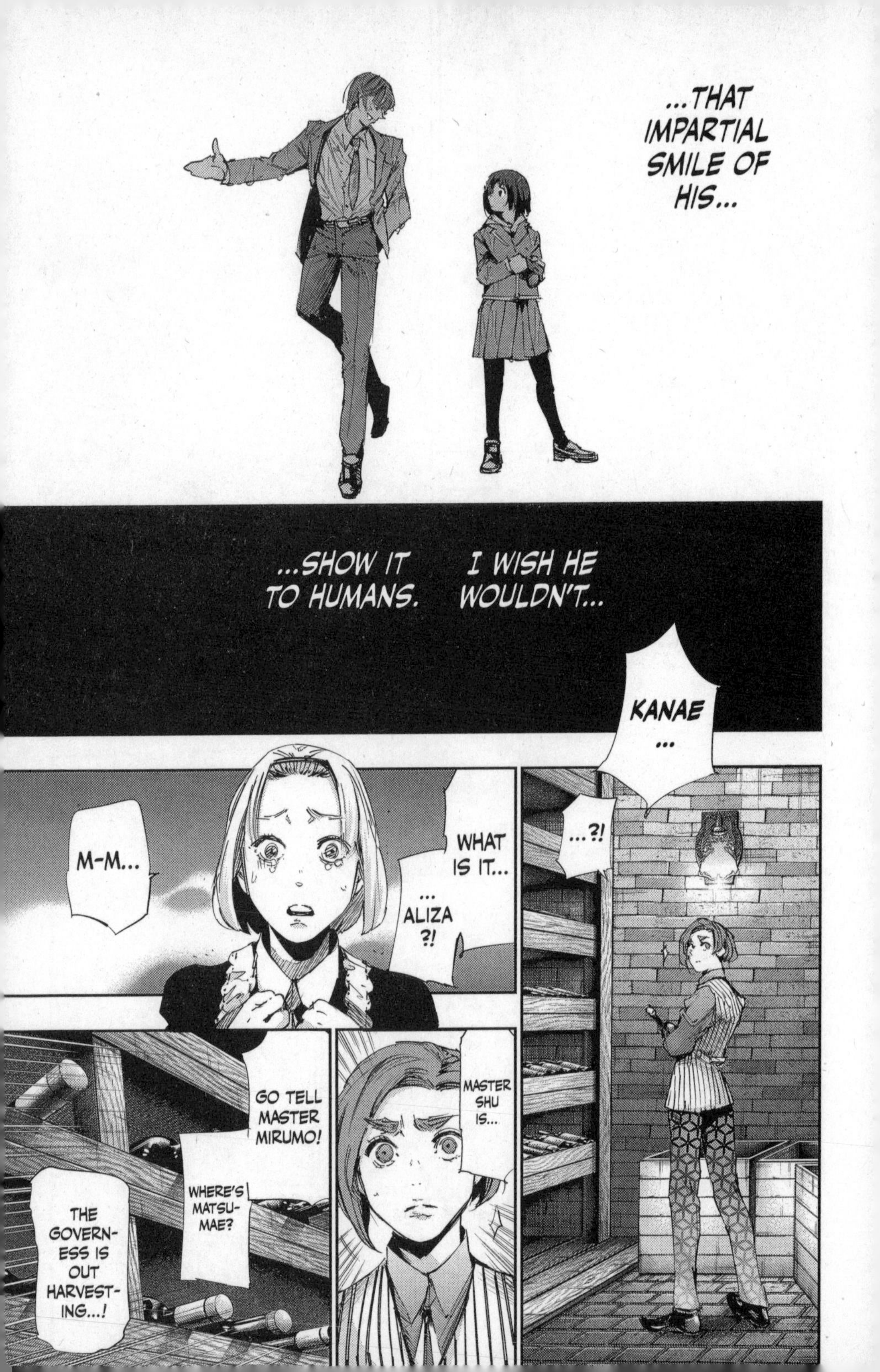
...THAT IMPARTIAL SMILE OF HIS...
I WISH HE WOULDN'T...
...SHOW IT TO HUMANS.
KANAE ...
...?!
WHAT IS IT...
... ALIZA ?!
M-M...
MASTER SHU IS...
GO TELL MASTER MIRUMO!
WHERE'S MATSU-MAE?
THE GOVERN-ESS IS OUT HARVEST-ING...!

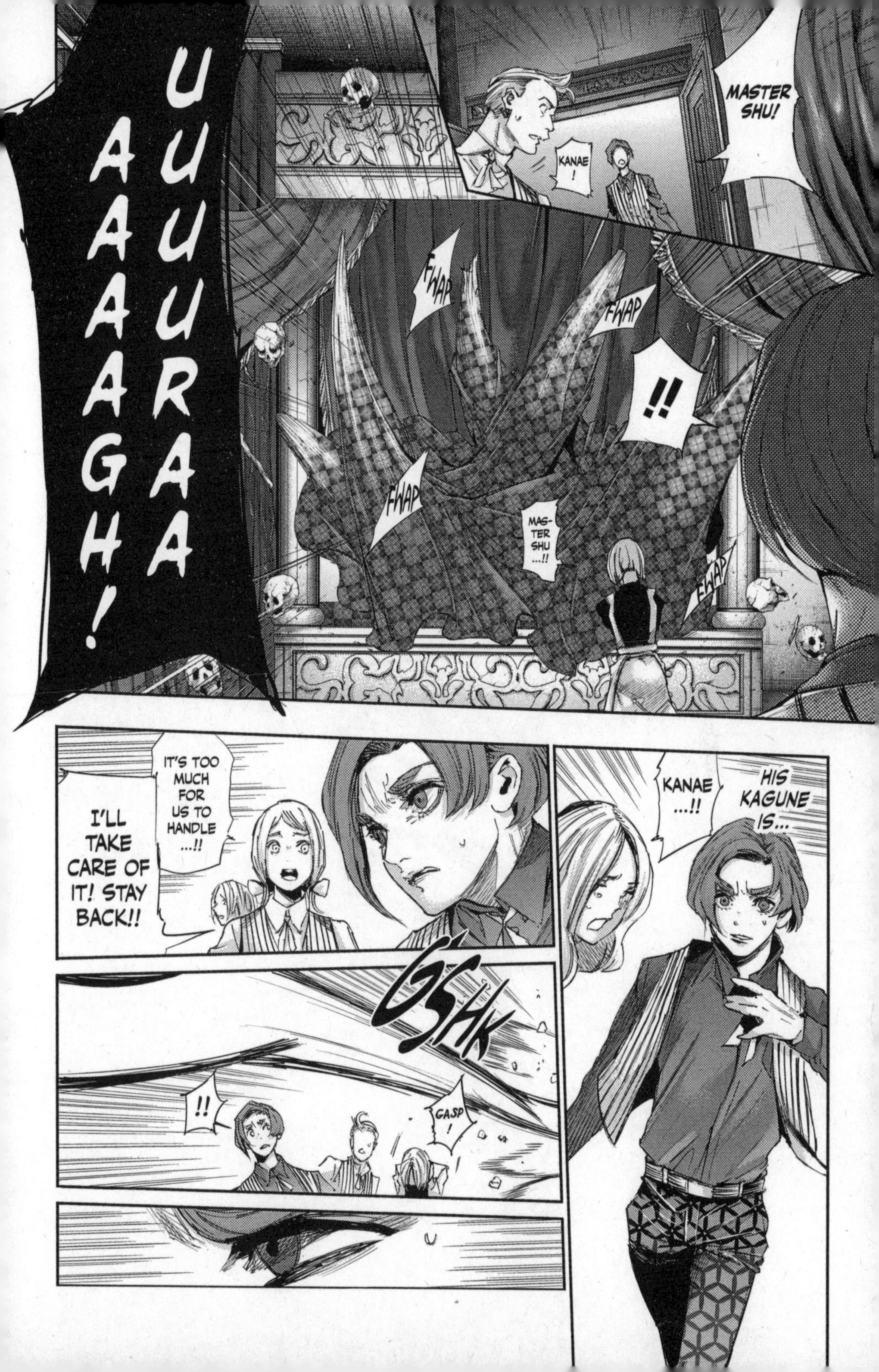
MASTER SHU!
KANAE !
!!
FWAP
FWAP
FWAP
MASTER SHU ...!!
FWAP
UUUURAA AAAAAGH!
HIS KAGUNE IS...
KANAE ...!!
IT'S TOO MUCH FOR US TO HANDLE ...!!
I'LL TAKE CARE OF IT! STAY BACK!!
GSHK
GASP !
!!

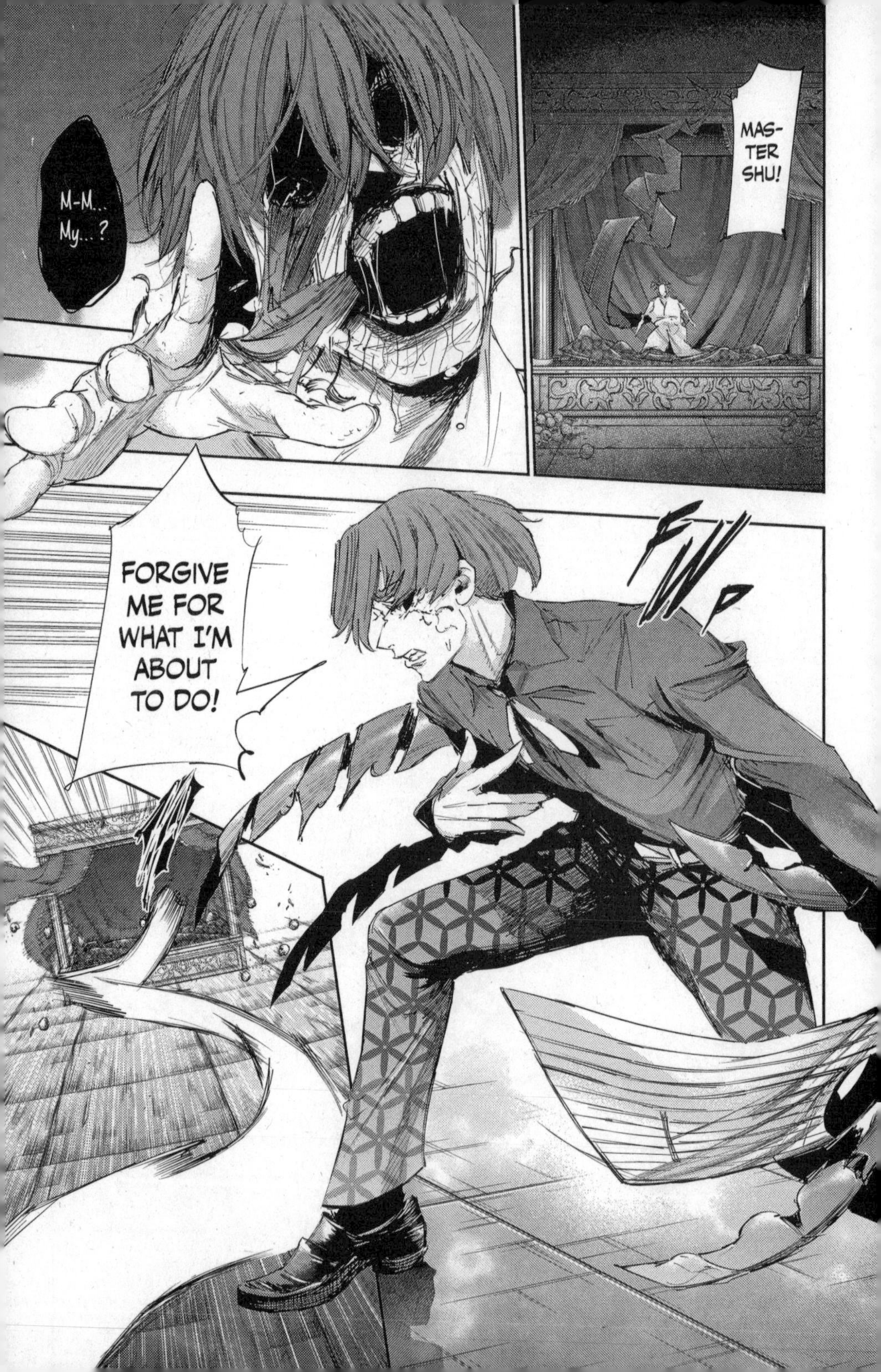
MAS-
TER
SHU!
M-M...
My...?
FWP
FORGIVE ME FOR WHAT I'M ABOUT TO DO!

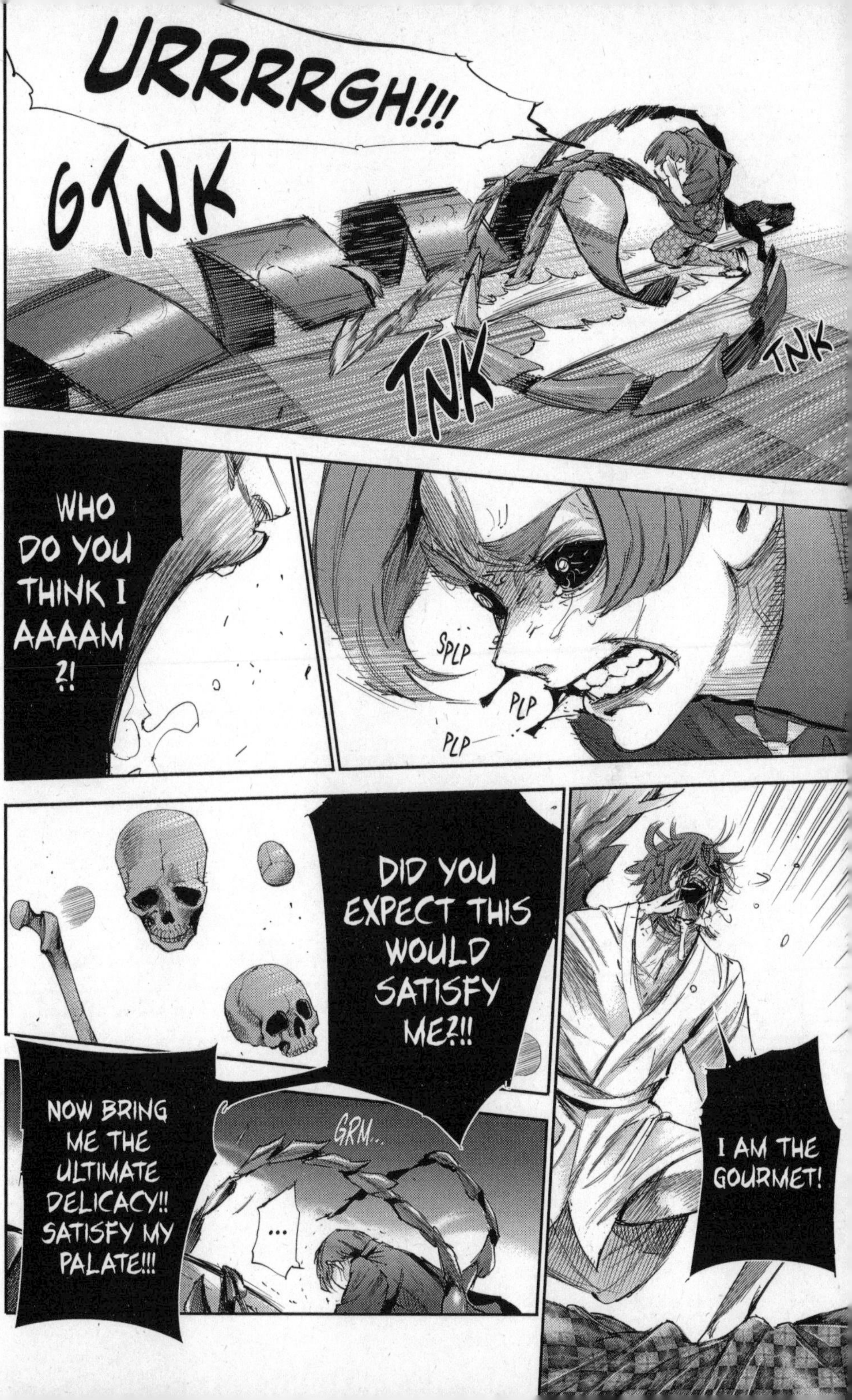
URRRRGH!!!
GTNK
TNK
TNK
!!
SPLP
PLP
PLP
WHO DO YOU THINK I AAAAM?!
I AM THE GOURMET!
DID YOU EXPECT THIS WOULD SATISFY ME?!!
NOW BRING ME THE ULTIMATE DELICACY!! SATISFY MY PALATE!!!
GRM..
...

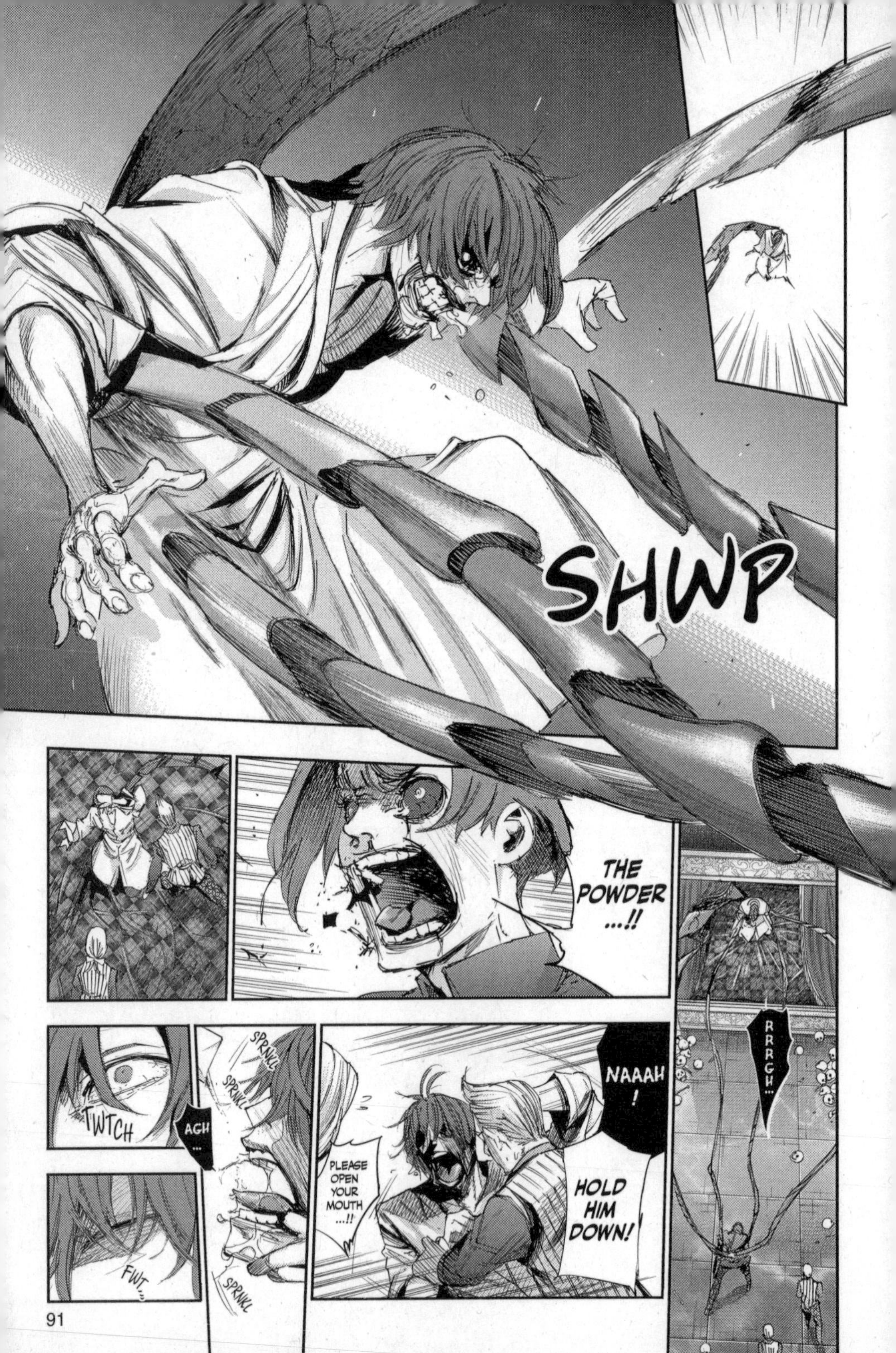
SHWP
RRRGH...
THE POWDER ...!!
NAAAH!
HOLD HIM DOWN!
PLEASE OPEN YOUR MOUTH ...!!
SPRNKL
SPRNKL
AGH...
SPRNKL
TWTCH
FWT...

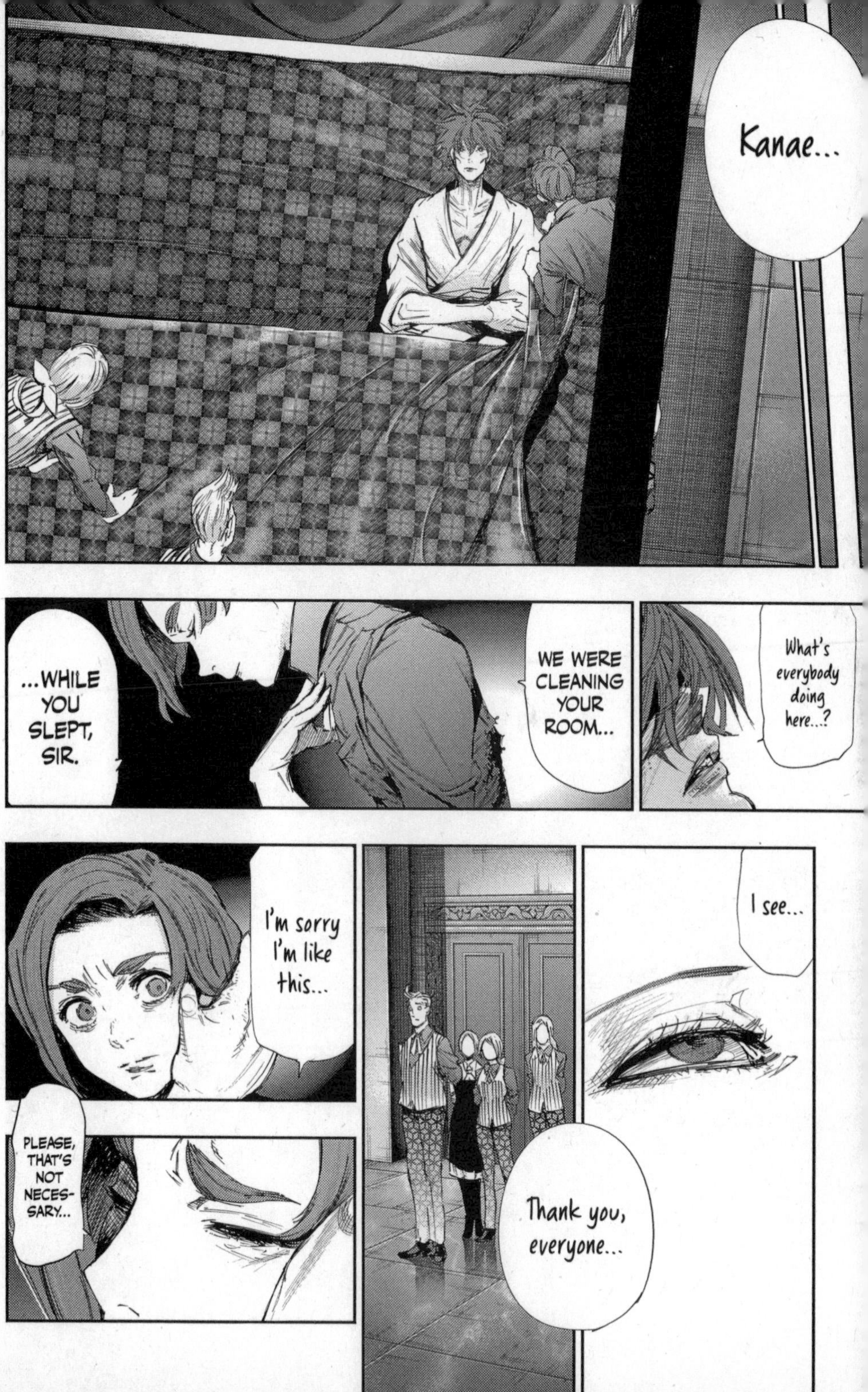
Kanae...
What's everybody doing here...?
WE WERE CLEANING YOUR ROOM...
...WHILE YOU SLEPT, SIR.
I see...
Thank you, everyone...
I'm sorry I'm like this...
PLEASE, THAT'S NOT NECES-SARY...

Please...

Keep taking care of this family....

...

YES, SIR.

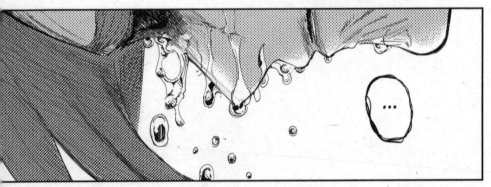

...

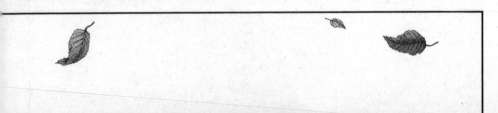

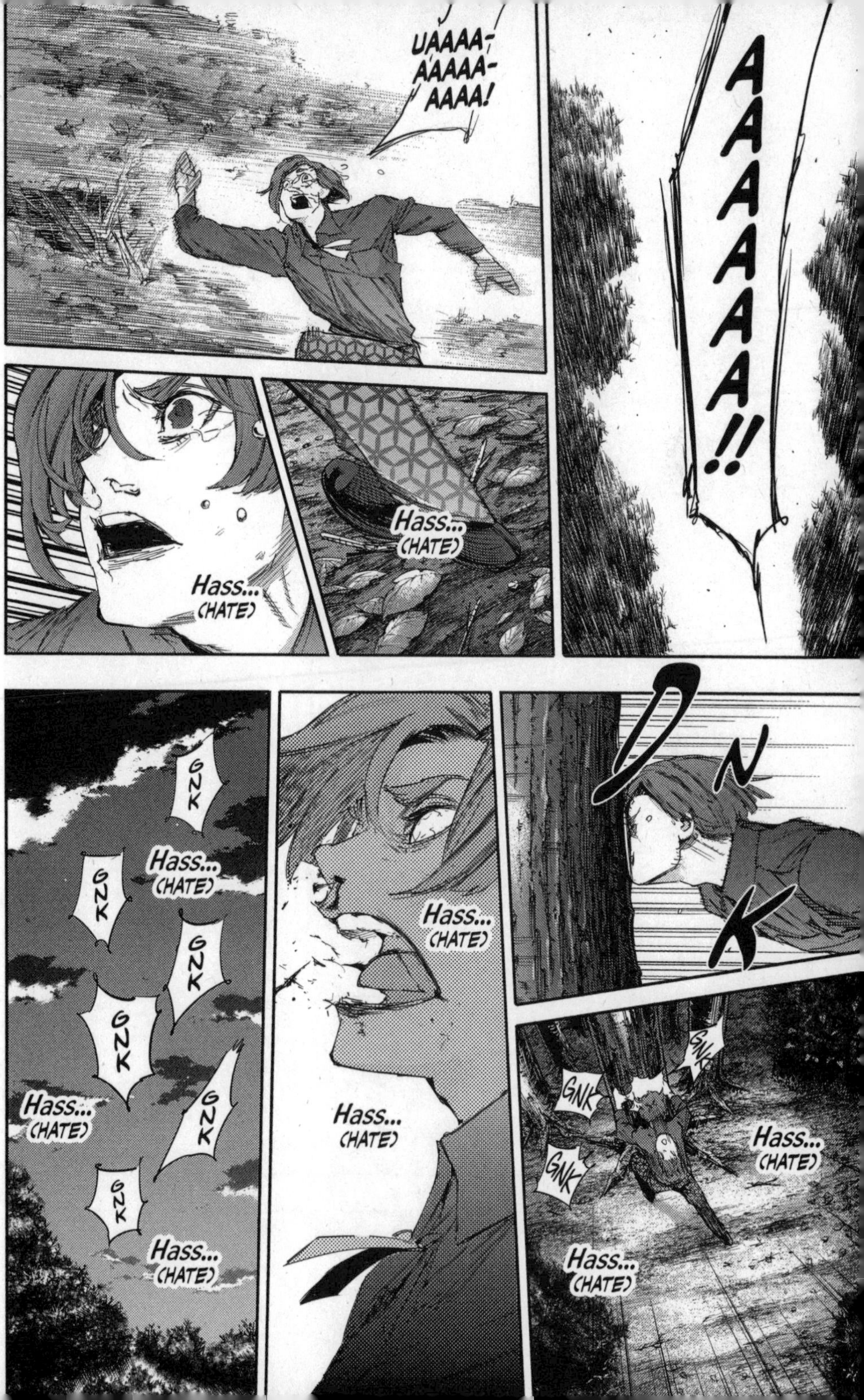
AAAAAAA!!
UAAAA-AAAAA-AAAA!
Hass... (HATE)
Hass... (HATE)
DNK
GNK
GNK
GNK
Hass... (HATE)
Hass... (HATE)
Hass... (HATE)
Hass... (HATE)
GNK
Hass... (HATE)
GNK
GNK
GNK
Hass... (HATE)
GNK
GNK
Hass... (HATE)

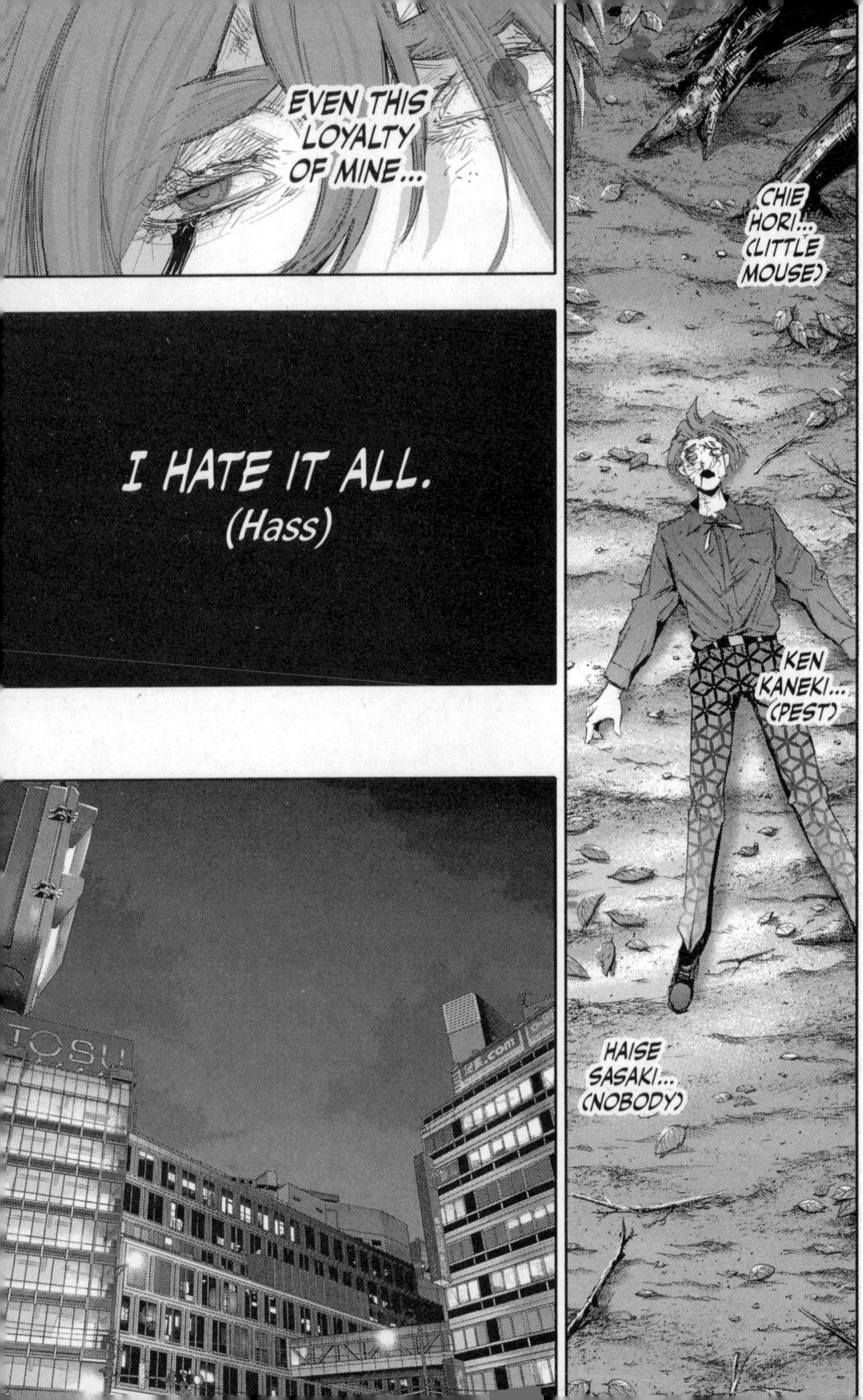
(CHIE HORI... (LITTLE MOUSE)
KEN KANEKI... (PEST)
HAISE SASAKI... (NOBODY)
EVEN THIS LOYALTY OF MINE...
I HATE IT ALL.
(Hass)
TOSU
RE.com

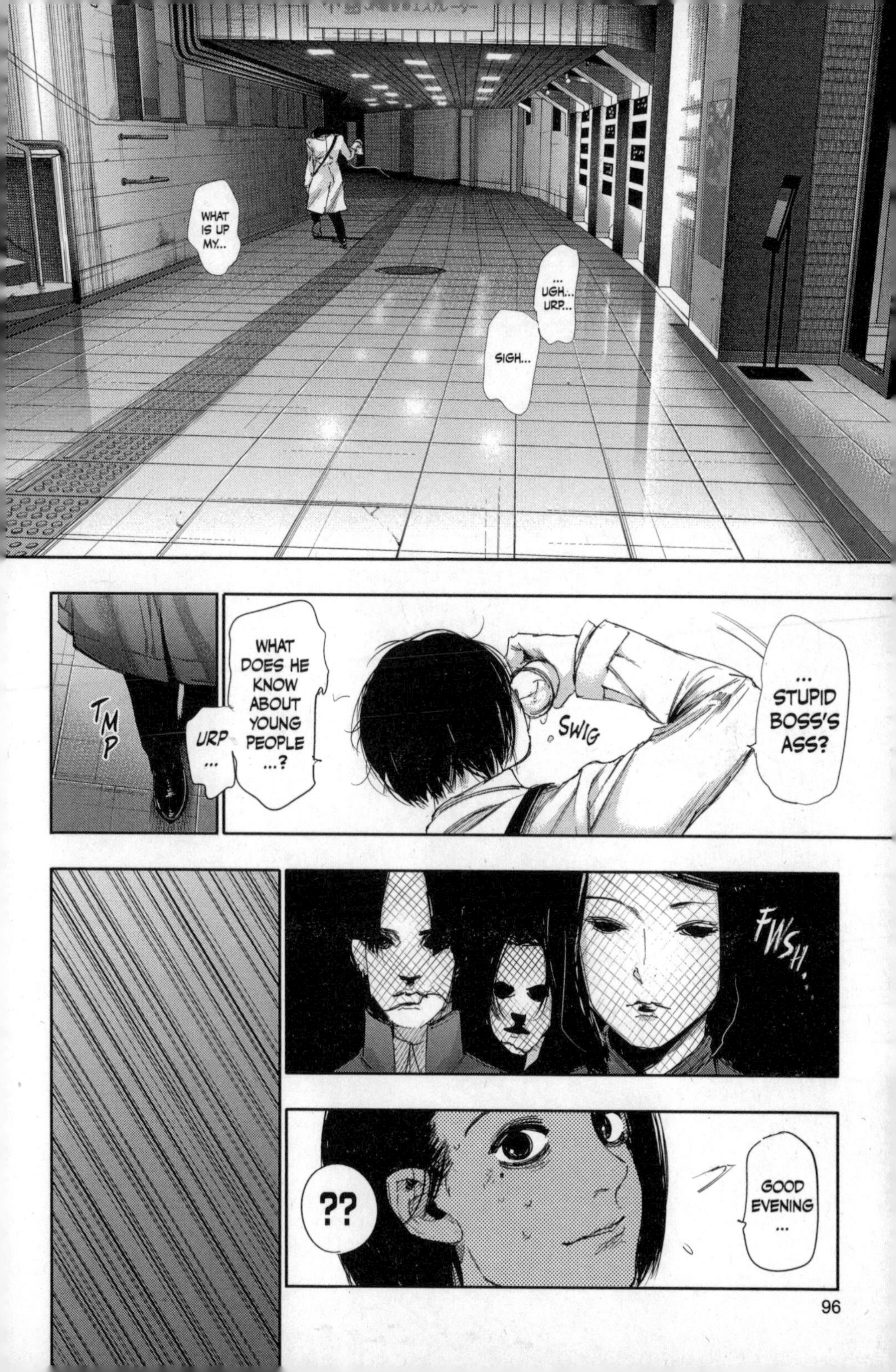
... UGH... URP...
SIGH...
WHAT IS UP MY...
... STUPID BOSS'S ASS?
SWIG
WHAT DOES HE KNOW ABOUT YOUNG PEOPLE ...?
URP ...
TMP
FWSH...
GOOD EVENING ...
??

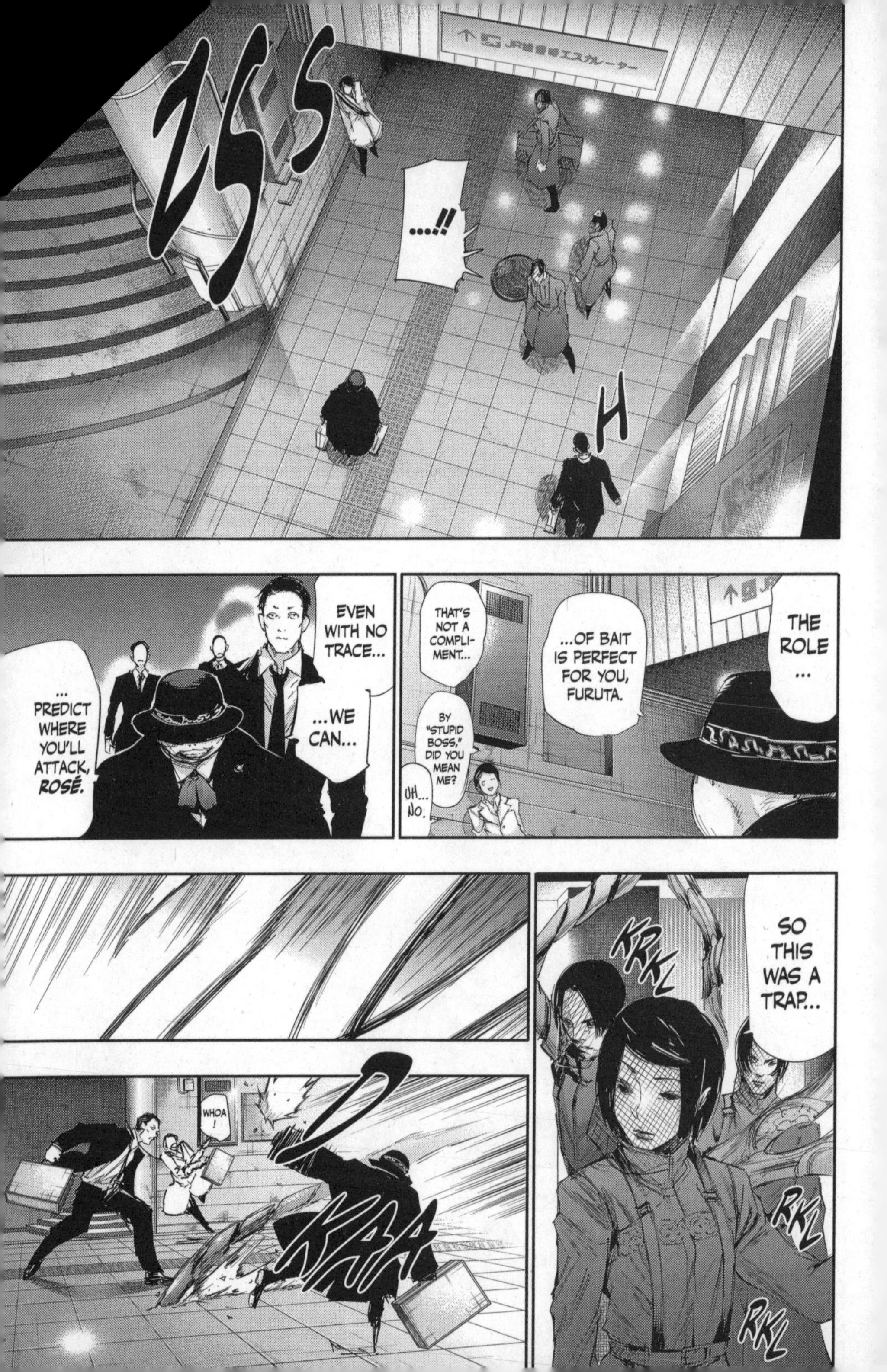
ZSS
...!!
H
THE ROLE...
...OF BAIT IS PERFECT FOR YOU, FURUTA.
THAT'S NOT A COMPLIMENT...
BY "STUPID BOSS," DID YOU MEAN ME?
UH... NO.
EVEN WITH NO TRACE...
...WE CAN...
...PREDICT WHERE YOU'LL ATTACK, ROSÉ.
SO THIS WAS A TRAP...
KRKL
RKL
RKL
WHOA!
D
KAA

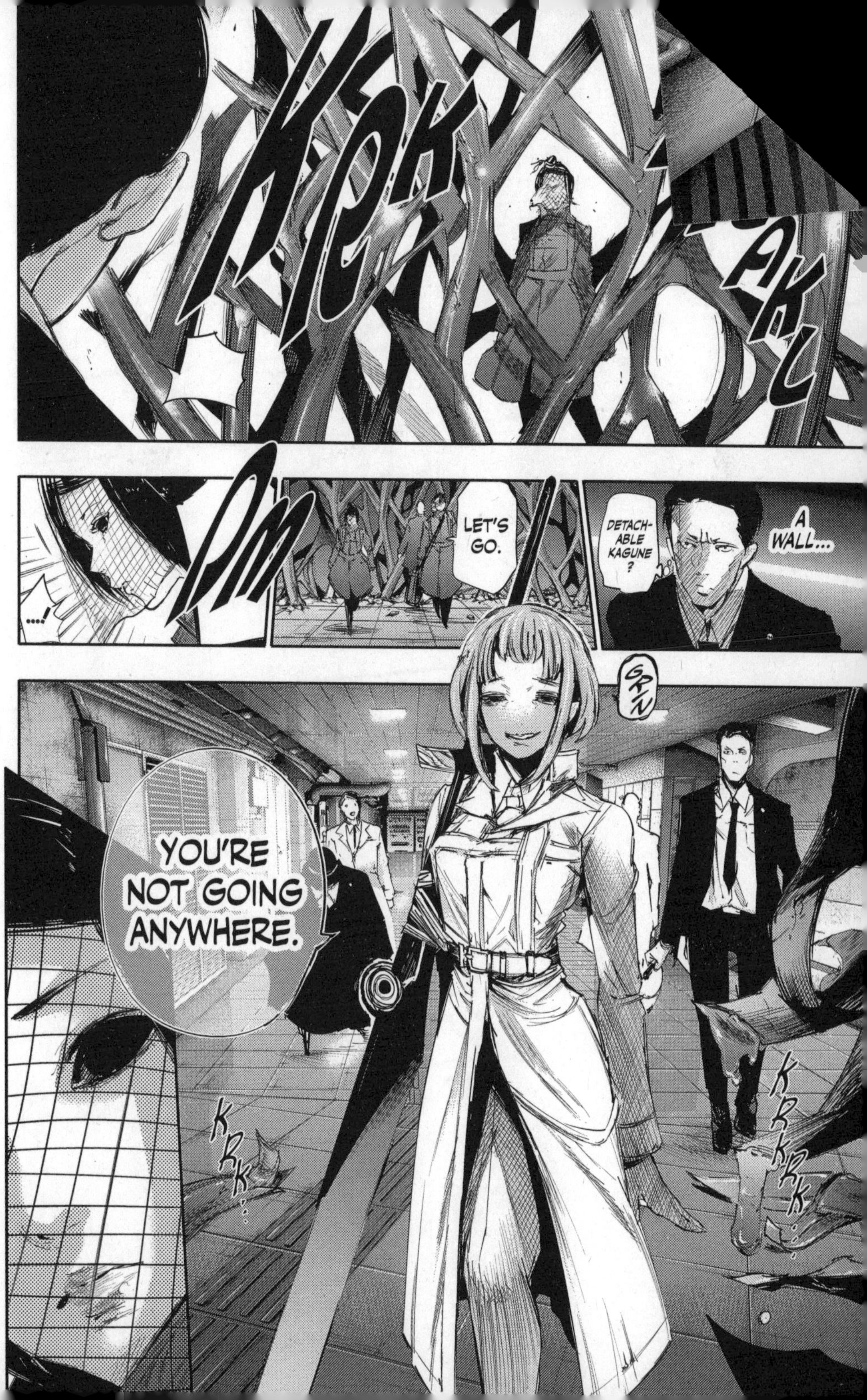
A WALL...
DETACH-
ABLE
KAGUNE
?
LET'S
GO.
...!
GRIN
YOU'RE
NOT GOING
ANYWHERE.
KRKRK...
KRK...

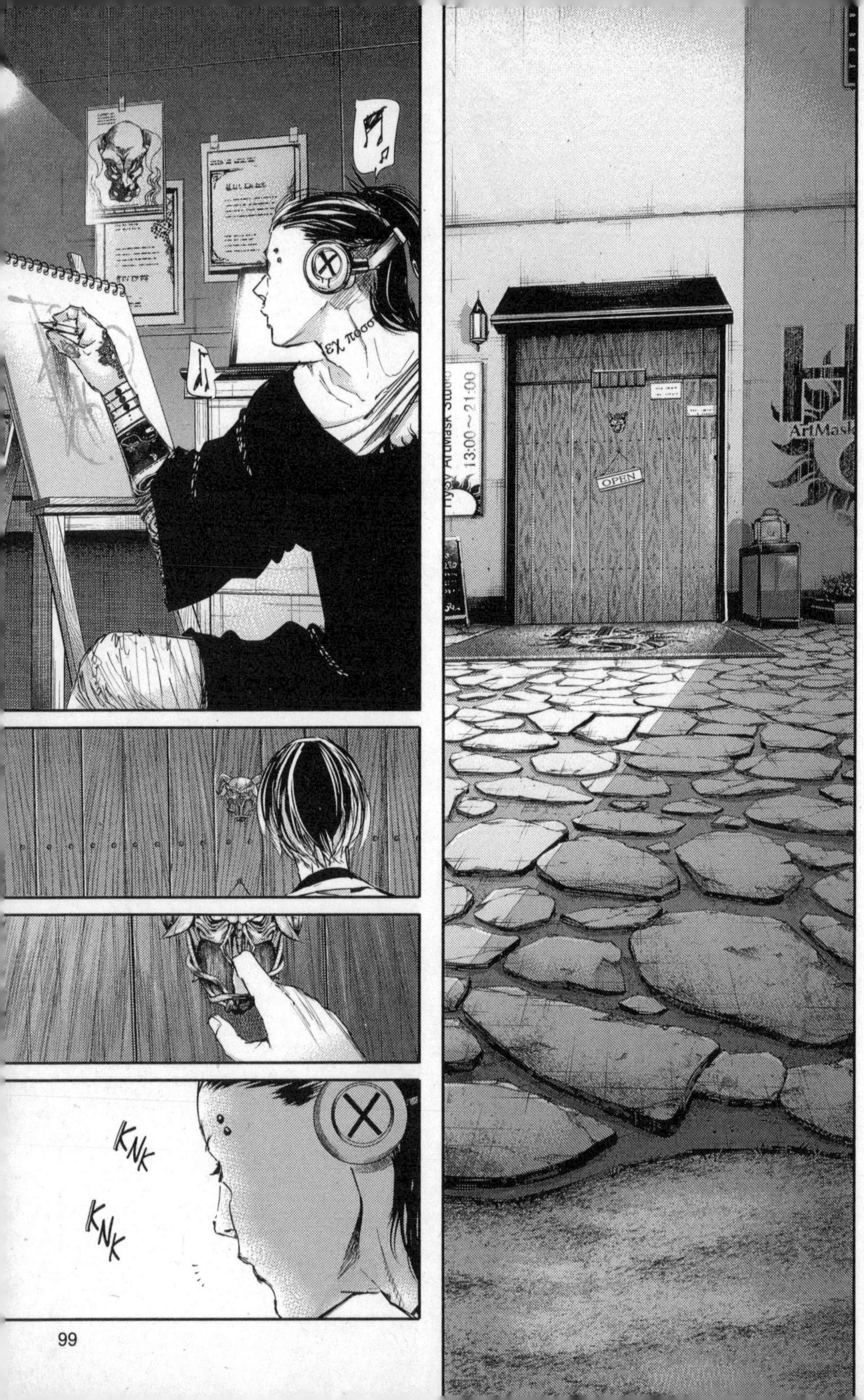
ArtMask Studio
13:00～21:00
OPEN
ArtMask
KNK
KNK

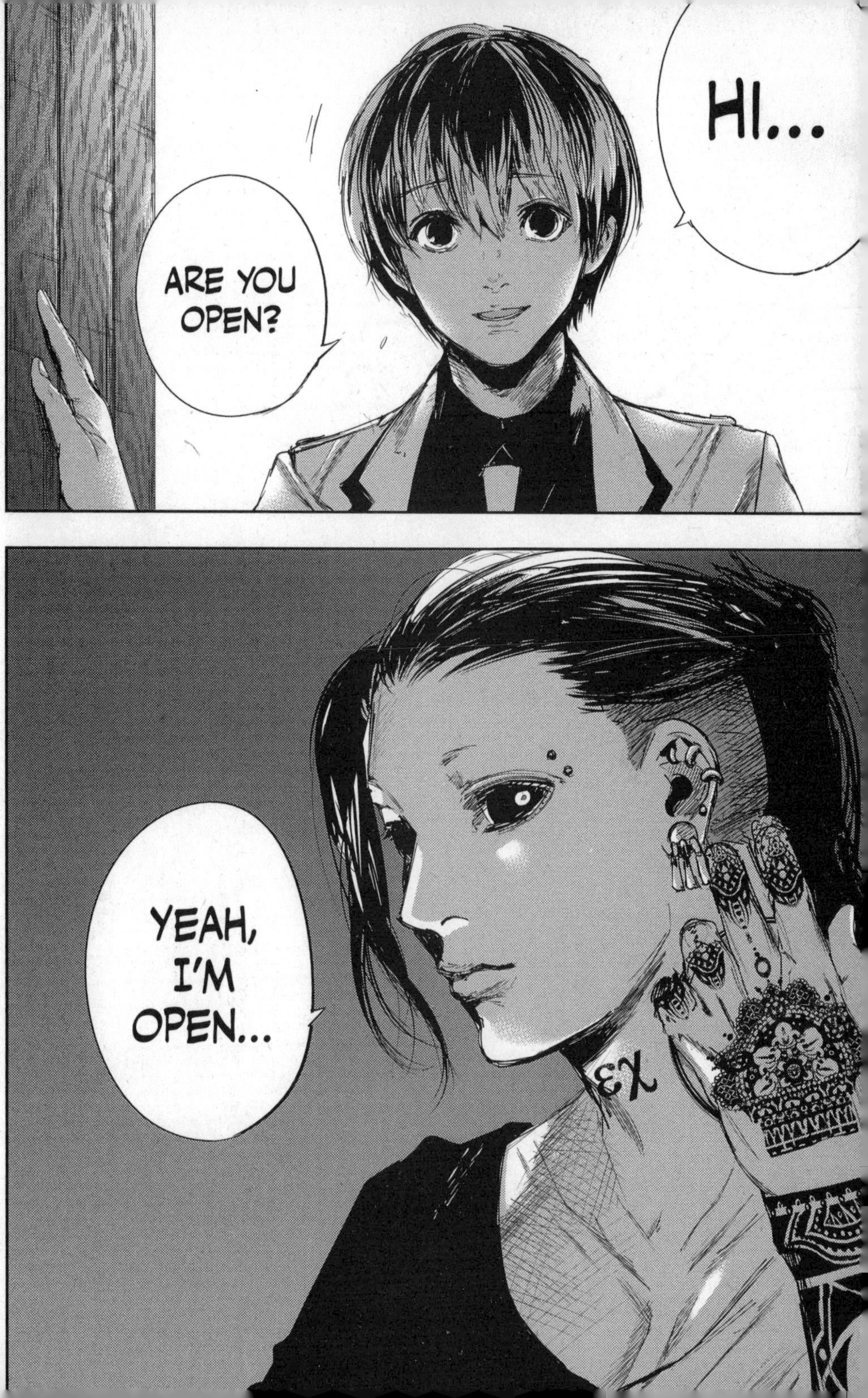
HI...
ARE YOU OPEN?
YEAH, I'M OPEN...

I wonder how long it's been since I broke up with my girlfriend?

It's lonely sleeping alone at night.
I feel like I'm going to lose my mind without that silky skin to hold in my arms.

I can't imagine why people feel joy, anger, sadness.
What's the trick to not losing someone?

Souls can't be seen, so it feels like everyone else is a meat-filled automaton.

Is that because I'm a Ghoul or because I am unique, even among Ghouls?

The only conciousness I can recognize is my own.
That's called a Philosophical Zombie.

A zombie. The living dead.
Maybe that's exactly what I covet. A zombie.

But one that stays and listens quietly to what I have to say.
A gentle zombie. A lover.

Because I have no empathy, I can't communicate, and I want it to sit and listen quietly until I can.

My previous lovers did not (could not) go anywhere, but they never tried to accept me either.

Their insults, pleas, ringing in my ears.
Looks of disdain.
It makes me sick just thinking about it.

And so they lose their faces.

And only the shadow of her left in the corpse comforts me.

Those eyes, that small nose, that mouth, those brow lines, that round forehead. How comforting it would've been if only they had accepted me.

Now, I don't even need a face any more.
Because I know I will never be accepted.

I can't trust anybody with arms and legs.

But right now… I'm thinking "Just maybe."
Even I, hopelessly apathetic, may actually be capable of loving somebody.

Toru.

I haven't felt this passionate in a while.
It's been more than a while. I don't recall feeling this strongly even in my earliest years.

As a Ghoul investigator, she has many secrets.
Beginning with her gender, her big, glistening eyes outlined by thick eyelashes, the numerous scars on her tanned skin. And…

I feel a strange oneness with her…

She and I must be the same.
I can't explain it, but I know.

That's what truth is.
Truth has no reasoning. It's not necessary.

I think she'll understand if I have the time to explain it.
Because I've released myself over you many times.

I want to feel you. The part that's thin from being ripped open.

The scar that lets us become a millimeter closer.

[From Karao Saeki (The Torso)]

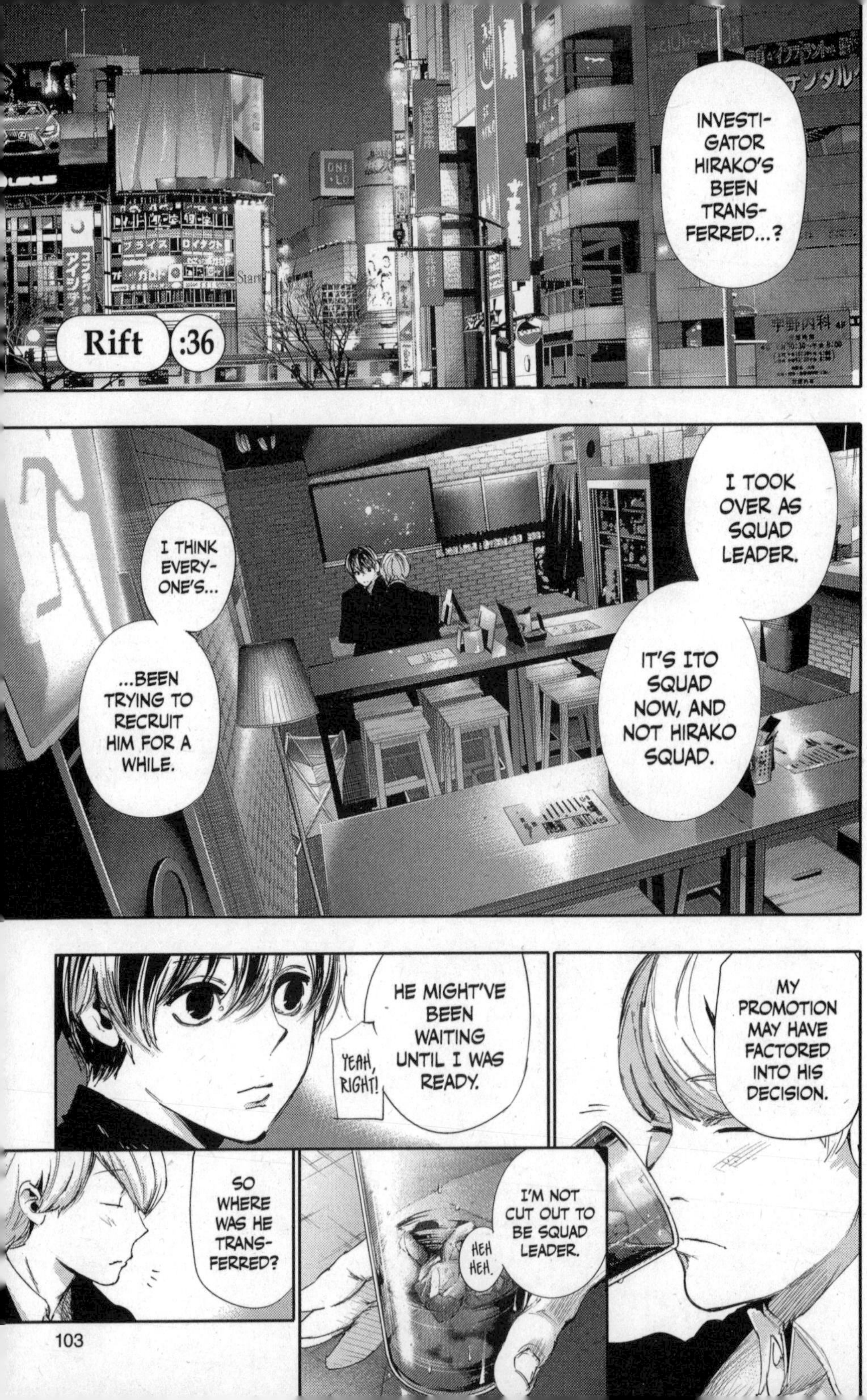
Rift :36
INVESTIGATOR HIRAKO'S BEEN TRANSFERRED...?
I TOOK OVER AS SQUAD LEADER.
IT'S ITO SQUAD NOW, AND NOT HIRAKO SQUAD.
I THINK EVERYONE'S...
...BEEN TRYING TO RECRUIT HIM FOR A WHILE.
MY PROMOTION MAY HAVE FACTORED INTO HIS DECISION.
HE MIGHT'VE BEEN WAITING UNTIL I WAS READY.
YEAH, RIGHT!
I'M NOT CUT OUT TO BE SQUAD LEADER.
HEH HEH.
SO WHERE WAS HE TRANSFERRED?

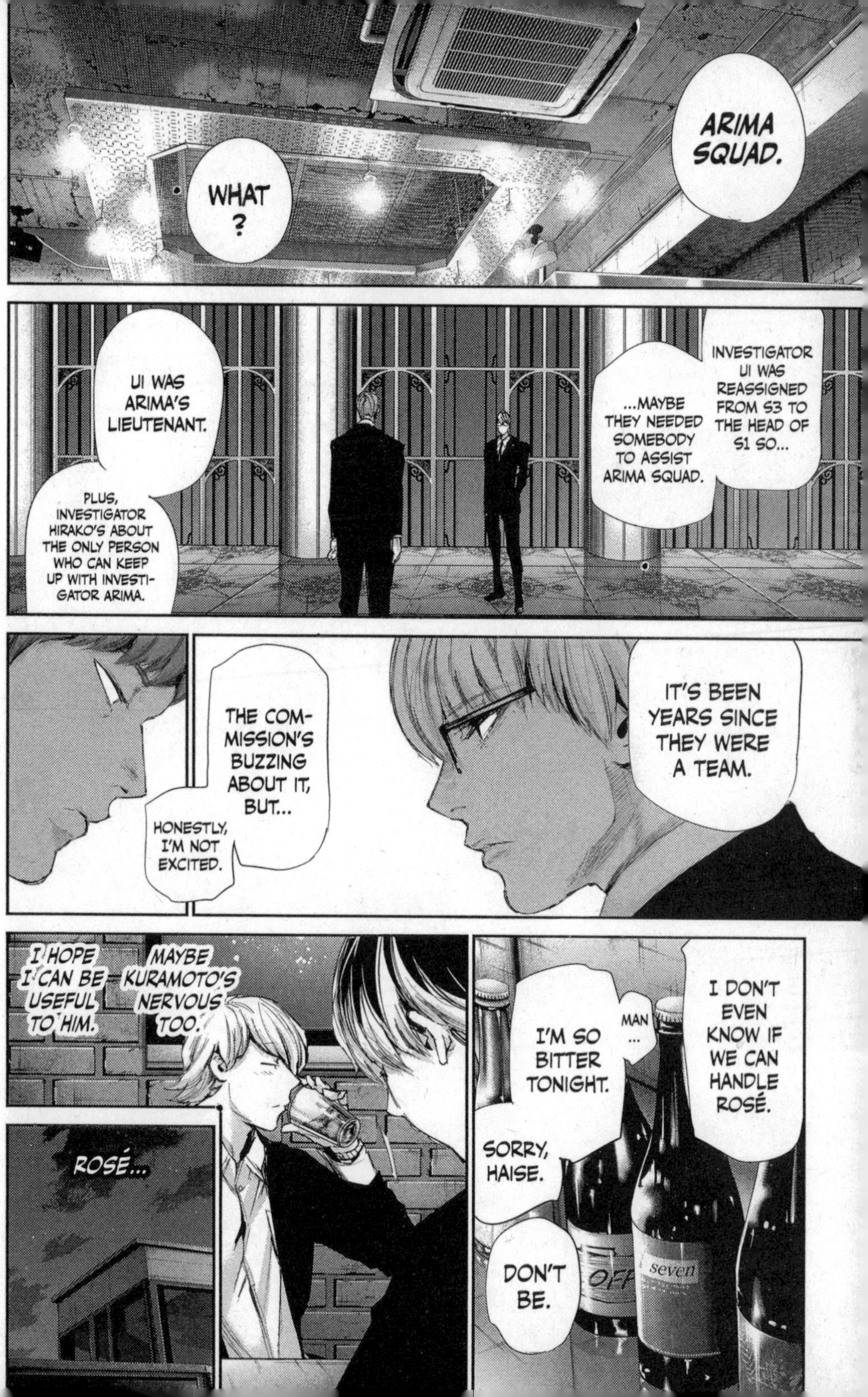
ARIMA SQUAD.
WHAT ?
INVESTIGATOR UI WAS REASSIGNED FROM S3 TO THE HEAD OF S1 SO...
...MAYBE THEY NEEDED SOMEBODY TO ASSIST ARIMA SQUAD.
UI WAS ARIMA'S LIEUTENANT.
PLUS, INVESTIGATOR HIRAKO'S ABOUT THE ONLY PERSON WHO CAN KEEP UP WITH INVESTI-GATOR ARIMA.
IT'S BEEN YEARS SINCE THEY WERE A TEAM.
THE COM-MISSION'S BUZZING ABOUT IT, BUT...
HONESTLY, I'M NOT EXCITED.
I DON'T EVEN KNOW IF WE CAN HANDLE ROSÉ.
MAN ...
I'M SO BITTER TONIGHT.
SORRY, HAISE.
DON'T BE.
OFF
seven
MAYBE KURAMOTO'S NERVOUS TOO.
I HOPE I CAN BE USEFUL TO HIM.
ROSÉ...

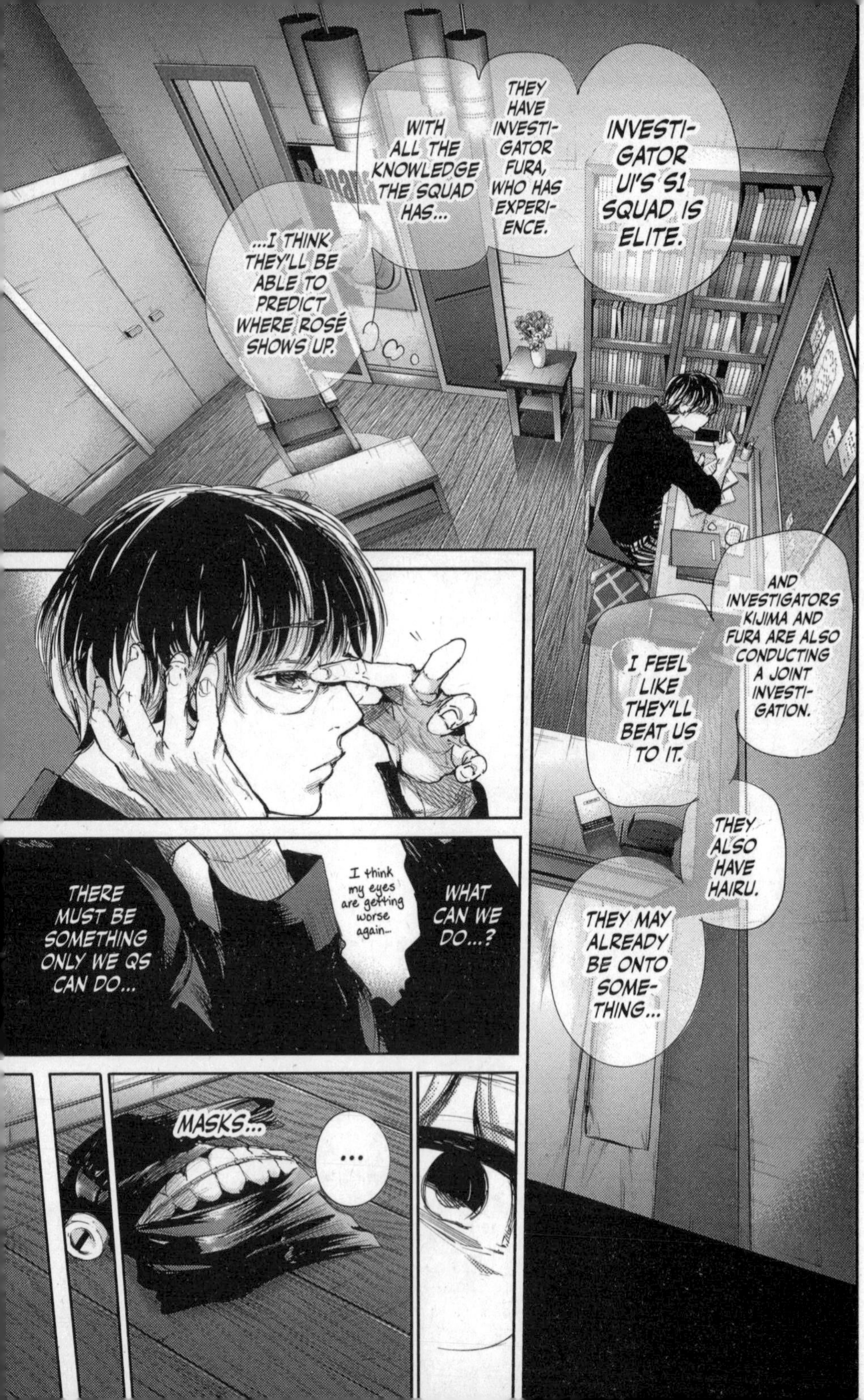
INVESTIGATOR UI'S S1 SQUAD IS ELITE.
THEY HAVE INVESTIGATOR FURA, WHO HAS EXPERIENCE.
WITH ALL THE KNOWLEDGE THE SQUAD HAS...
...I THINK THEY'LL BE ABLE TO PREDICT WHERE ROSÉ SHOWS UP.
AND INVESTIGATORS KIJIMA AND FURA ARE ALSO CONDUCTING A JOINT INVESTIGATION.
I FEEL LIKE THEY'LL BEAT US TO IT.
THEY ALSO HAVE HAIRU.
THEY MAY ALREADY BE ONTO SOMETHING...
WHAT CAN WE DO...?
I think my eyes are getting worse again...
THERE MUST BE SOMETHING ONLY WE QS CAN DO...
...
MASKS...

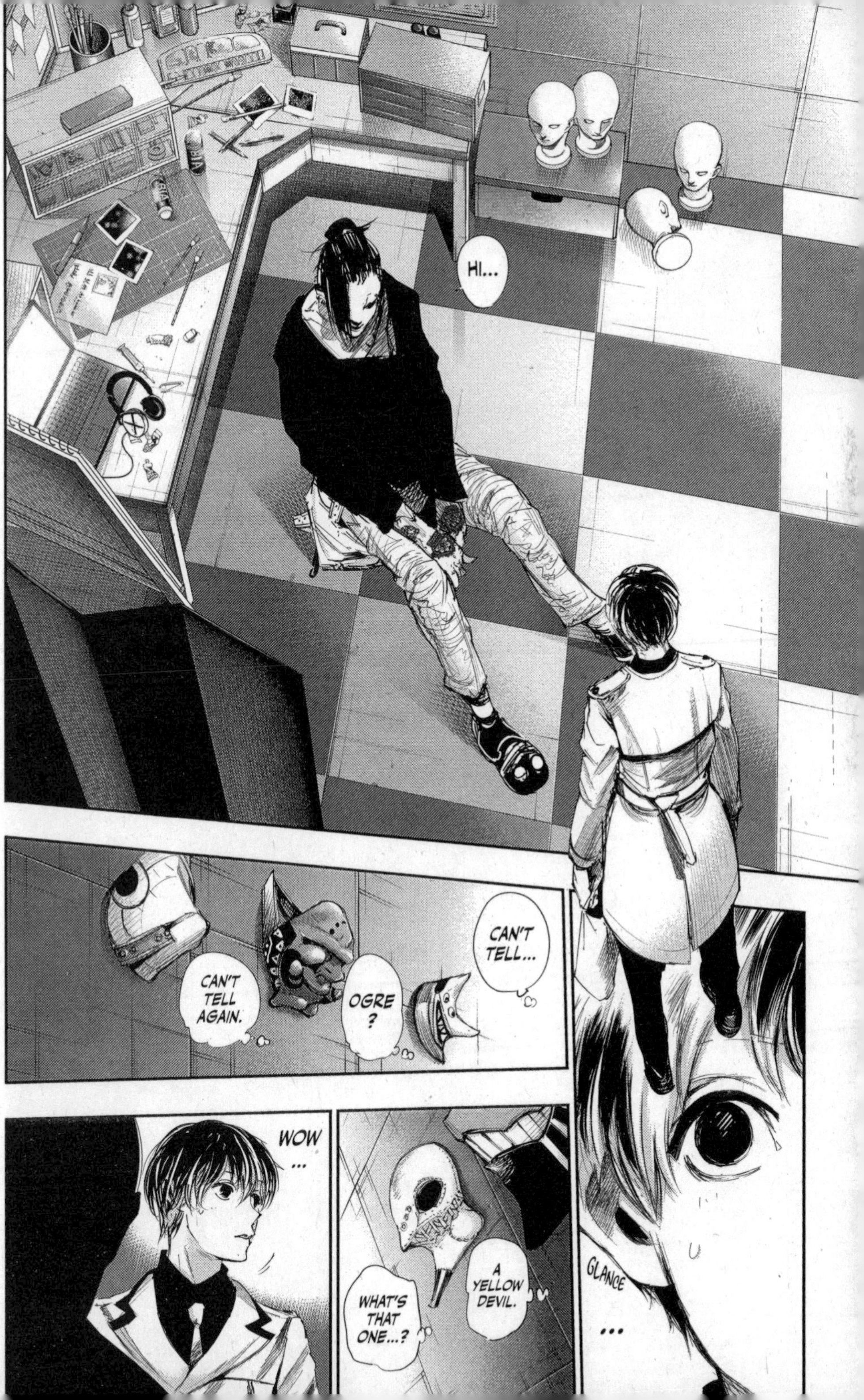
HI...
GLANCE
...
CAN'T TELL...
OGRE?
CAN'T TELL AGAIN.
A YELLOW DEVIL.
WHAT'S THAT ONE...?
WOW...

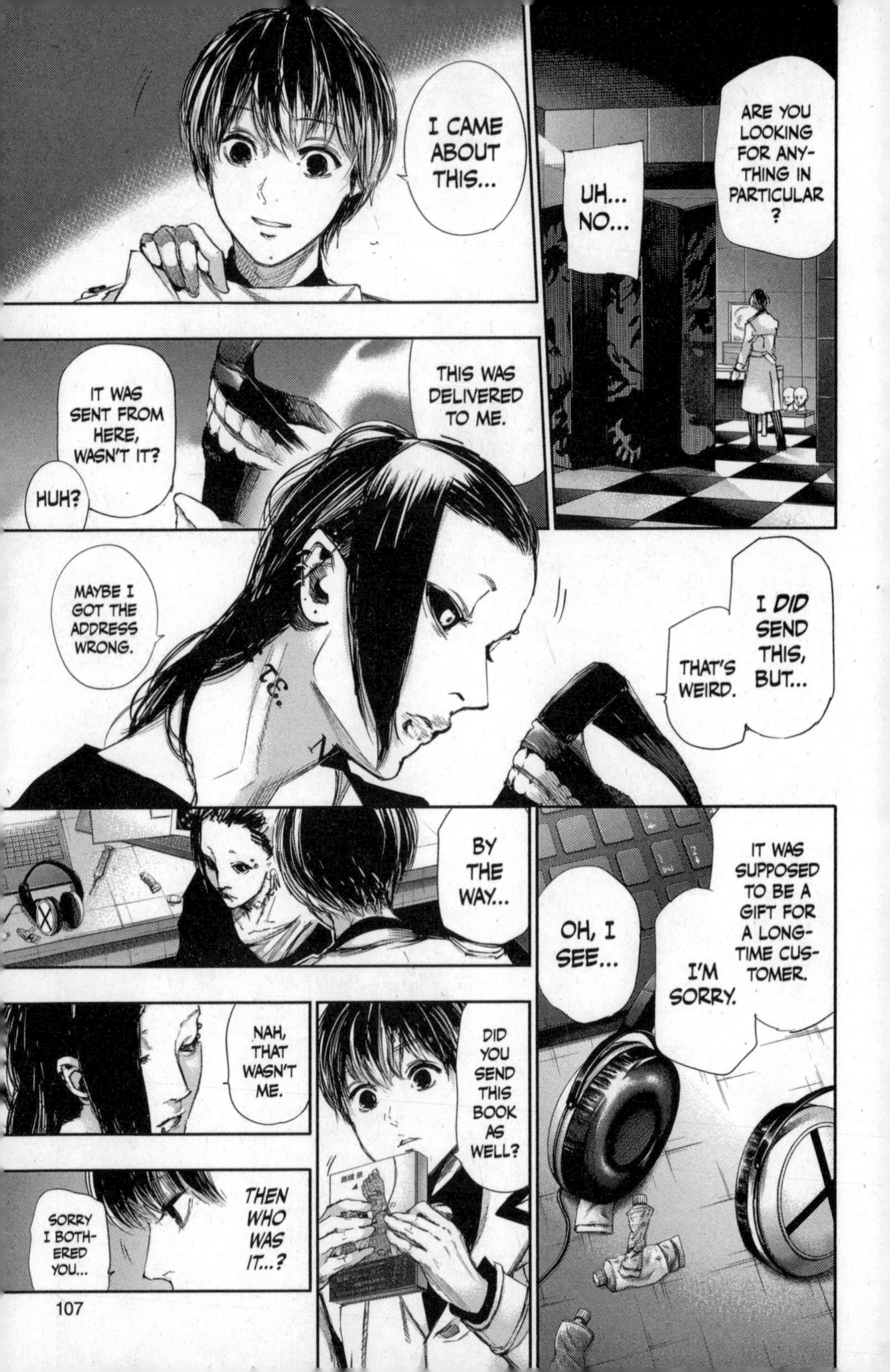
ARE YOU LOOKING FOR ANY-THING IN PARTICULAR?
UH... NO...
I CAME ABOUT THIS...
THIS WAS DELIVERED TO ME.
IT WAS SENT FROM HERE, WASN'T IT?
HUH?
I *DID* SEND THIS, BUT...
THAT'S WEIRD.
MAYBE I GOT THE ADDRESS WRONG.
IT WAS SUPPOSED TO BE A GIFT FOR A LONG-TIME CUS-TOMER.
I'M SORRY.
OH, I SEE...
BY THE WAY...
DID YOU SEND THIS BOOK AS WELL?
NAH, THAT WASN'T ME.
THEN WHO WAS IT...?
SORRY I BOTH-ERED YOU...

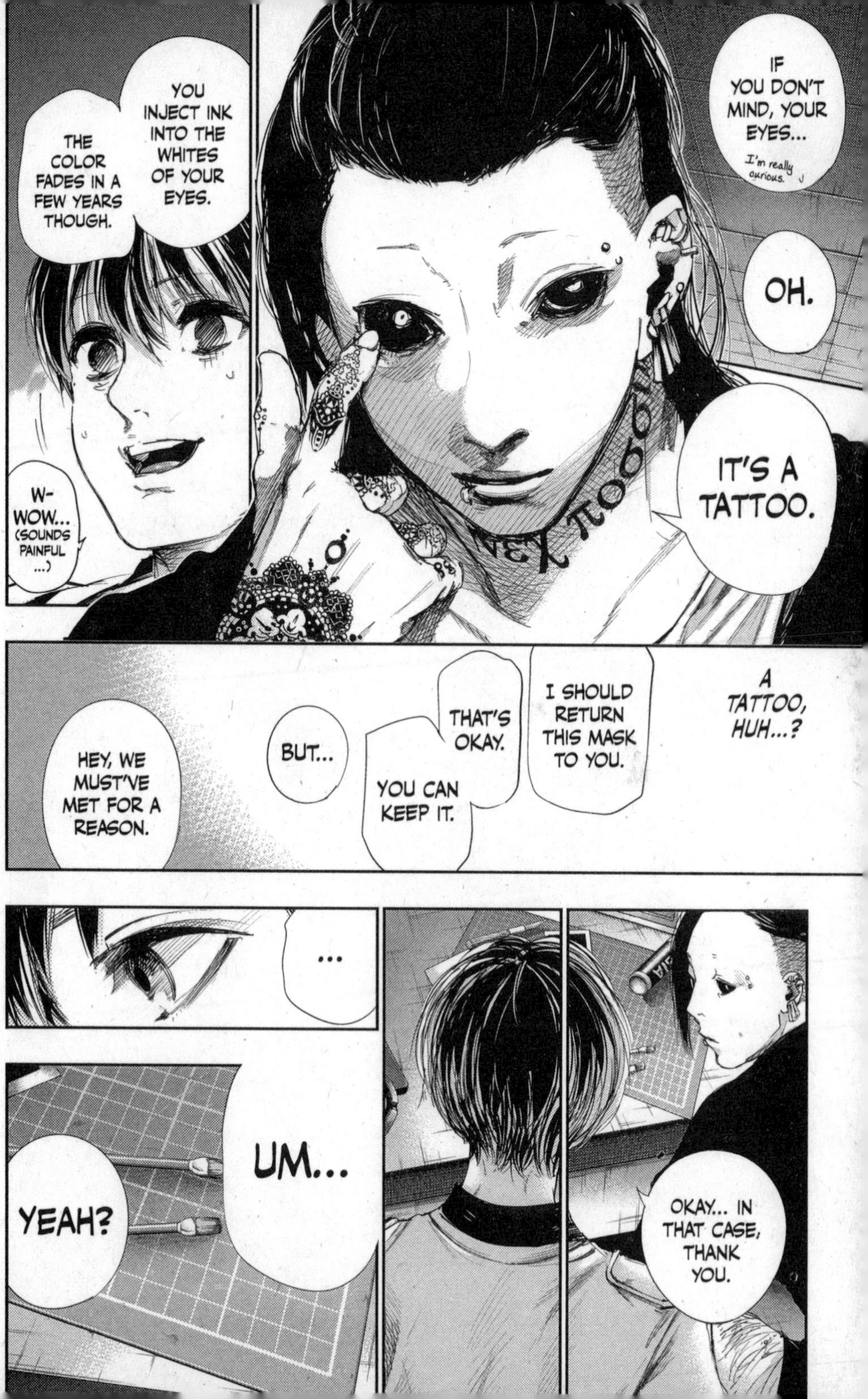
IF YOU DON'T MIND, YOUR EYES...
I'm really curious.
OH.
IT'S A TATTOO.
YOU INJECT INK INTO THE WHITES OF YOUR EYES.
THE COLOR FADES IN A FEW YEARS THOUGH.
W-WOW... (SOUNDS PAINFUL...)
A TATTOO, HUH...?
I SHOULD RETURN THIS MASK TO YOU.
THAT'S OKAY.
YOU CAN KEEP IT.
BUT...
HEY, WE MUST'VE MET FOR A REASON.
OKAY... IN THAT CASE, THANK YOU.
...
UM...
YEAH?

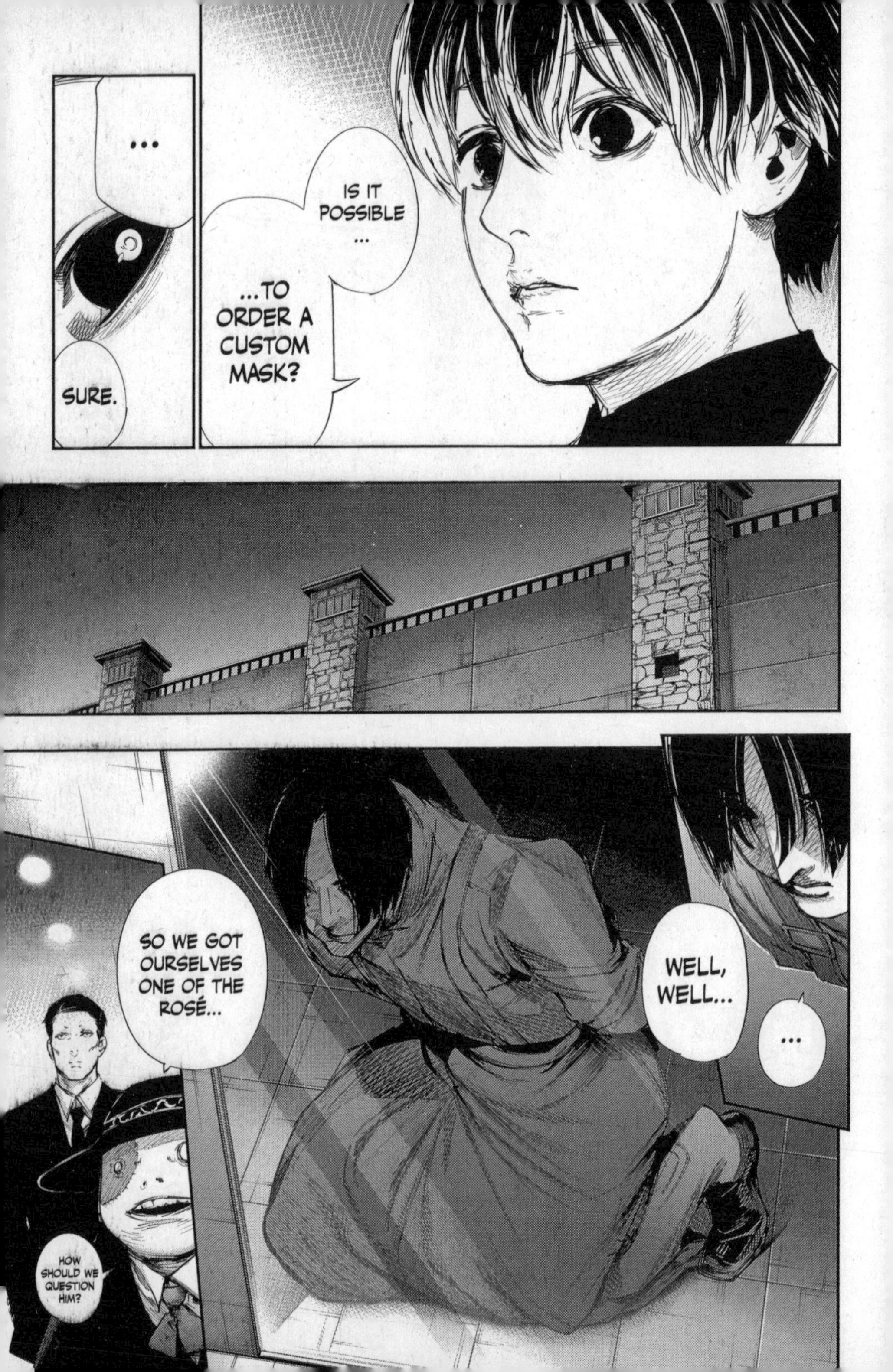
IS IT POSSIBLE ...
...TO ORDER A CUSTOM MASK?
...
SURE.
WELL, WELL...
...
SO WE GOT OURSELVES ONE OF THE ROSÉ...
HOW SHOULD WE QUESTION HIM?

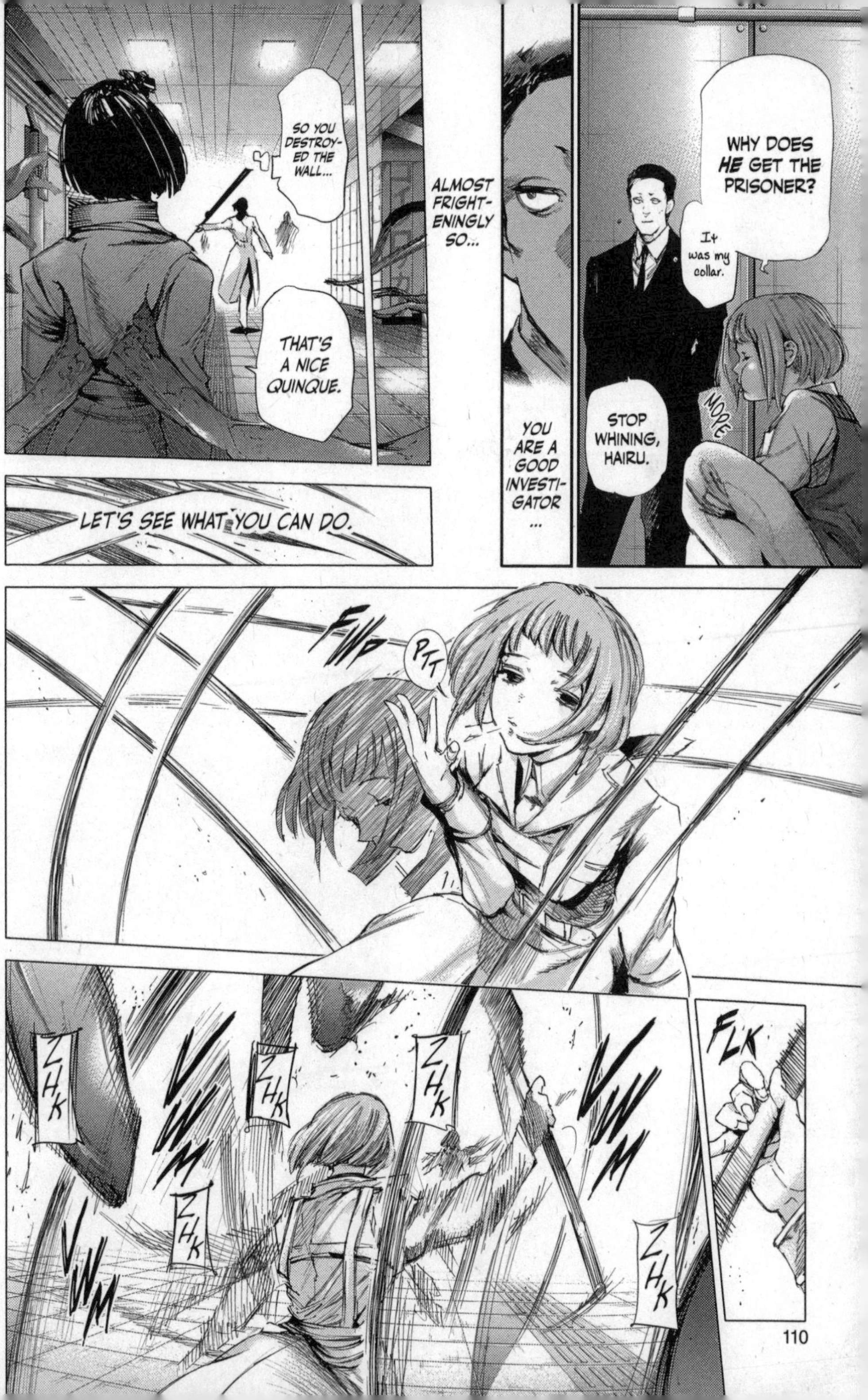
WHY DOES HE GET THE PRISONER?
It was my collar.
STOP WHINING, HAIRU.
MOPE
YOU ARE A GOOD INVESTIGATOR ...
ALMOST FRIGHTENINGLY SO...
SO YOU DESTROYED THE WALL...
THAT'S A NICE QUINQUE.
LET'S SEE WHAT YOU CAN DO.
FWP
PTT
FLK
ZHK
VWM
ZHK
ZHK
VWM
ZHK
VWM
ZHK

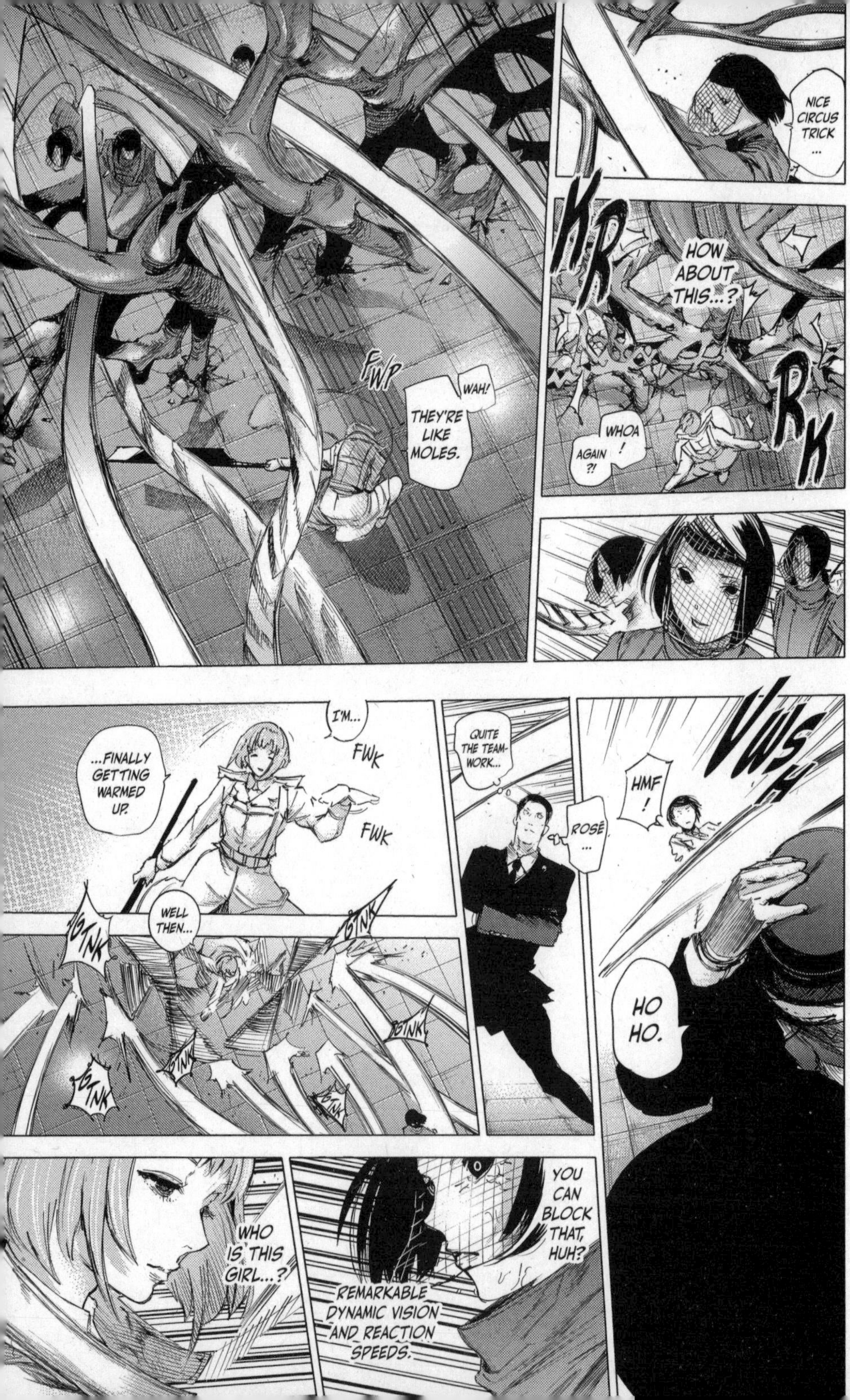
NICE CIRCUS TRICK ...
KR
HOW ABOUT THIS...?
RK
WHOA!
AGAIN?!
FWP
WAH!
THEY'RE LIKE MOLES.
VWSH
HMF!
HO HO.
QUITE THE TEAMWORK...
ROSÉ...
I'M...
...FINALLY GETTING WARMED UP.
FWK
FWK
WELL THEN...
GTNK
GTNK
GTNK
GTNK
GTNK
GTNK
YOU CAN BLOCK THAT, HUH?
REMARKABLE DYNAMIC VISION AND REACTION SPEEDS.
WHO IS THIS GIRL...?

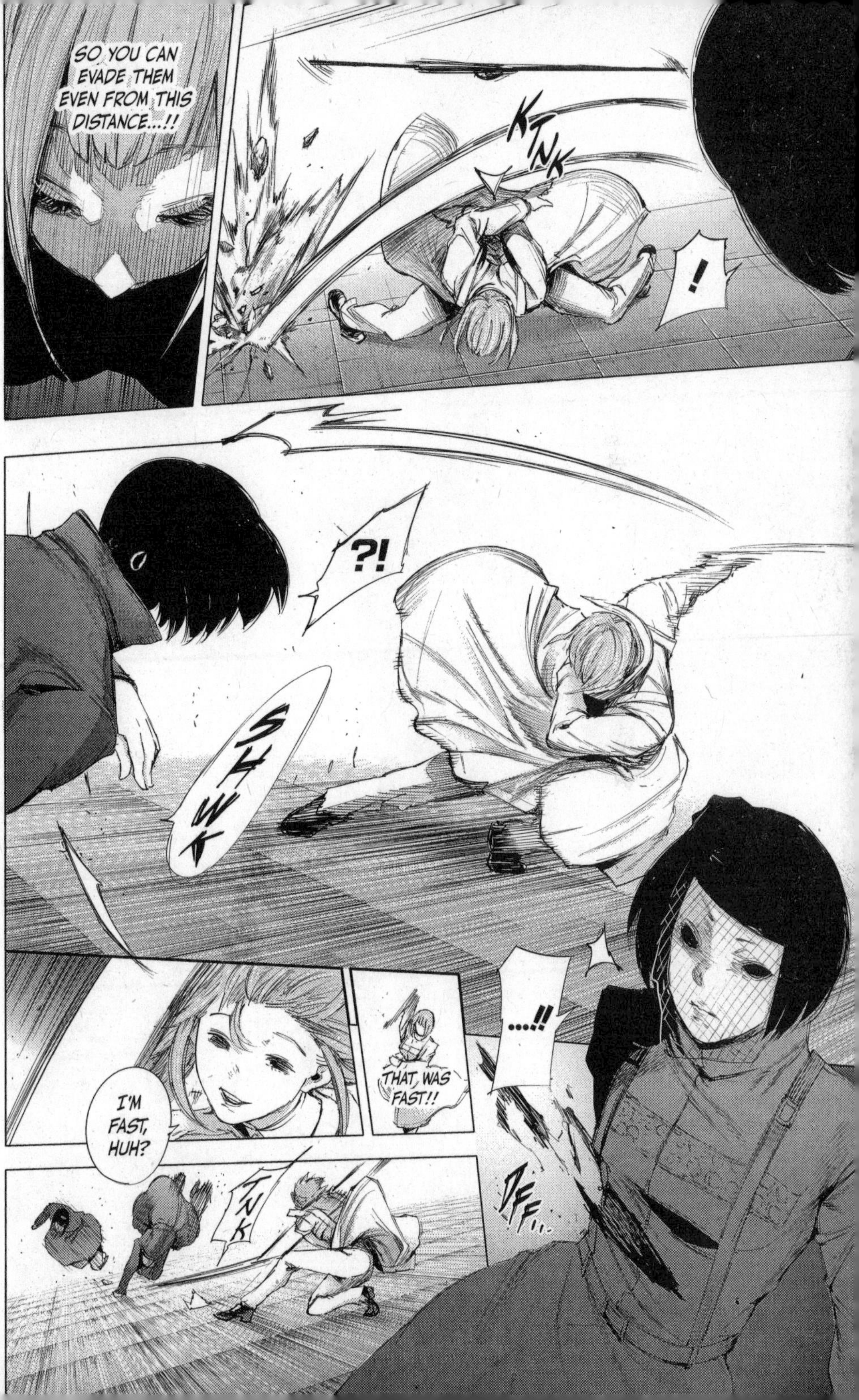
KTINK
!
SO YOU CAN EVADE THEM EVEN FROM THIS DISTANCE...!!
?!
SHUNK
...!!
DFF..
THAT WAS FAST!!
I'M FAST, HUH?
TINK

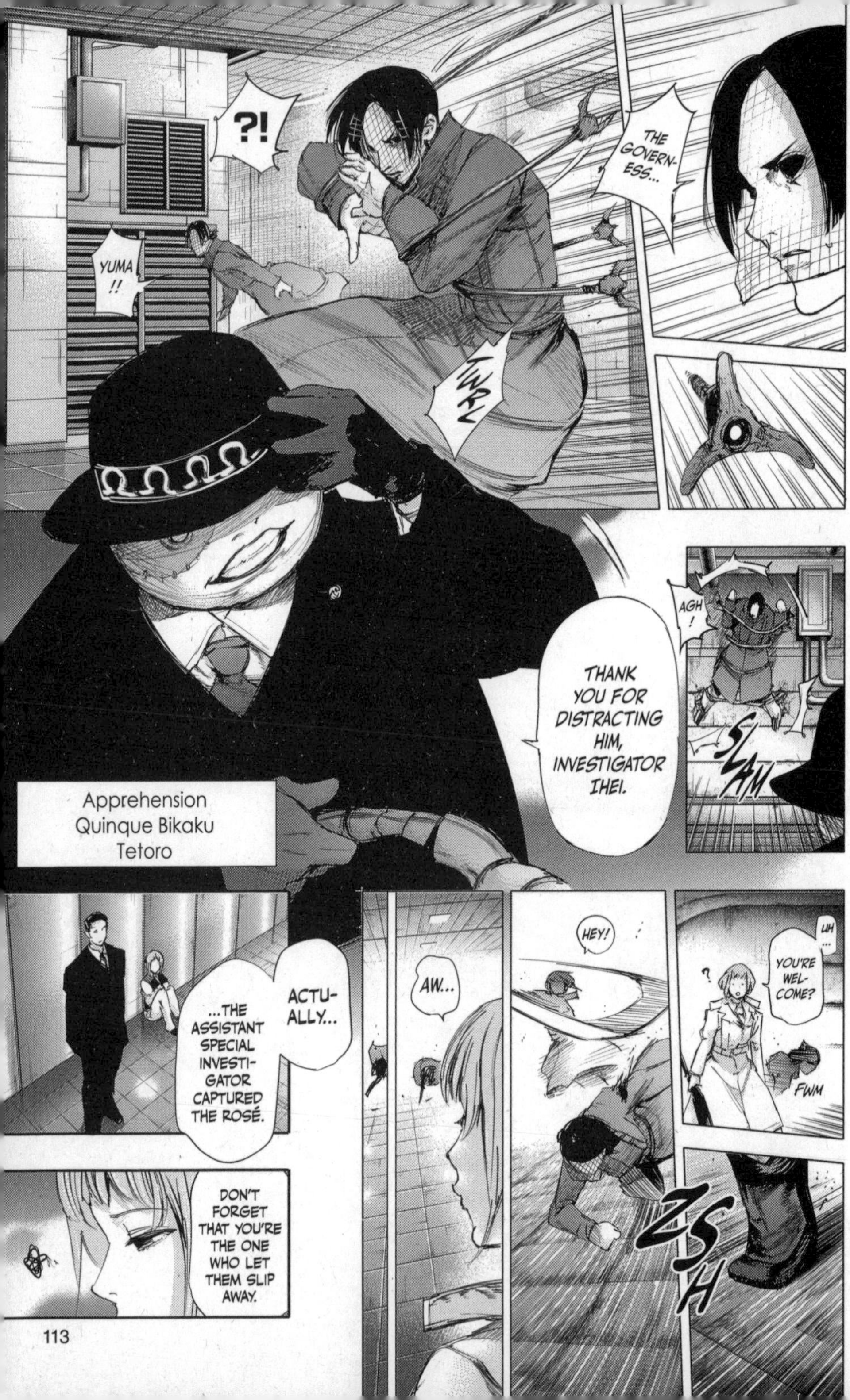

THE GOVERN-ESS...
?!
YUMA!!
TWRL
AGH!
SLAM
THANK YOU FOR DISTRACTING HIM, INVESTIGATOR IHEI.
Apprehension Quinque Bikaku Tetoro
UH...
YOU'RE WEL-COME?
FWM
HEY!
AW...
ACTU-ALLY...
...THE ASSISTANT SPECIAL INVESTI-GATOR CAPTURED THE ROSÉ.
ZSH
DON'T FORGET THAT YOU'RE THE ONE WHO LET THEM SLIP AWAY.

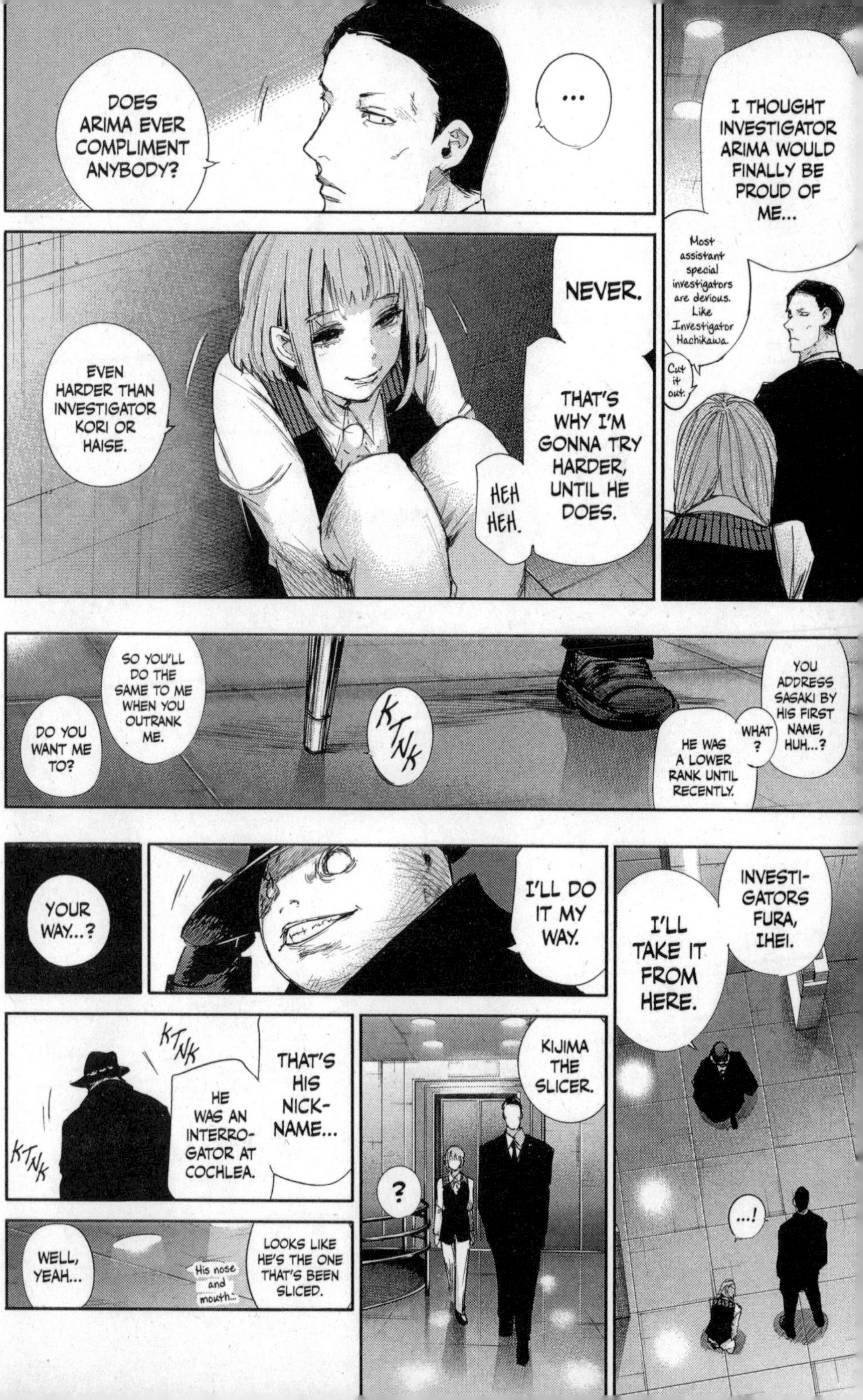

I THOUGHT INVESTIGATOR ARIMA WOULD FINALLY BE PROUD OF ME...
Most assistant special investigators are devious. Like Investigator Hachikawa.
Cut it out.
...
DOES ARIMA EVER COMPLIMENT ANYBODY?
NEVER.
THAT'S WHY I'M GONNA TRY HARDER, UNTIL HE DOES.
HEH HEH.
EVEN HARDER THAN INVESTIGATOR KORI OR HAISE.
YOU ADDRESS SASAKI BY HIS FIRST NAME, HUH...?
WHAT?
HE WAS A LOWER RANK UNTIL RECENTLY.
KTNK
SO YOU'LL DO THE SAME TO ME WHEN YOU OUTRANK ME.
DO YOU WANT ME TO?
INVESTI-GATORS FURA, IHEI.
I'LL TAKE IT FROM HERE.
...!
I'LL DO IT MY WAY.
YOUR WAY...?
KIJIMA THE SLICER.
?
THAT'S HIS NICK-NAME...
HE WAS AN INTERRO-GATOR AT COCHLEA.
KTNK
KTNK
LOOKS LIKE HE'S THE ONE THAT'S BEEN SLICED.
His nose and mouth...
WELL, YEAH...

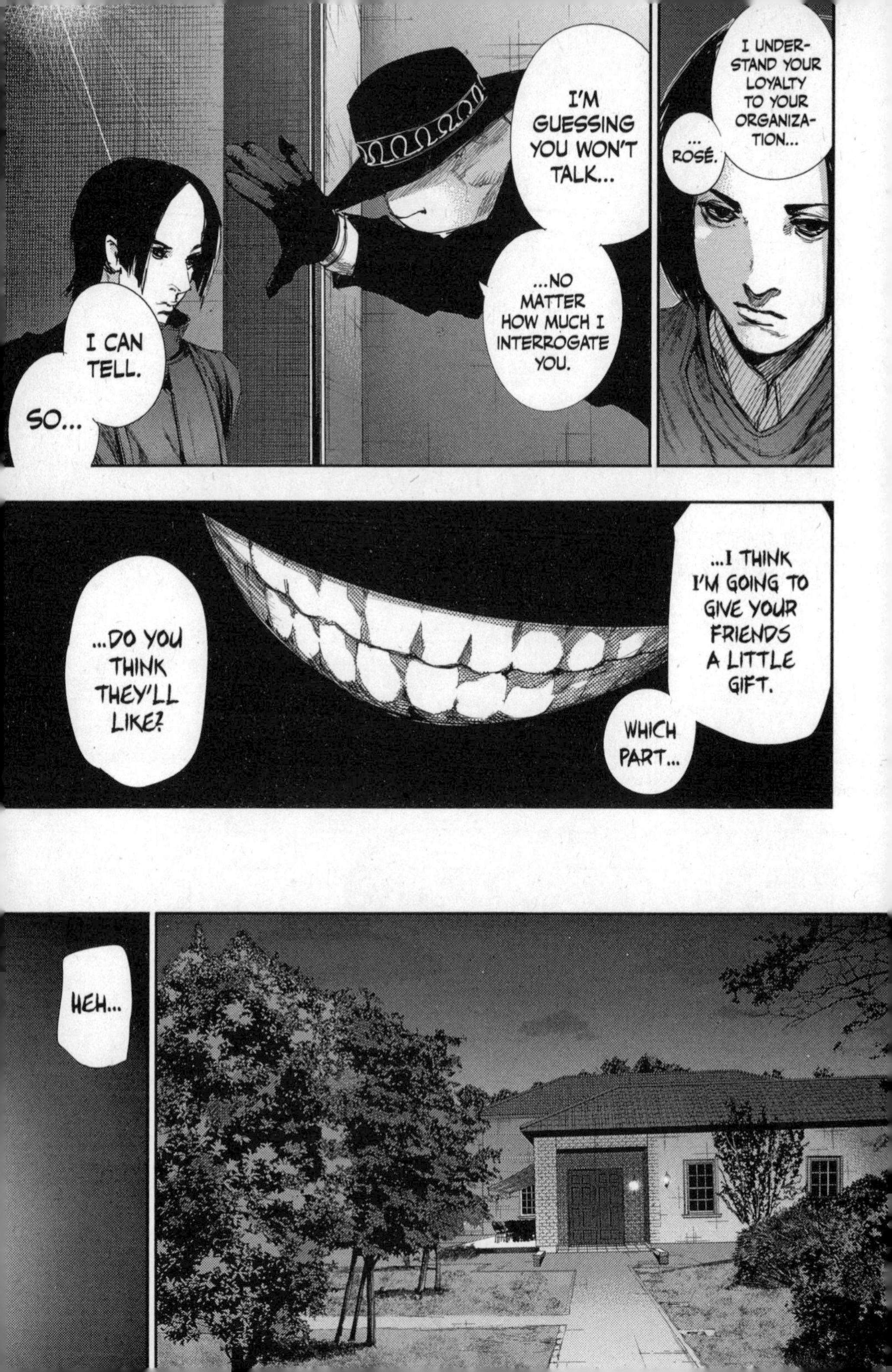
I UNDER-STAND YOUR LOYALTY TO YOUR ORGANIZA-TION...
... ROSÉ.
I'M GUESSING YOU WON'T TALK...
...NO MATTER HOW MUCH I INTERROGATE YOU.
I CAN TELL.
SO...
...I THINK I'M GOING TO GIVE YOUR FRIENDS A LITTLE GIFT.
WHICH PART...
...DO YOU THINK THEY'LL LIKE?
HEH...

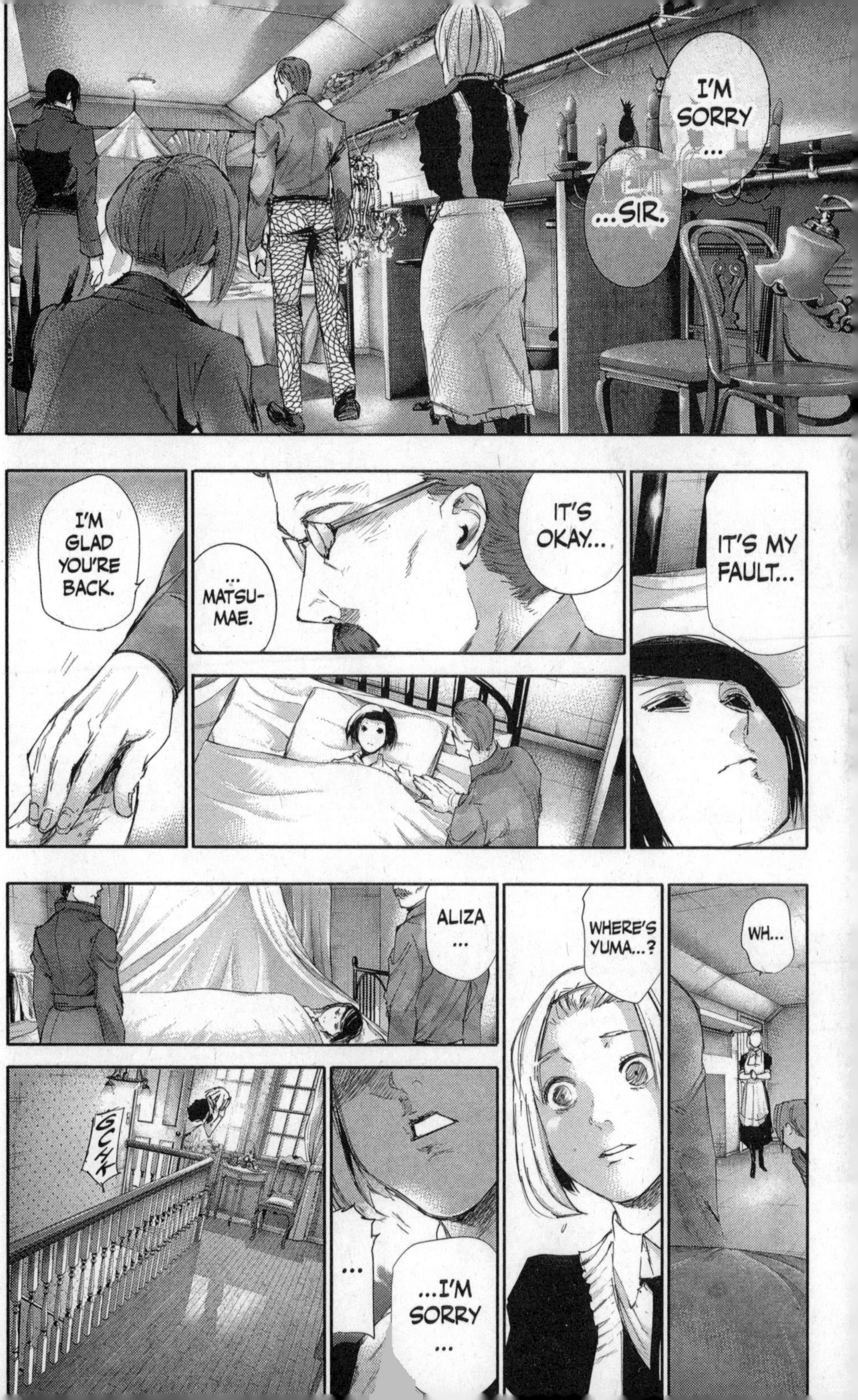
I'M SORRY ...
...SIR.
IT'S MY FAULT...
IT'S OKAY...
... MATSU-MAE.
I'M GLAD YOU'RE BACK.
WH...
WHERE'S YUMA...?
ALIZA ...
...
...I'M SORRY ...
GCHK

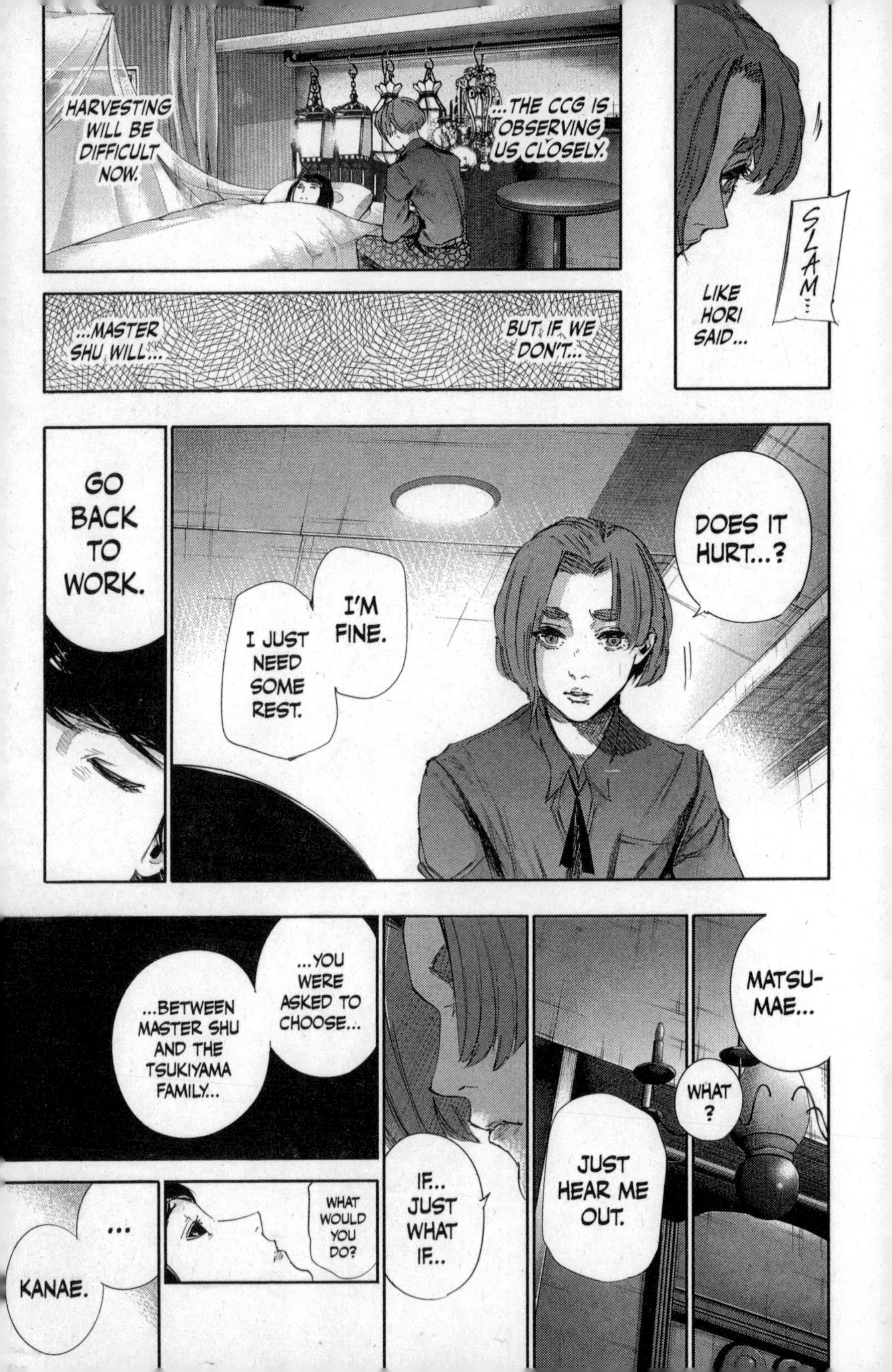
SLAM...
LIKE HORI SAID...
...THE CCG IS OBSERVING US CLOSELY.
HARVESTING WILL BE DIFFICULT NOW.
BUT IF WE DON'T...
...MASTER SHU WILL...
DOES IT HURT...?
I'M FINE.
I JUST NEED SOME REST.
GO BACK TO WORK.
MATSU-MAE...
WHAT?
JUST HEAR ME OUT.
IF... JUST WHAT IF...
...YOU WERE ASKED TO CHOOSE...
...BETWEEN MASTER SHU AND THE TSUKIYAMA FAMILY...
WHAT WOULD YOU DO?
...
KANAE.

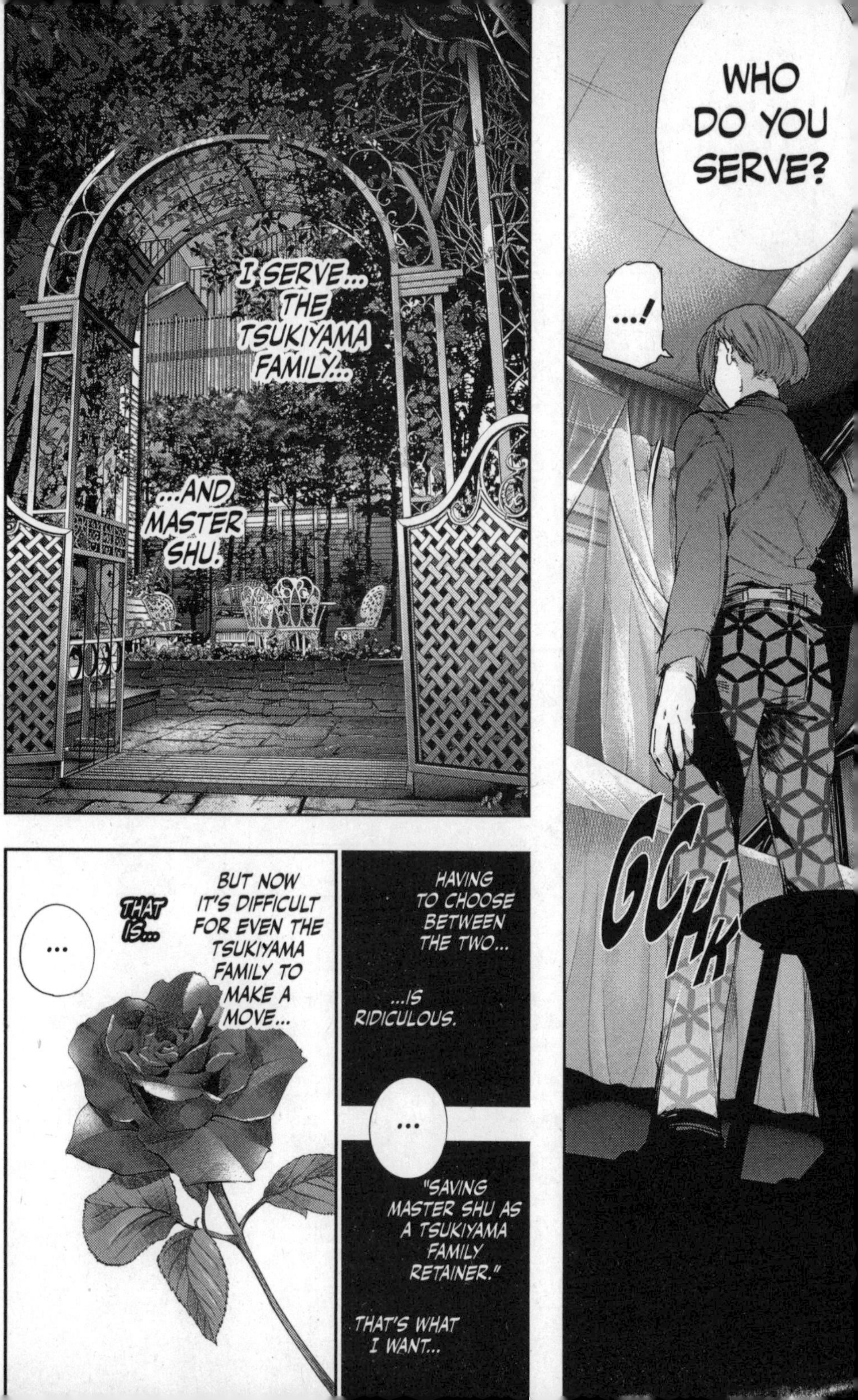
WHO DO YOU SERVE?
...!
GCHK
I SERVE... THE TSUKIYAMA FAMILY...
...AND MASTER SHU.
HAVING TO CHOOSE BETWEEN THE TWO...
...IS RIDICULOUS.
...
"SAVING MASTER SHU AS A TSUKIYAMA FAMILY RETAINER."
THAT'S WHAT I WANT...
BUT NOW IT'S DIFFICULT FOR EVEN THE TSUKIYAMA FAMILY TO MAKE A MOVE...
THAT IS...
...

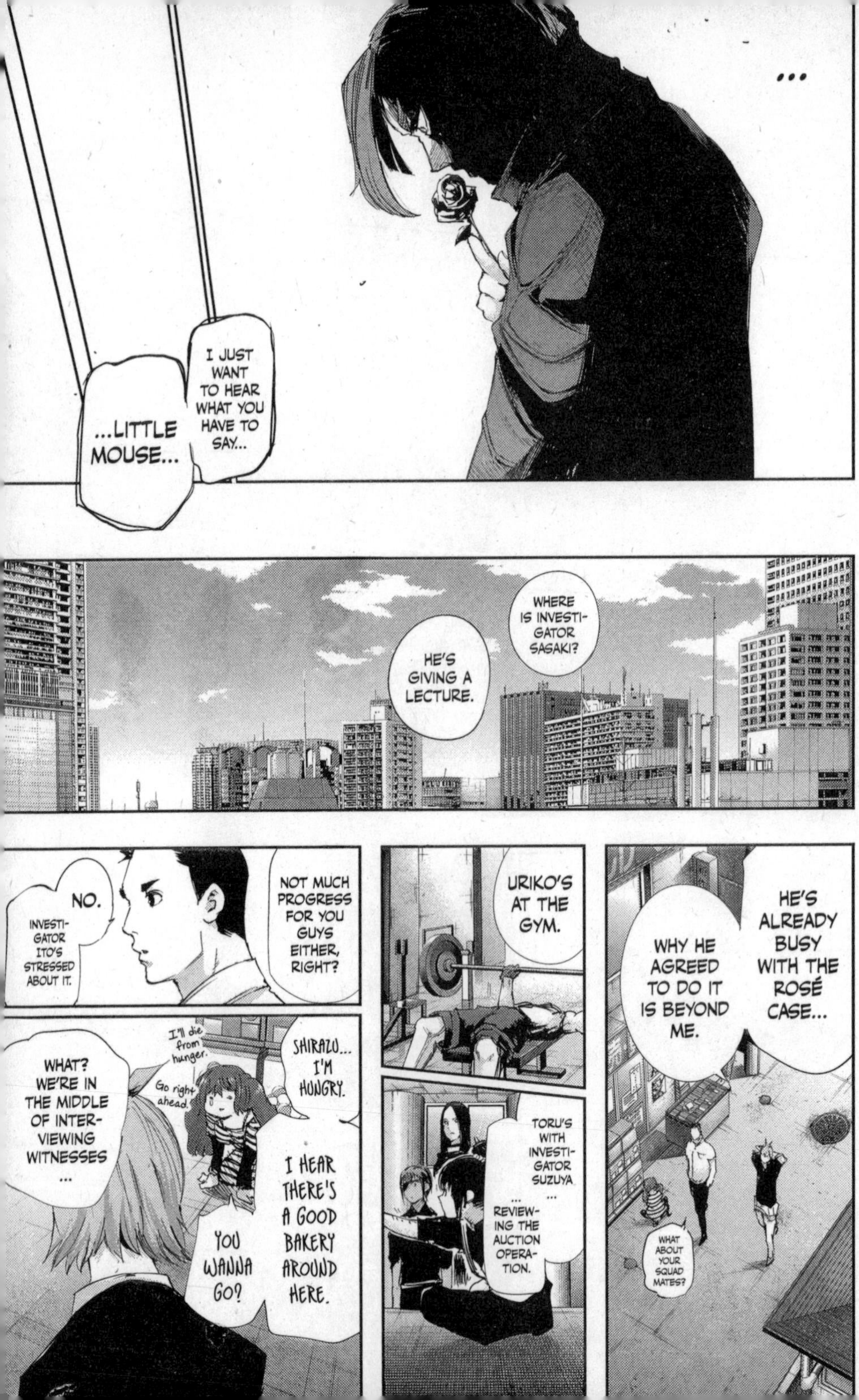
...
I JUST WANT TO HEAR WHAT YOU HAVE TO SAY...
...LITTLE MOUSE...
WHERE IS INVESTIGATOR SASAKI?
HE'S GIVING A LECTURE.
HE'S ALREADY BUSY WITH THE ROSÉ CASE...
WHY HE AGREED TO DO IT IS BEYOND ME.
WHAT ABOUT YOUR SQUAD MATES?
URIKO'S AT THE GYM.
TORU'S WITH INVESTIGATOR SUZUYA... REVIEWING THE AUCTION OPERATION.
NOT MUCH PROGRESS FOR YOU GUYS EITHER, RIGHT?
NO.
INVESTIGATOR ITO'S STRESSED ABOUT IT.
SHIRAZU... I'M HUNGRY.
I HEAR THERE'S A GOOD BAKERY AROUND HERE.
YOU WANNA GO?
WHAT? WE'RE IN THE MIDDLE OF INTERVIEWING WITNESSES...
I'll die from hunger.
Go right ahead.

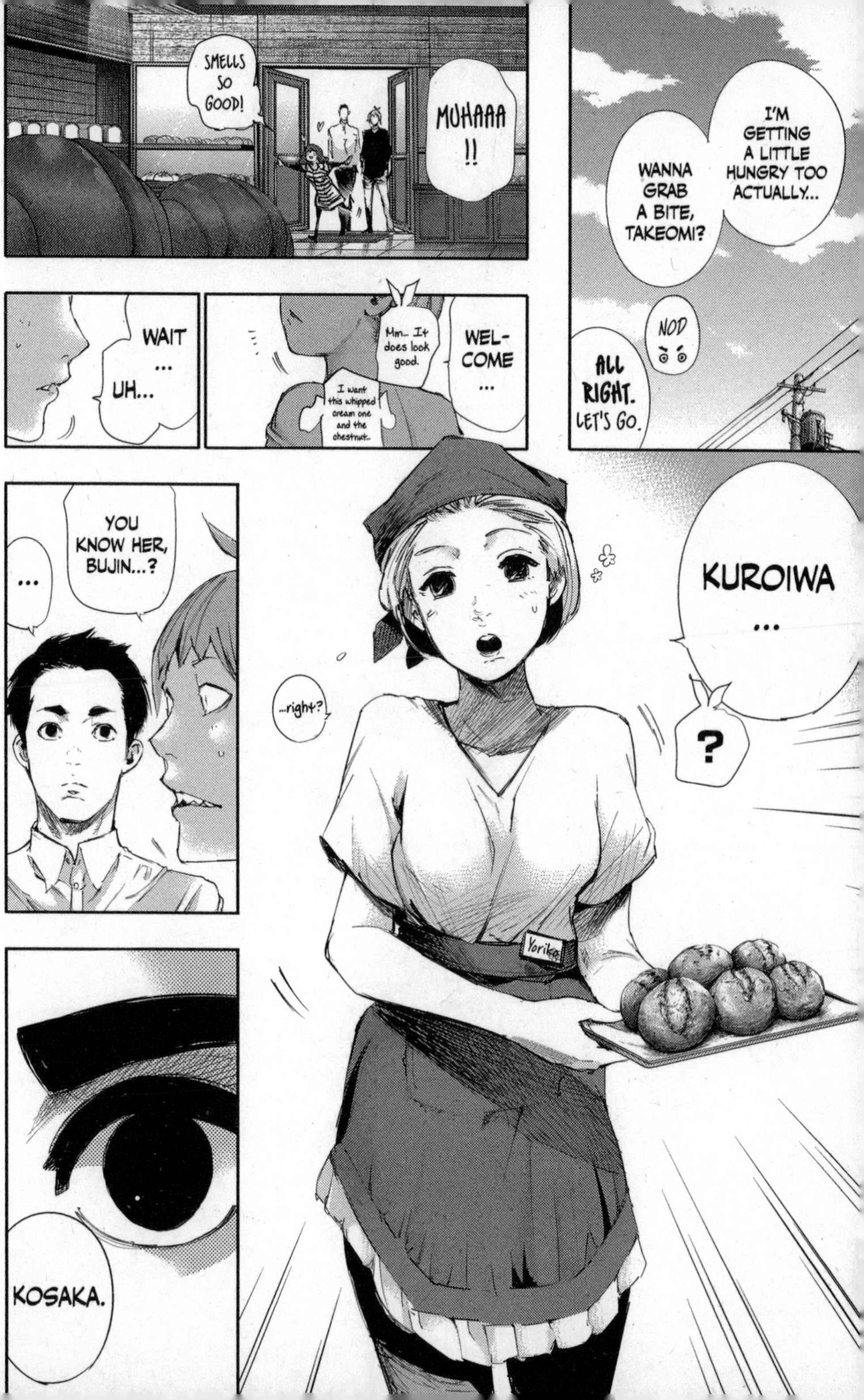
I'M GETTING A LITTLE HUNGRY TOO ACTUALLY...
WANNA GRAB A BITE, TAKEOMI?
NOD
ALL RIGHT. LET'S GO.
MUHAAA !!
SMELLS SO GOOD!
WEL-COME ...
Mm... It does look good.
I want this whipped cream one and the chestnut...
WAIT ... UH...
KUROIWA ...
?
...right?
YOU KNOW HER, BUJIN...?
...
KOSAKA.

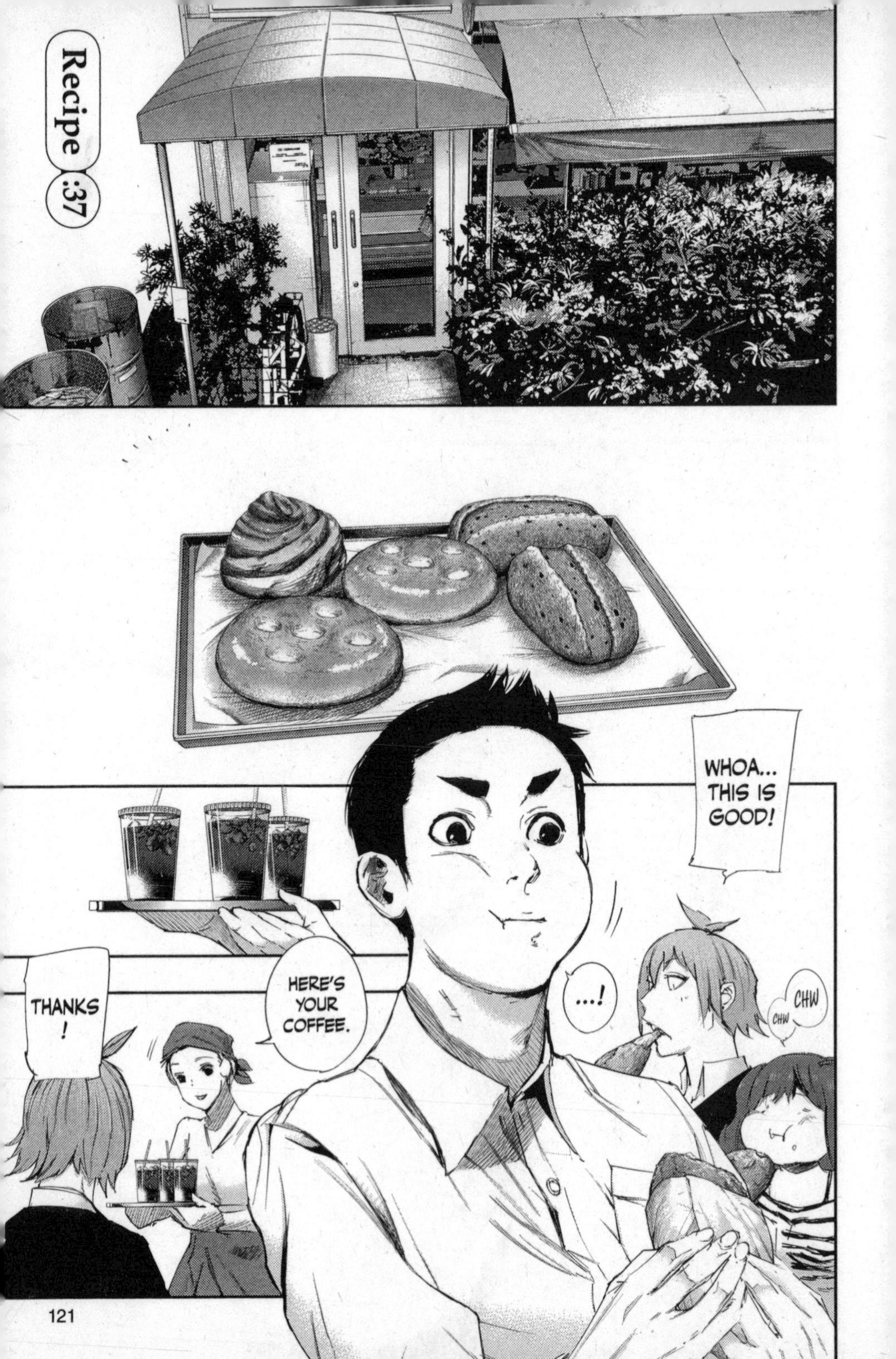
Recipe :37
WHOA... THIS IS GOOD!
CHW
CHW
...!
HERE'S YOUR COFFEE.
THANKS!

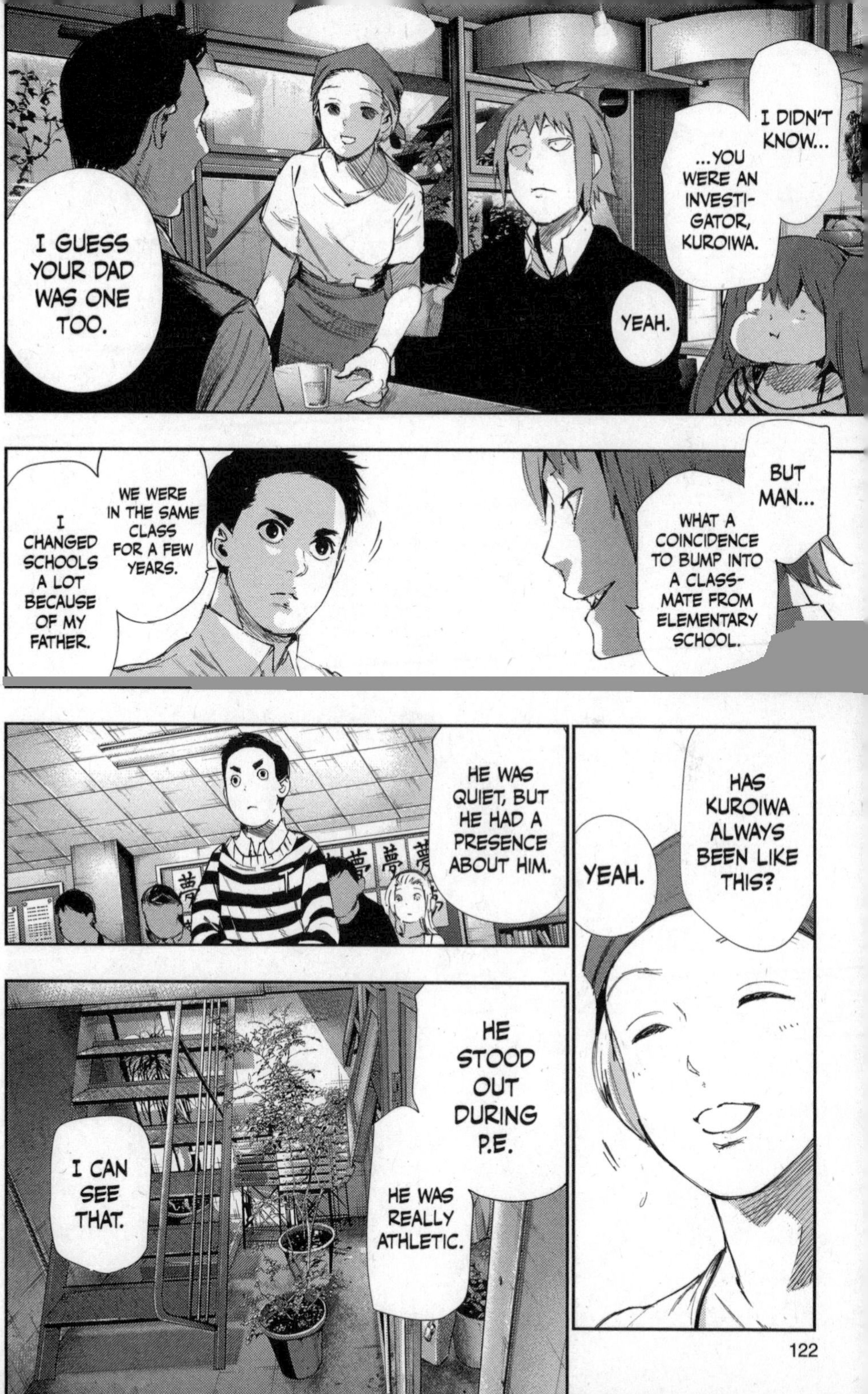
I DIDN'T KNOW...
...YOU WERE AN INVESTI-GATOR, KUROIWA.
YEAH.
I GUESS YOUR DAD WAS ONE TOO.
BUT MAN...
WHAT A COINCIDENCE TO BUMP INTO A CLASS-MATE FROM ELEMENTARY SCHOOL.
WE WERE IN THE SAME CLASS FOR A FEW YEARS.
I CHANGED SCHOOLS A LOT BECAUSE OF MY FATHER.
HAS KUROIWA ALWAYS BEEN LIKE THIS?
YEAH.
HE WAS QUIET, BUT HE HAD A PRESENCE ABOUT HIM.
HE STOOD OUT DURING P.E.
HE WAS REALLY ATHLETIC.
I CAN SEE THAT.

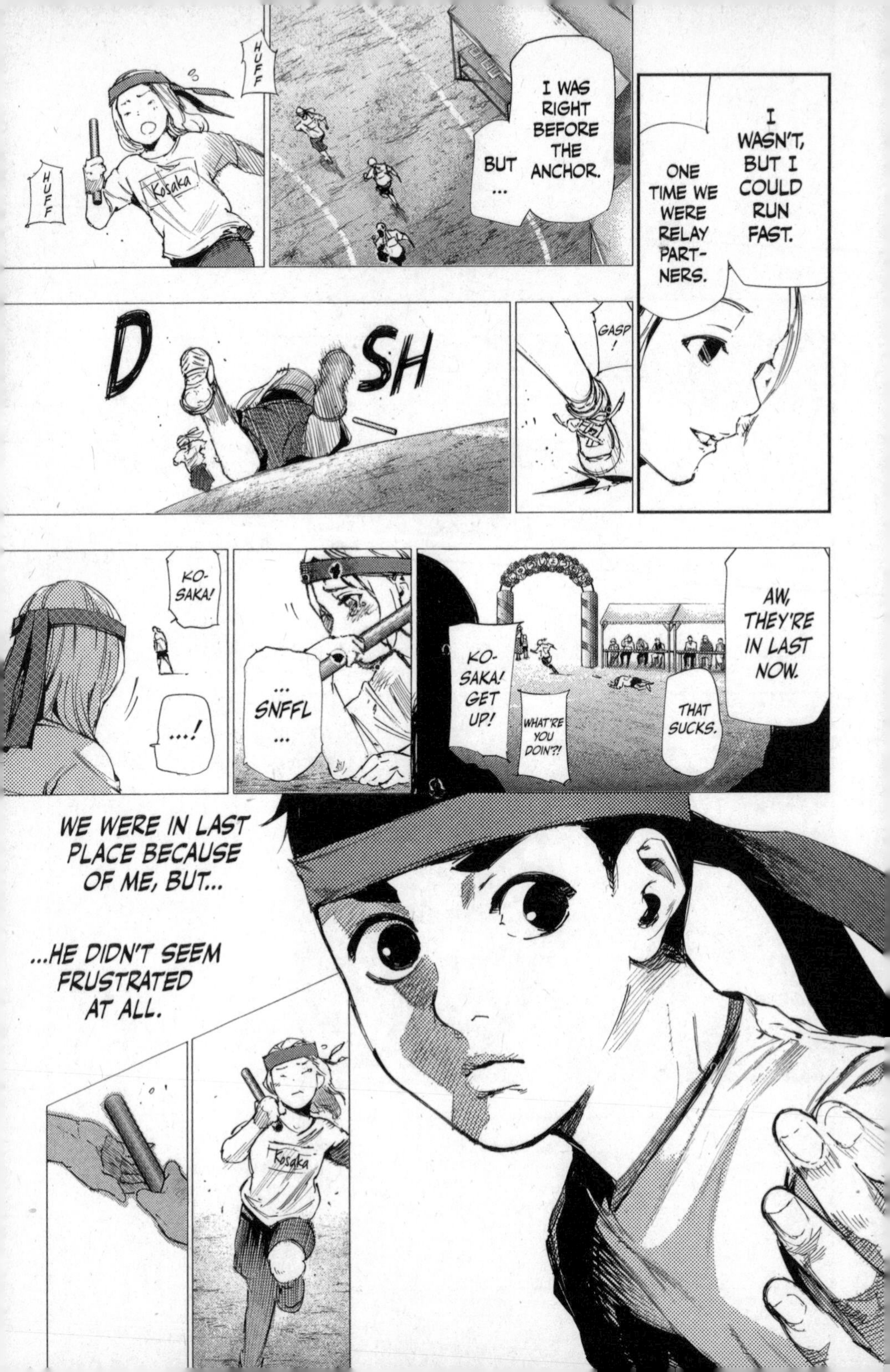
I WASN'T, BUT I COULD RUN FAST.
ONE TIME WE WERE RELAY PARTNERS.
I WAS RIGHT BEFORE THE ANCHOR.
BUT ...
HUFF
HUFF
Kosaka
GASP!
DASH
AW, THEY'RE IN LAST NOW.
THAT SUCKS.
KO-SAKA! GET UP!
WHAT'RE YOU DOIN'?!
... SNFFL ...
KO-SAKA!
...!
WE WERE IN LAST PLACE BECAUSE OF ME, BUT...
...HE DIDN'T SEEM FRUSTRATED AT ALL.
Kosaka

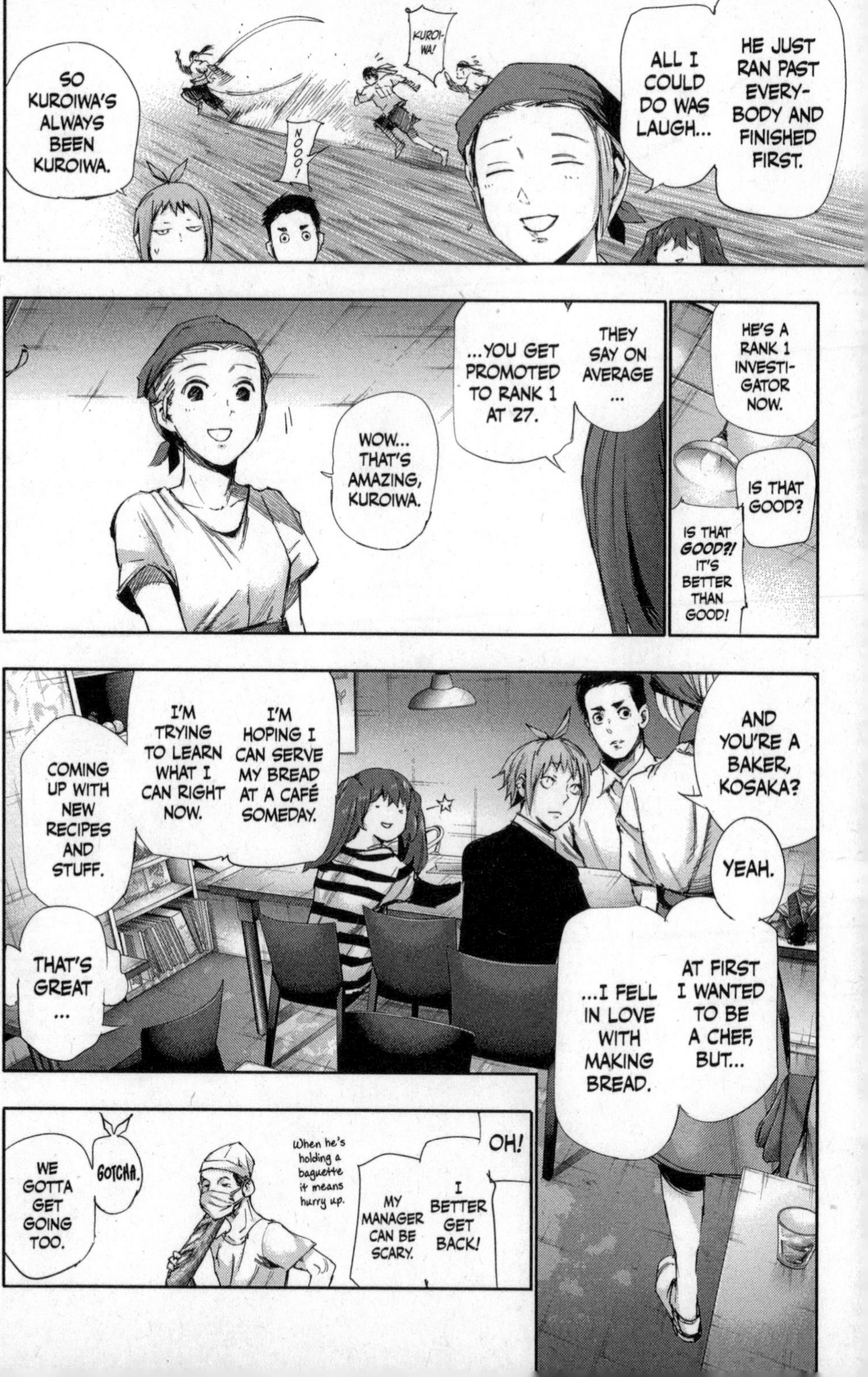
HE JUST RAN PAST EVERY-BODY AND FINISHED FIRST.
ALL I COULD DO WAS LAUGH...
KUROI-WA!
NOOOO!
SO KUROIWA'S ALWAYS BEEN KUROIWA.
HE'S A RANK 1 INVESTI-GATOR NOW.
IS THAT GOOD?
IS THAT *GOOD?!* IT'S BETTER THAN GOOD!
THEY SAY ON AVERAGE ...
...YOU GET PROMOTED TO RANK 1 AT 27.
WOW... THAT'S AMAZING, KUROIWA.
AND YOU'RE A BAKER, KOSAKA?
YEAH.
AT FIRST I WANTED TO BE A CHEF, BUT...
...I FELL IN LOVE WITH MAKING BREAD.
I'M HOPING I CAN SERVE MY BREAD AT A CAFÉ SOMEDAY.
I'M TRYING TO LEARN WHAT I CAN RIGHT NOW.
COMING UP WITH NEW RECIPES AND STUFF.
THAT'S GREAT ...
OH!
I BETTER GET BACK!
MY MANAGER CAN BE SCARY.
When he's holding a baguette it means hurry up.
GOTCHA.
WE GOTTA GET GOING TOO.

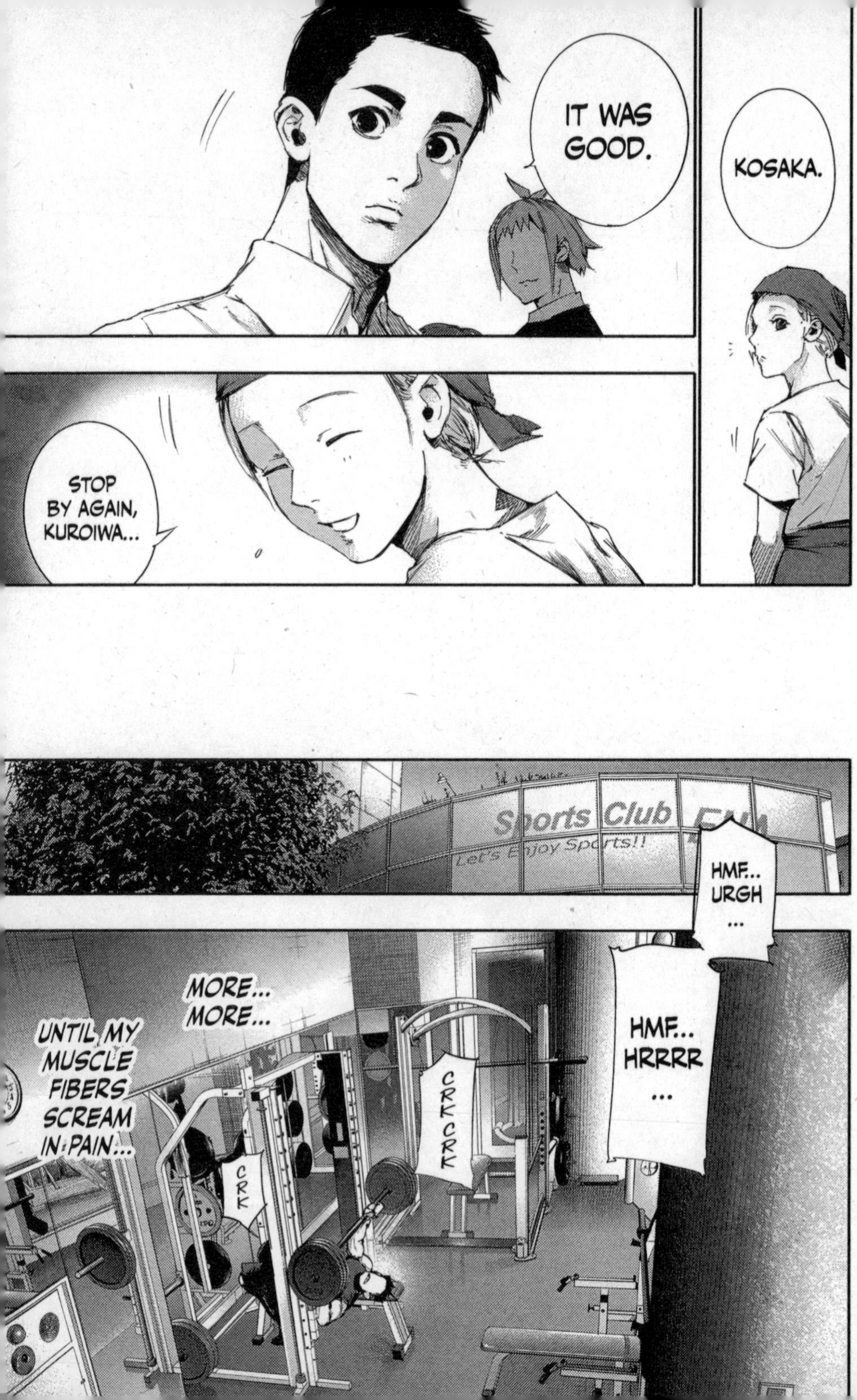
KOSAKA.
IT WAS GOOD.
STOP BY AGAIN, KUROIWA...
Sports Club
Let's Enjoy Sports!!
HMF... URGH ...
HMF... HRRRR ...
CRK CRK
CRK
MORE... MORE...
UNTIL MY MUSCLE FIBERS SCREAM IN PAIN...

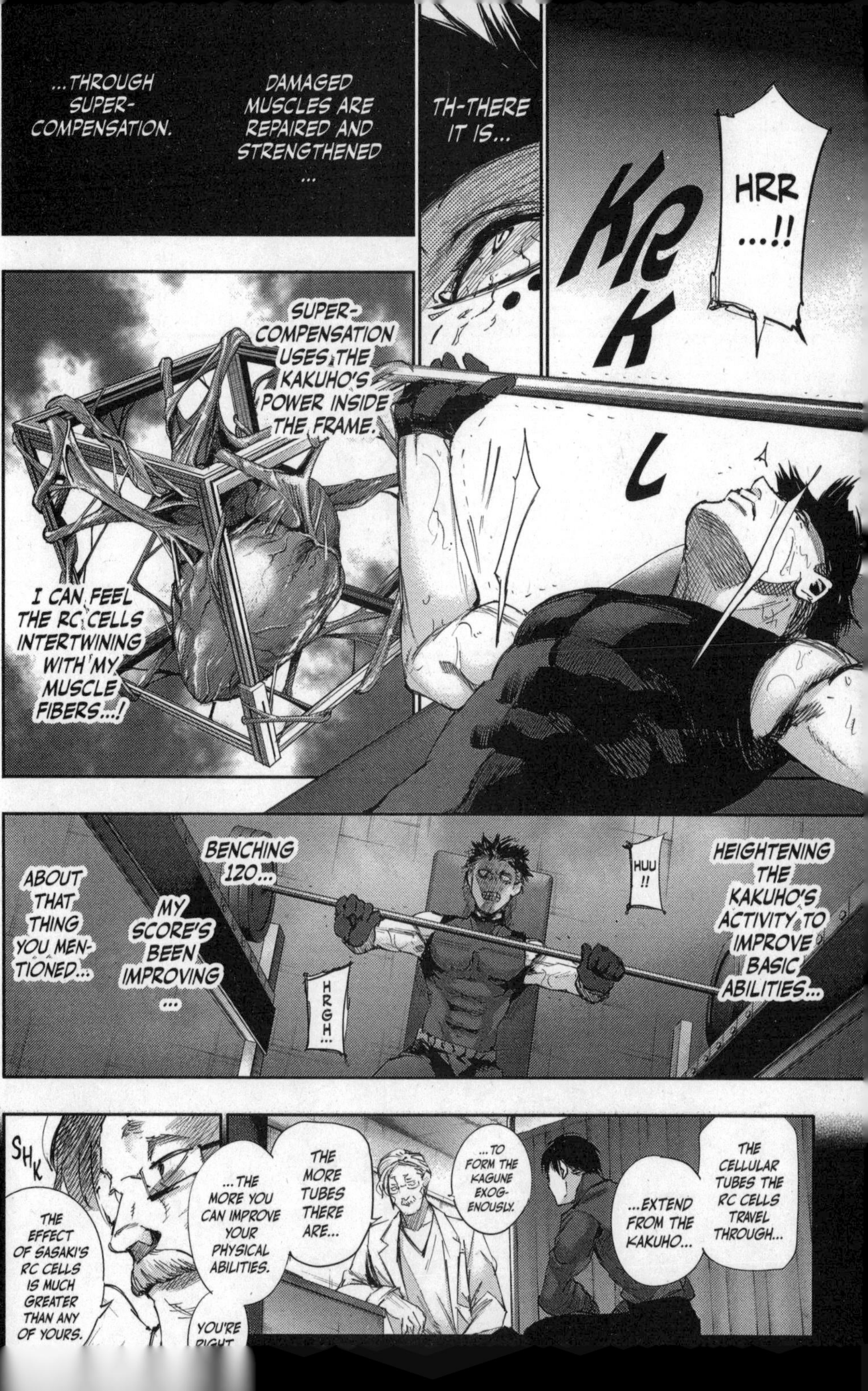
HRR ...!!
TH-THERE IT IS...
KREK
DAMAGED MUSCLES ARE REPAIRED AND STRENGTHENED ...
...THROUGH SUPER-COMPENSATION.
SUPER-COMPENSATION USES THE KAKUHO'S POWER INSIDE THE FRAME.
I CAN FEEL THE RC CELLS INTERTWINING WITH MY MUSCLE FIBERS...!
HEIGHTENING THE KAKUHO'S ACTIVITY TO IMPROVE BASIC ABILITIES...
HUU !!
BENCHING 120...
MY SCORE'S BEEN IMPROVING ...
HRGH...
ABOUT THAT THING YOU MENTIONED...
THE CELLULAR TUBES THE RC CELLS TRAVEL THROUGH...
...EXTEND FROM THE KAKUHO...
...TO FORM THE KAGUNE EXOGENOUSLY.
THE MORE TUBES THERE ARE...
...THE MORE YOU CAN IMPROVE YOUR PHYSICAL ABILITIES.
SHK
THE EFFECT OF SASAKI'S RC CELLS IS MUCH GREATER THAN ANY OF YOURS.
YOU'RE

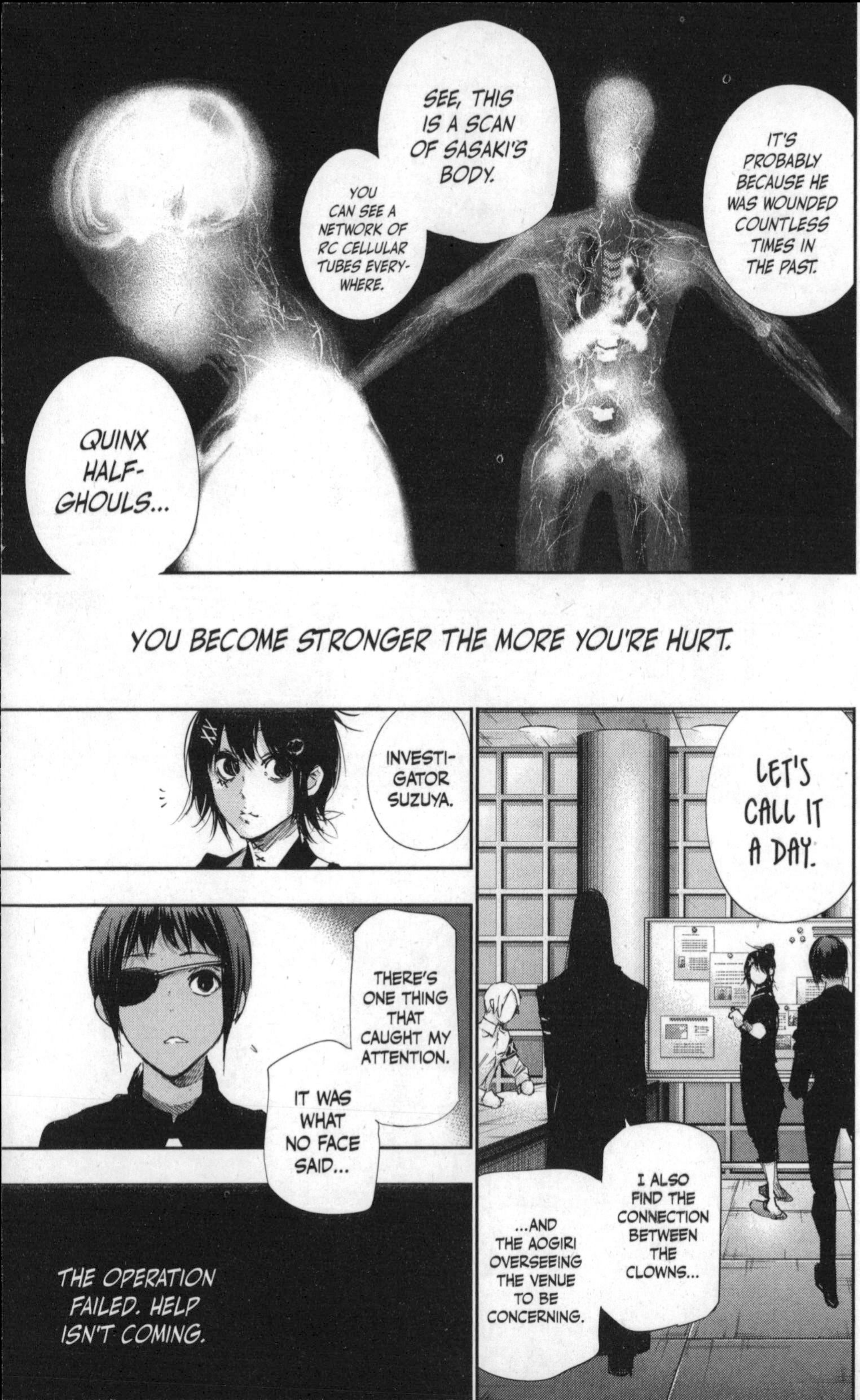
SEE, THIS IS A SCAN OF SASAKI'S BODY.
YOU CAN SEE A NETWORK OF RC CELLULAR TUBES EVERY-WHERE.
IT'S PROBABLY BECAUSE HE WAS WOUNDED COUNTLESS TIMES IN THE PAST.
QUINX HALF-GHOULS...
YOU BECOME STRONGER THE MORE YOU'RE HURT.
LET'S CALL IT A DAY.
I ALSO FIND THE CONNECTION BETWEEN THE CLOWNS...
...AND THE AOGIRI OVERSEEING THE VENUE TO BE CONCERNING.
INVESTI-GATOR SUZUYA.
THERE'S ONE THING THAT CAUGHT MY ATTENTION.
IT WAS WHAT NO FACE SAID...
THE OPERATION FAILED. HELP ISN'T COMING.

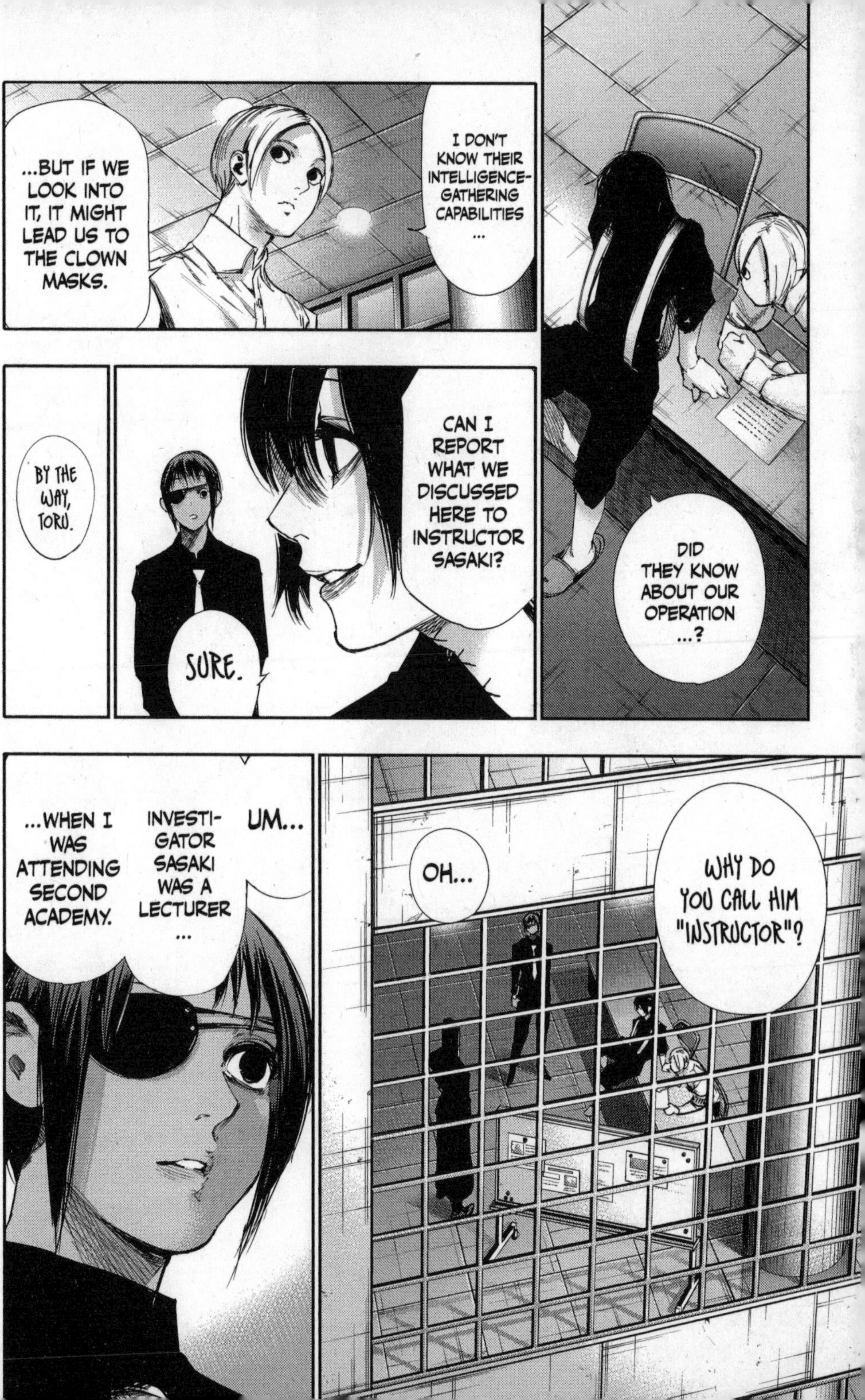
DID THEY KNOW ABOUT OUR OPERATION ...?
I DON'T KNOW THEIR INTELLIGENCE-GATHERING CAPABILITIES ...
...BUT IF WE LOOK INTO IT, IT MIGHT LEAD US TO THE CLOWN MASKS.
CAN I REPORT WHAT WE DISCUSSED HERE TO INSTRUCTOR SASAKI?
SURE.
BY THE WAY, TORU.
WHY DO YOU CALL HIM "INSTRUCTOR"?
OH...
UM...
INVESTI-GATOR SASAKI WAS A LECTURER ...
...WHEN I WAS ATTENDING SECOND ACADEMY.

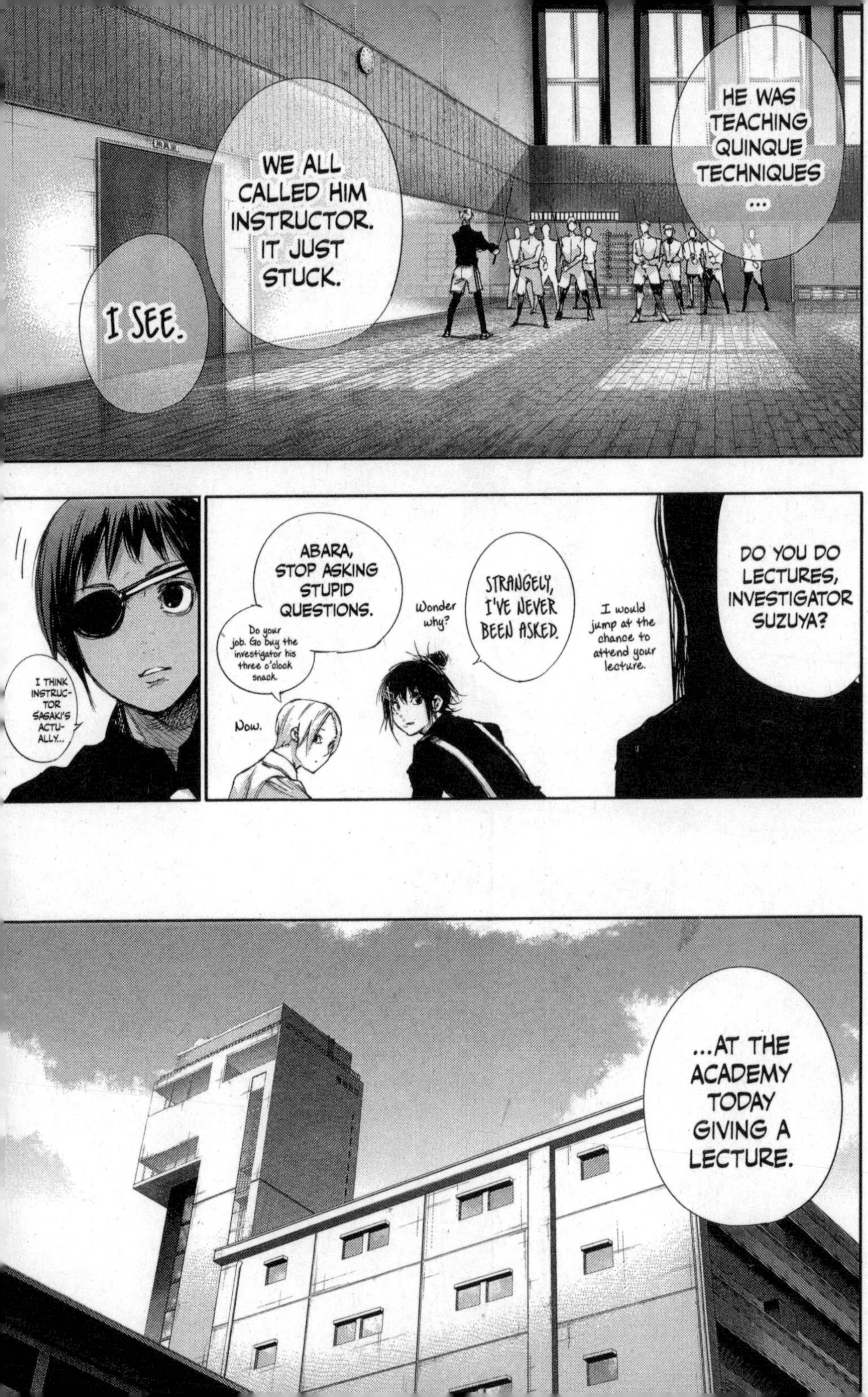
HE WAS TEACHING QUINQUE TECHNIQUES...
WE ALL CALLED HIM INSTRUCTOR. IT JUST STUCK.
I SEE.
DO YOU DO LECTURES, INVESTIGATOR SUZUYA?
I would jump at the chance to attend your lecture.
STRANGELY, I'VE NEVER BEEN ASKED.
Wonder why?
ABARA, STOP ASKING STUPID QUESTIONS.
Do your job. Go buy the investigator his three o'clock snack.
Now.
I THINK INSTRUCTOR SASAKI'S ACTUALLY...
...AT THE ACADEMY TODAY GIVING A LECTURE.

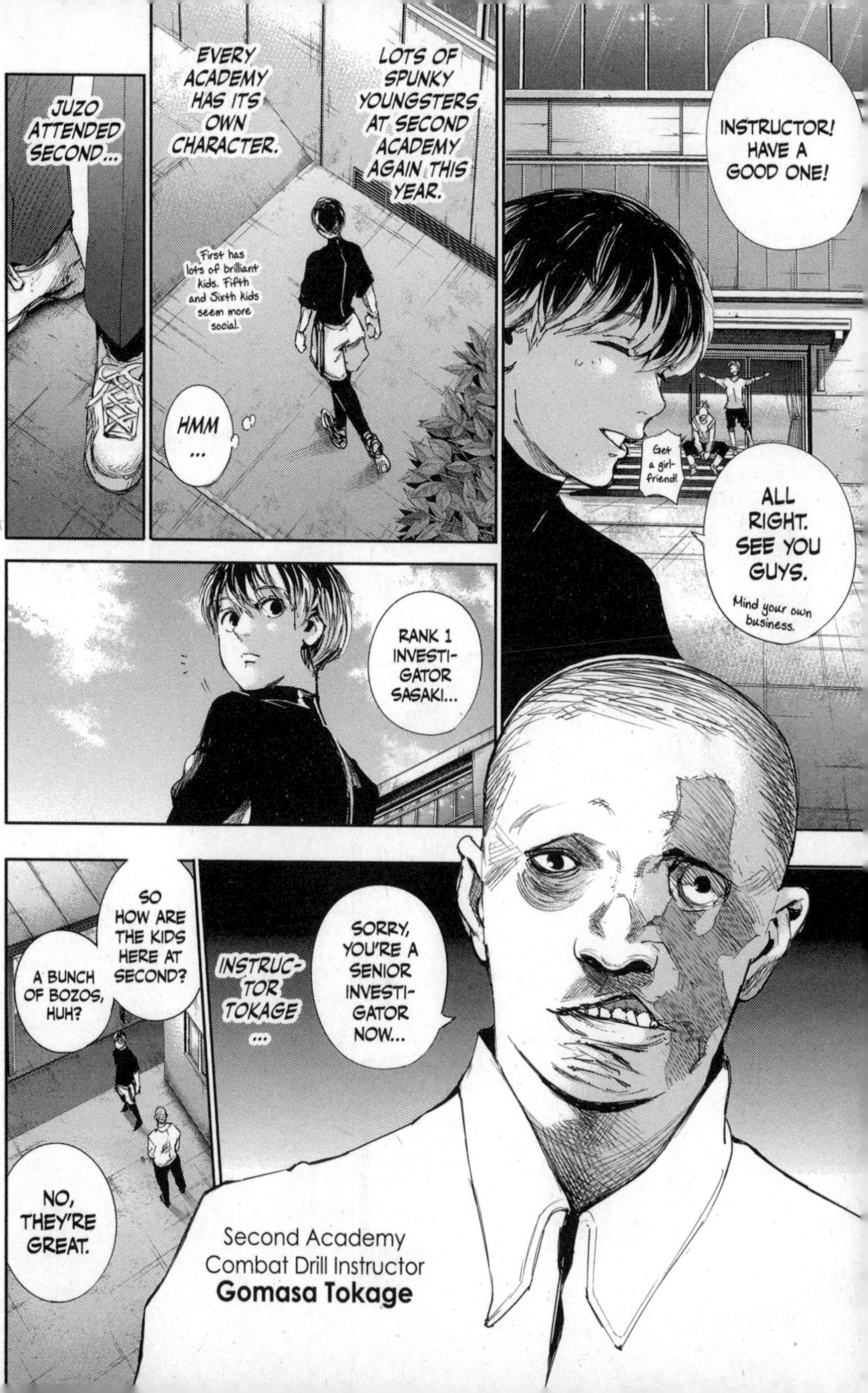
INSTRUCTOR! HAVE A GOOD ONE!
Get a girlfriend!
ALL RIGHT. SEE YOU GUYS.
Mind your own business.
LOTS OF SPUNKY YOUNGSTERS AT SECOND ACADEMY AGAIN THIS YEAR.
EVERY ACADEMY HAS ITS OWN CHARACTER.
First has lots of brilliant kids. Fifth and Sixth kids seem more social.
HMM ...
JUZO ATTENDED SECOND...
RANK 1 INVESTIGATOR SASAKI...
INSTRUCTOR TOKAGE ...
SORRY, YOU'RE A SENIOR INVESTIGATOR NOW...
Second Academy
Combat Drill Instructor
Gomasa Tokage
SO HOW ARE THE KIDS HERE AT SECOND?
A BUNCH OF BOZOS, HUH?
NO, THEY'RE GREAT.

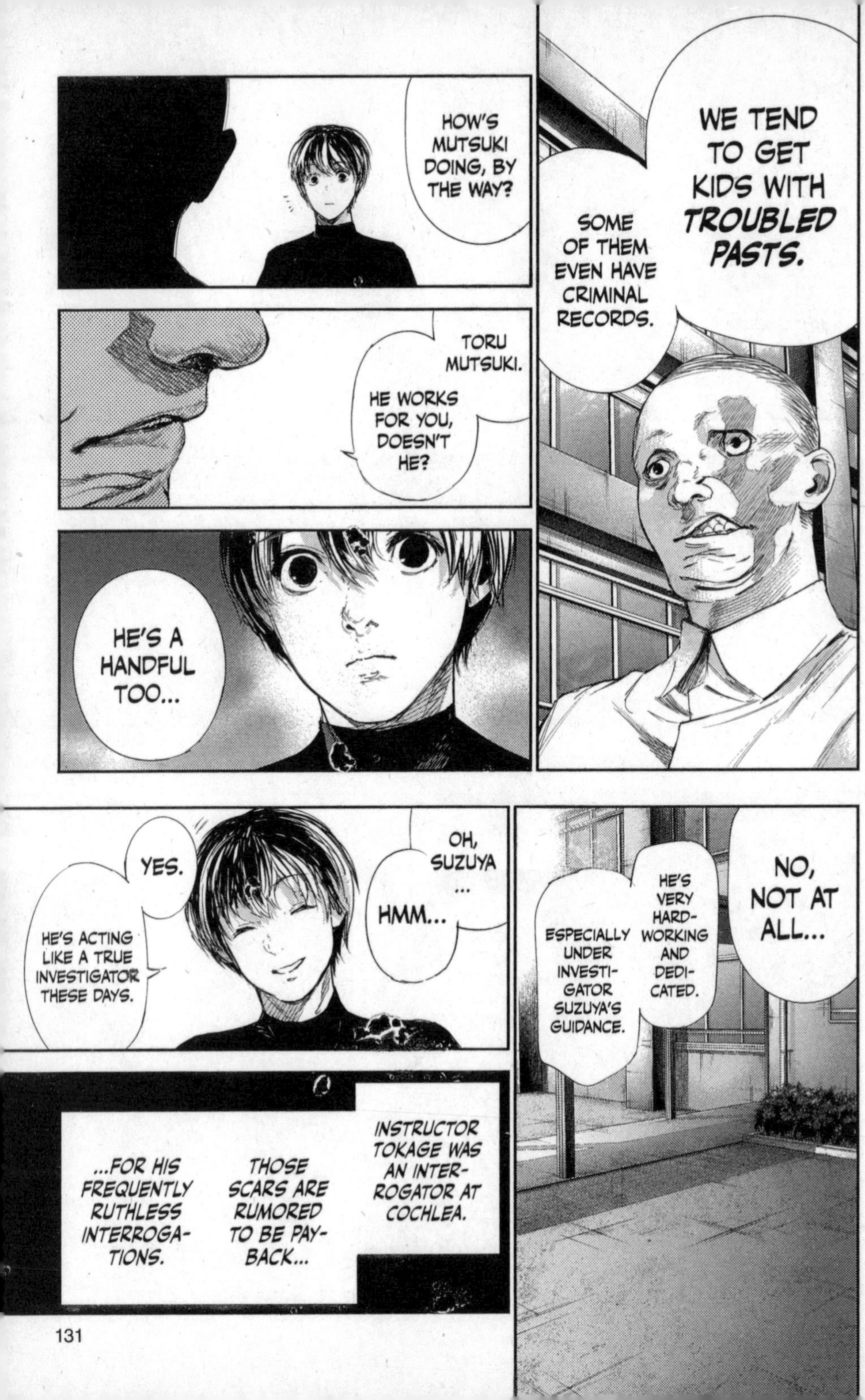
WE TEND TO GET KIDS WITH TROUBLED PASTS.
SOME OF THEM EVEN HAVE CRIMINAL RECORDS.
HOW'S MUTSUKI DOING, BY THE WAY?
TORU MUTSUKI.
HE WORKS FOR YOU, DOESN'T HE?
HE'S A HANDFUL TOO...
NO, NOT AT ALL...
HE'S VERY HARD-WORKING AND DEDICATED.
ESPECIALLY UNDER INVESTIGATOR SUZUYA'S GUIDANCE.
OH, SUZUYA...
HMM...
YES.
HE'S ACTING LIKE A TRUE INVESTIGATOR THESE DAYS.
INSTRUCTOR TOKAGE WAS AN INTERROGATOR AT COCHLEA.
THOSE SCARS ARE RUMORED TO BE PAYBACK...
...FOR HIS FREQUENTLY RUTHLESS INTERROGATIONS.

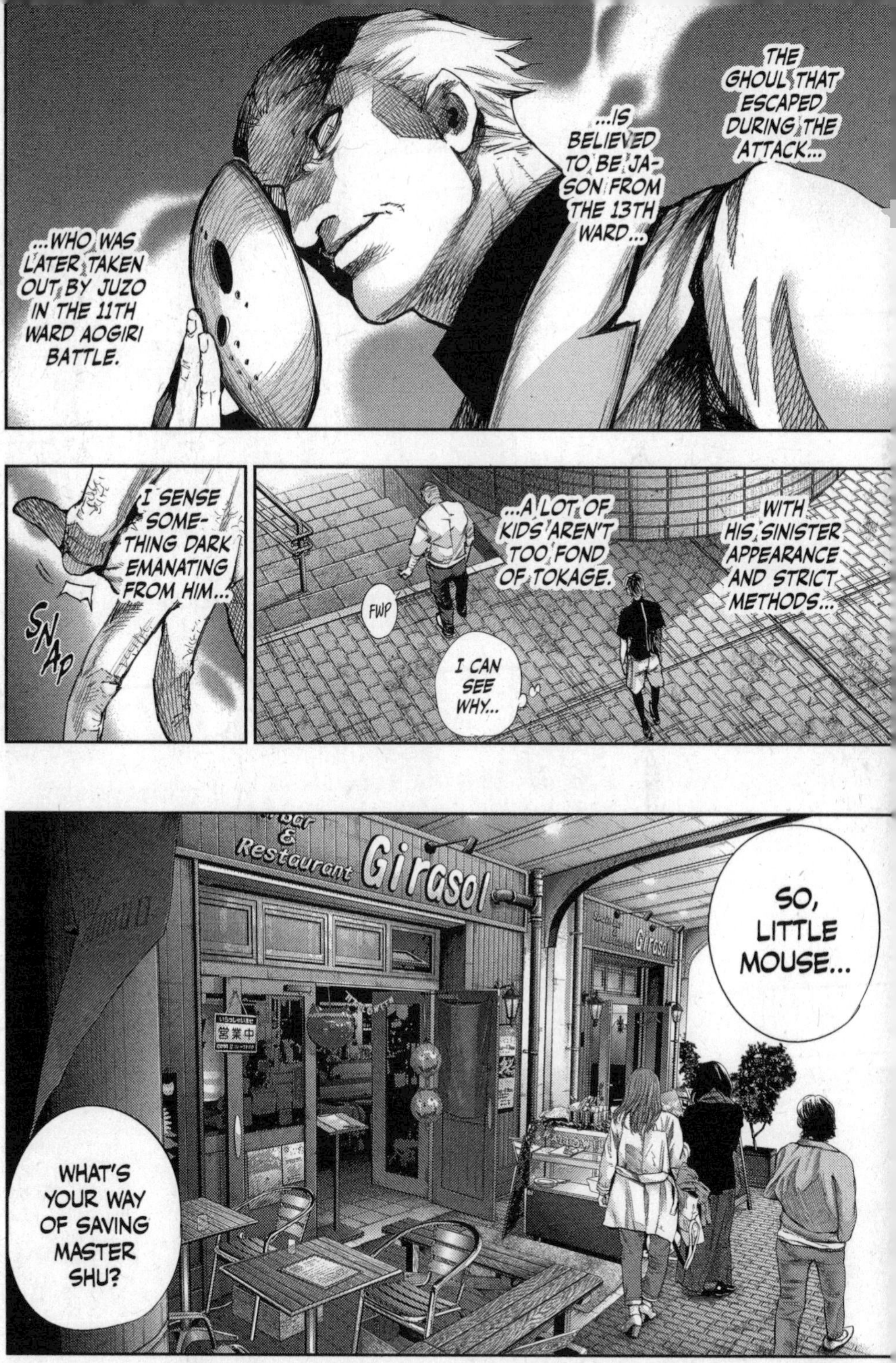
THE GHOUL THAT ESCAPED DURING THE ATTACK...
...IS BELIEVED TO BE JASON FROM THE 13TH WARD...
...WHO WAS LATER TAKEN OUT BY JUZO IN THE 11TH WARD AOGIRI BATTLE.
WITH HIS SINISTER APPEARANCE AND STRICT METHODS...
...A LOT OF KIDS AREN'T TOO FOND OF TOKAGE.
FWP
I CAN SEE WHY...
I SENSE SOMETHING DARK EMANATING FROM HIM...
SNAP
&
Restaurant Girasol
営業中
SO, LITTLE MOUSE...
WHAT'S YOUR WAY OF SAVING MASTER SHU?

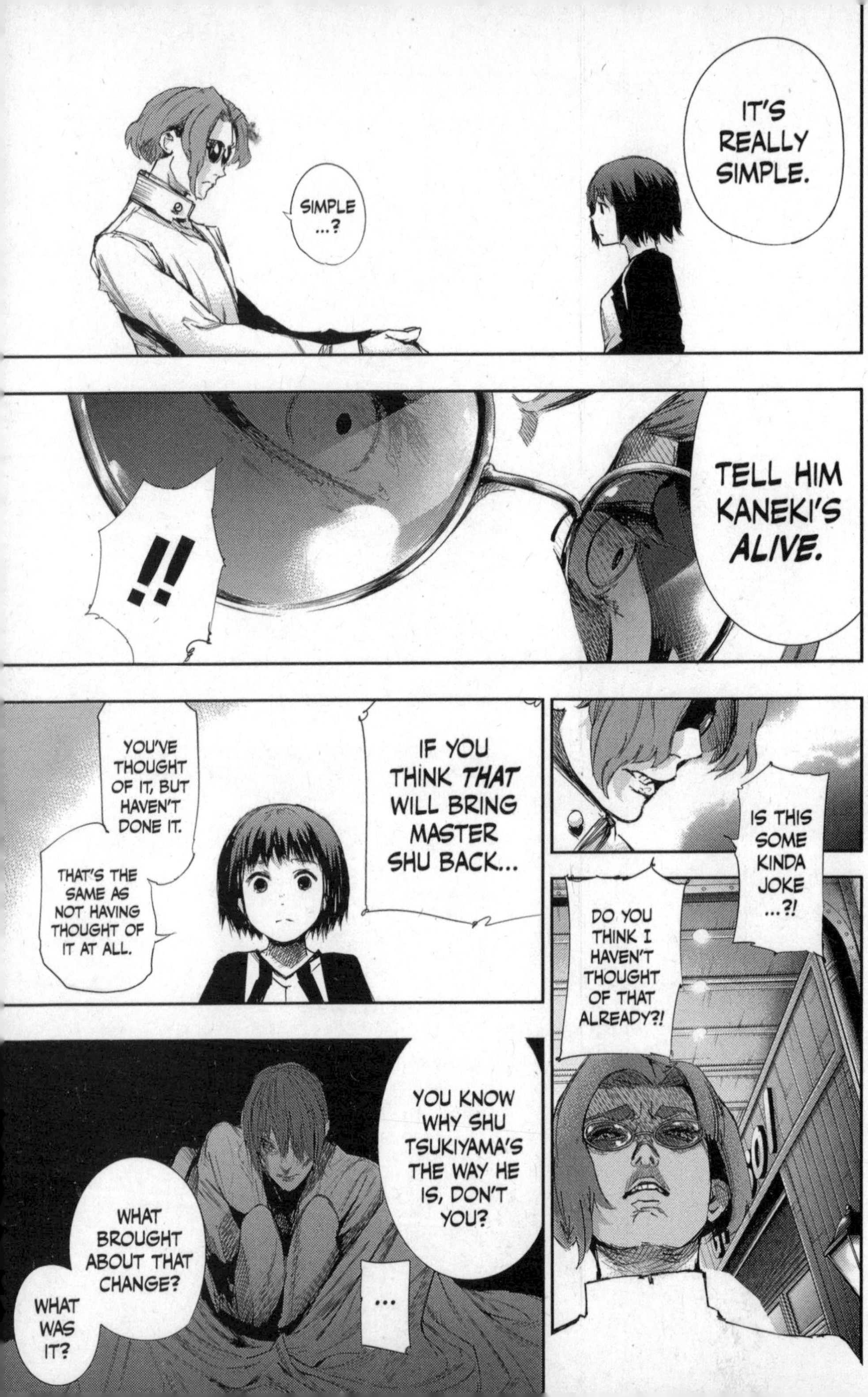
IT'S REALLY SIMPLE.
SIMPLE ...?
TELL HIM KANEKI'S *ALIVE.*
!!
IS THIS SOME KINDA JOKE ...?!
DO YOU THINK I HAVEN'T THOUGHT OF THAT ALREADY?!
IF YOU THINK *THAT* WILL BRING MASTER SHU BACK...
YOU'VE THOUGHT OF IT, BUT HAVEN'T DONE IT.
THAT'S THE SAME AS NOT HAVING THOUGHT OF IT AT ALL.
YOU KNOW WHY SHU TSUKIYAMA'S THE WAY HE IS, DON'T YOU?
...
WHAT BROUGHT ABOUT THAT CHANGE?
WHAT WAS IT?

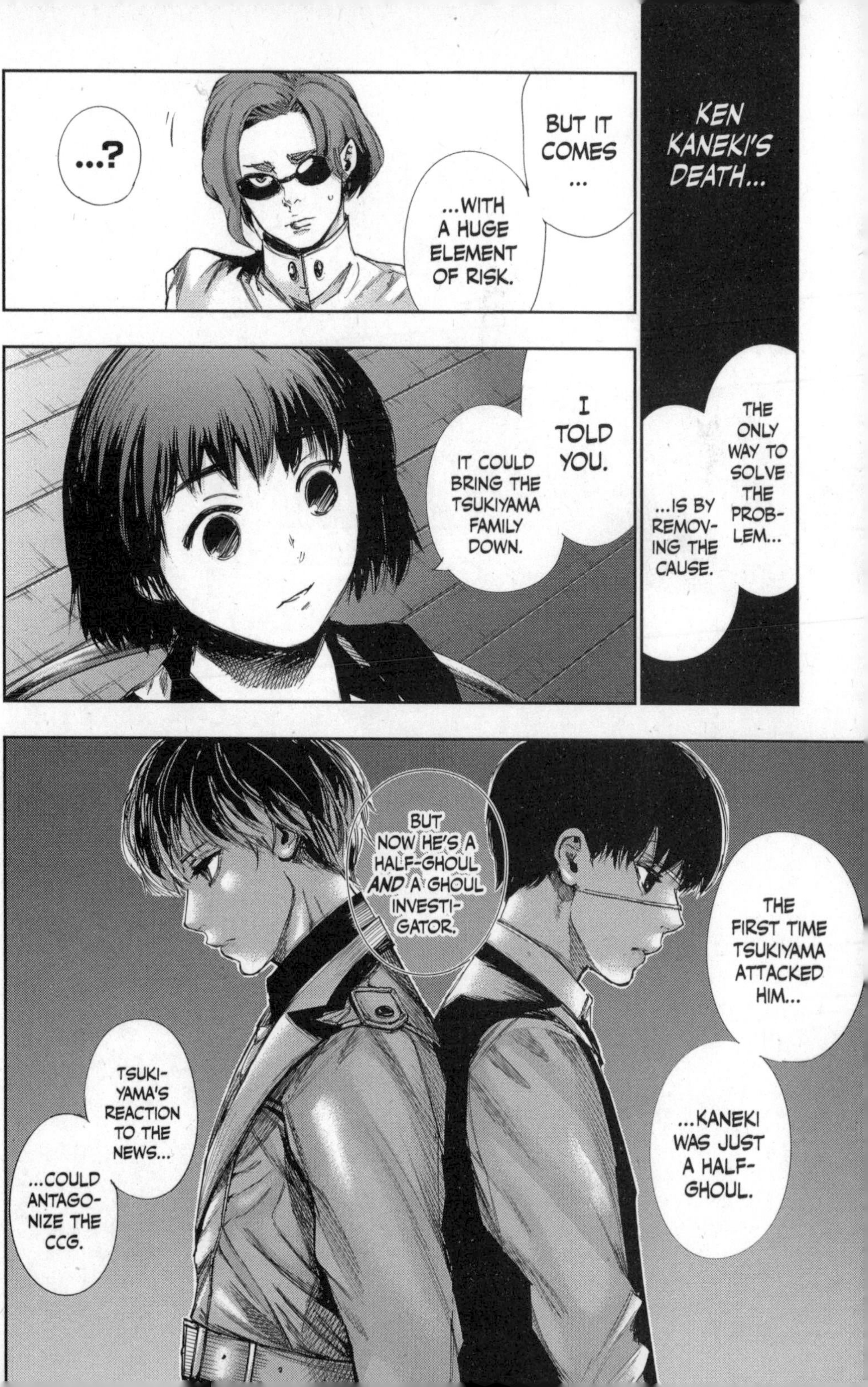
KEN KANEKI'S DEATH...
THE ONLY WAY TO SOLVE THE PROBLEM...
...IS BY REMOVING THE CAUSE.
BUT IT COMES...
...WITH A HUGE ELEMENT OF RISK.
...?
I TOLD YOU.
IT COULD BRING THE TSUKIYAMA FAMILY DOWN.
THE FIRST TIME TSUKIYAMA ATTACKED HIM...
...KANEKI WAS JUST A HALF-GHOUL.
BUT NOW HE'S A HALF-GHOUL *AND* A GHOUL INVESTIGATOR.
TSUKIYAMA'S REACTION TO THE NEWS...
...COULD ANTAGONIZE THE CCG.

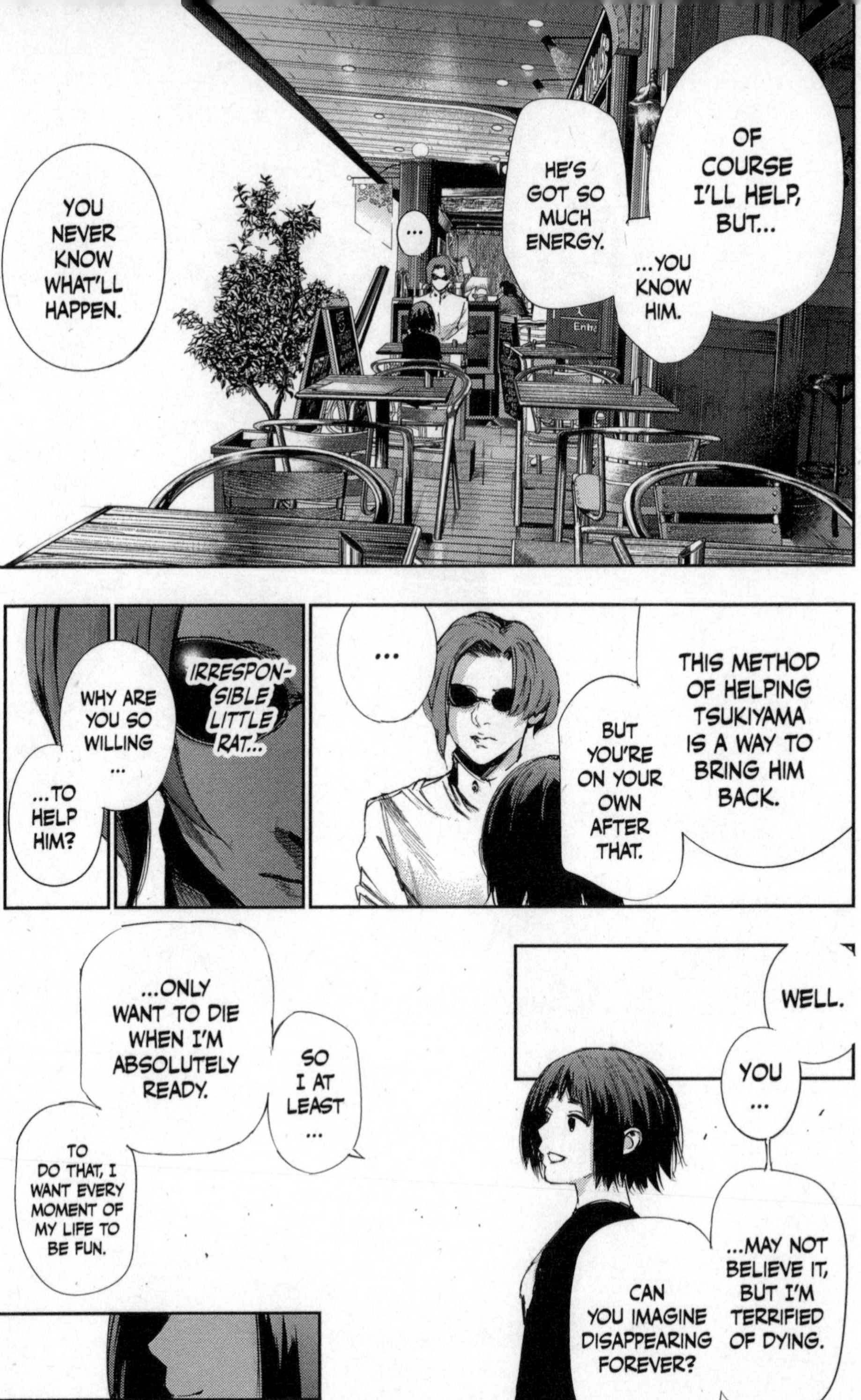
OF COURSE I'LL HELP, BUT...
...YOU KNOW HIM.
HE'S GOT SO MUCH ENERGY.
...
YOU NEVER KNOW WHAT'LL HAPPEN.
THIS METHOD OF HELPING TSUKIYAMA IS A WAY TO BRING HIM BACK.
BUT YOU'RE ON YOUR OWN AFTER THAT.
...
IRRESPON-SIBLE LITTLE RAT...
WHY ARE YOU SO WILLING ...
...TO HELP HIM?
WELL.
YOU ...
...MAY NOT BELIEVE IT, BUT I'M TERRIFIED OF DYING.
CAN YOU IMAGINE DISAPPEARING FOREVER?
SO I AT LEAST ...
...ONLY WANT TO DIE WHEN I'M ABSOLUTELY READY.
TO DO THAT, I WANT EVERY MOMENT OF MY LIFE TO BE FUN.

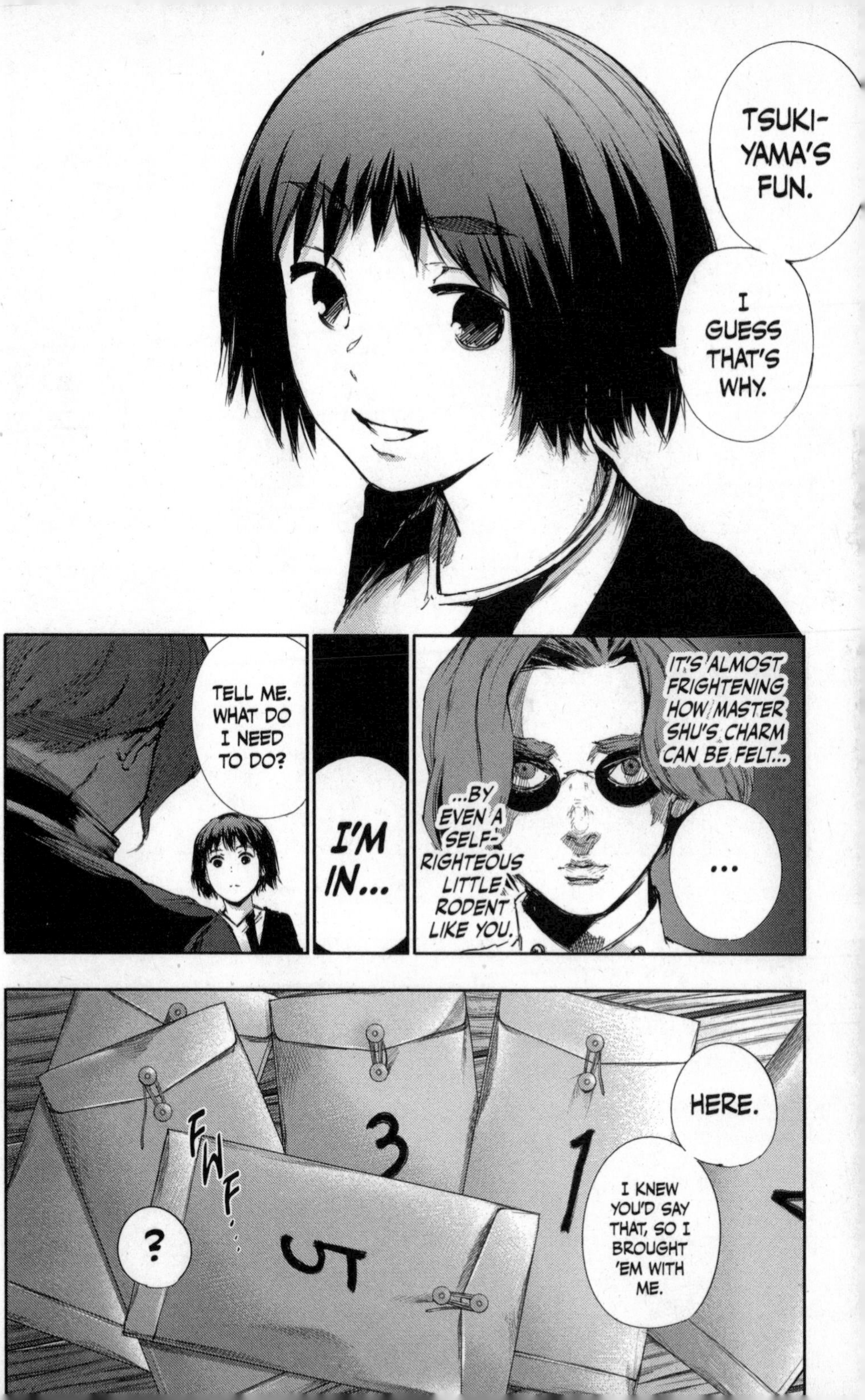
TSUKI-YAMA'S FUN.
I GUESS THAT'S WHY.
IT'S ALMOST FRIGHTENING HOW MASTER SHU'S CHARM CAN BE FELT...
...BY EVEN A SELF-RIGHTEOUS LITTLE RODENT LIKE YOU.
...
I'M IN...
TELL ME. WHAT DO I NEED TO DO?
HERE.
I KNEW YOU'D SAY THAT, SO I BROUGHT 'EM WITH ME.
FWF...
?

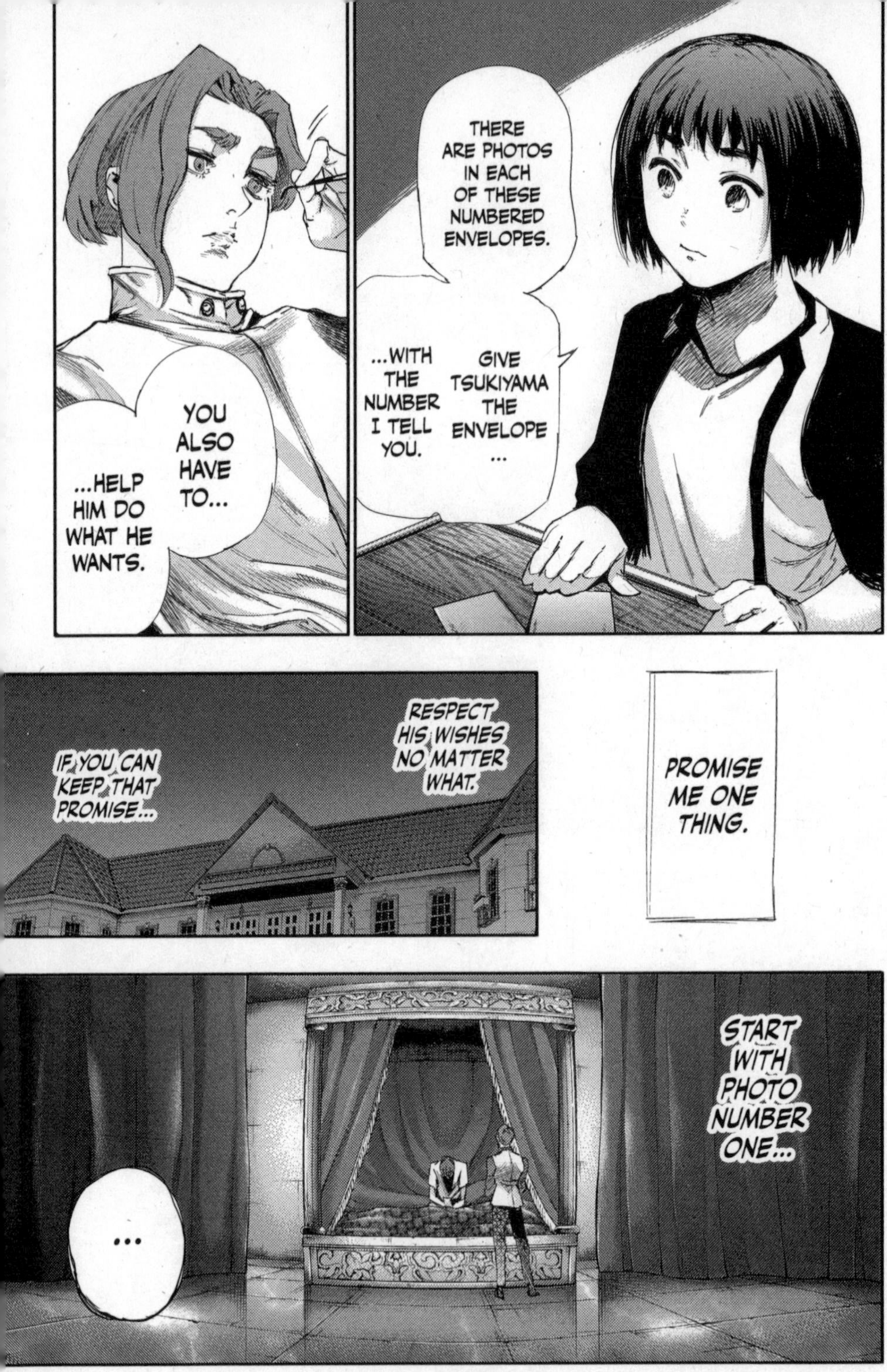
THERE ARE PHOTOS IN EACH OF THESE NUMBERED ENVELOPES.
GIVE TSUKIYAMA THE ENVELOPE ...
...WITH THE NUMBER I TELL YOU.
YOU ALSO HAVE TO...
...HELP HIM DO WHAT HE WANTS.
PROMISE ME ONE THING.
RESPECT HIS WISHES NO MATTER WHAT.
IF YOU CAN KEEP THAT PROMISE...
START WITH PHOTO NUMBER ONE...
...

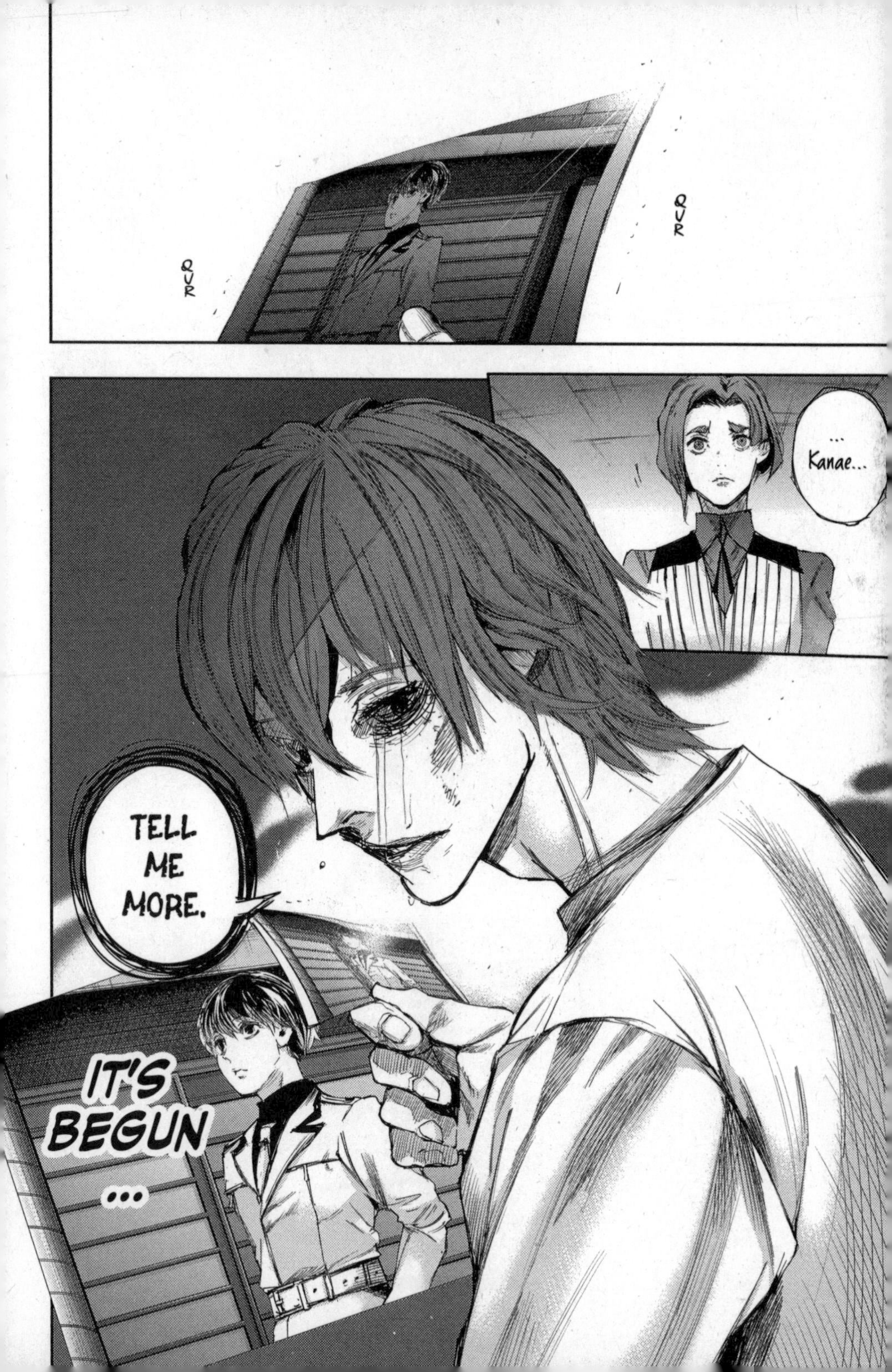
QUR
QUR
... Kanae...
TELL ME MORE.
IT'S BEGUN ...

•Shu likes playing soccer.

I'm the goalie and Shu shoots.
You wouldn't know he's a six-year-old from his powerful shots!
Perhaps he has a future playing in an overseas league.
Daddy is so proud of his very athletic son.

•Shu is good at the piano!

Once he started taking piano lessons, he was able to play Beyer just like that. His original composition *Daddy's Eyeglasses* was brilliant. He'll either be a soccer player, a pianist, or perhaps a conductor. I'd love to listen to his orchestra someday!

•Shu has an interest in foreign languages?

He wanted to know what I do for work, so I showed him some of my business documents. I thought they were too difficult for him to read, but he showed lots of interest. His eyes sparkled looking at presentations written in French and English. I felt my blood in him. Let's take a trip together soon.

•Shu is a kind boy.

"You eat humans? Isn't that mean?"
That took me by surprise.
It's something us proud Ghouls never even question.
I was overwhelmed by his innocent, childlike question.
That's why I told him,
"Humans appreciate being eaten by Ghouls like you, Shu. You have to eat a lot of them so you can be strong."
When I told him that, he understood completely!
I like seeing you eat a lot, Shu.

•Shu is a ladies' man.

Shu received lots of chocolate at school.
It's what they call Valentine's Day.
We can't eat chocolate, so I threw it all away.
Being the nice boy that he is, he looked sad.

He received a surprising amount. He must be quite popular with the girls. I'm worried he will end up a ladies' man like his grandfather…

I want Shu to find passionate love with a pretty, noble Ghoul woman like I did. I hope you get married and have grandchildren as sweet as you are, Shu.

•Shu and his mother.

"What was mommy like?"
He asked me out of nowhere. It took me by surprise.
I felt such guilt. Because I decided I would give him twice the love.
It made me reflect on how I must have made him feel lonely, that I didn't care enough about him.

That's why I told him to look in the mirror.
"Your big eyes and gentle face are like your mother's. We are reflected in your face and in your body even after we're gone."

He looked puzzled, but one day he'll understand.

Daddy loves you, Shu.

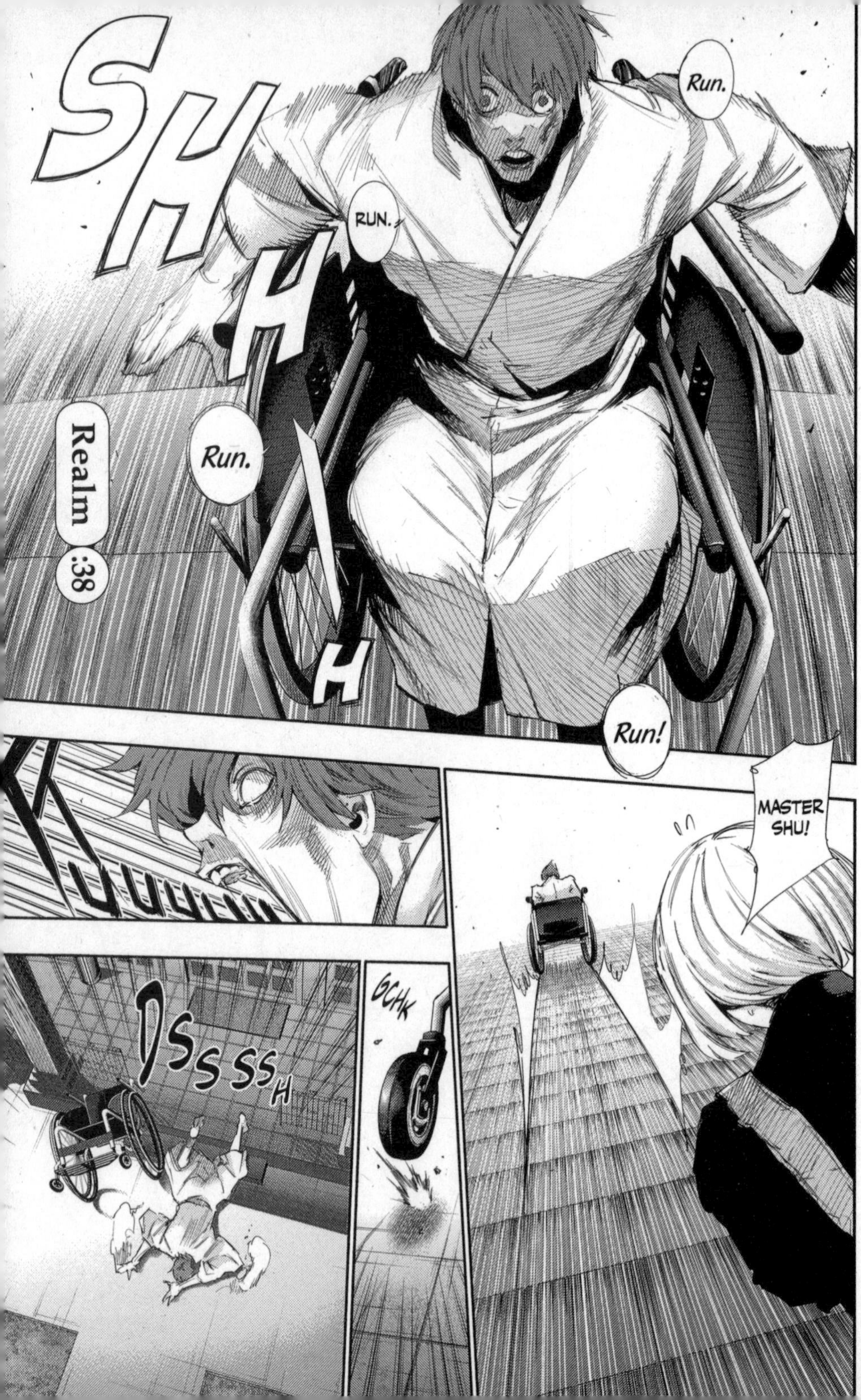
Run.
SHHH
RUN.
Realm :38
Run.
Run!
MASTER SHU!
GCHK
DSSSSH

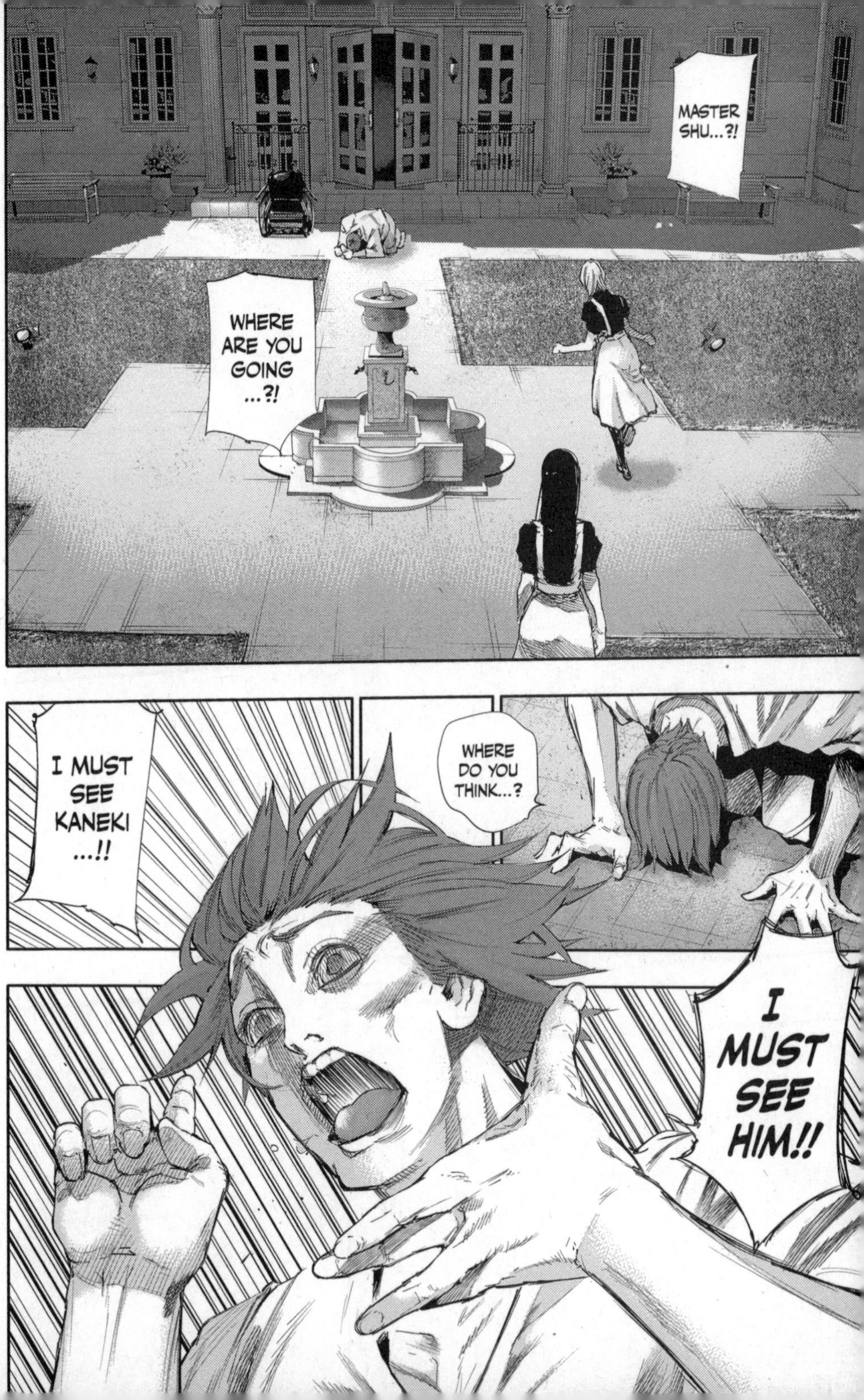
MASTER SHU...?!
WHERE ARE YOU GOING ...?!
WHERE DO YOU THINK...?
I MUST SEE KANEKI ...!!
I MUST SEE HIM!!

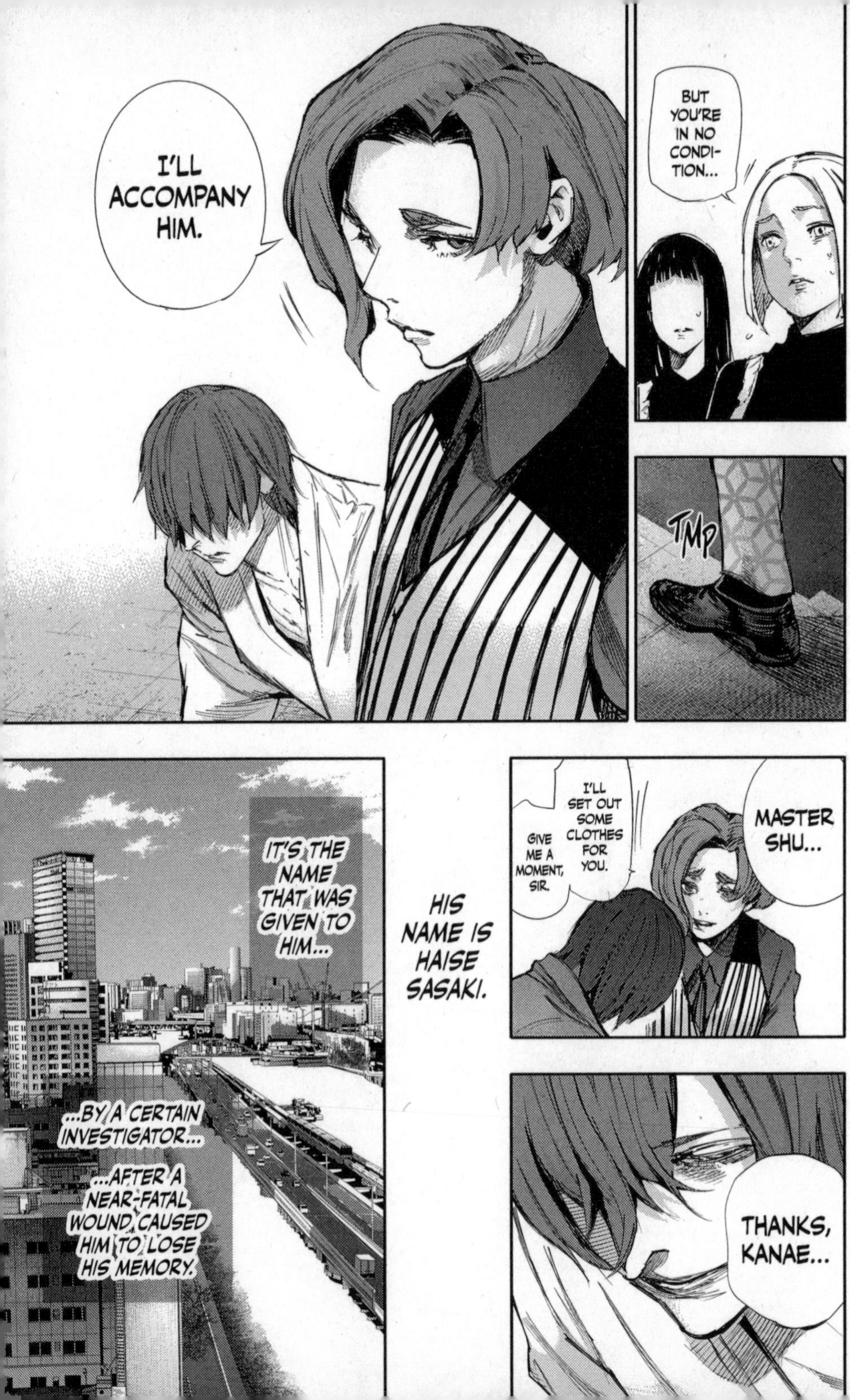
BUT YOU'RE IN NO CONDITION...
TMP
I'LL ACCOMPANY HIM.
MASTER SHU...
I'LL SET OUT SOME CLOTHES FOR YOU.
GIVE ME A MOMENT, SIR.
THANKS, KANAE...
HIS NAME IS HAISE SASAKI.
IT'S THE NAME THAT WAS GIVEN TO HIM...
...BY A CERTAIN INVESTIGATOR...
...AFTER A NEAR-FATAL WOUND CAUSED HIM TO LOSE HIS MEMORY.

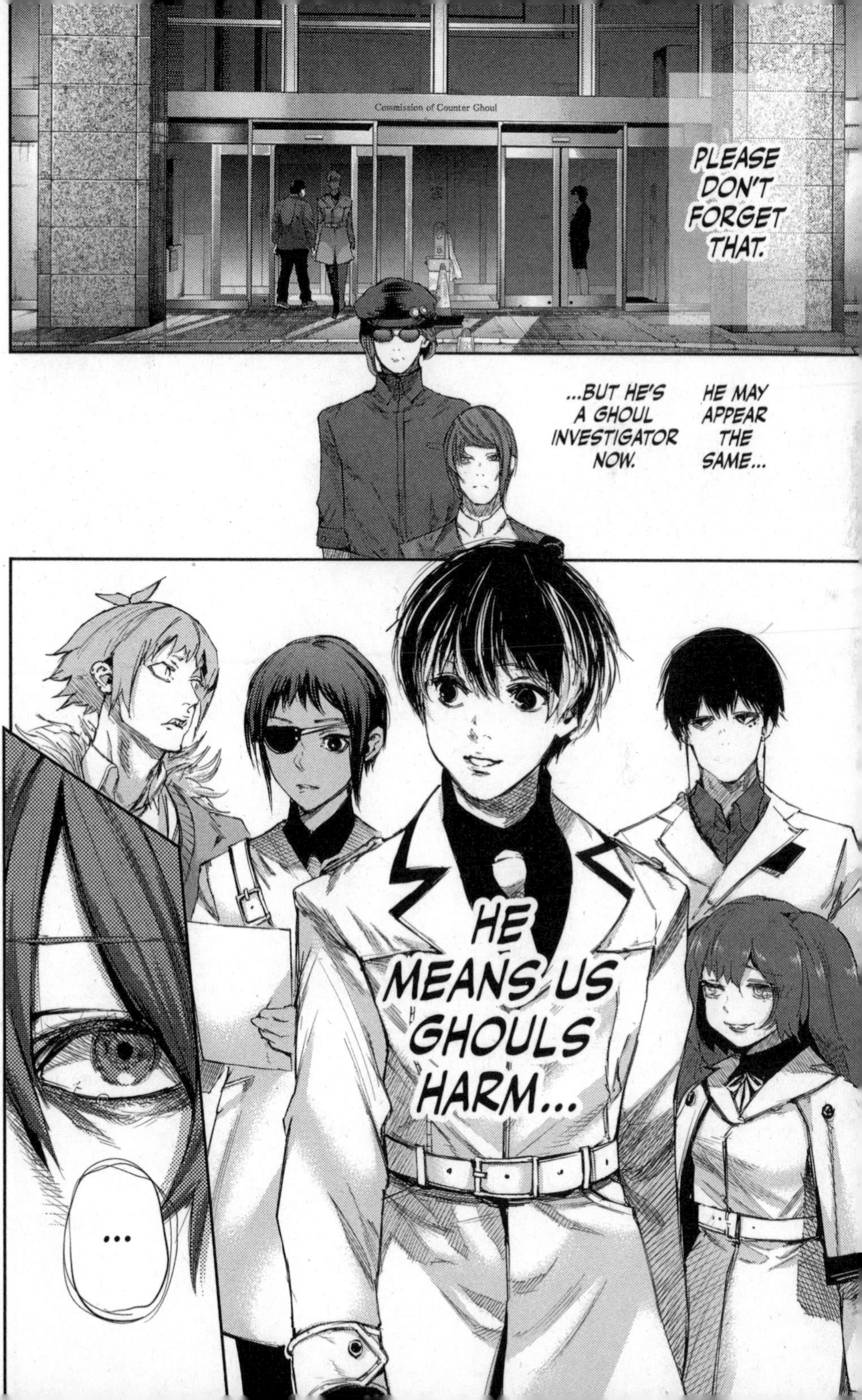

Commission of Counter Ghoul
PLEASE DON'T FORGET THAT.
HE MAY APPEAR THE SAME...
...BUT HE'S A GHOUL INVESTIGATOR NOW.
HE MEANS US GHOULS HARM...
...

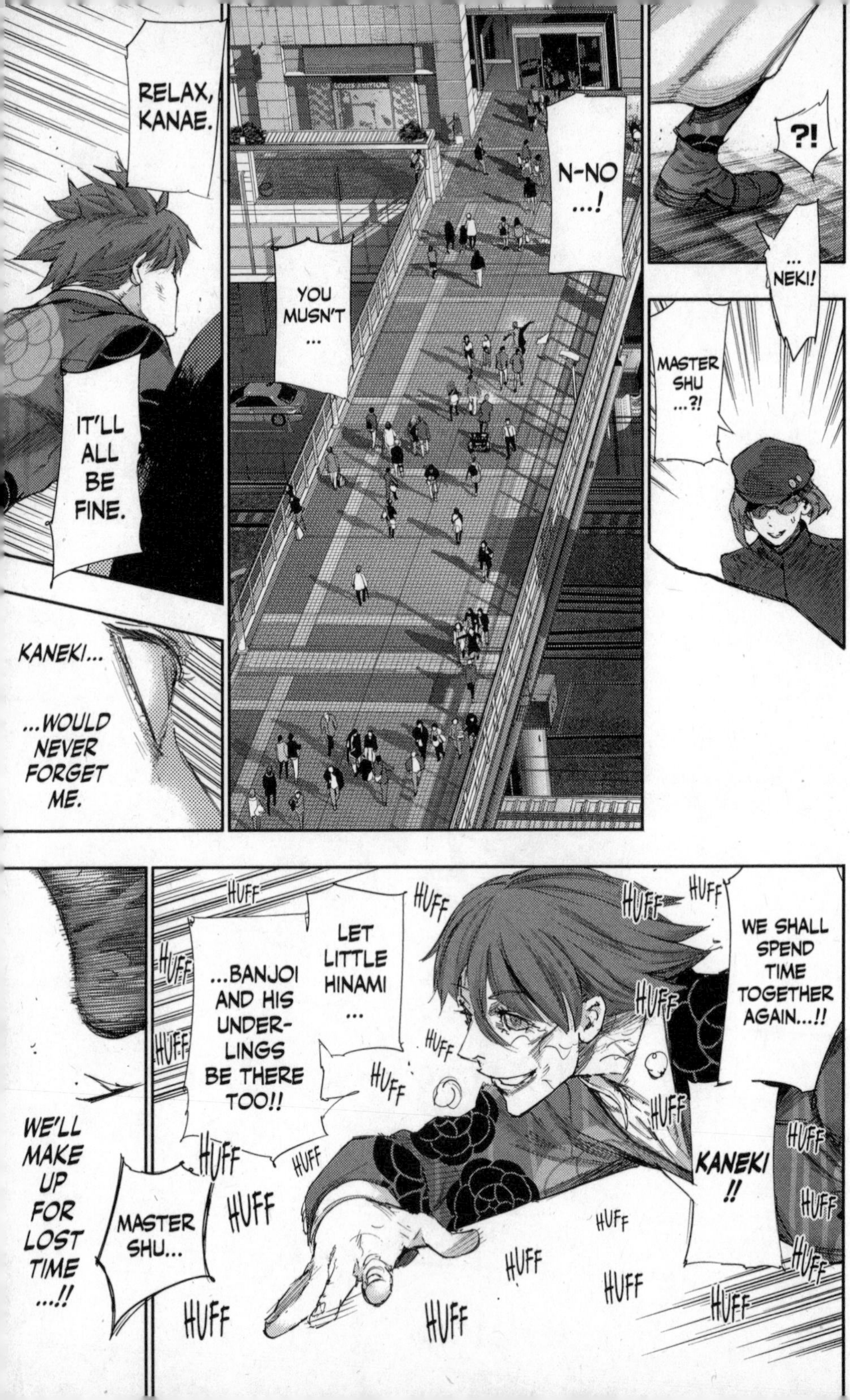

?!
... NEKI!
MASTER SHU ...?!
N-NO ...!
YOU MUSN'T ...
RELAX, KANAE.
IT'LL ALL BE FINE.
KANEKI...
...WOULD NEVER FORGET ME.
HUFF
WE SHALL SPEND TIME TOGETHER AGAIN...!!
HUFF
LET LITTLE HINAMI ...
...BANJOI AND HIS UNDER-LINGS BE THERE TOO!!
HUFF
KANEKI !!
HUFF
MASTER SHU...
HUFF
WE'LL MAKE UP FOR LOST TIME ...!!

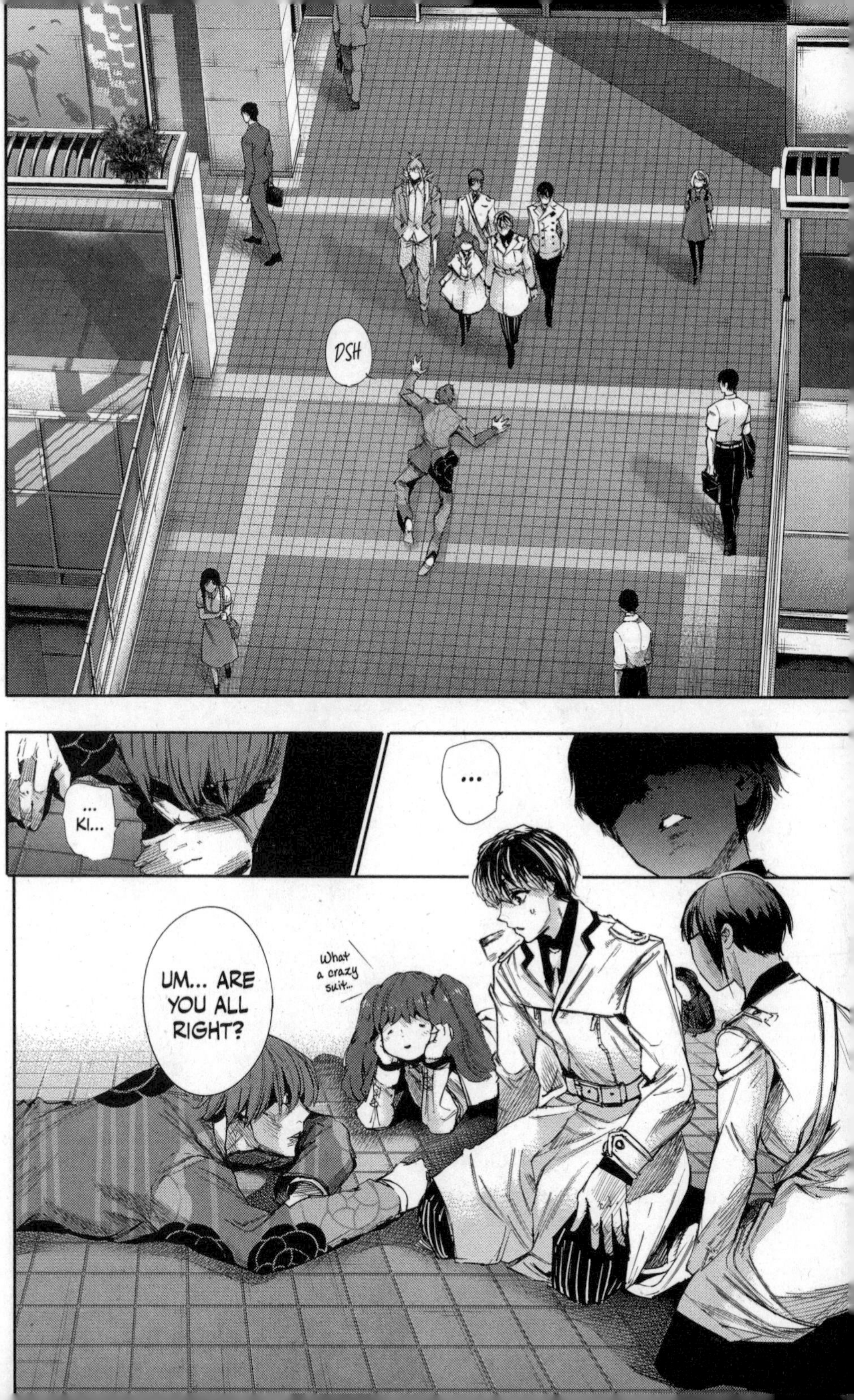
DSH
...
... KI...
What a crazy suit...
UM... ARE YOU ALL RIGHT?

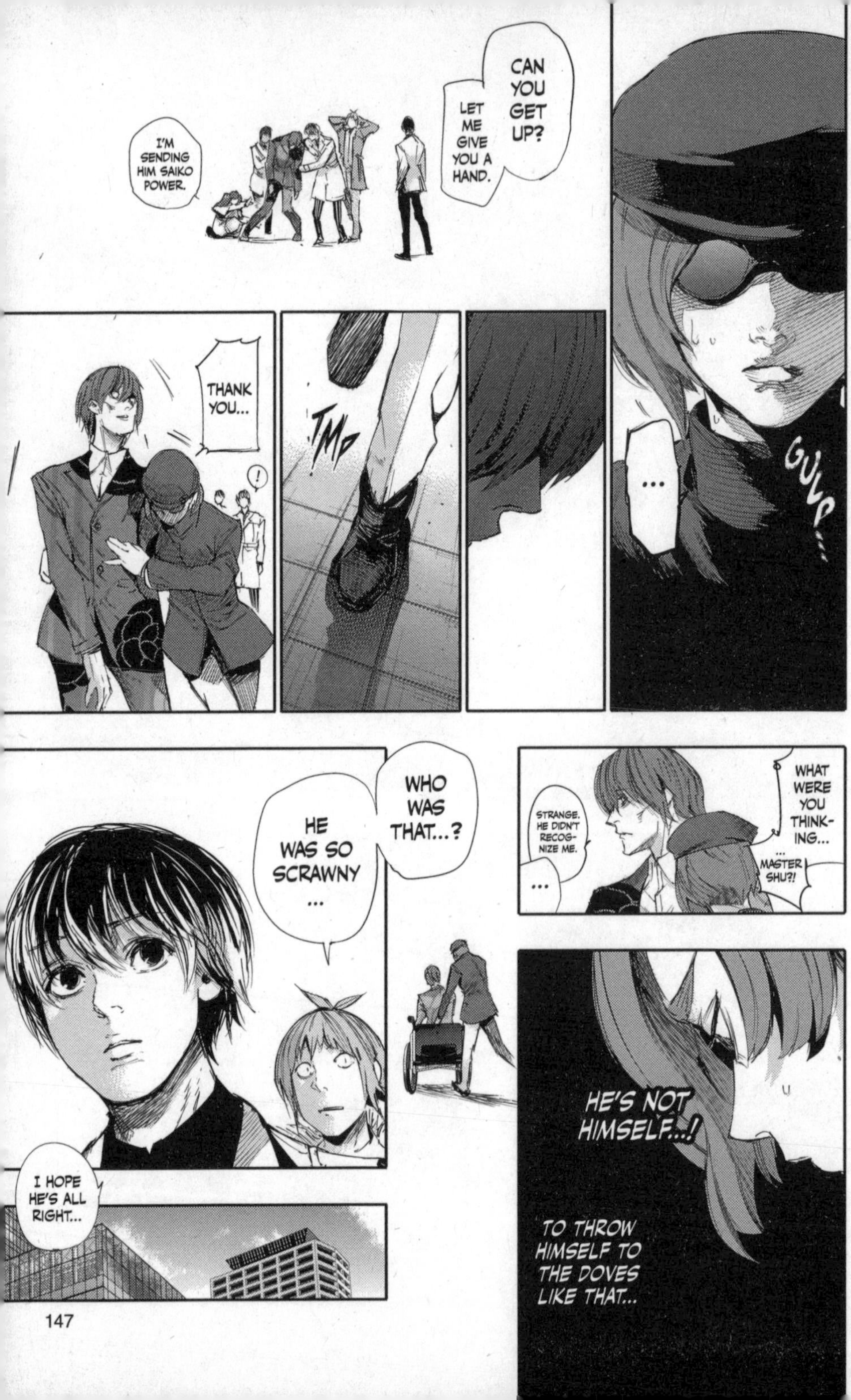
...
GULP...
CAN YOU GET UP?
LET ME GIVE YOU A HAND.
I'M SENDING HIM SAIKO POWER.
TMP
THANK YOU...
!
WHAT WERE YOU THINKING... ... MASTER SHU?!
STRANGE. HE DIDN'T RECOGNIZE ME.
...
HE'S NOT HIMSELF...!
TO THROW HIMSELF TO THE DOVES LIKE THAT...
WHO WAS THAT...?
HE WAS SO SCRAWNY...
I HOPE HE'S ALL RIGHT...

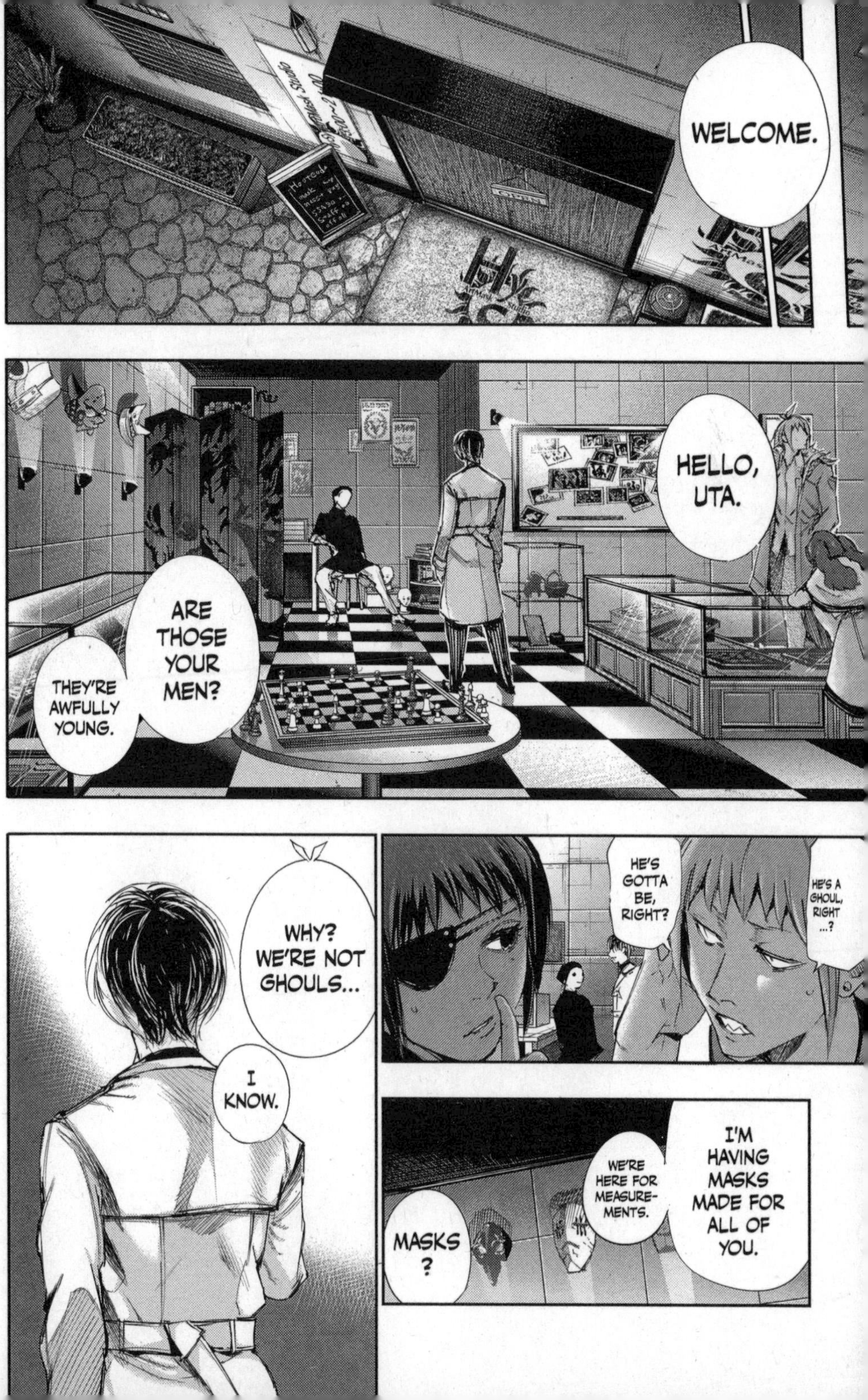
WELCOME.
HELLO, UTA.
ARE THOSE YOUR MEN?
THEY'RE AWFULLY YOUNG.
HE'S A GHOUL, RIGHT ...?
HE'S GOTTA BE, RIGHT?
I'M HAVING MASKS MADE FOR ALL OF YOU.
WE'RE HERE FOR MEASUREMENTS.
MASKS?
WHY? WE'RE NOT GHOULS...
I KNOW.

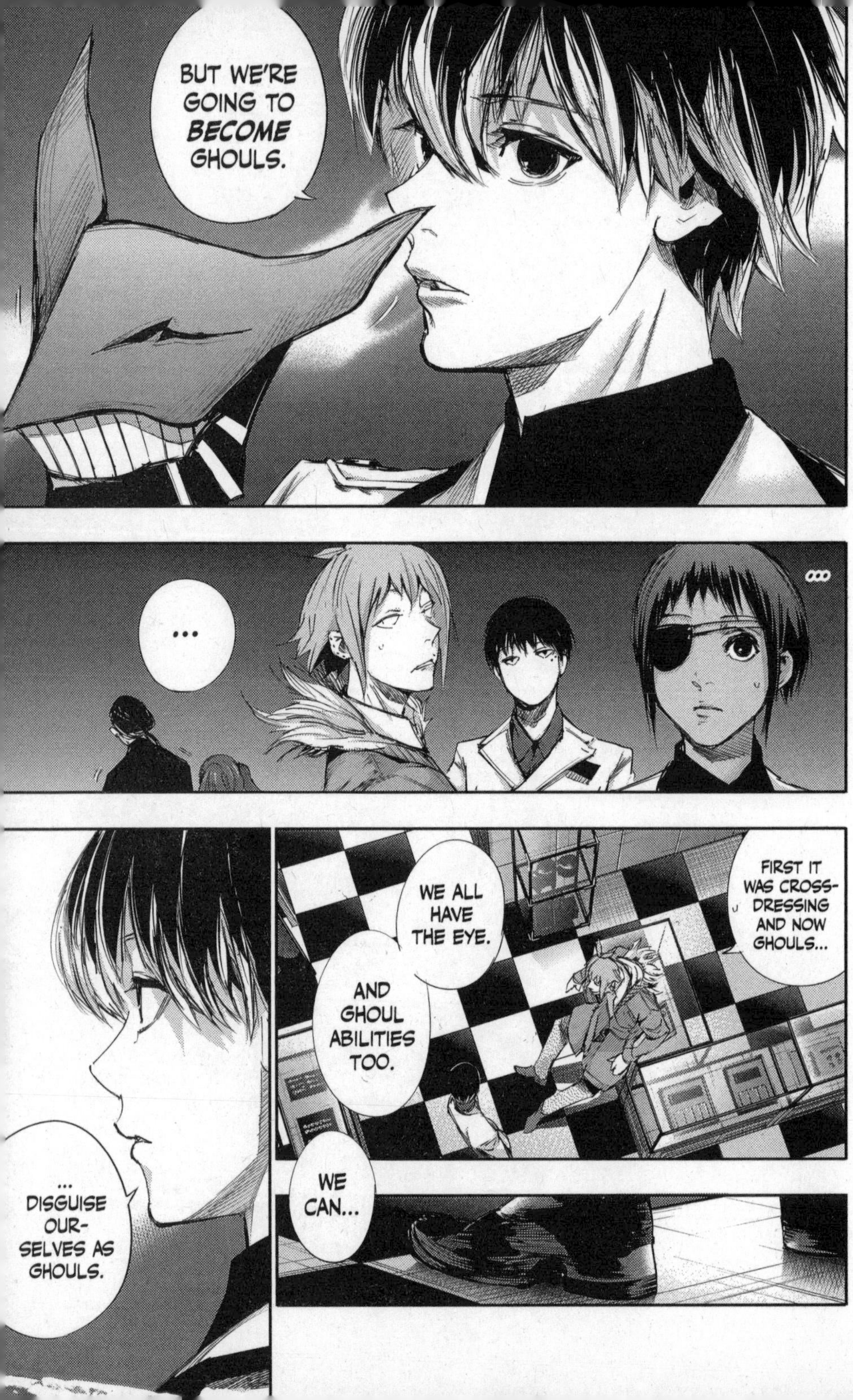
BUT WE'RE GOING TO *BECOME* GHOULS.
...
...
FIRST IT WAS CROSS-DRESSING AND NOW GHOULS...
WE ALL HAVE THE EYE.
AND GHOUL ABILITIES TOO.
WE CAN...
... DISGUISE OURSELVES AS GHOULS.

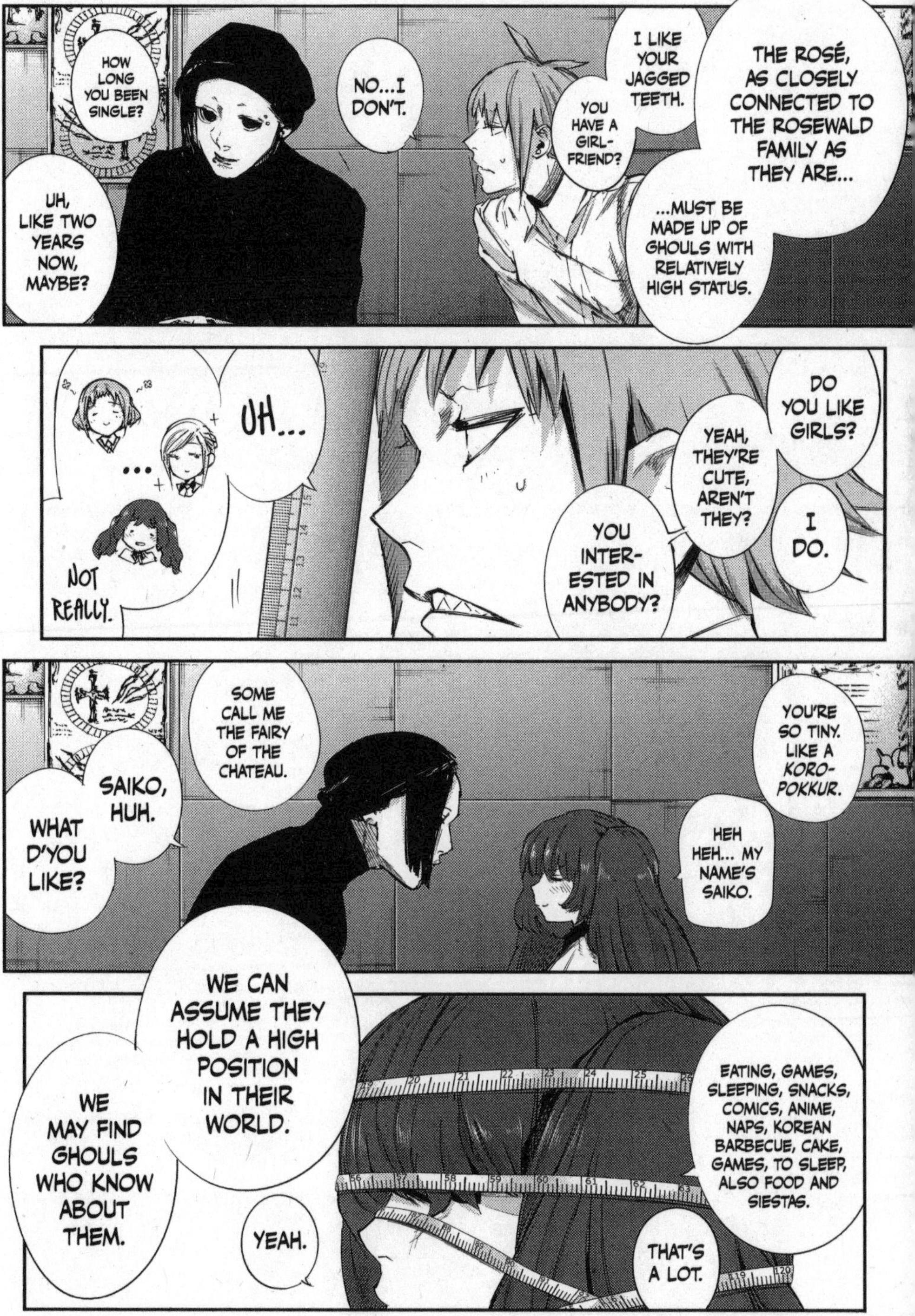
THE ROSÉ, AS CLOSELY CONNECTED TO THE ROSEWALD FAMILY AS THEY ARE...
...MUST BE MADE UP OF GHOULS WITH RELATIVELY HIGH STATUS.
I LIKE YOUR JAGGED TEETH.
YOU HAVE A GIRL-FRIEND?
NO...I DON'T.
HOW LONG YOU BEEN SINGLE?
UH, LIKE TWO YEARS NOW, MAYBE?
DO YOU LIKE GIRLS?
I DO.
YEAH, THEY'RE CUTE, AREN'T THEY?
YOU INTER-ESTED IN ANYBODY?
UH...
... NOT REALLY.
YOU'RE SO TINY. LIKE A KORO-POKKUR.
HEH HEH... MY NAME'S SAIKO.
SOME CALL ME THE FAIRY OF THE CHATEAU.
SAIKO, HUH.
WHAT D'YOU LIKE?
EATING, GAMES, SLEEPING, SNACKS, COMICS, ANIME, NAPS, KOREAN BARBECUE, CAKE, GAMES, TO SLEEP, ALSO FOOD AND SIESTAS.
THAT'S A LOT.
WE CAN ASSUME THEY HOLD A HIGH POSITION IN THEIR WORLD.
WE MAY FIND GHOULS WHO KNOW ABOUT THEM.
YEAH.

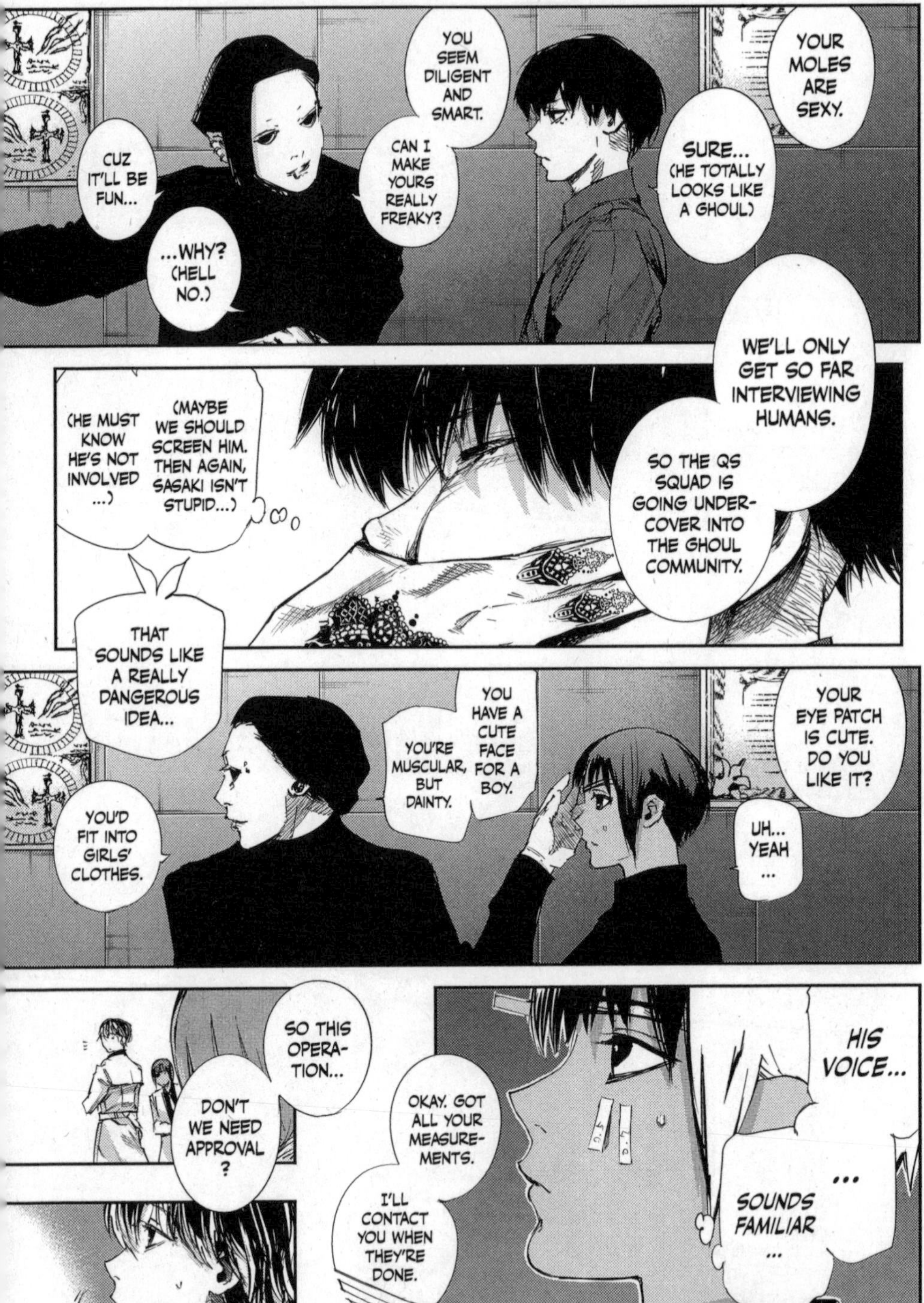
YOUR MOLES ARE SEXY.
SURE... (HE TOTALLY LOOKS LIKE A GHOUL)
YOU SEEM DILIGENT AND SMART.
CAN I MAKE YOURS REALLY FREAKY?
CUZ IT'LL BE FUN...
...WHY? (HELL NO.)
WE'LL ONLY GET SO FAR INTERVIEWING HUMANS.
SO THE QS SQUAD IS GOING UNDER-COVER INTO THE GHOUL COMMUNITY.
(MAYBE WE SHOULD SCREEN HIM. THEN AGAIN, SASAKI ISN'T STUPID...)
(HE MUST KNOW HE'S NOT INVOLVED ...)
THAT SOUNDS LIKE A REALLY DANGEROUS IDEA...
YOUR EYE PATCH IS CUTE. DO YOU LIKE IT?
UH... YEAH ...
YOU HAVE A CUTE FACE FOR A BOY.
YOU'RE MUSCULAR, BUT DAINTY.
YOU'D FIT INTO GIRLS' CLOTHES.
HIS VOICE...
... SOUNDS FAMILIAR ...
OKAY. GOT ALL YOUR MEASURE-MENTS.
I'LL CONTACT YOU WHEN THEY'RE DONE.
SO THIS OPERA-TION...
DON'T WE NEED APPROVAL ?

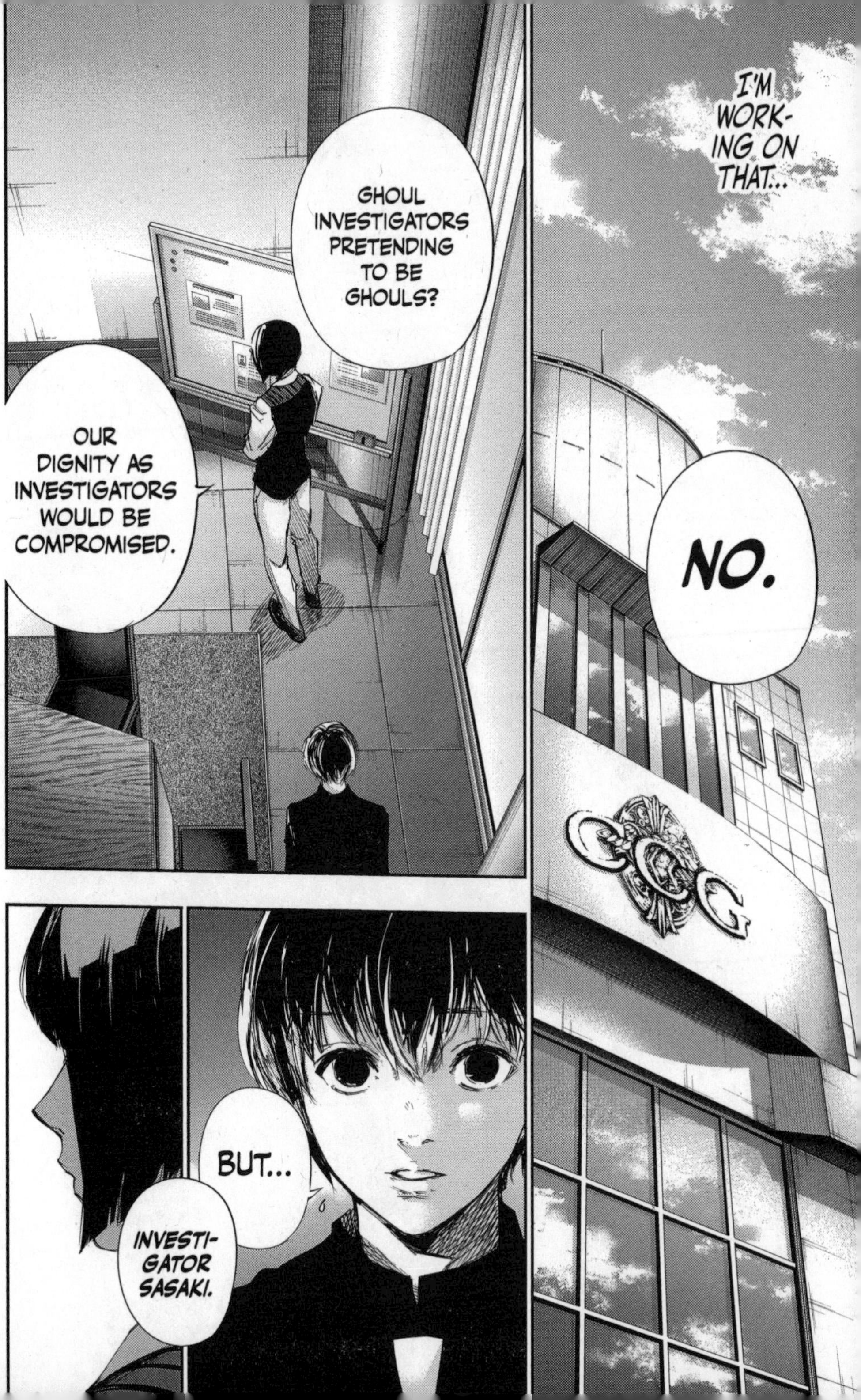
I'M WORKING-ING ON THAT...
NO.
GHOUL INVESTIGATORS PRETENDING TO BE GHOULS?
OUR DIGNITY AS INVESTIGATORS WOULD BE COMPROMISED.
BUT...
INVESTI-GATOR SASAKI.

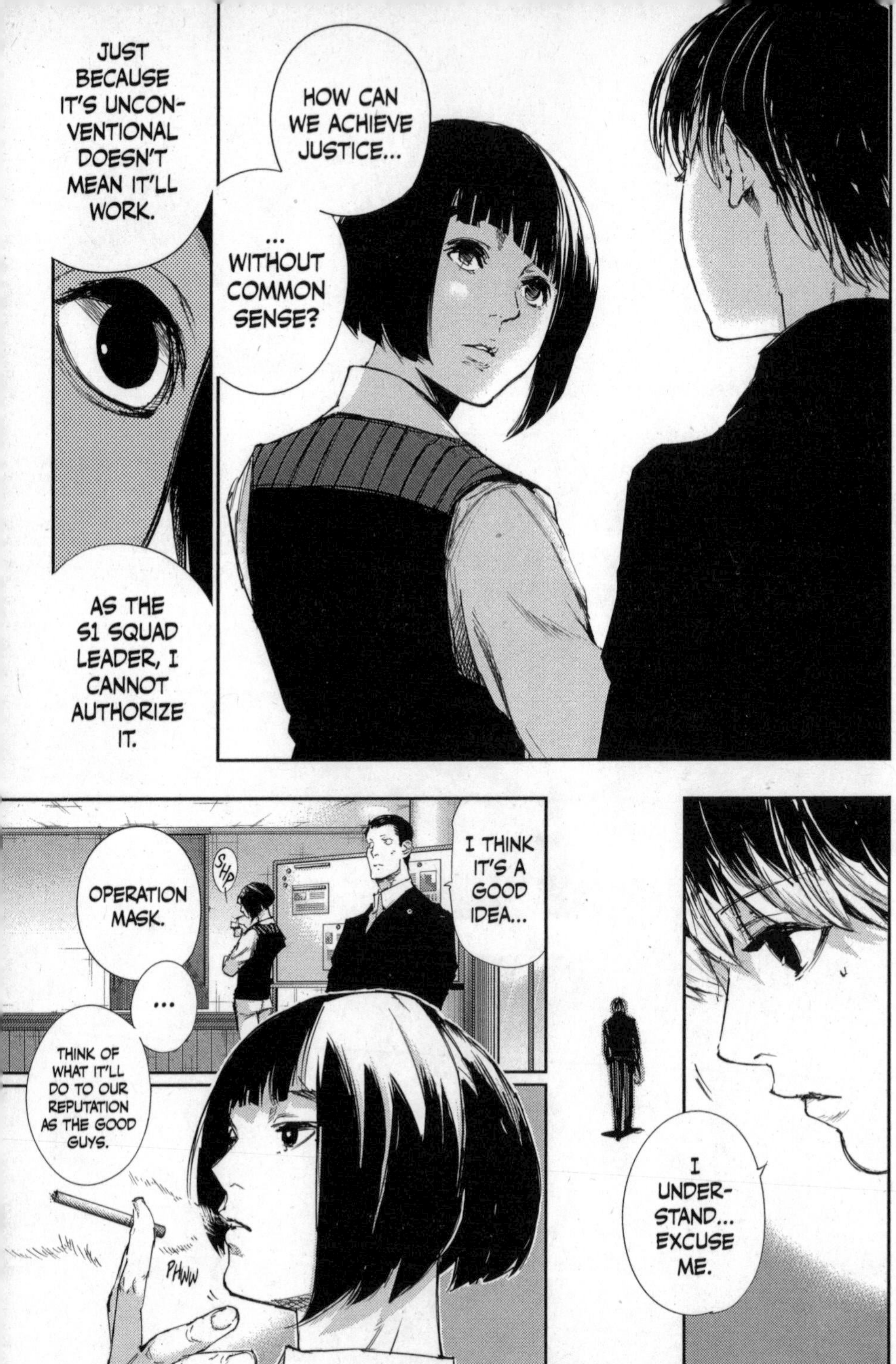
HOW CAN WE ACHIEVE JUSTICE...
...WITHOUT COMMON SENSE?
JUST BECAUSE IT'S UNCON-VENTIONAL DOESN'T MEAN IT'LL WORK.
AS THE S1 SQUAD LEADER, I CANNOT AUTHORIZE IT.
I UNDER-STAND... EXCUSE ME.
I THINK IT'S A GOOD IDEA...
SHP
OPERATION MASK.
...
THINK OF WHAT IT'LL DO TO OUR REPUTATION AS THE GOOD GUYS.
PHNW

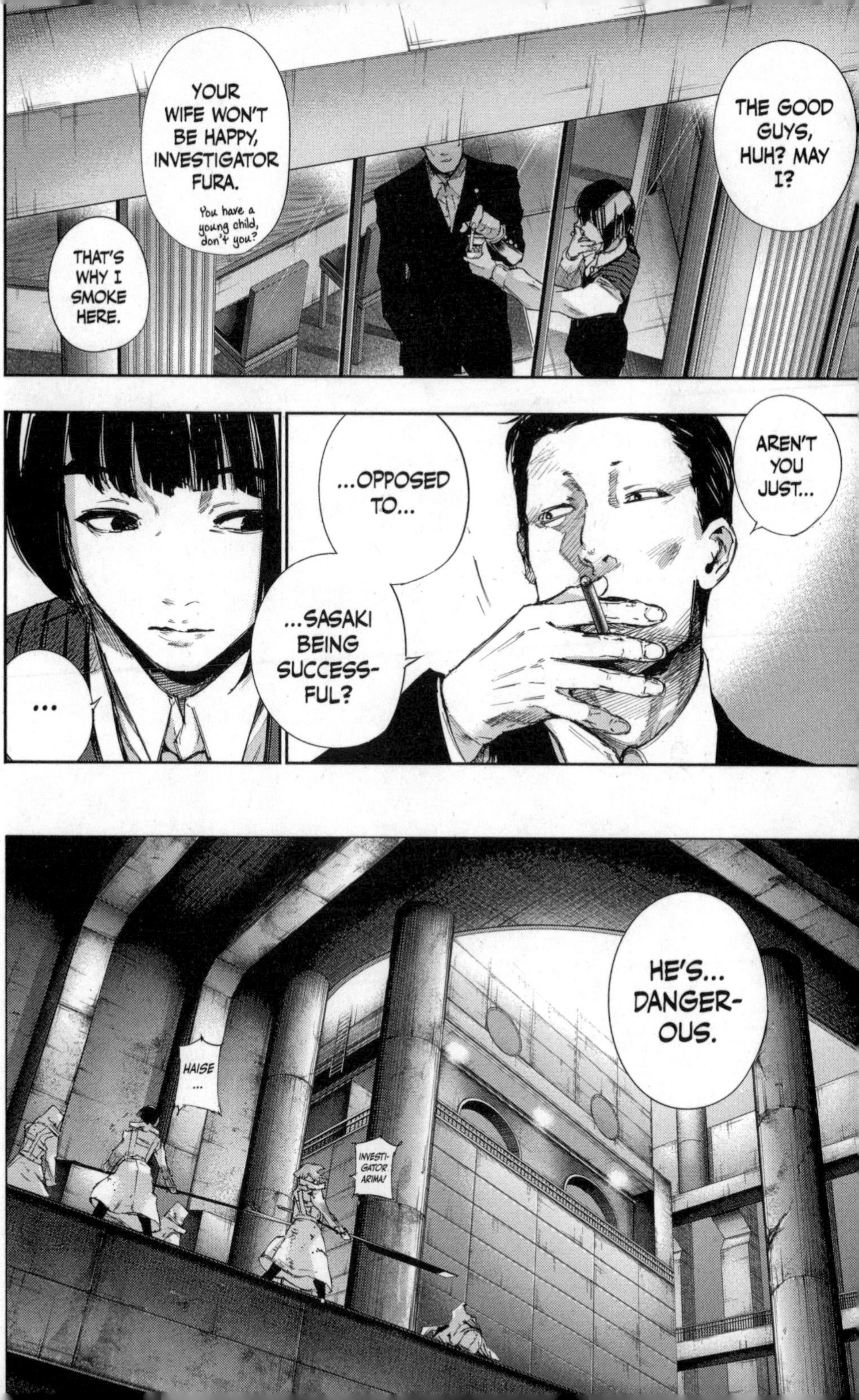
THE GOOD GUYS, HUH? MAY I?
YOUR WIFE WON'T BE HAPPY, INVESTIGATOR FURA.
You have a young child, don't you?
THAT'S WHY I SMOKE HERE.
AREN'T YOU JUST...
...OPPOSED TO...
...SASAKI BEING SUCCESS-FUL?
...
HE'S... DANGER-OUS.
HAISE...
INVESTI-GATOR ARIMA!

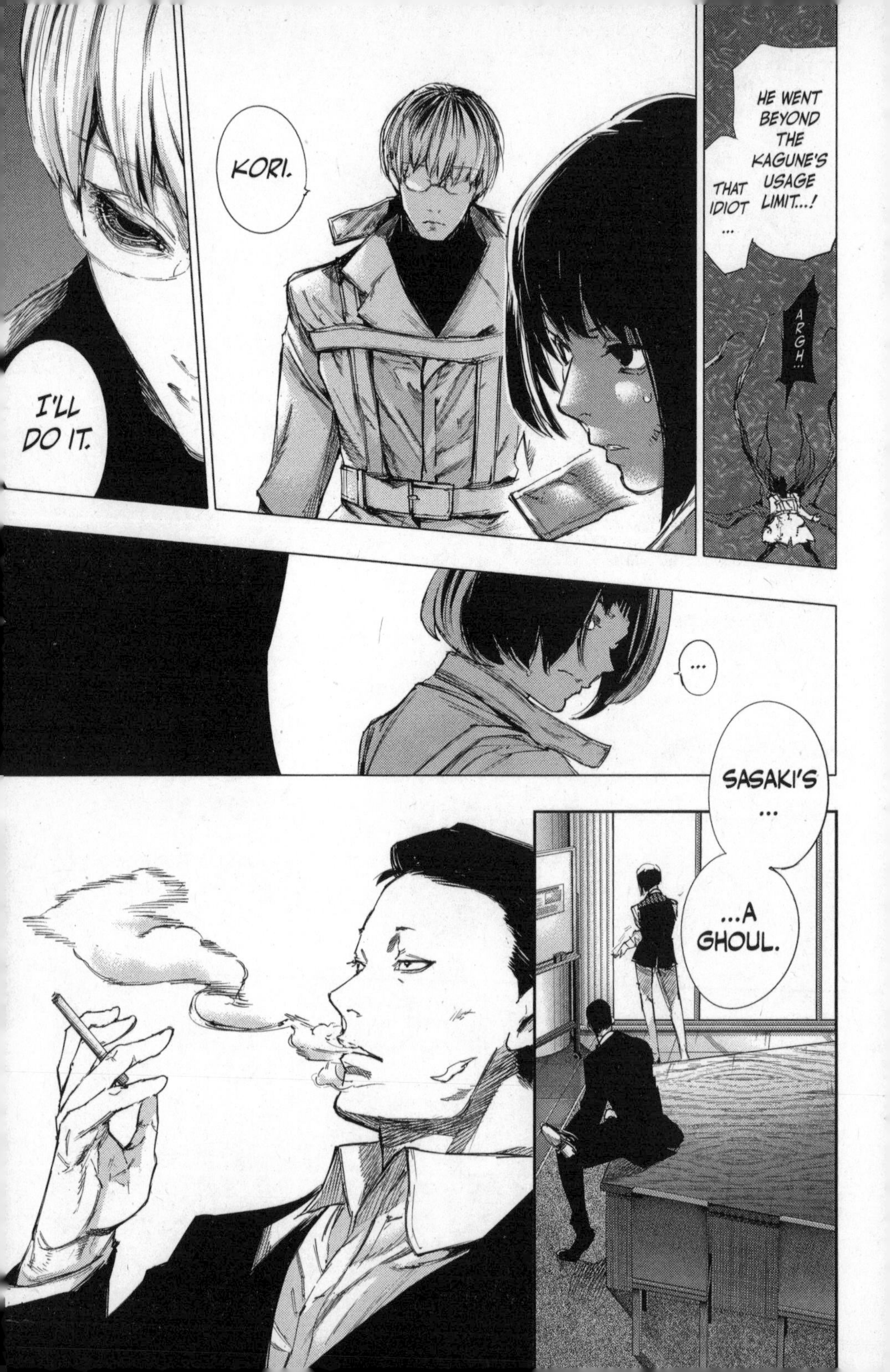
HE WENT BEYOND THE KAGUNE'S USAGE LIMIT...!
THAT IDIOT ...
ARGH...
KORI.
I'LL DO IT.
...
SASAKI'S ...
...A GHOUL.

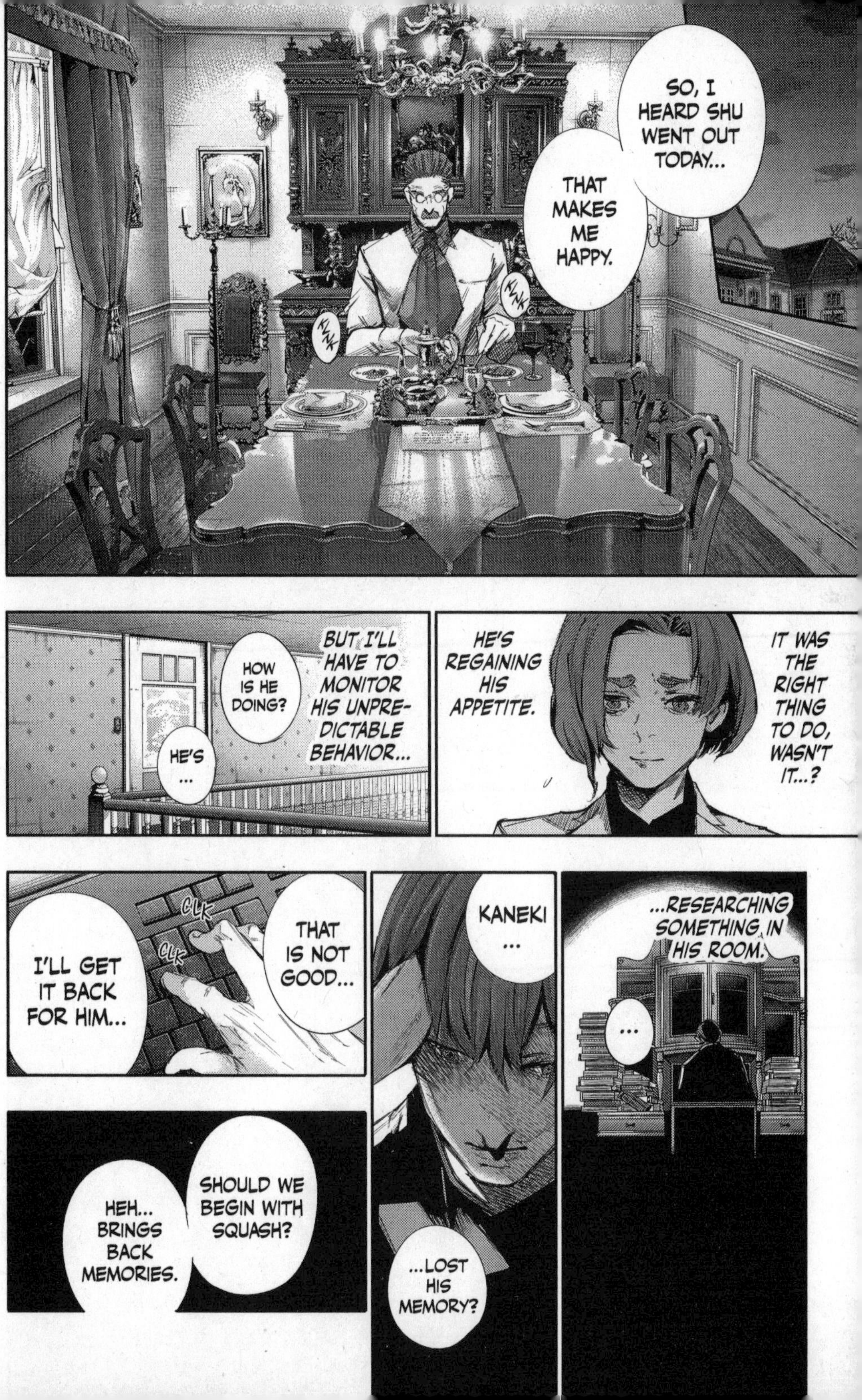
SO, I HEARD SHU WENT OUT TODAY...
THAT MAKES ME HAPPY.
KLINK
KLINK
IT WAS THE RIGHT THING TO DO, WASN'T IT...?
HE'S REGAINING HIS APPETITE.
BUT I'LL HAVE TO MONITOR HIS UNPREDICTABLE BEHAVIOR...
HOW IS HE DOING?
HE'S ...
...RESEARCHING SOMETHING IN HIS ROOM.
...
KANEKI ...
...LOST HIS MEMORY?
THAT IS NOT GOOD...
CLK
CLK
I'LL GET IT BACK FOR HIM...
SHOULD WE BEGIN WITH SQUASH?
HEH... BRINGS BACK MEMORIES.

CVK CVK

SIR ...

THIS WAS POSTED ON THE CCG WEBSITE...

TO ROSÉ ...?

"What you are about... contains shocking material... Viewer discretion is advis...

Dane...

...FOR CONVE-NIENCE.

THAT'S WHAT WE CALL YOU...

HELLO, ROSÉ.

I THOUGHT I'D GIVE YOU AN UPDATE ON ONE OF YOUR APPREHENDED MEMBERS.

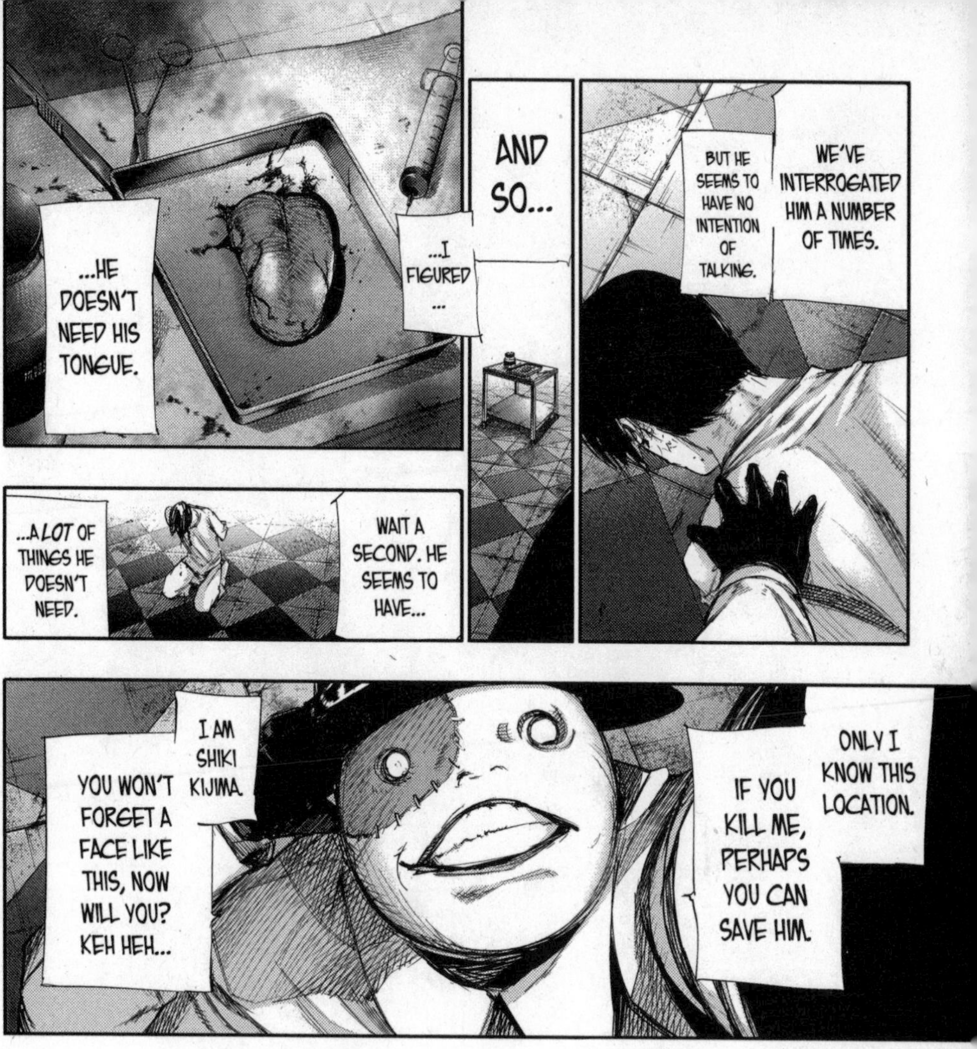
WE'VE INTERROGATED HIM A NUMBER OF TIMES.
BUT HE SEEMS TO HAVE NO INTENTION OF TALKING.
AND SO...
...I FIGURED...
...HE DOESN'T NEED HIS TONGUE.
WAIT A SECOND. HE SEEMS TO HAVE...
...A *LOT* OF THINGS HE DOESN'T NEED.
ONLY I KNOW THIS LOCATION.
IF YOU KILL ME, PERHAPS YOU CAN SAVE HIM.
I AM SHIKI KIJIMA.
YOU WON'T FORGET A FACE LIKE THIS, NOW WILL YOU? KEH HEH...

COME KILL ME. DAY OR NIGHT.

I'LL BE WAITING, ROSÉ.

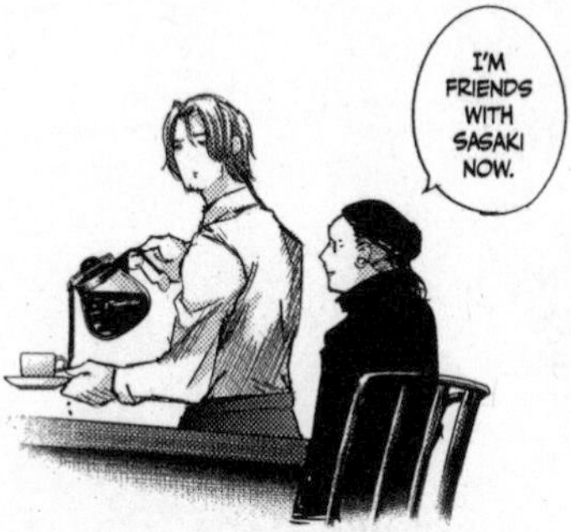
I'M FRIENDS WITH SASAKI NOW.

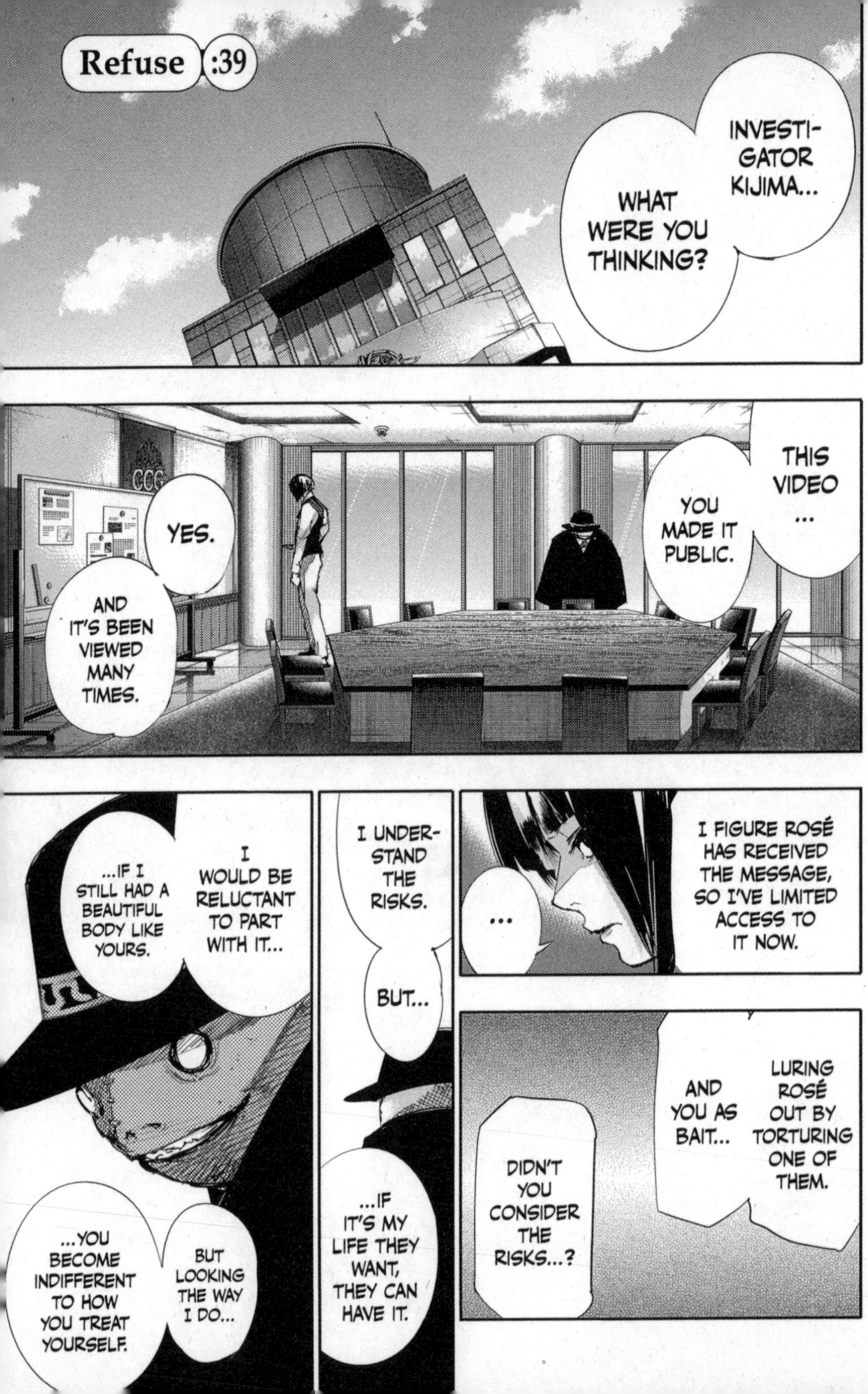
Refuse :39
INVESTIGATOR KIJIMA...
WHAT WERE YOU THINKING?
THIS VIDEO...
YOU MADE IT PUBLIC.
YES.
AND IT'S BEEN VIEWED MANY TIMES.
I FIGURE ROSÉ HAS RECEIVED THE MESSAGE, SO I'VE LIMITED ACCESS TO IT NOW.
...
LURING ROSÉ OUT BY TORTURING ONE OF THEM.
AND YOU AS BAIT...
DIDN'T YOU CONSIDER THE RISKS...?
I UNDERSTAND THE RISKS.
BUT...
...IF IT'S MY LIFE THEY WANT, THEY CAN HAVE IT.
I WOULD BE RELUCTANT TO PART WITH IT...
...IF I STILL HAD A BEAUTIFUL BODY LIKE YOURS.
BUT LOOKING THE WAY I DO...
...YOU BECOME INDIFFERENT TO HOW YOU TREAT YOURSELF.

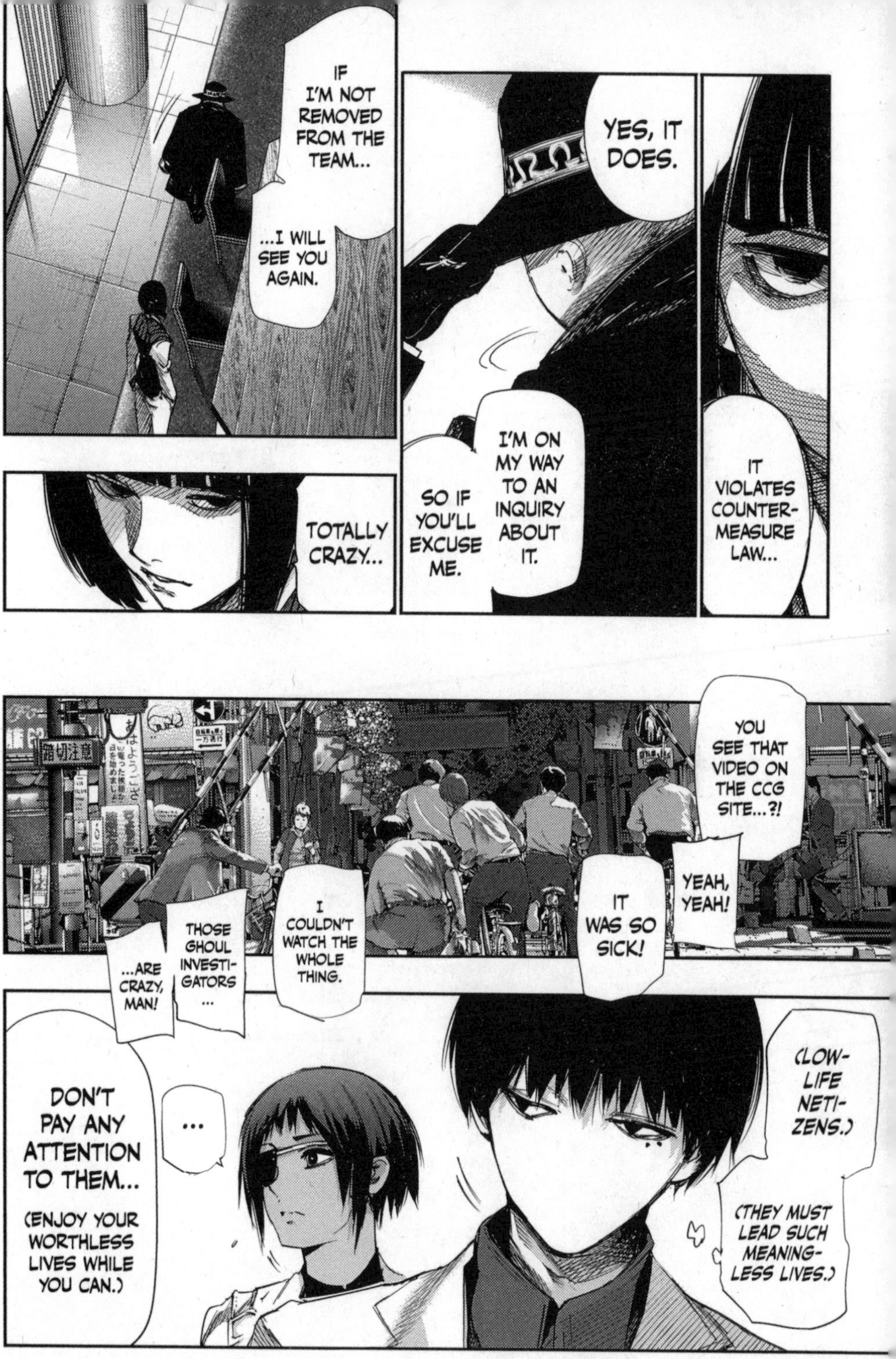
IT VIOLATES COUNTER-MEASURE LAW...
YES, IT DOES.
I'M ON MY WAY TO AN INQUIRY ABOUT IT.
SO IF YOU'LL EXCUSE ME.
IF I'M NOT REMOVED FROM THE TEAM...
...I WILL SEE YOU AGAIN.
TOTALLY CRAZY...
YOU SEE THAT VIDEO ON THE CCG SITE...?!
YEAH, YEAH!
踏切注意
IT WAS SO SICK!
I COULDN'T WATCH THE WHOLE THING.
THOSE GHOUL INVESTI-GATORS...
...ARE CRAZY, MAN!
(LOW-LIFE NETI-ZENS.)
(THEY MUST LEAD SUCH MEANING-LESS LIVES.)
...
DON'T PAY ANY ATTENTION TO THEM...
(ENJOY YOUR WORTHLESS LIVES WHILE YOU CAN.)

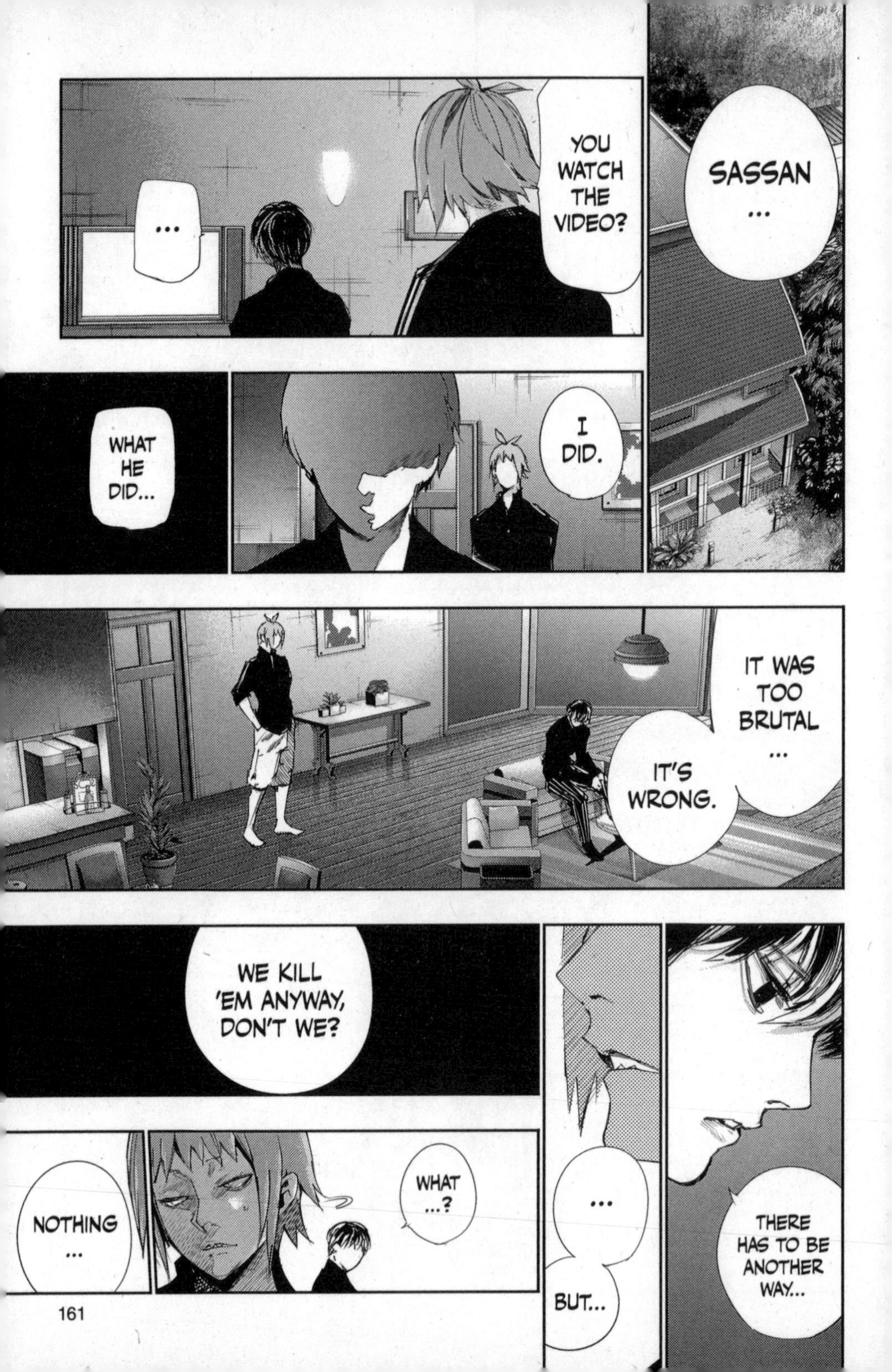
SASSAN...
YOU WATCH THE VIDEO?
...
I DID.
WHAT HE DID...
IT WAS TOO BRUTAL...
IT'S WRONG.
THERE HAS TO BE ANOTHER WAY...
...
BUT...
WE KILL 'EM ANYWAY, DON'T WE?
WHAT...?
NOTHING...

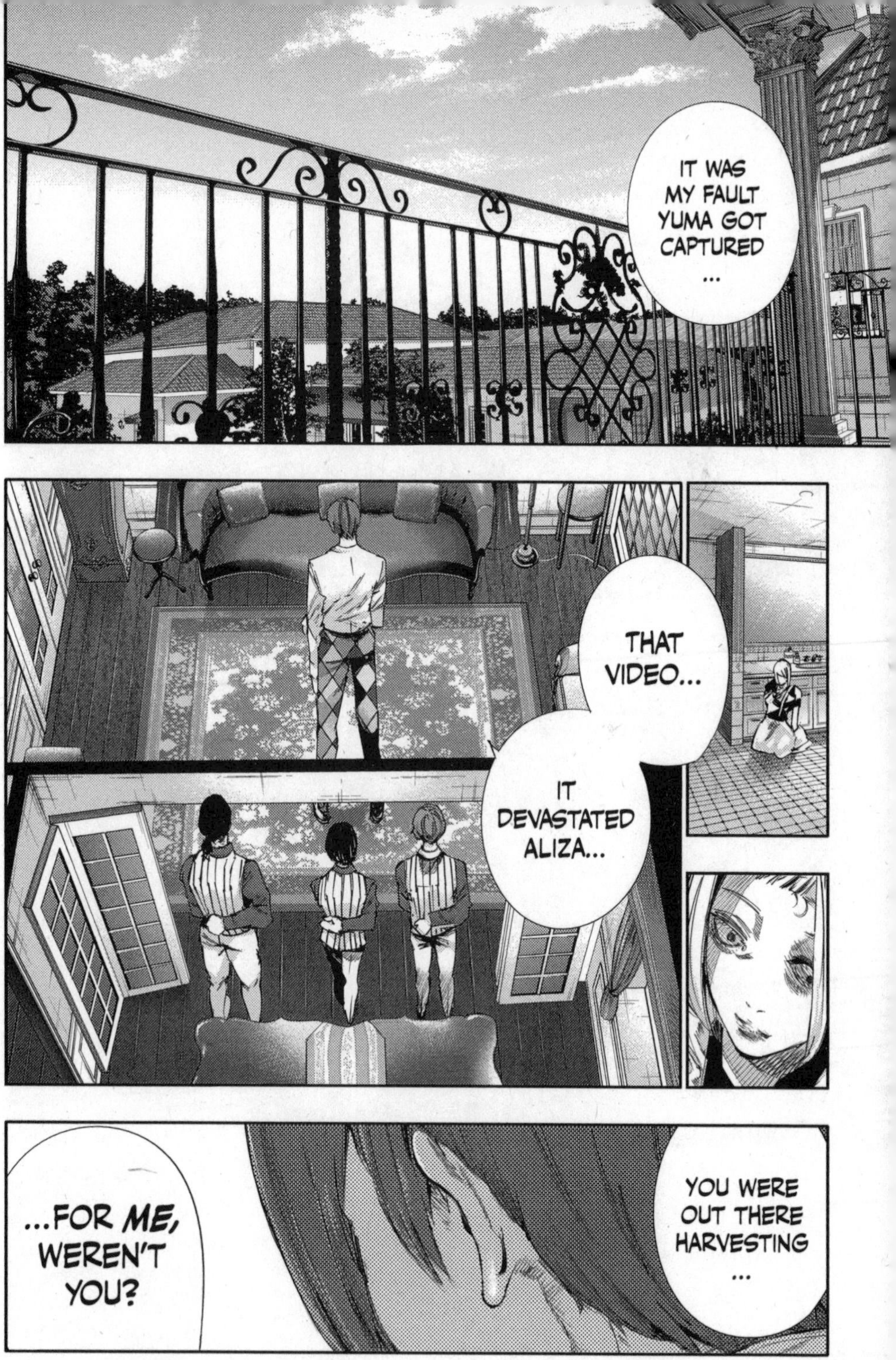

IT WAS MY FAULT YUMA GOT CAPTURED ...
THAT VIDEO...
IT DEVASTATED ALIZA...
YOU WERE OUT THERE HARVESTING ...
...FOR *ME*, WEREN'T YOU?

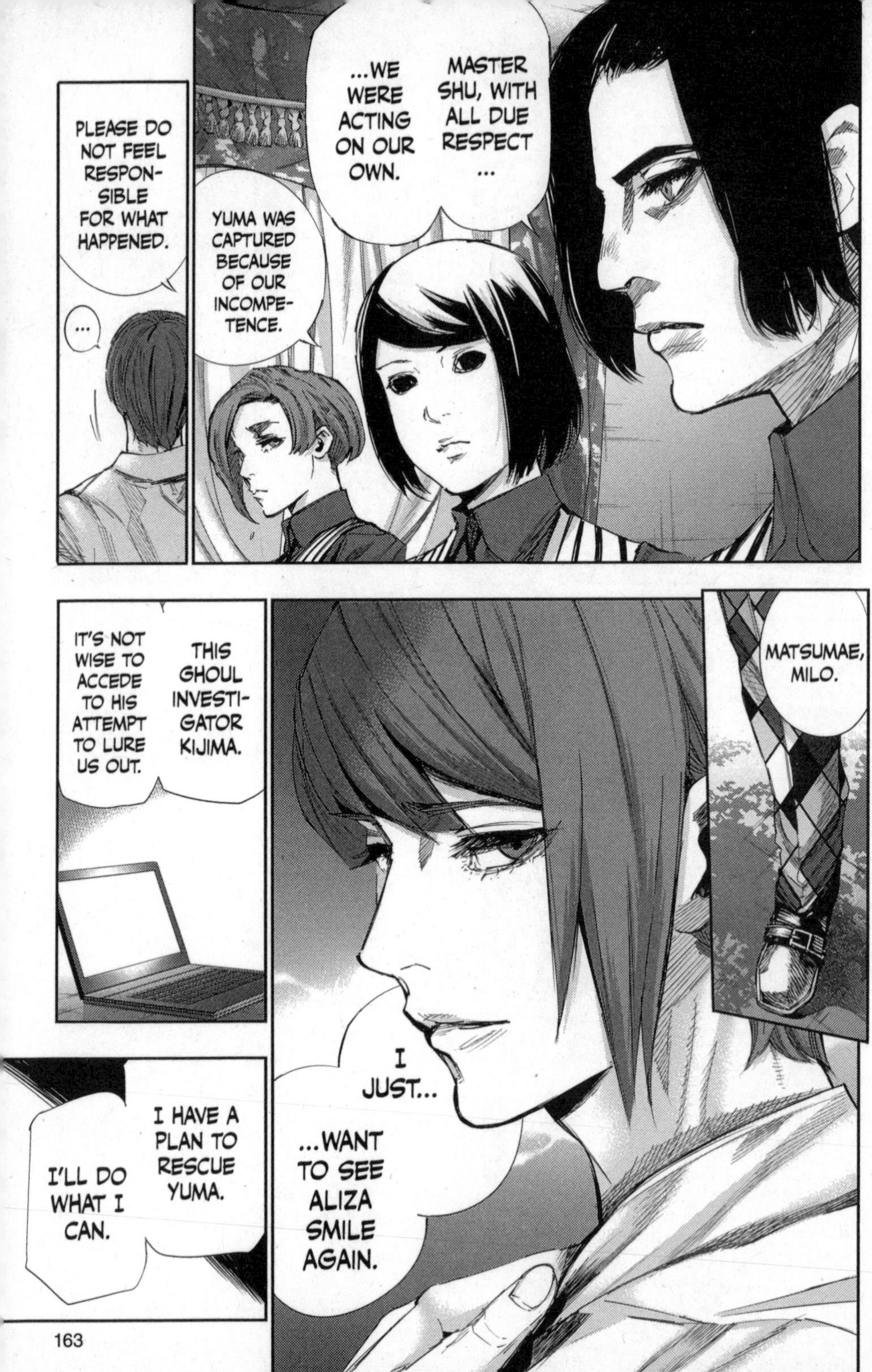
MASTER SHU, WITH ALL DUE RESPECT ...
...WE WERE ACTING ON OUR OWN.
YUMA WAS CAPTURED BECAUSE OF OUR INCOMPETENCE.
PLEASE DO NOT FEEL RESPON-SIBLE FOR WHAT HAPPENED.
...
MATSUMAE, MILO.
I JUST...
...WANT TO SEE ALIZA SMILE AGAIN.
THIS GHOUL INVESTI-GATOR KIJIMA.
IT'S NOT WISE TO ACCEDE TO HIS ATTEMPT TO LURE US OUT.
I HAVE A PLAN TO RESCUE YUMA.
I'LL DO WHAT I CAN.

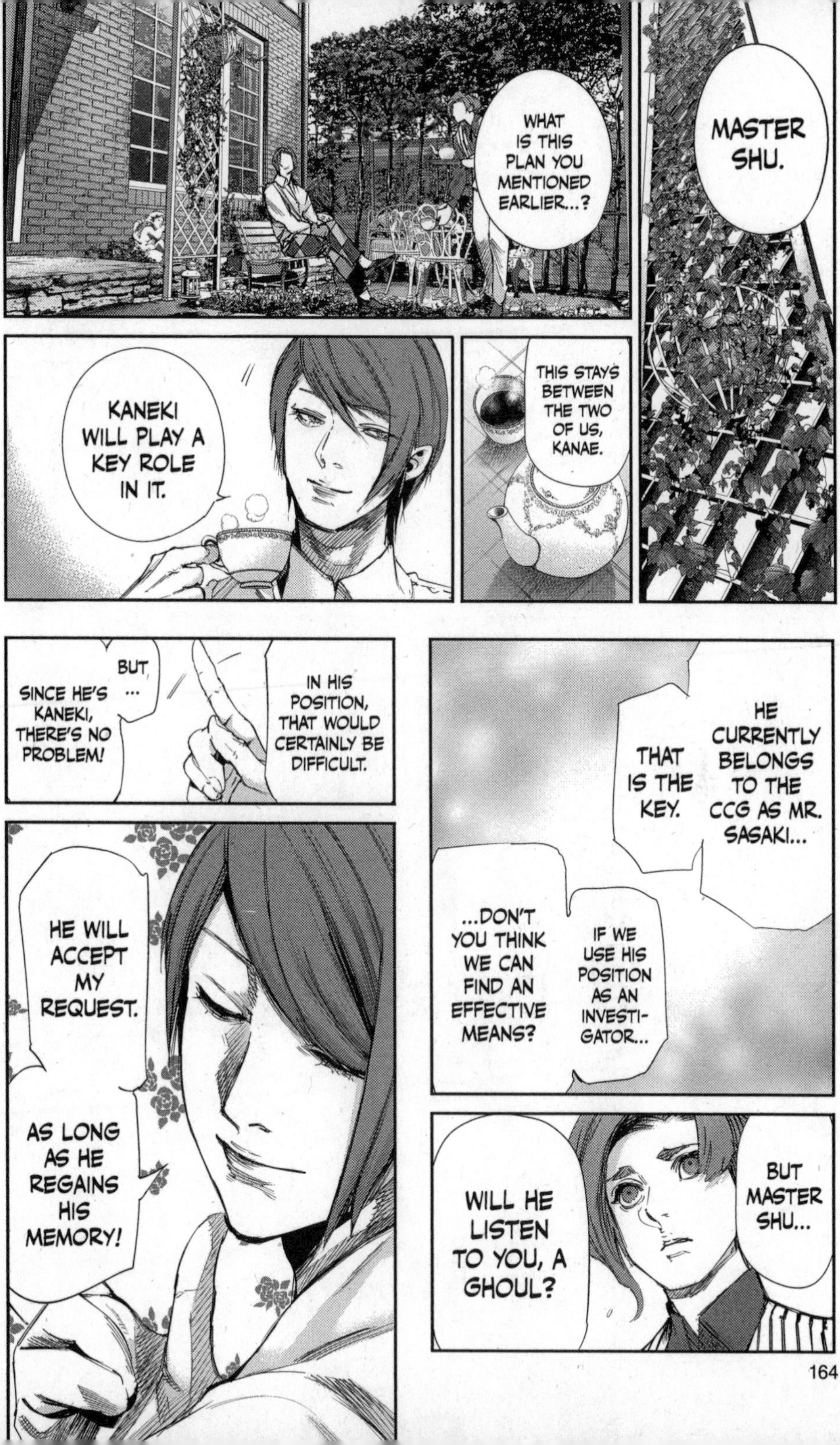
MASTER SHU.
WHAT IS THIS PLAN YOU MENTIONED EARLIER...?
THIS STAYS BETWEEN THE TWO OF US, KANAE.
KANEKI WILL PLAY A KEY ROLE IN IT.
HE CURRENTLY BELONGS TO THE CCG AS MR. SASAKI...
THAT IS THE KEY.
IF WE USE HIS POSITION AS AN INVESTIGATOR...
...DON'T YOU THINK WE CAN FIND AN EFFECTIVE MEANS?
BUT MASTER SHU...
WILL HE LISTEN TO YOU, A GHOUL?
IN HIS POSITION, THAT WOULD CERTAINLY BE DIFFICULT.
BUT...
SINCE HE'S KANEKI, THERE'S NO PROBLEM!
HE WILL ACCEPT MY REQUEST.
AS LONG AS HE REGAINS HIS MEMORY!

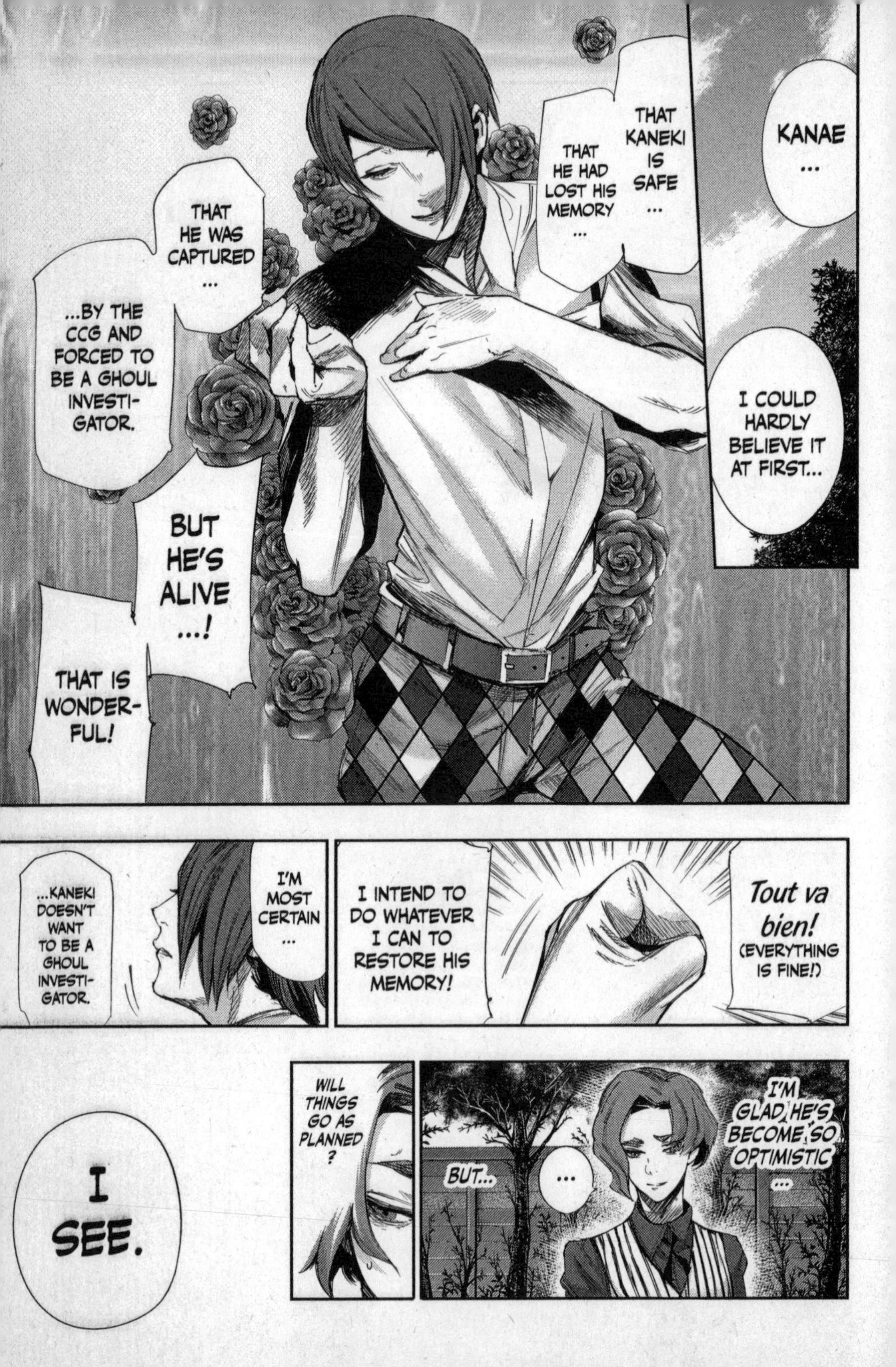
KANAE ...
I COULD HARDLY BELIEVE IT AT FIRST...
THAT KANEKI IS SAFE ...
THAT HE HAD LOST HIS MEMORY ...
THAT HE WAS CAPTURED ...
...BY THE CCG AND FORCED TO BE A GHOUL INVESTI-GATOR.
BUT HE'S ALIVE ...!
THAT IS WONDER-FUL!
Tout va bien! (EVERYTHING IS FINE!)
I INTEND TO DO WHATEVER I CAN TO RESTORE HIS MEMORY!
I'M MOST CERTAIN ...
...KANEKI DOESN'T WANT TO BE A GHOUL INVESTI-GATOR.
I'M GLAD HE'S BECOME SO OPTIMISTIC ...
...
BUT...
WILL THINGS GO AS PLANNED ?
I SEE.

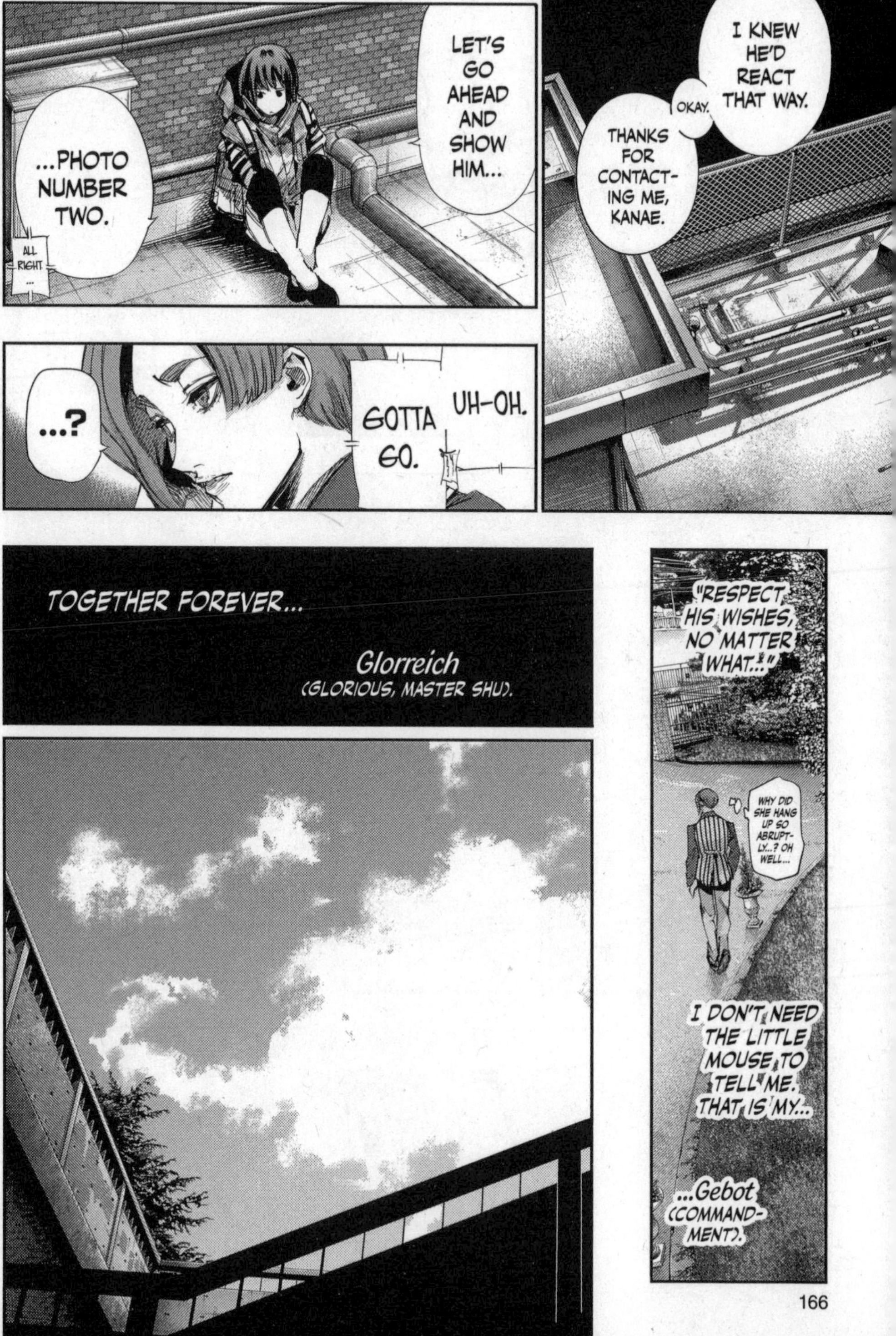
I KNEW HE'D REACT THAT WAY.
OKAY.
THANKS FOR CONTACTING ME, KANAE.
LET'S GO AHEAD AND SHOW HIM...
...PHOTO NUMBER TWO.
ALL RIGHT. ...
UH-OH.
GOTTA GO.
...?
"RESPECT HIS WISHES, NO MATTER WHAT..."
WHY DID SHE HANG UP SO ABRUPTLY...? OH WELL...
I DON'T NEED THE LITTLE MOUSE TO TELL ME. THAT IS MY...
...Gebot (COMMANDMENT).
TOGETHER FOREVER...
Glorreich (GLORIOUS, MASTER SHU).

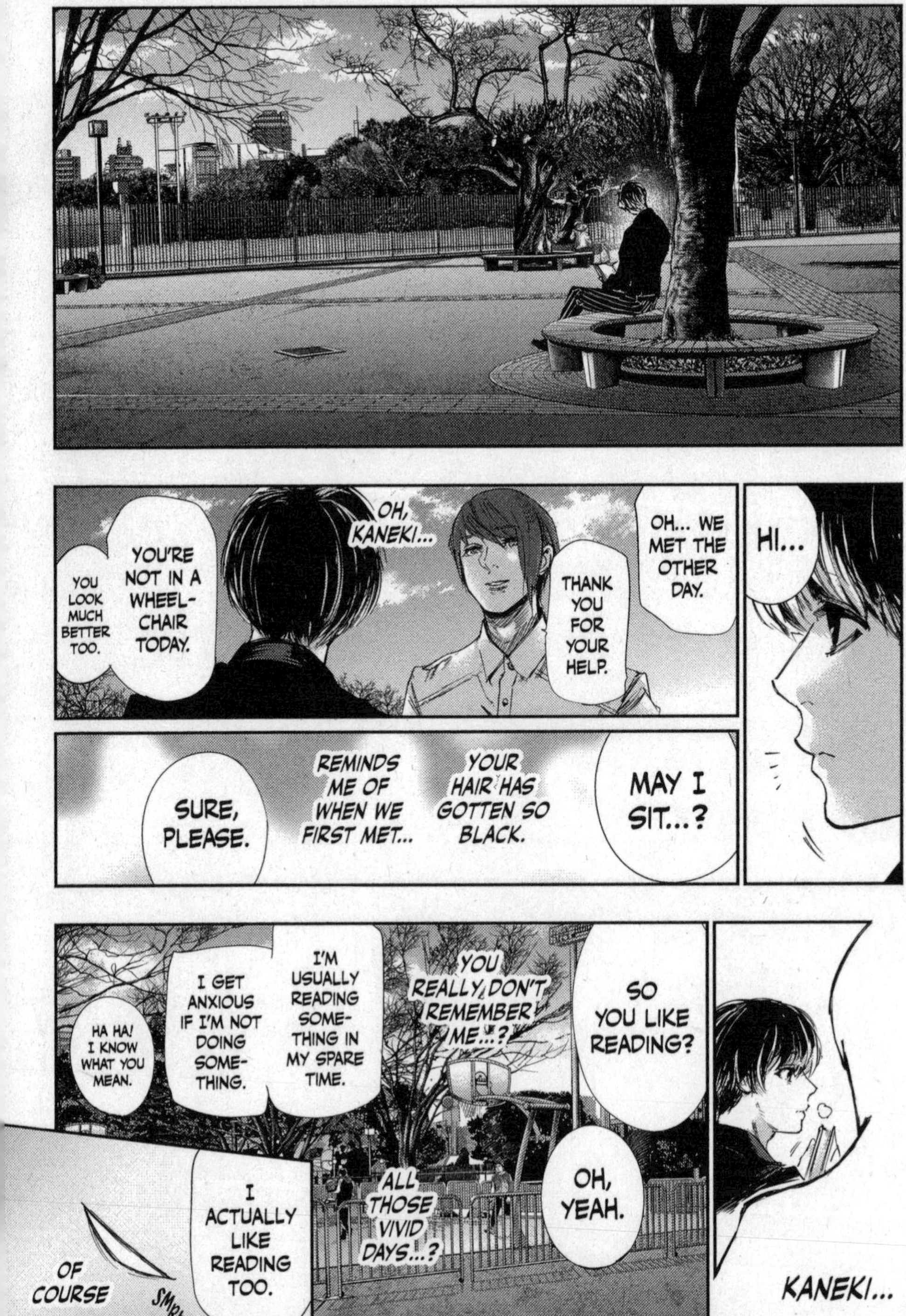
HI...
OH... WE MET THE OTHER DAY.
THANK YOU FOR YOUR HELP.
OH, KANEKI...
YOU'RE NOT IN A WHEEL-CHAIR TODAY.
YOU LOOK MUCH BETTER TOO.
MAY I SIT...?
YOUR HAIR HAS GOTTEN SO BLACK.
REMINDS ME OF WHEN WE FIRST MET...
SURE, PLEASE.
KANEKI...
SO YOU LIKE READING?
YOU REALLY DON'T REMEMBER ME...?
I'M USUALLY READING SOME-THING IN MY SPARE TIME.
I GET ANXIOUS IF I'M NOT DOING SOME-THING.
HA HA! I KNOW WHAT YOU MEAN.
OH, YEAH.
ALL THOSE VIVID DAYS...?
I ACTUALLY LIKE READING TOO.
SMRK
OF COURSE...

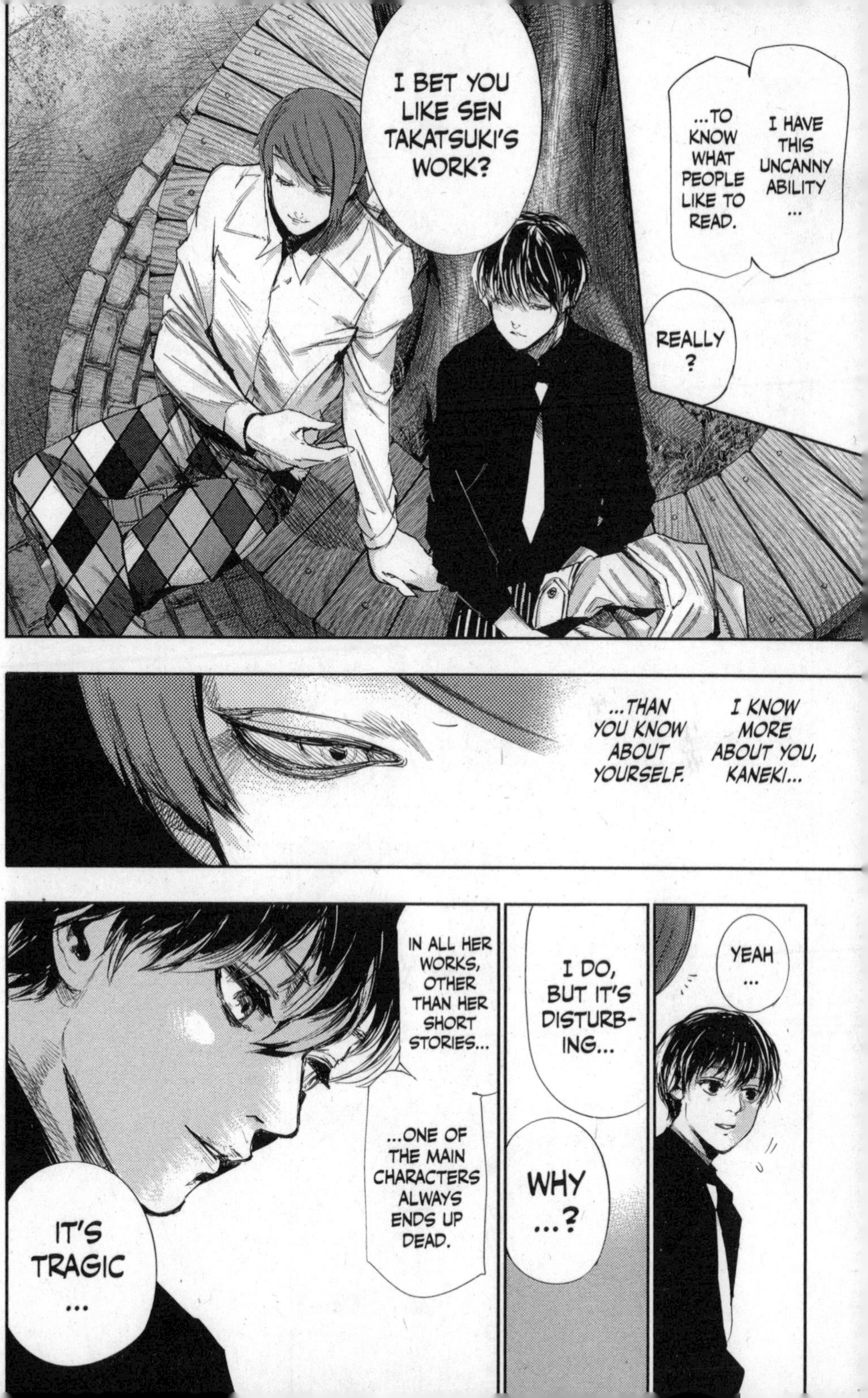
I HAVE THIS UNCANNY ABILITY...
...TO KNOW WHAT PEOPLE LIKE TO READ.
I BET YOU LIKE SEN TAKATSUKI'S WORK?
REALLY?
I KNOW MORE ABOUT YOU, KANEKI...
...THAN YOU KNOW ABOUT YOURSELF.
YEAH...
I DO, BUT IT'S DISTURB-ING...
WHY...?
IN ALL HER WORKS, OTHER THAN HER SHORT STORIES...
...ONE OF THE MAIN CHARACTERS ALWAYS ENDS UP DEAD.
IT'S TRAGIC...

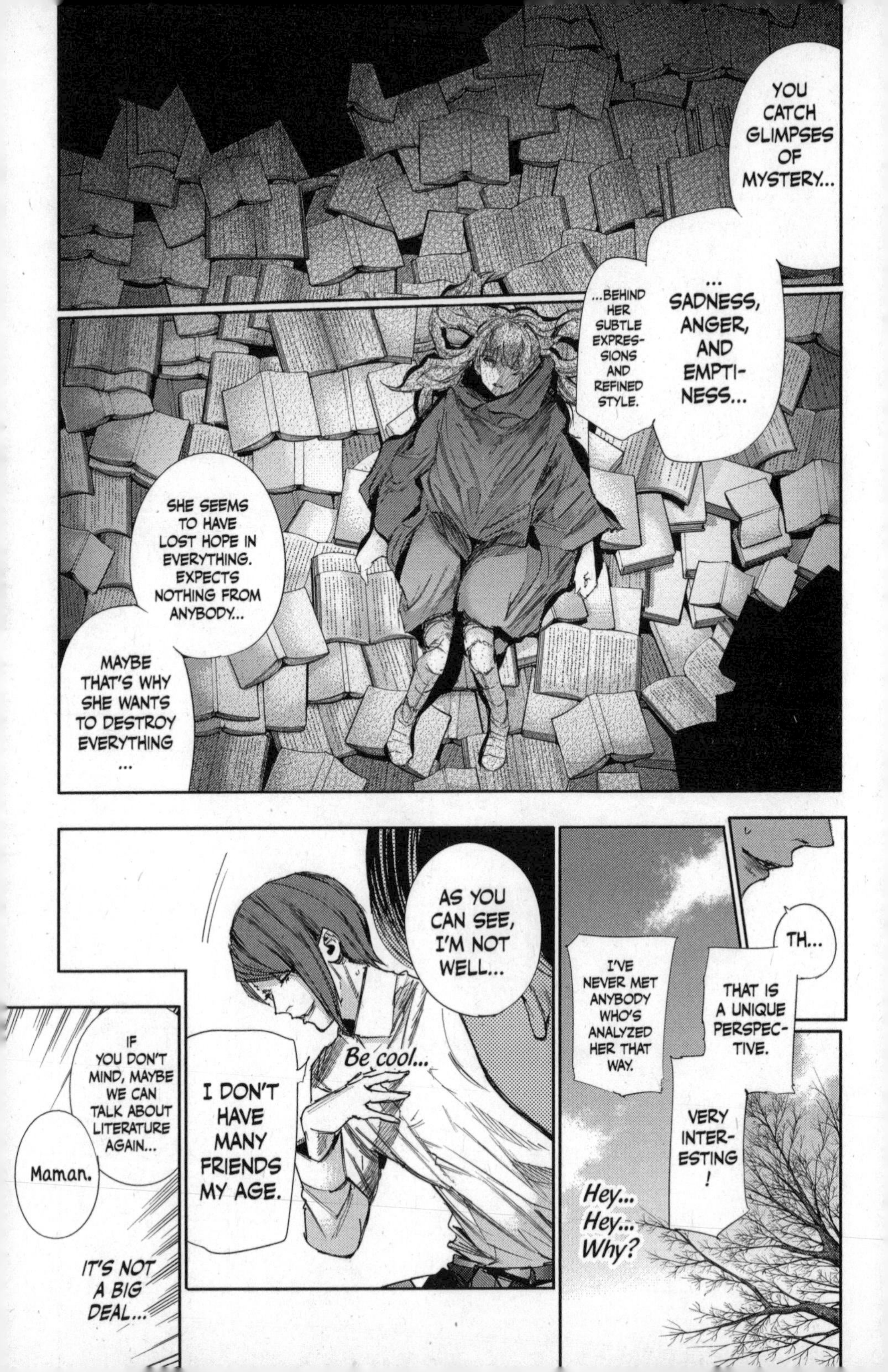
YOU CATCH GLIMPSES OF MYSTERY...
... SADNESS, ANGER, AND EMPTINESS...
...BEHIND HER SUBTLE EXPRESSIONS AND REFINED STYLE.
SHE SEEMS TO HAVE LOST HOPE IN EVERYTHING. EXPECTS NOTHING FROM ANYBODY...
MAYBE THAT'S WHY SHE WANTS TO DESTROY EVERYTHING ...
TH...
THAT IS A UNIQUE PERSPECTIVE.
I'VE NEVER MET ANYBODY WHO'S ANALYZED HER THAT WAY.
VERY INTERESTING!
Hey... Hey... Why?
AS YOU CAN SEE, I'M NOT WELL...
Be cool...
I DON'T HAVE MANY FRIENDS MY AGE.
IF YOU DON'T MIND, MAYBE WE CAN TALK ABOUT LITERATURE AGAIN...
Maman.
IT'S NOT A BIG DEAL...

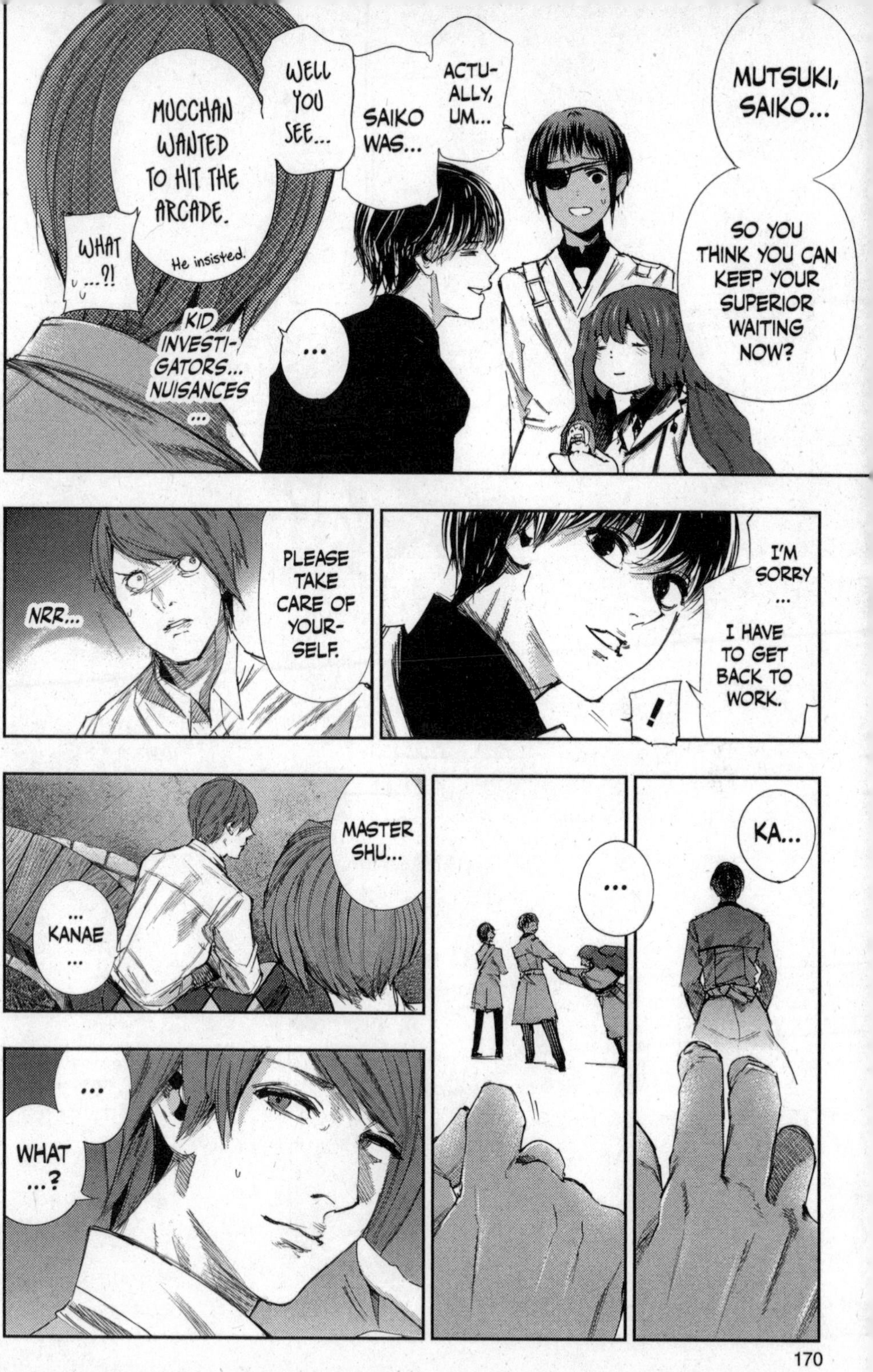
MUTSUKI, SAIKO...
SO YOU THINK YOU CAN KEEP YOUR SUPERIOR WAITING NOW?
ACTU-ALLY, UM...
SAIKO WAS...
WELL YOU SEE...
MUCCHAN WANTED TO HIT THE ARCADE.
He insisted.
WHAT ...?!
...
KID INVESTI-GATORS... NUISANCES ...
I'M SORRY ...
I HAVE TO GET BACK TO WORK.
!
PLEASE TAKE CARE OF YOUR-SELF.
NRR...
KA...
...
MASTER SHU...
... KANAE ...
...
WHAT ...?

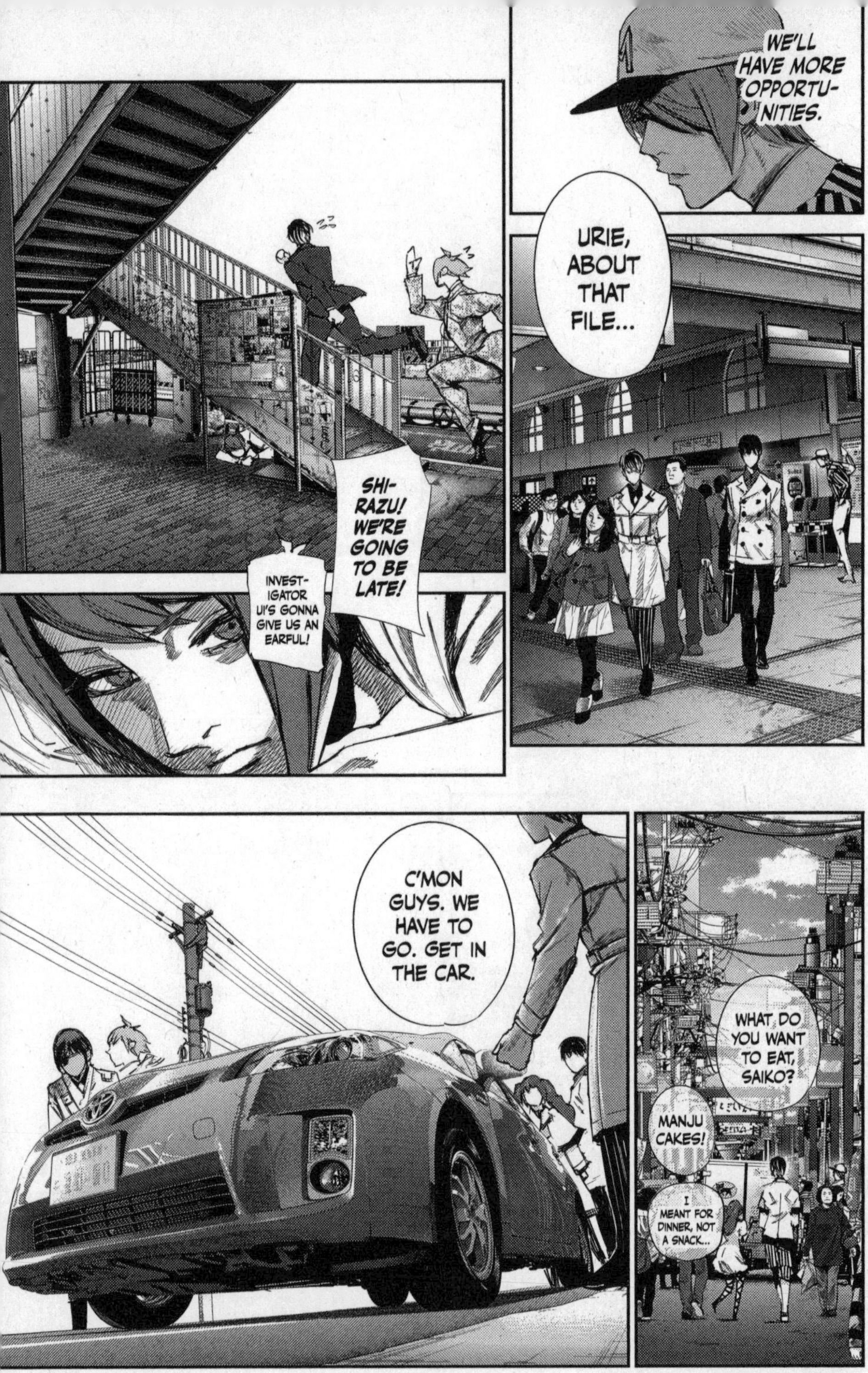
WE'LL HAVE MORE OPPORTU-NITIES.
URIE, ABOUT THAT FILE...
SHI-RAZU! WE'RE GOING TO BE LATE!
INVEST-IGATOR UI'S GONNA GIVE US AN EARFUL!
WHAT DO YOU WANT TO EAT, SAIKO?
MANJU CAKES!
I MEANT FOR DINNER, NOT A SNACK...
C'MON GUYS. WE HAVE TO GO. GET IN THE CAR.

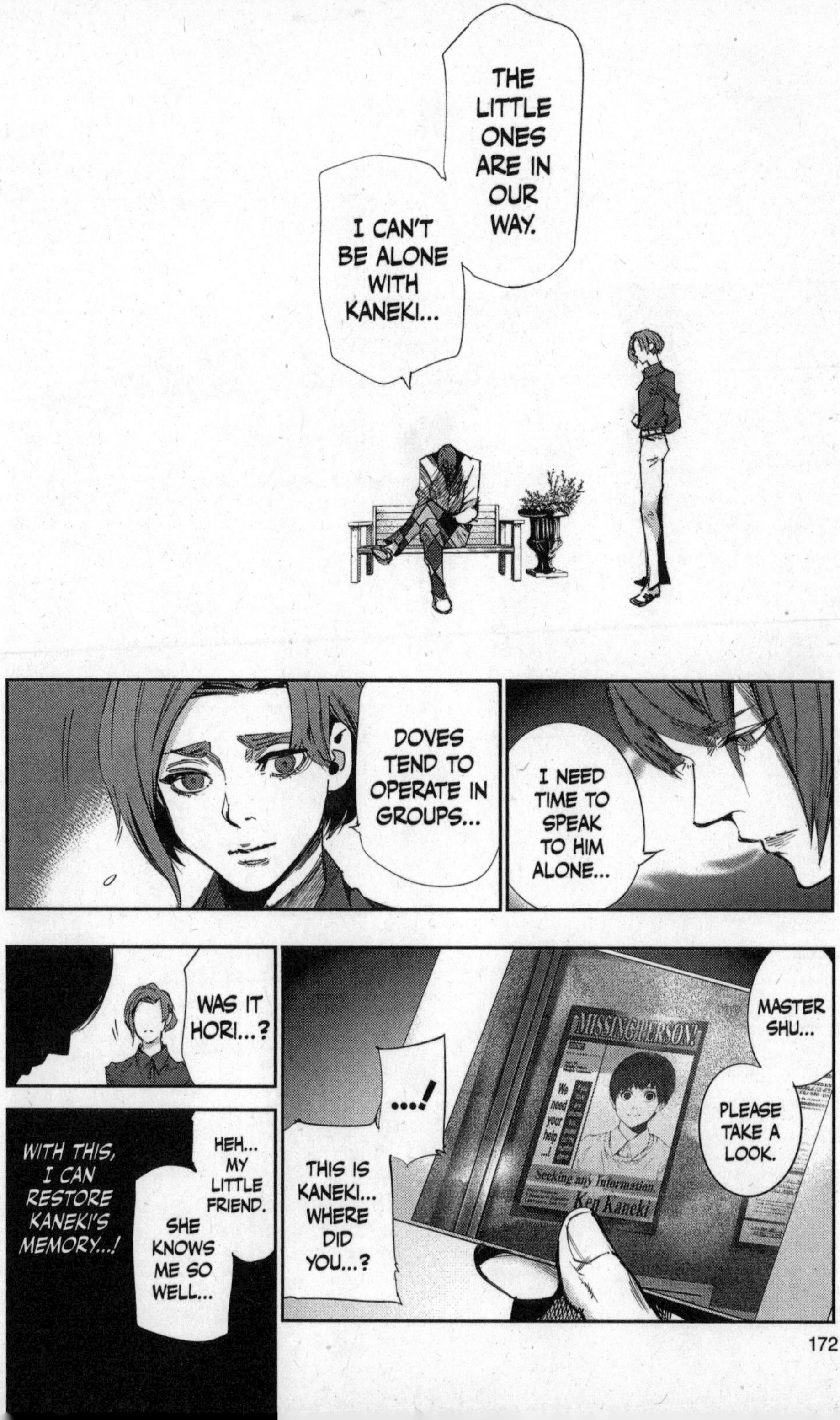
THE LITTLE ONES ARE IN OUR WAY.
I CAN'T BE ALONE WITH KANEKI...
I NEED TIME TO SPEAK TO HIM ALONE...
DOVES TEND TO OPERATE IN GROUPS...
MASTER SHU...
PLEASE TAKE A LOOK.
MISSING PERSON!
We need your help ...!
Seeking any Information
Ken Kaneki
...!
THIS IS KANEKI... WHERE DID YOU...?
WAS IT HORI...?
HEH... MY LITTLE FRIEND.
SHE KNOWS ME SO WELL...
WITH THIS, I CAN RESTORE KANEKI'S MEMORY...!

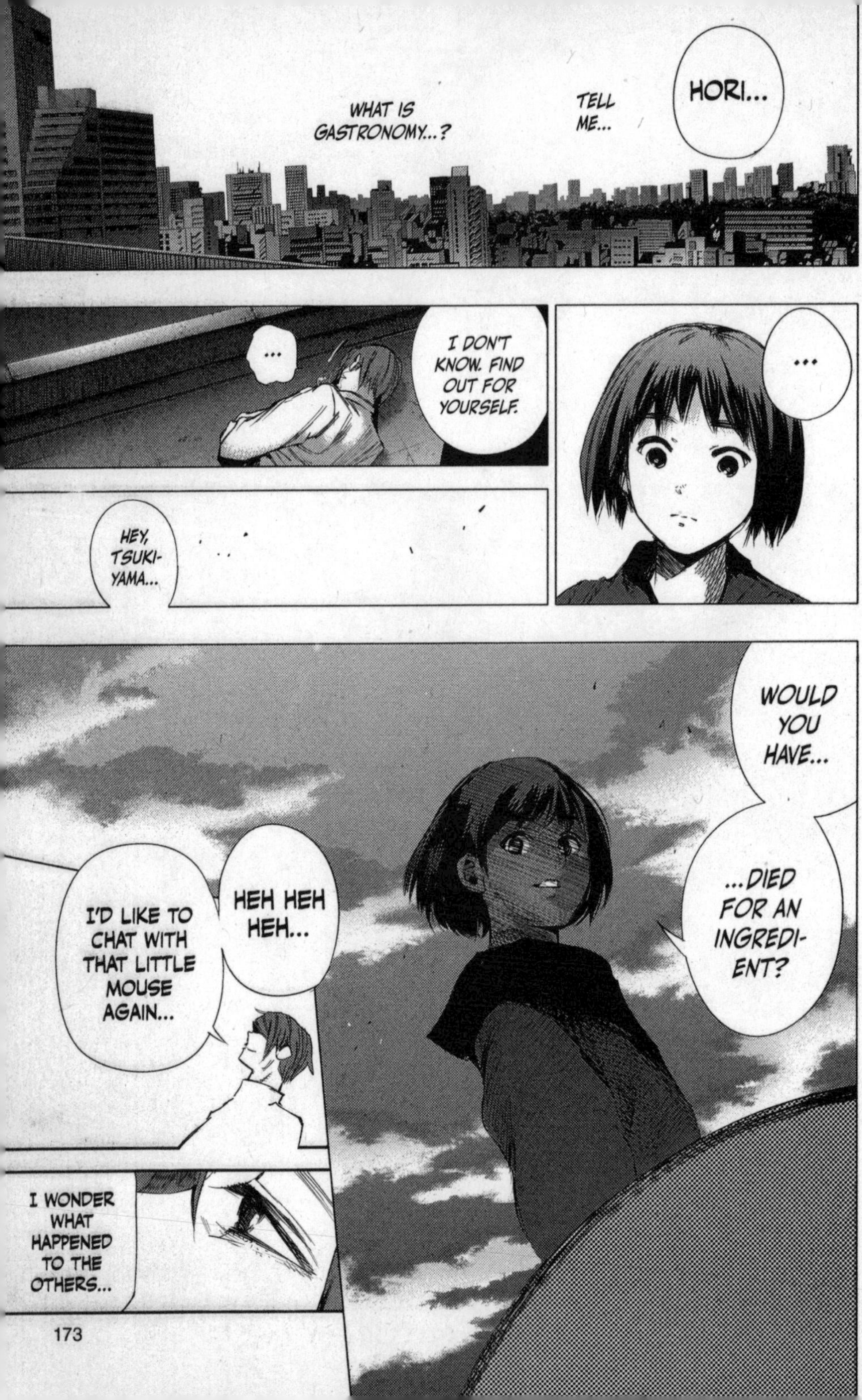

HORI...
TELL ME...
WHAT IS GASTRONOMY...?
...
I DON'T KNOW. FIND OUT FOR YOURSELF.
...
HEY, TSUKIYAMA...
WOULD YOU HAVE...
...DIED FOR AN INGREDIENT?
HEH HEH HEH...
I'D LIKE TO CHAT WITH THAT LITTLE MOUSE AGAIN...
I WONDER WHAT HAPPENED TO THE OTHERS...

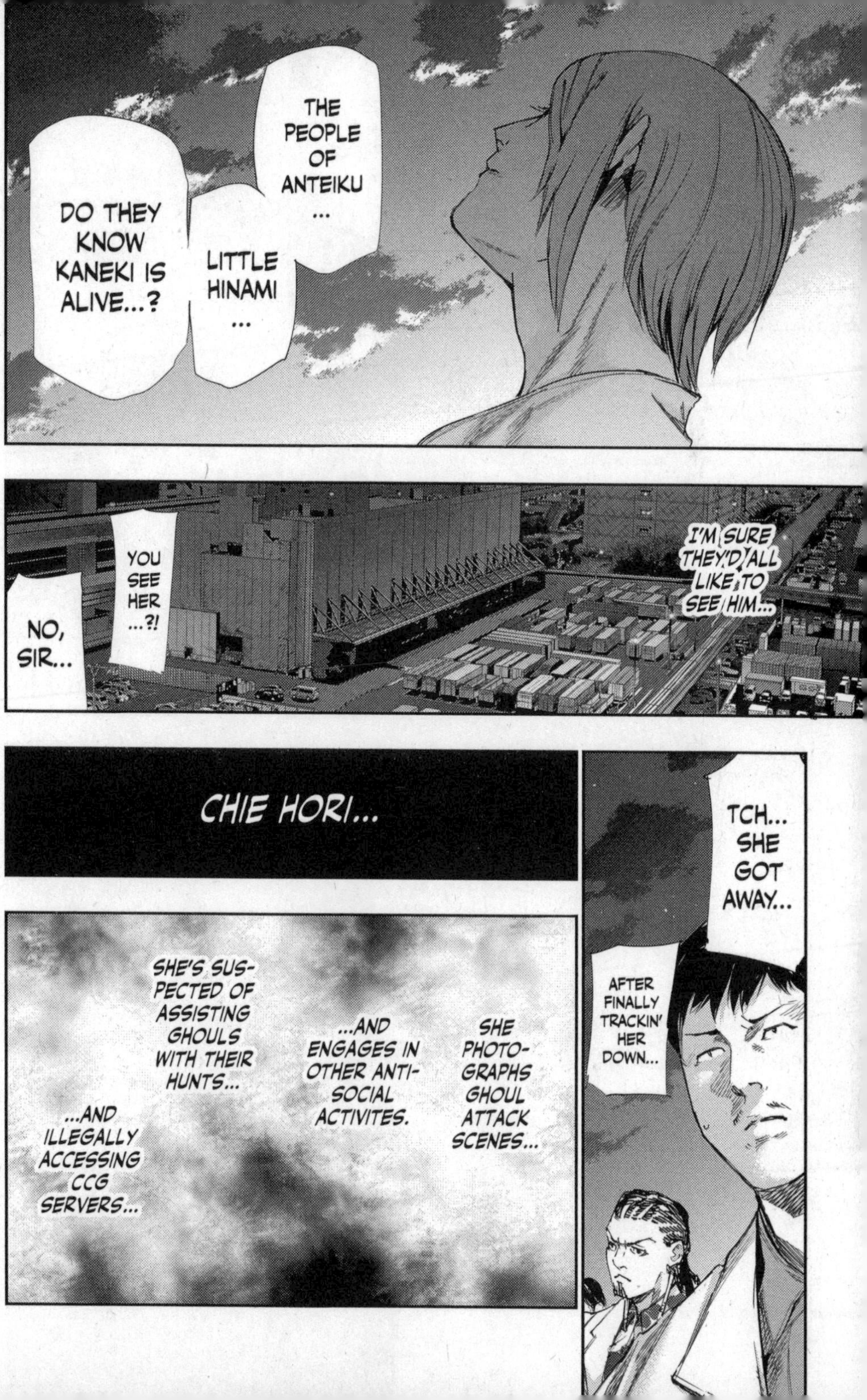
THE PEOPLE OF ANTEIKU ...
LITTLE HINAMI ...
DO THEY KNOW KANEKI IS ALIVE...?
I'M SURE THEY'D ALL LIKE TO SEE HIM...
YOU SEE HER ...?!
NO, SIR...
TCH... SHE GOT AWAY...
AFTER FINALLY TRACKIN' HER DOWN...
CHIE HORI...
SHE PHOTO-GRAPHS GHOUL ATTACK SCENES...
...AND ENGAGES IN OTHER ANTI-SOCIAL ACTIVITES.
SHE'S SUS-PECTED OF ASSISTING GHOULS WITH THEIR HUNTS...
...AND ILLEGALLY ACCESSING CCG SERVERS...

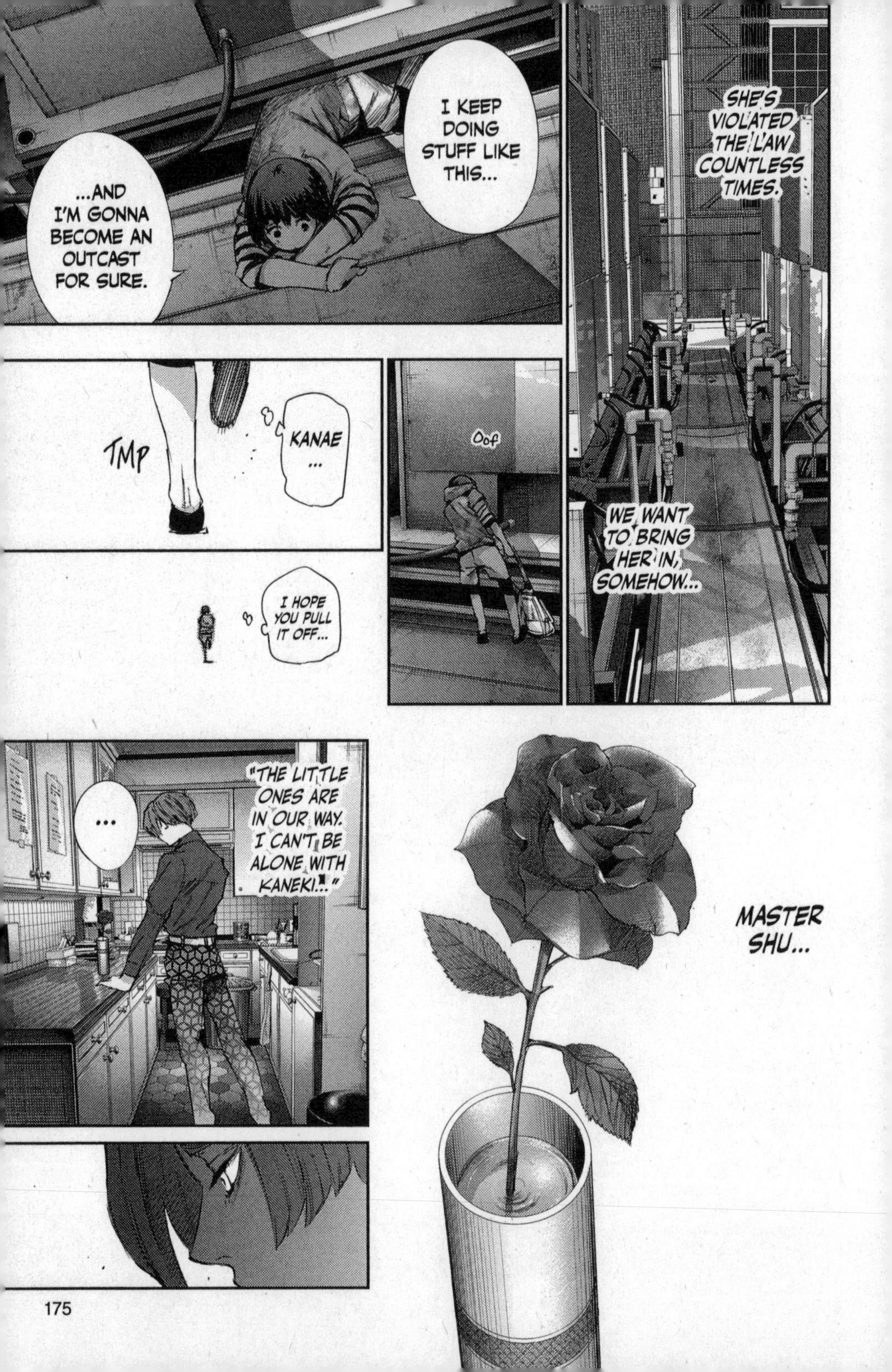

SHE'S VIOLATED THE LAW COUNTLESS TIMES.
WE WANT TO BRING HER IN, SOMEHOW...
I KEEP DOING STUFF LIKE THIS...
...AND I'M GONNA BECOME AN OUTCAST FOR SURE.
Oof
KANAE ...
TMP
I HOPE YOU PULL IT OFF...
MASTER SHU...
"THE LITTLE ONES ARE IN OUR WAY. I CAN'T BE ALONE WITH KANEKI..."
...

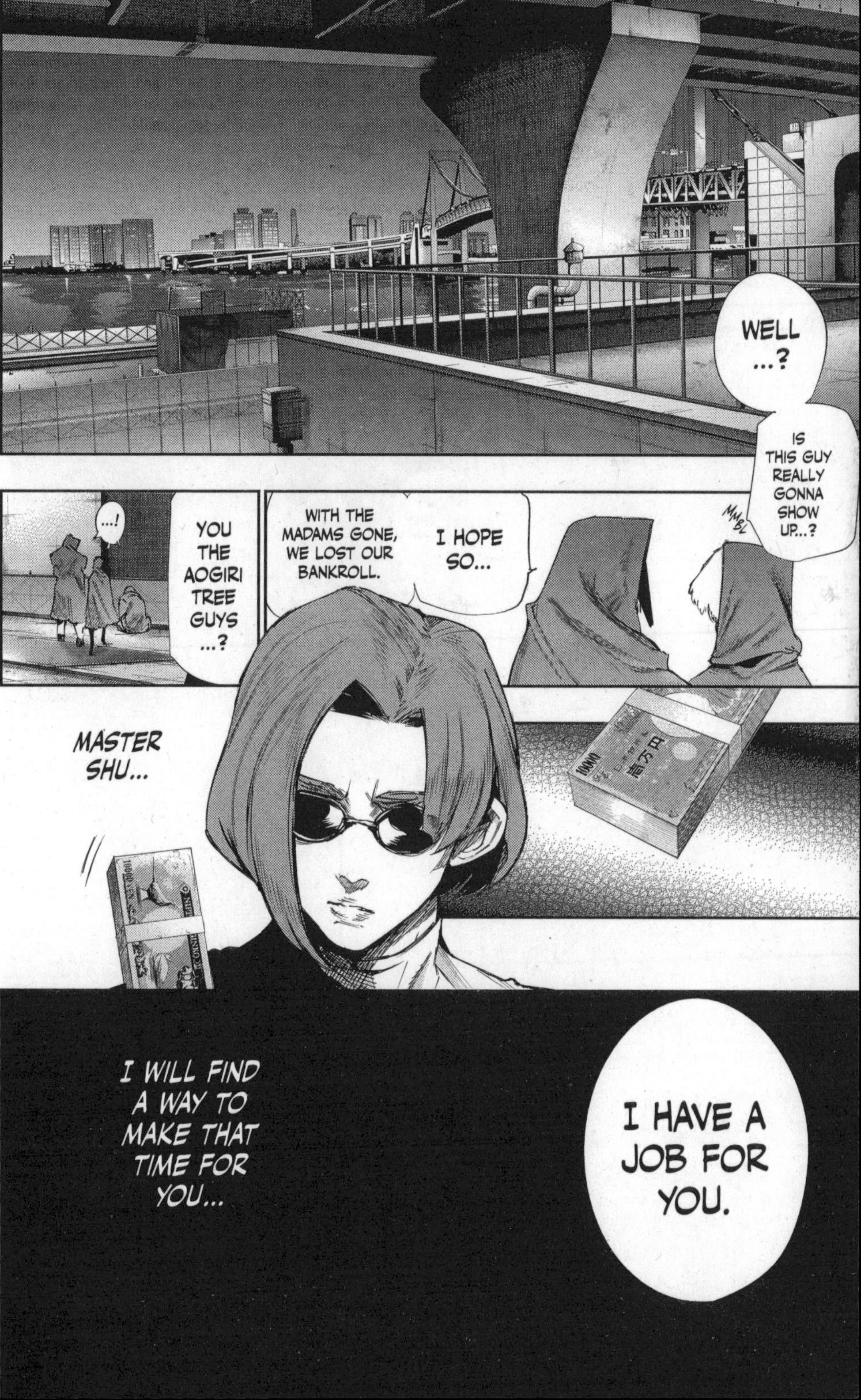
WELL ...?
IS THIS GUY REALLY GONNA SHOW UP...?
MMBL
I HOPE SO...
WITH THE MADAMS GONE, WE LOST OUR BANKROLL.
YOU THE AOGIRI TREE GUYS ...?
...!
MASTER SHU...
I HAVE A JOB FOR YOU.
I WILL FIND A WAY TO MAKE THAT TIME FOR YOU...

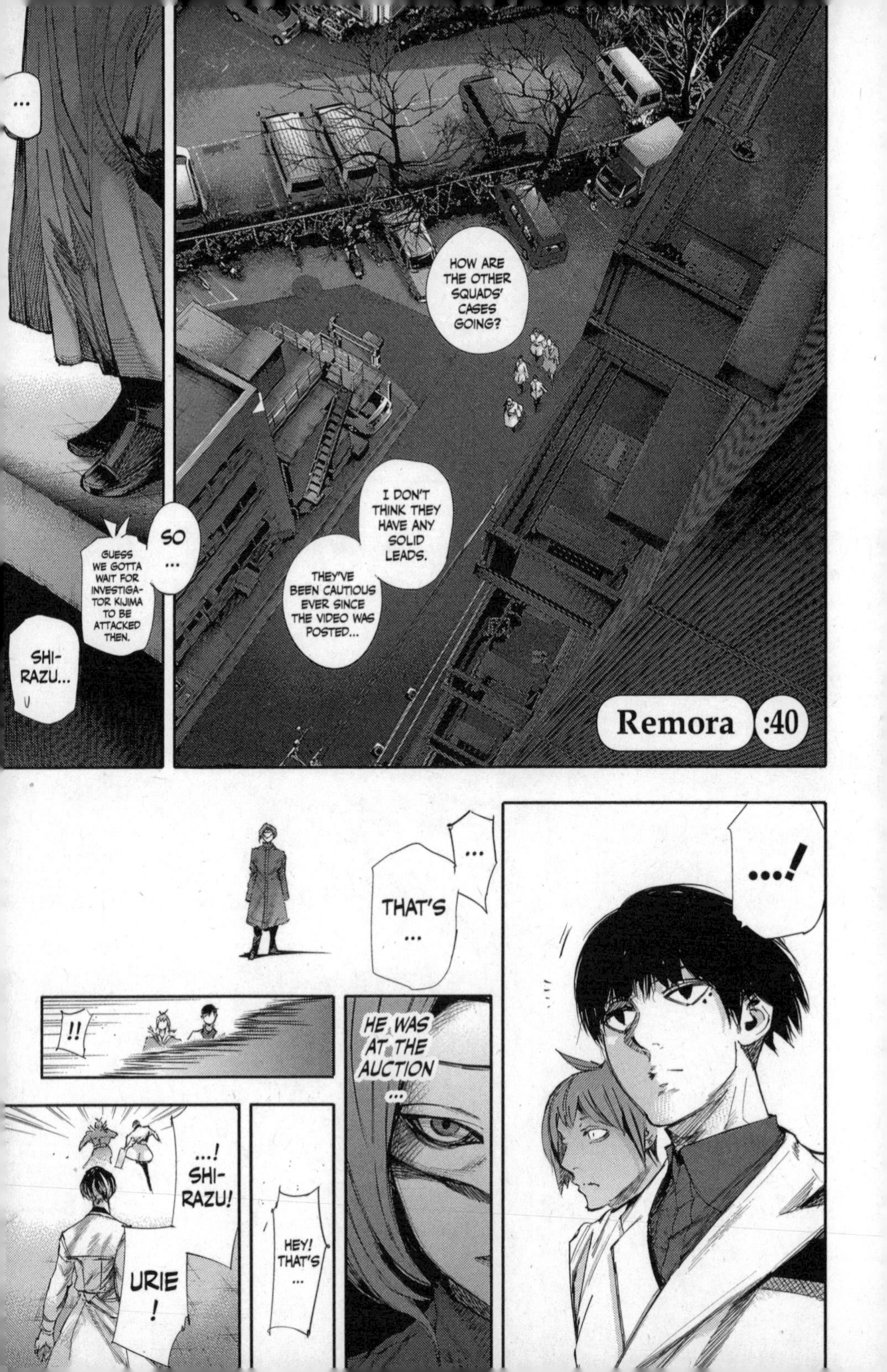
HOW ARE THE OTHER SQUADS' CASES GOING?
I DON'T THINK THEY HAVE ANY SOLID LEADS.
THEY'VE BEEN CAUTIOUS EVER SINCE THE VIDEO WAS POSTED...
SO ...
GUESS WE GOTTA WAIT FOR INVESTIGATOR KIJIMA TO BE ATTACKED THEN.
SHI-RAZU...
Remora :40
...
...!
...
THAT'S ...
HE WAS AT THE AUCTION ...
!!
HEY! THAT'S ...
...! SHI-RAZU!
URIE !

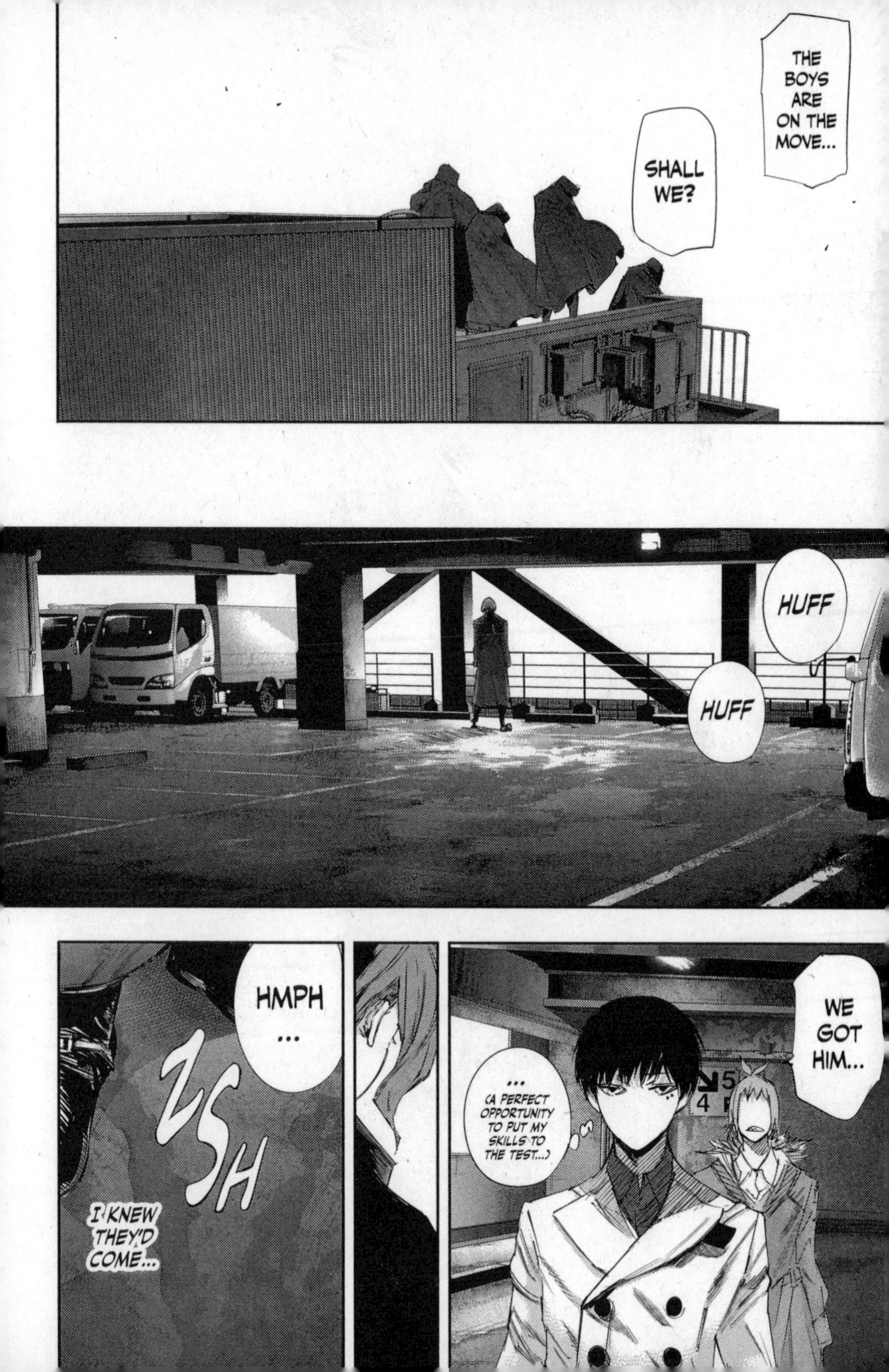
THE BOYS ARE ON THE MOVE...
SHALL WE?
HUFF
HUFF
WE GOT HIM...
...(A PERFECT OPPORTUNITY TO PUT MY SKILLS TO THE TEST...)
HMPH ...
ZSH
I KNEW THEY'D COME...

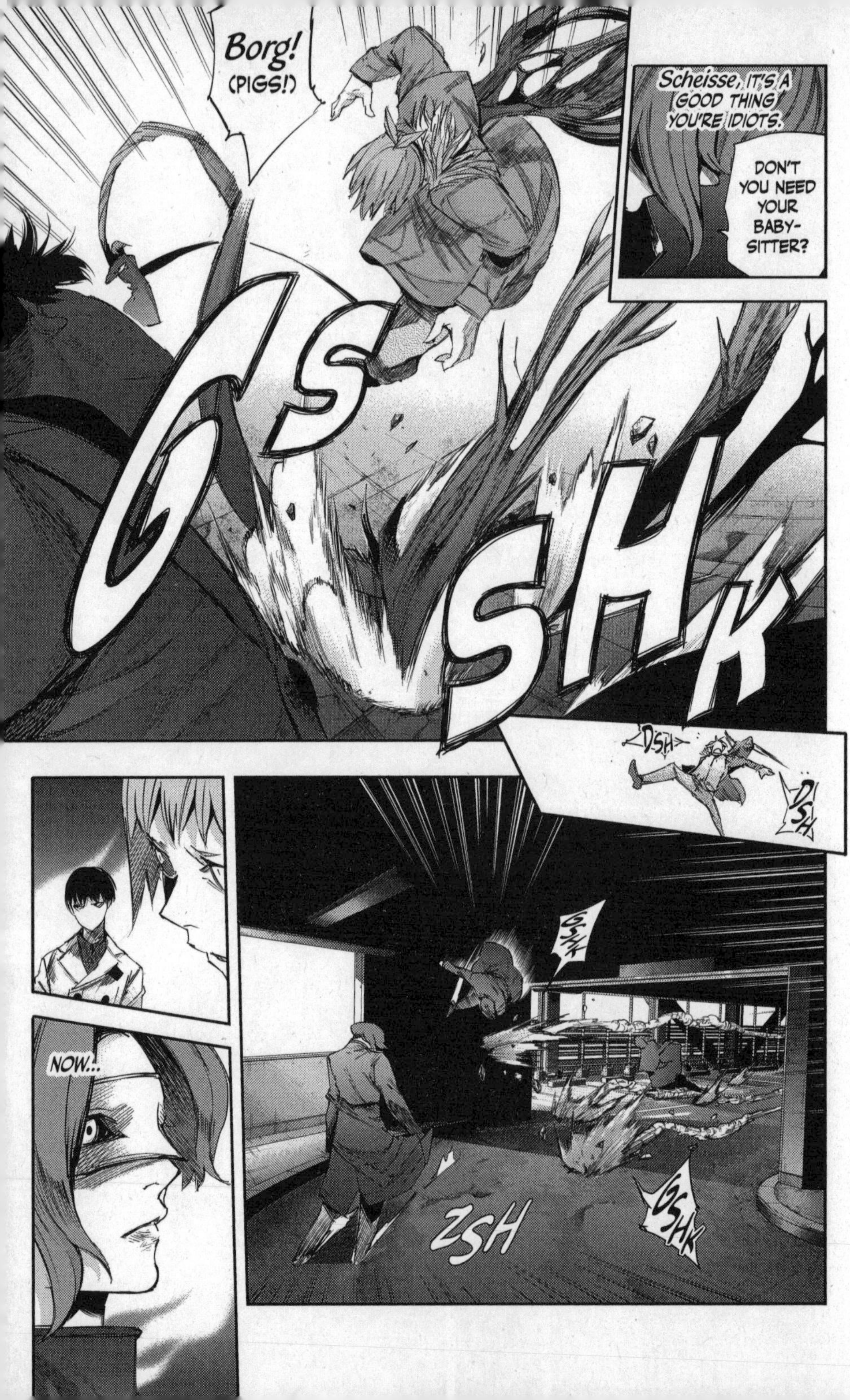
Scheisse, IT'S A GOOD THING YOU'RE IDIOTS.
DON'T YOU NEED YOUR BABY-SITTER?
Borg! (PIGS!)
GSSHK
DSH
DSH
GSHK
GSHK
ZSH
NOW...

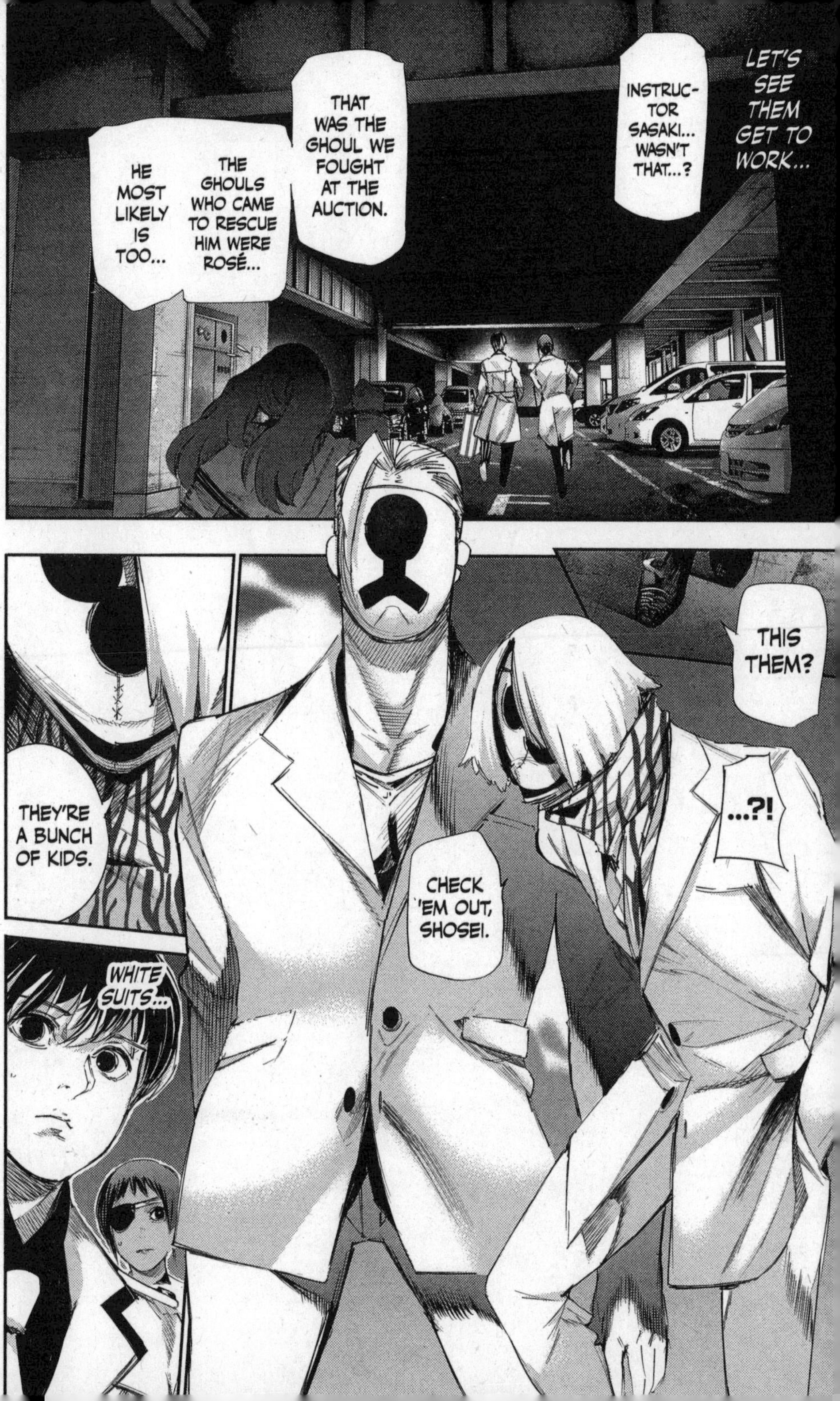
LET'S SEE THEM GET TO WORK...
INSTRUCTOR SASAKI... WASN'T THAT...?
THAT WAS THE GHOUL WE FOUGHT AT THE AUCTION.
THE GHOULS WHO CAME TO RESCUE HIM WERE ROSÉ...
HE MOST LIKELY IS TOO...
THIS THEM?
...?!
CHECK 'EM OUT, SHOSEI.
THEY'RE A BUNCH OF KIDS.
WHITE SUITS...

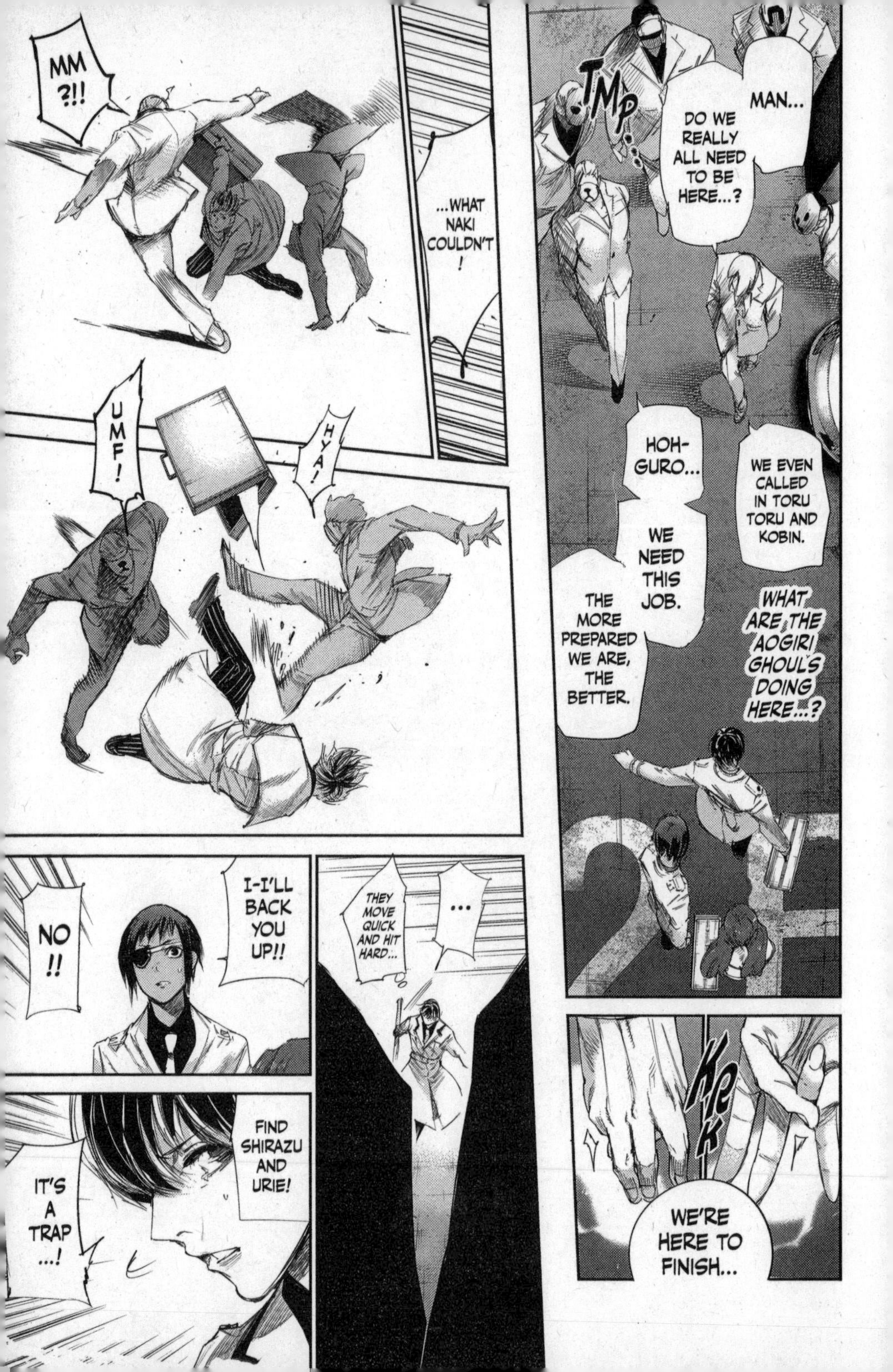
MAN...
DO WE REALLY ALL NEED TO BE HERE...?
TMP...
WE EVEN CALLED IN TORU TORU AND KOBIN.
HOH-GURO...
WE NEED THIS JOB.
THE MORE PREPARED WE ARE, THE BETTER.
WHAT ARE THE AOGIRI GHOULS DOING HERE...?
KRK
WE'RE HERE TO FINISH...
...WHAT NAKI COULDN'T!
MM?!!
HYA!
UMF!
...
THEY MOVE QUICK AND HIT HARD...
I-I'LL BACK YOU UP!!
NO!!
FIND SHIRAZU AND URIE!
IT'S A TRAP...!

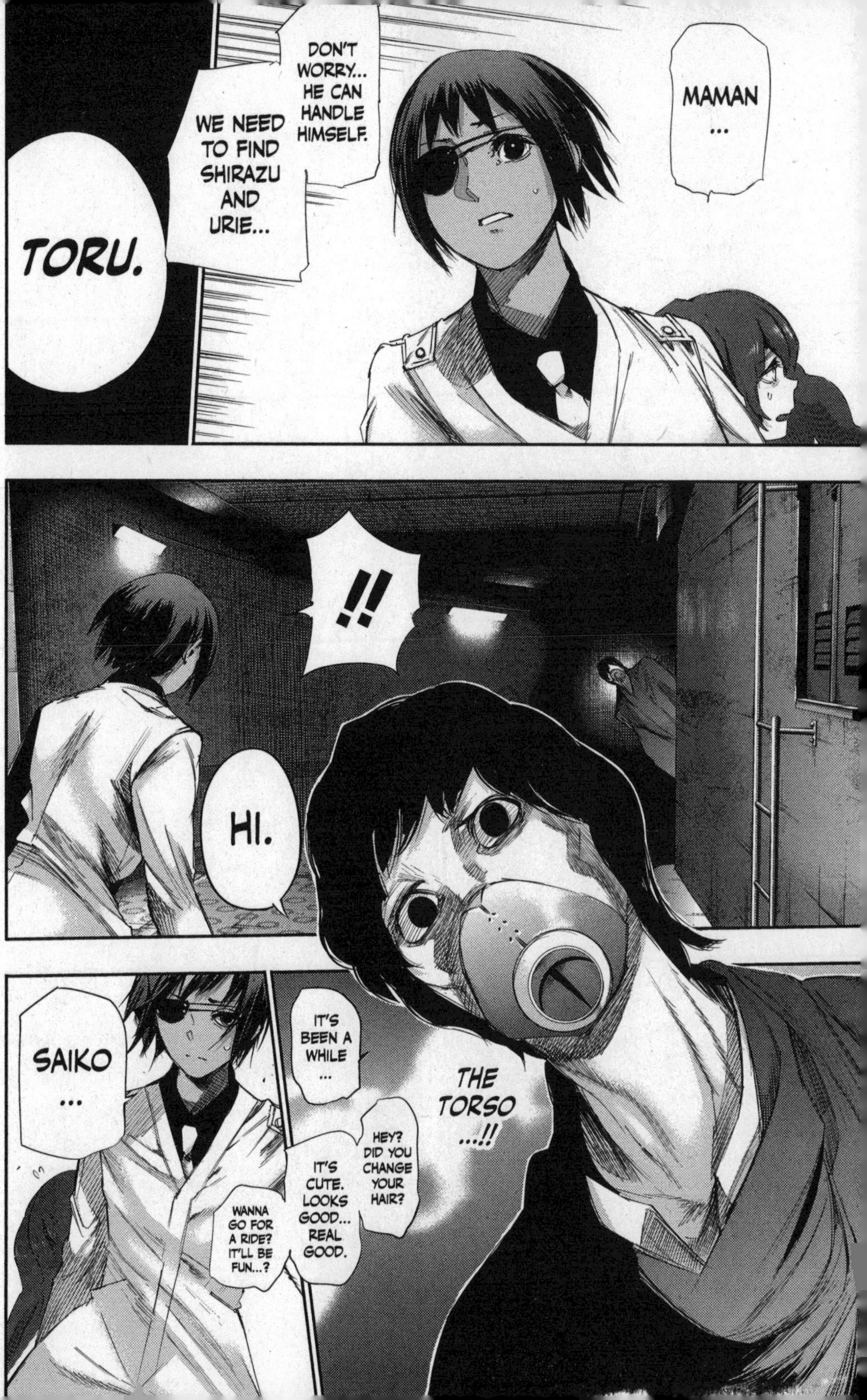
MAMAN ...
DON'T WORRY... HE CAN HANDLE HIMSELF.
WE NEED TO FIND SHIRAZU AND URIE...
TORU.
!!
HI.
THE TORSO ...!!
HEY? DID YOU CHANGE YOUR HAIR?
IT'S BEEN A WHILE ...
IT'S CUTE. LOOKS GOOD... REAL GOOD.
WANNA GO FOR A RIDE? IT'LL BE FUN...?
SAIKO ...

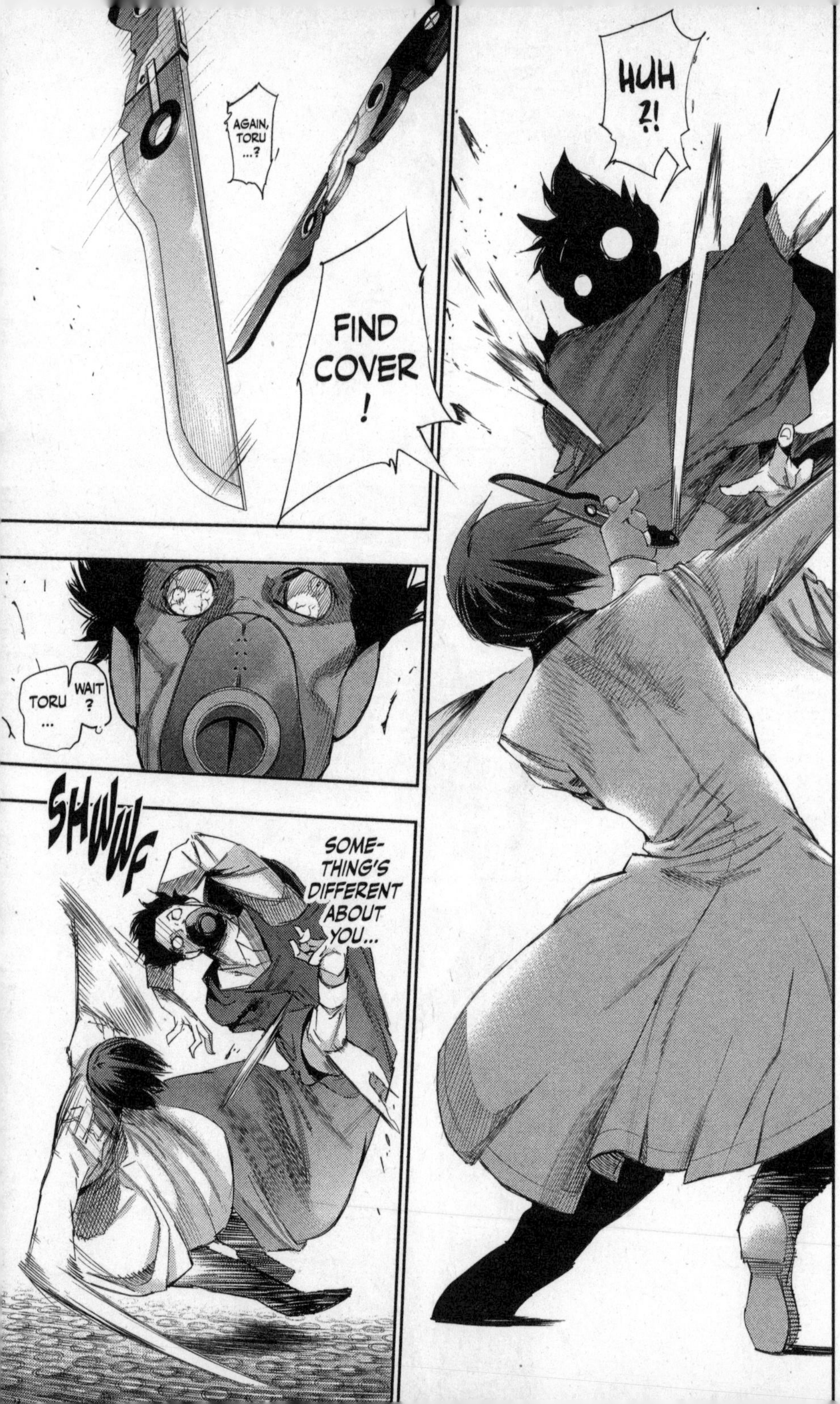
HUH ?!
AGAIN, TORU ...?
FIND COVER !
WAIT ?
TORU ...
SHWWF
SOME-THING'S DIFFERENT ABOUT YOU...

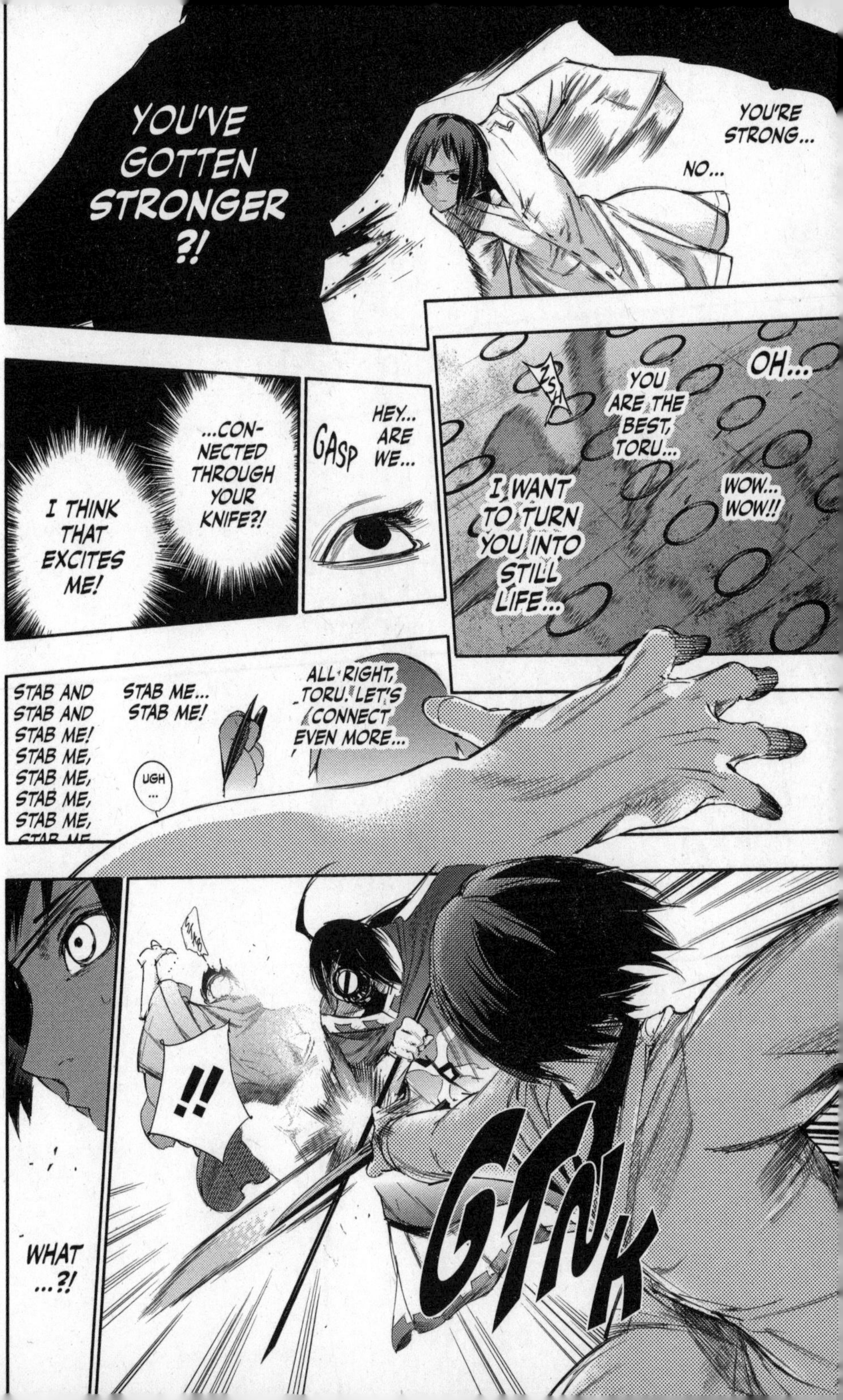
YOU'RE STRONG...
NO...
YOU'VE GOTTEN STRONGER ?!
OH...
YOU ARE THE BEST, TORU...
WOW... WOW!!
I WANT TO TURN YOU INTO STILL LIFE...
ZSH
HEY... ARE WE...
GASP
...CON-NECTED THROUGH YOUR KNIFE?!
I THINK THAT EXCITES ME!
ALL RIGHT, TORU. LET'S CONNECT EVEN MORE...
UGH ...
STAB ME... STAB ME!
STAB AND STAB AND STAB ME! STAB ME, STAB ME, STAB ME, STAB ME,
!!
GTCK
WHAT ...?!

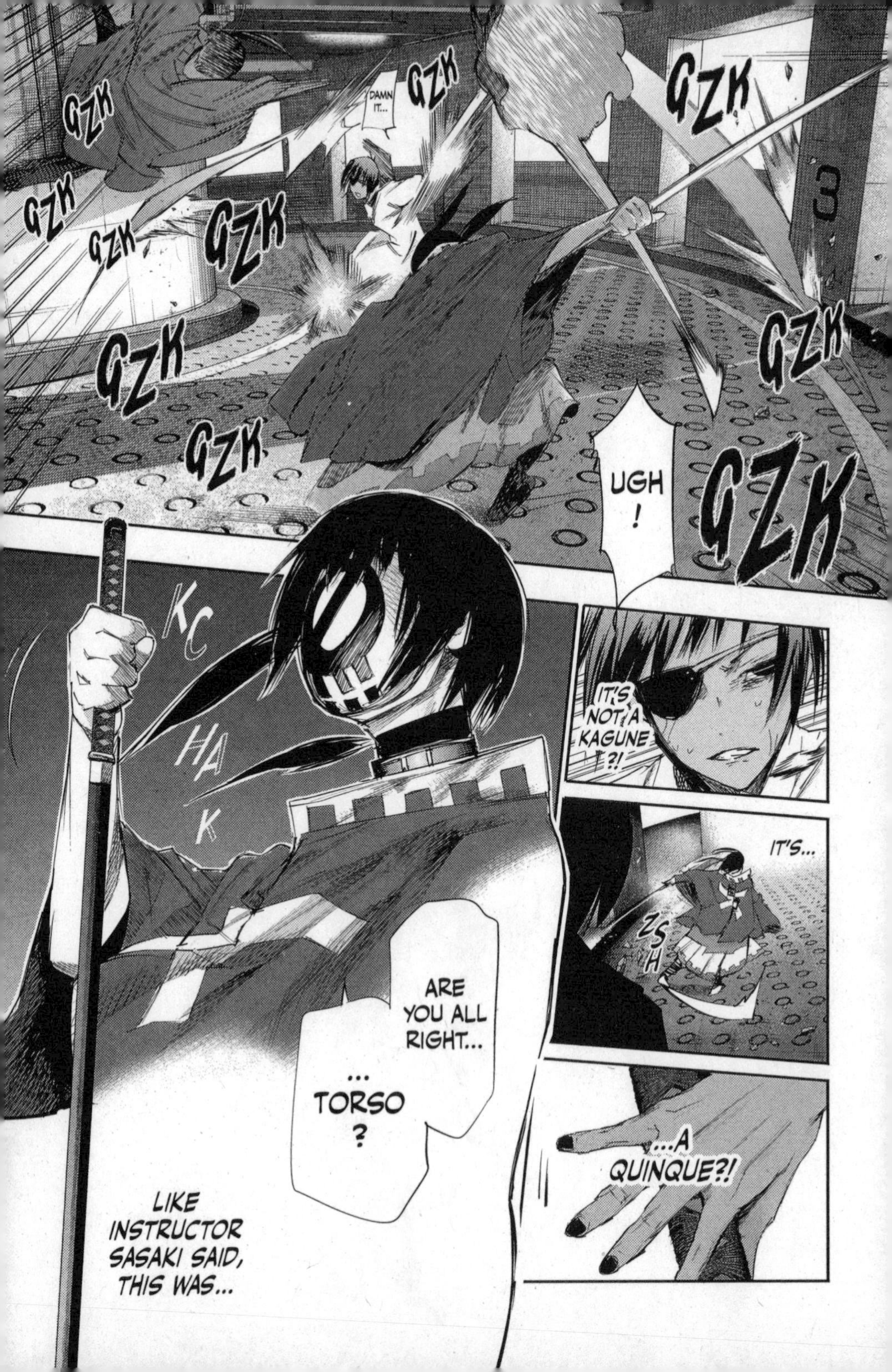
GZK
GZK
GZK
UGH!
GZK
DAMN IT...
GZK
GZK
GZK
GZK
GZK
GZK
IT'S NOT A KAGUNE?!
IT'S...
ZSH
...A QUINQUE?!
KCHAK
ARE YOU ALL RIGHT...
... TORSO?
LIKE INSTRUCTOR SASAKI SAID, THIS WAS...

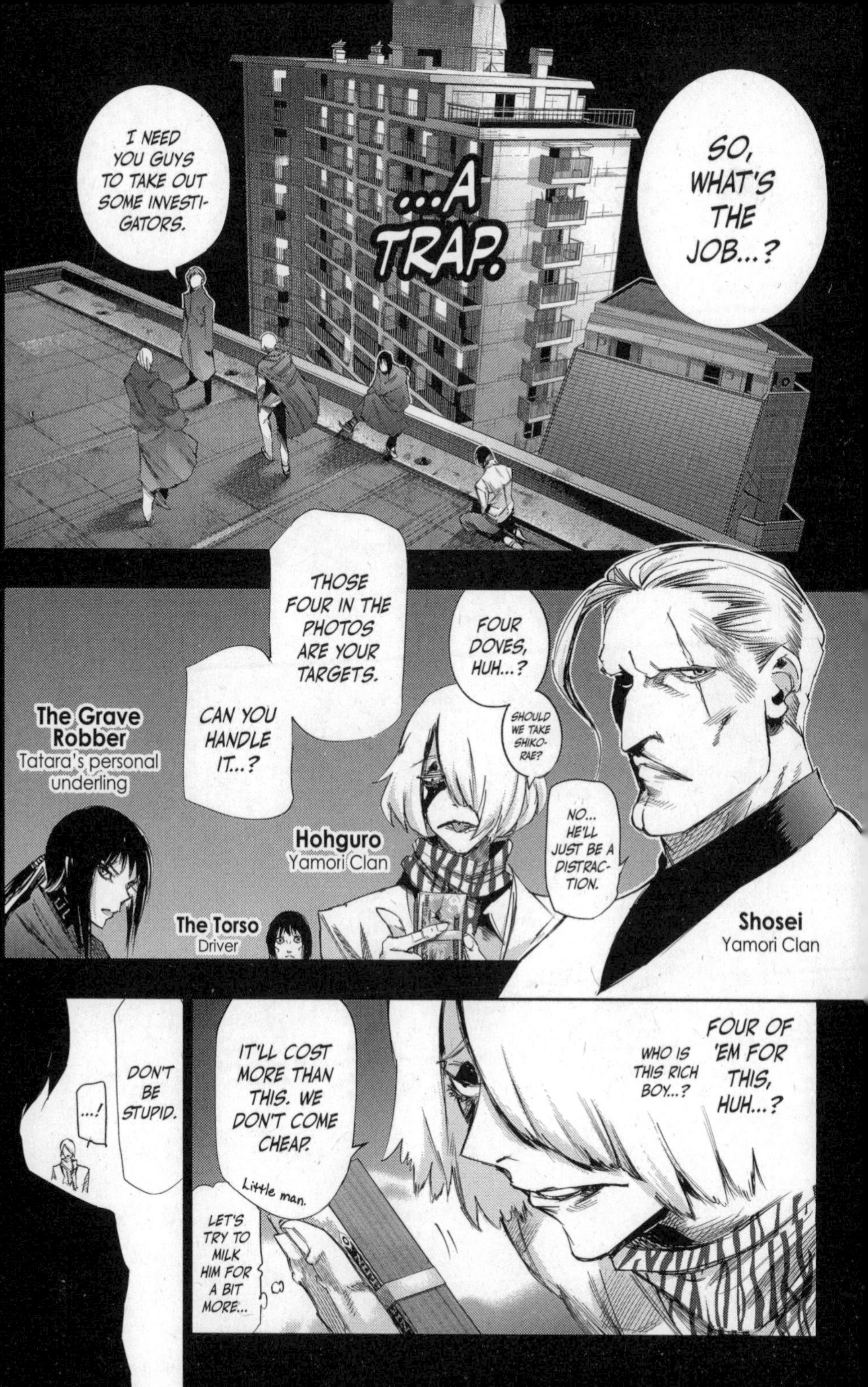
SO, WHAT'S THE JOB...?
...A TRAP.
I NEED YOU GUYS TO TAKE OUT SOME INVESTI-GATORS.
Shosei
Yamori Clan
FOUR DOVES, HUH...?
SHOULD WE TAKE SHIKO-RAE?
NO... HE'LL JUST BE A DISTRAC-TION.
THOSE FOUR IN THE PHOTOS ARE YOUR TARGETS.
CAN YOU HANDLE IT...?
Hohguro
Yamori Clan
The Torso
Driver
The Grave Robber
Tatara's personal underling
FOUR OF 'EM FOR THIS, HUH...?
WHO IS THIS RICH BOY...?
IT'LL COST MORE THAN THIS. WE DON'T COME CHEAP.
Little man.
LET'S TRY TO MILK HIM FOR A BIT MORE...
DON'T BE STUPID.
...!

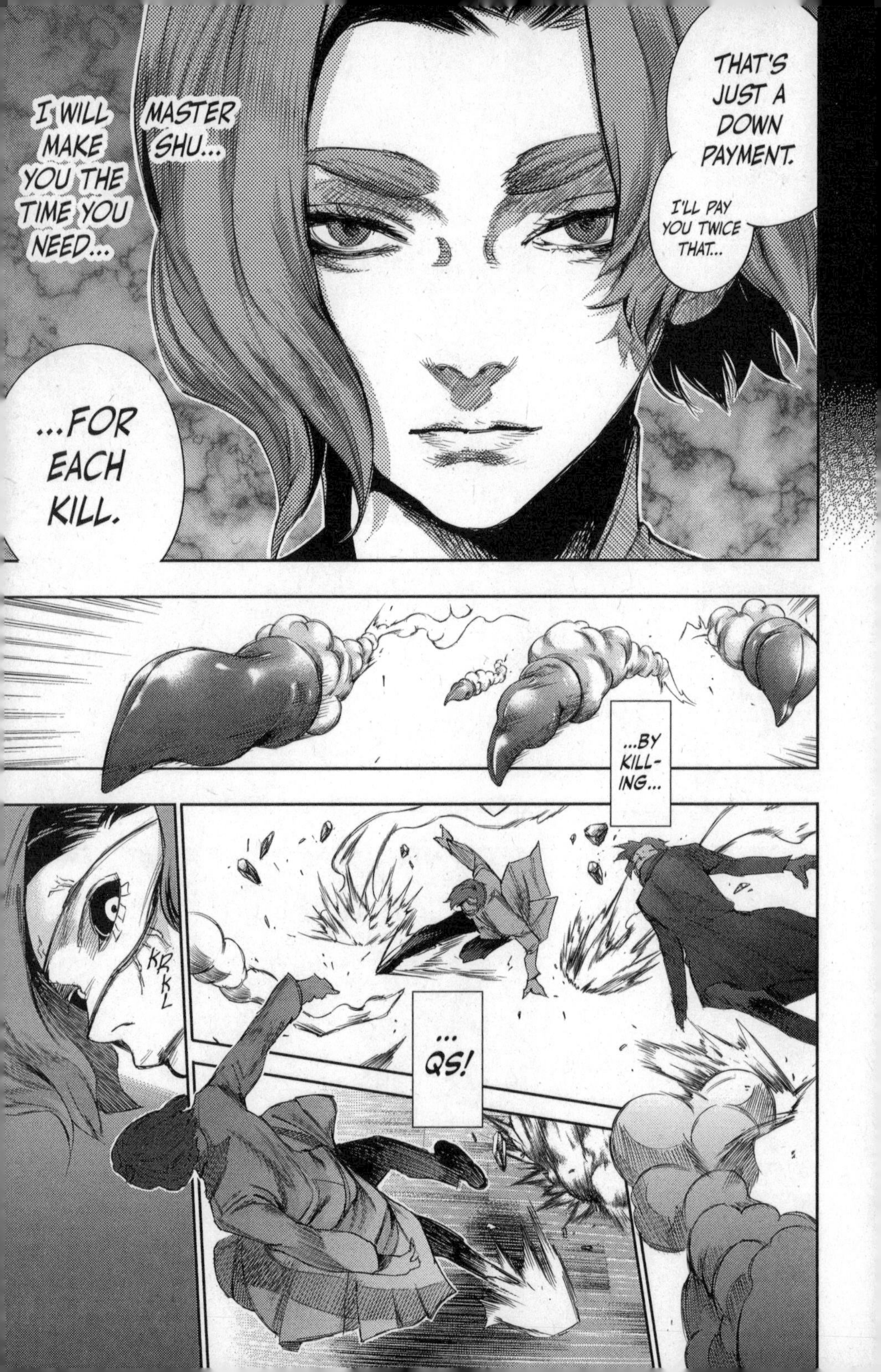
THAT'S JUST A DOWN PAYMENT.
I'LL PAY YOU TWICE THAT...
...FOR EACH KILL.
MASTER SHU...
I WILL MAKE YOU THE TIME YOU NEED...
...BY KILLING...
... QS!
KRKL

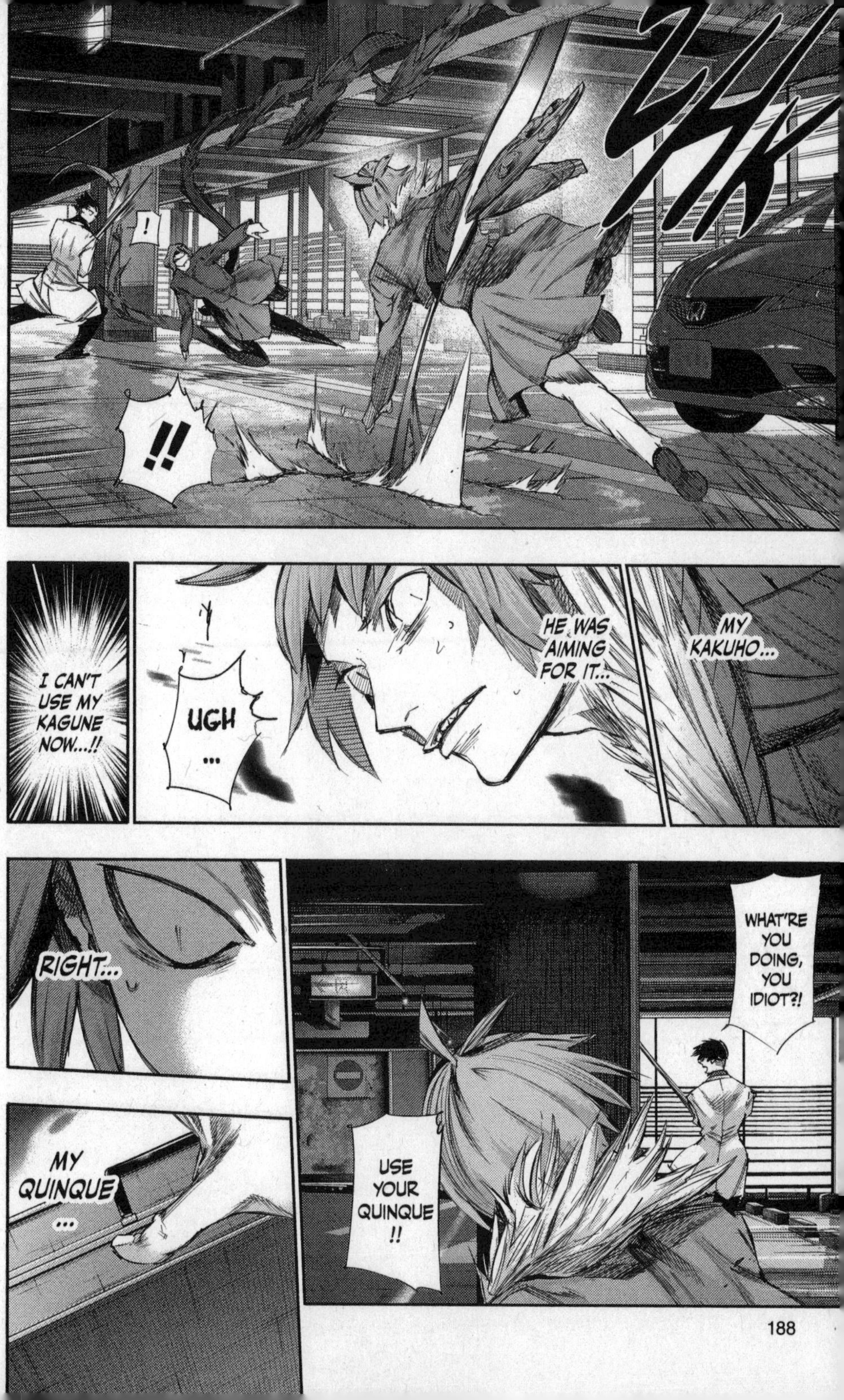
!
!!
MY KAKUHO...
HE WAS AIMING FOR IT...
UGH ...
I CAN'T USE MY KAGUNE NOW...!!
WHAT'RE YOU DOING, YOU IDIOT?!
USE YOUR QUINQUE !!
RIGHT...
MY QUINQUE ...

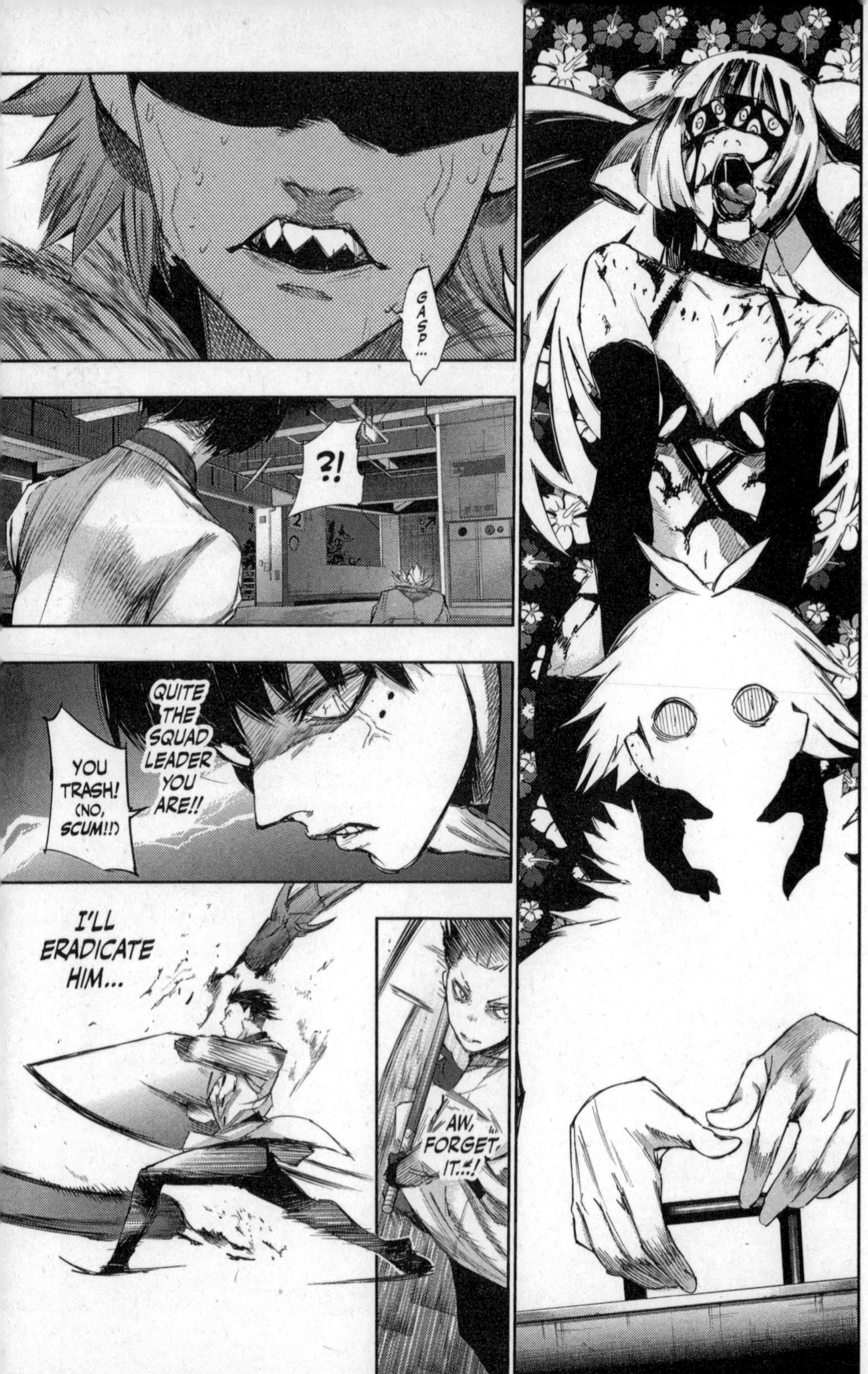
GASP...
?!
QUITE THE SQUAD LEADER YOU ARE!!
YOU TRASH! (NO, SCUM!!)
AW, FORGET IT...!
I'LL ERADICATE HIM...

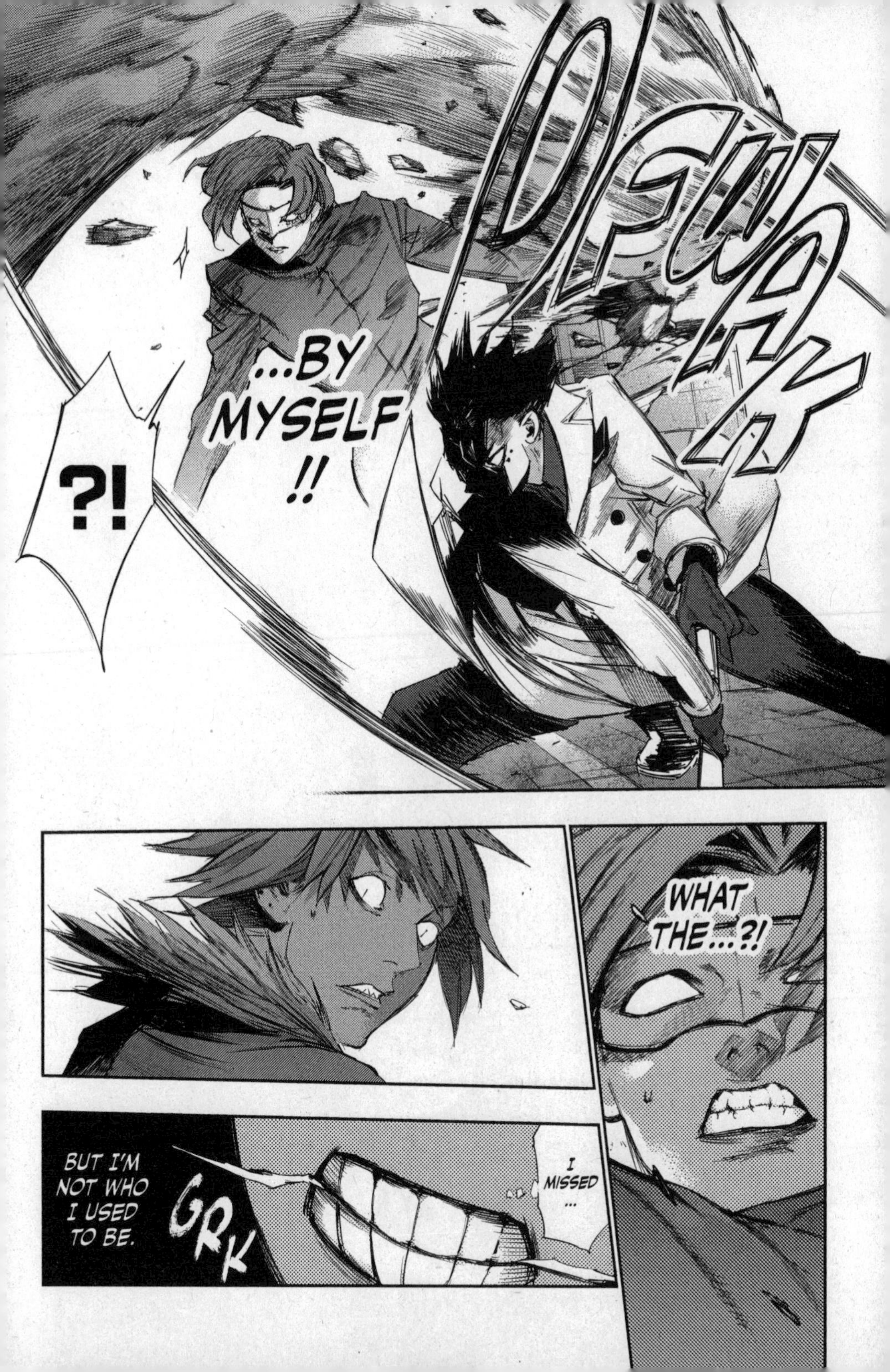
...BY MYSELF!!
?!
WHAT THE...?!
I MISSED...
GRK
BUT I'M NOT WHO I USED TO BE.

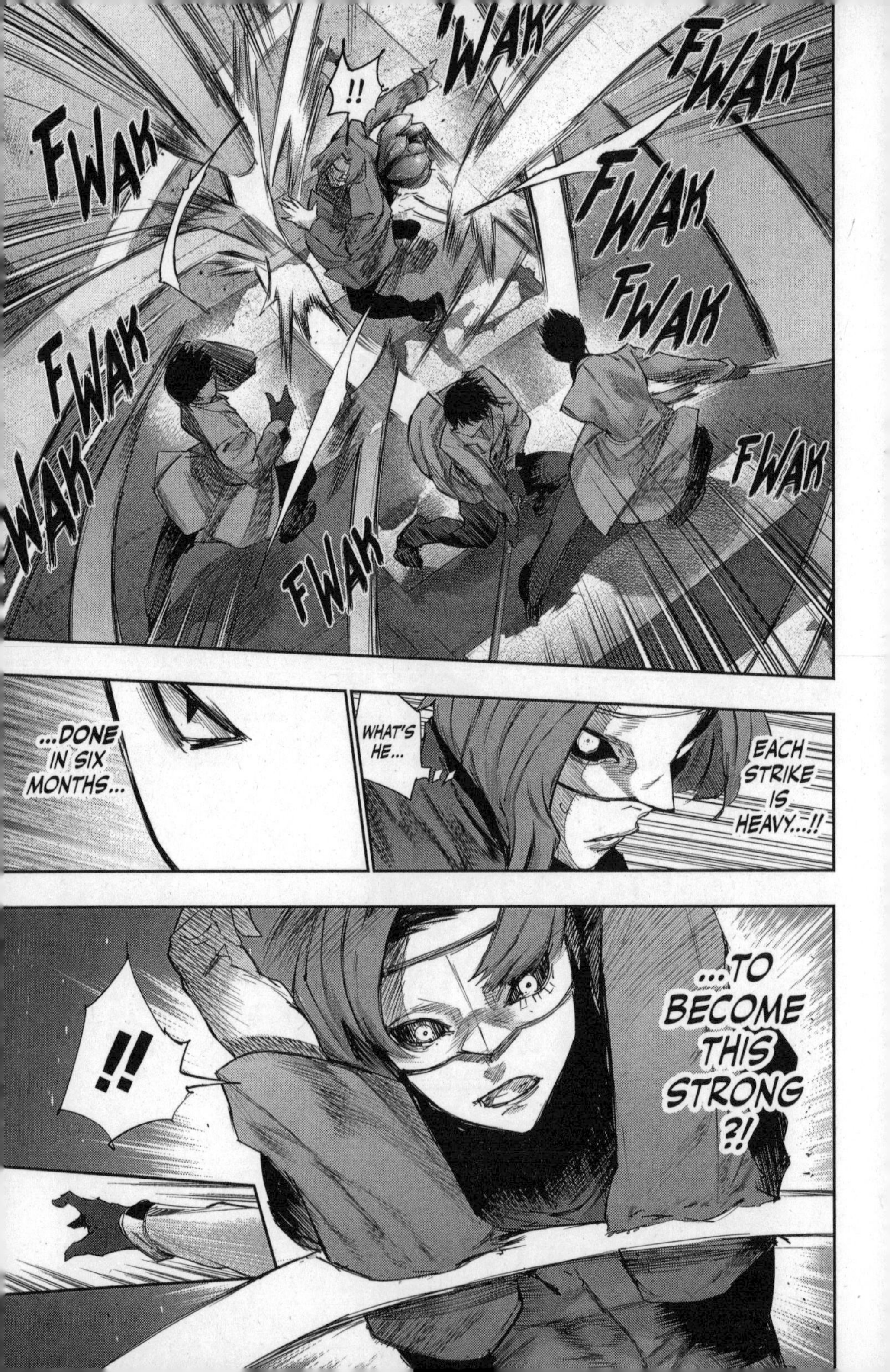

FWAK
'WAK
!!
FWAK
FWAK
FWAK
FWAK
WAK
FWAK
FWAK
EACH STRIKE IS HEAVY...!!
WHAT'S HE...
...DONE IN SIX MONTHS...
...TO BECOME THIS STRONG?!
!!

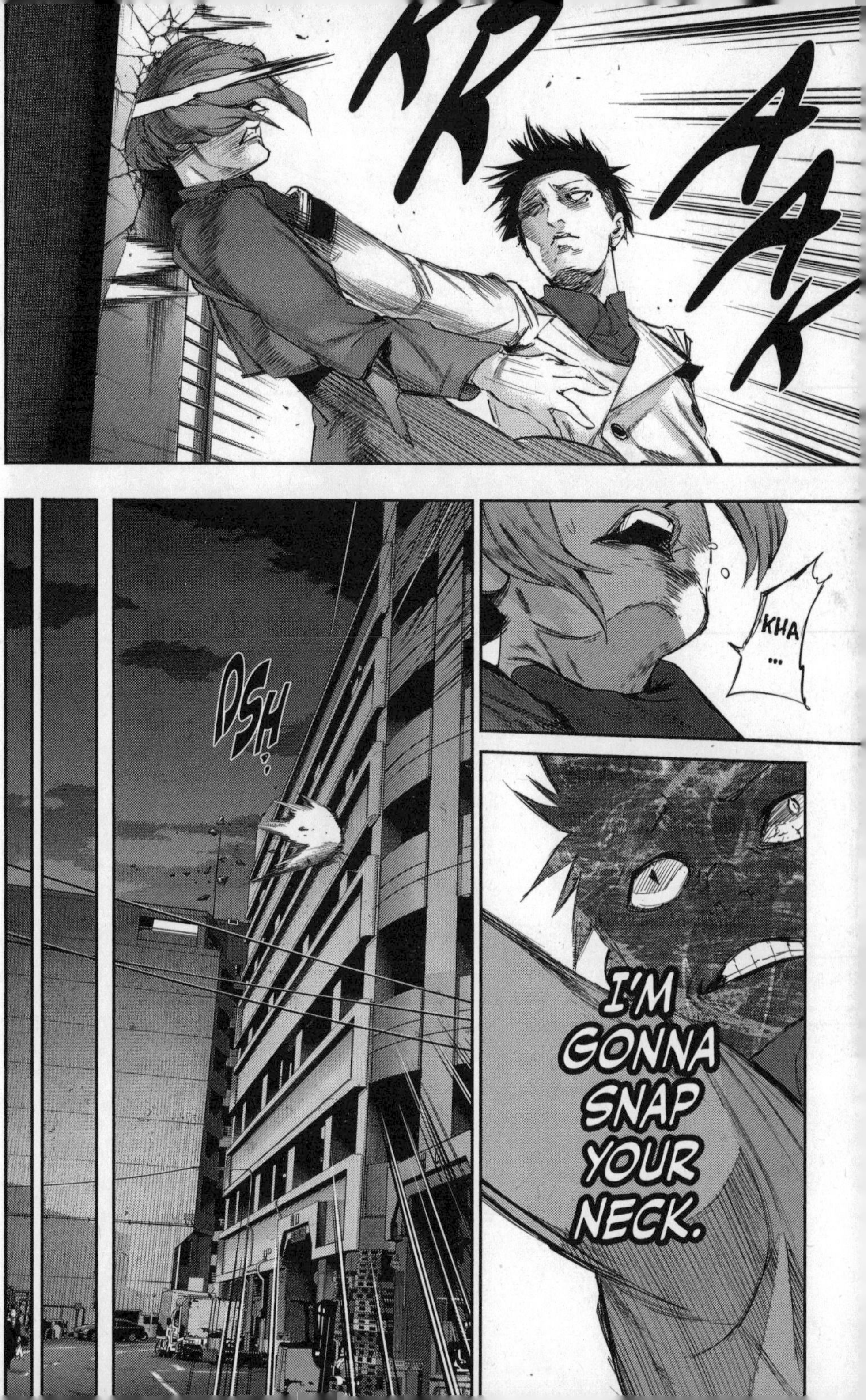
KRAAK
KHA …
I'M GONNA SNAP YOUR NECK.
PSH

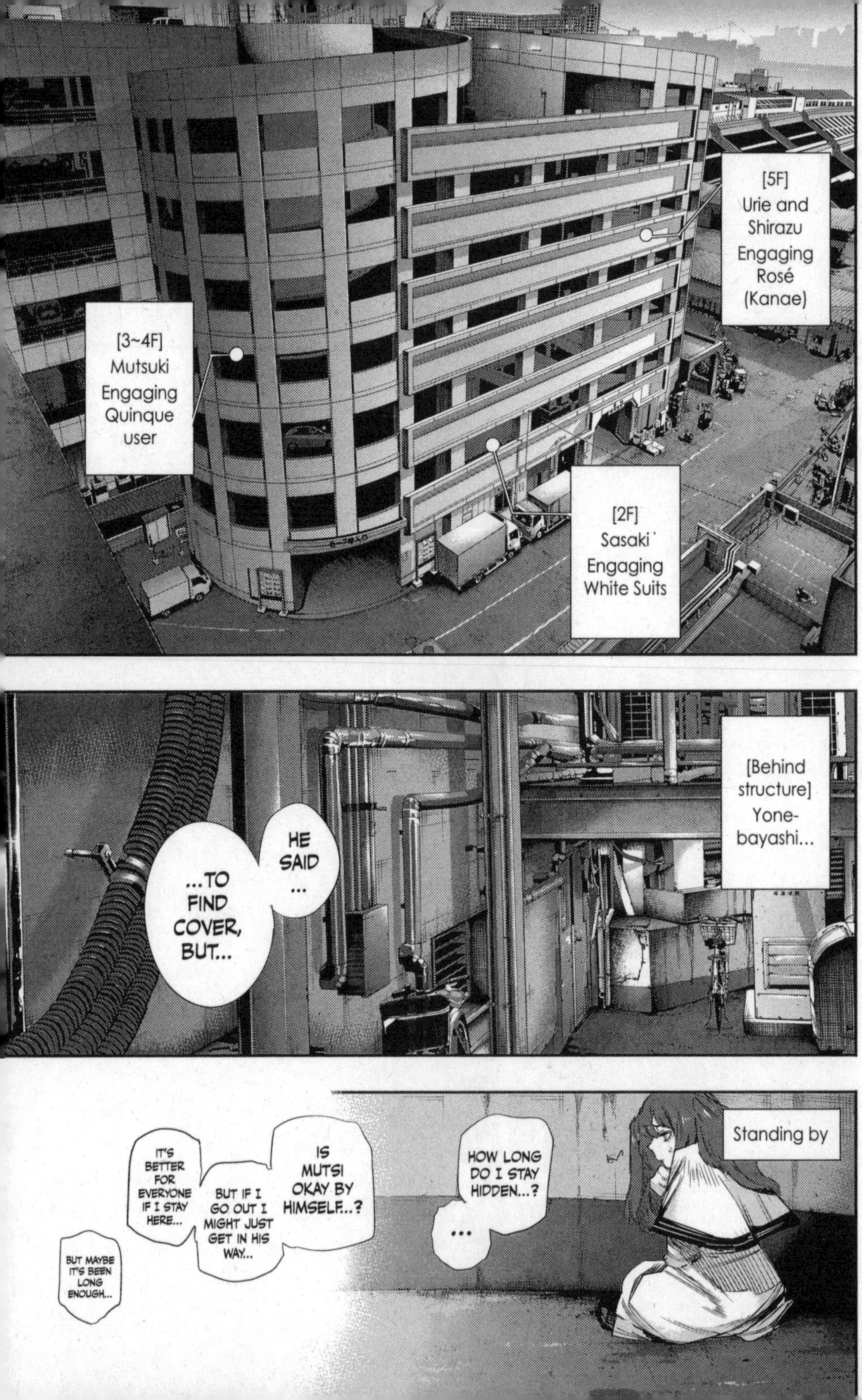
[5F] Urie and Shirazu Engaging Rosé (Kanae)
[2F] Sasaki Engaging White Suits
[3~4F] Mutsuki Engaging Quinque user
[Behind structure] Yone-bayashi...
HE SAID ...
...TO FIND COVER, BUT...
Standing by
HOW LONG DO I STAY HIDDEN...?
...
IS MUTSI OKAY BY HIMSELF...?
BUT IF I GO OUT I MIGHT JUST GET IN HIS WAY...
IT'S BETTER FOR EVERYONE IF I STAY HERE...
BUT MAYBE IT'S BEEN LONG ENOUGH...

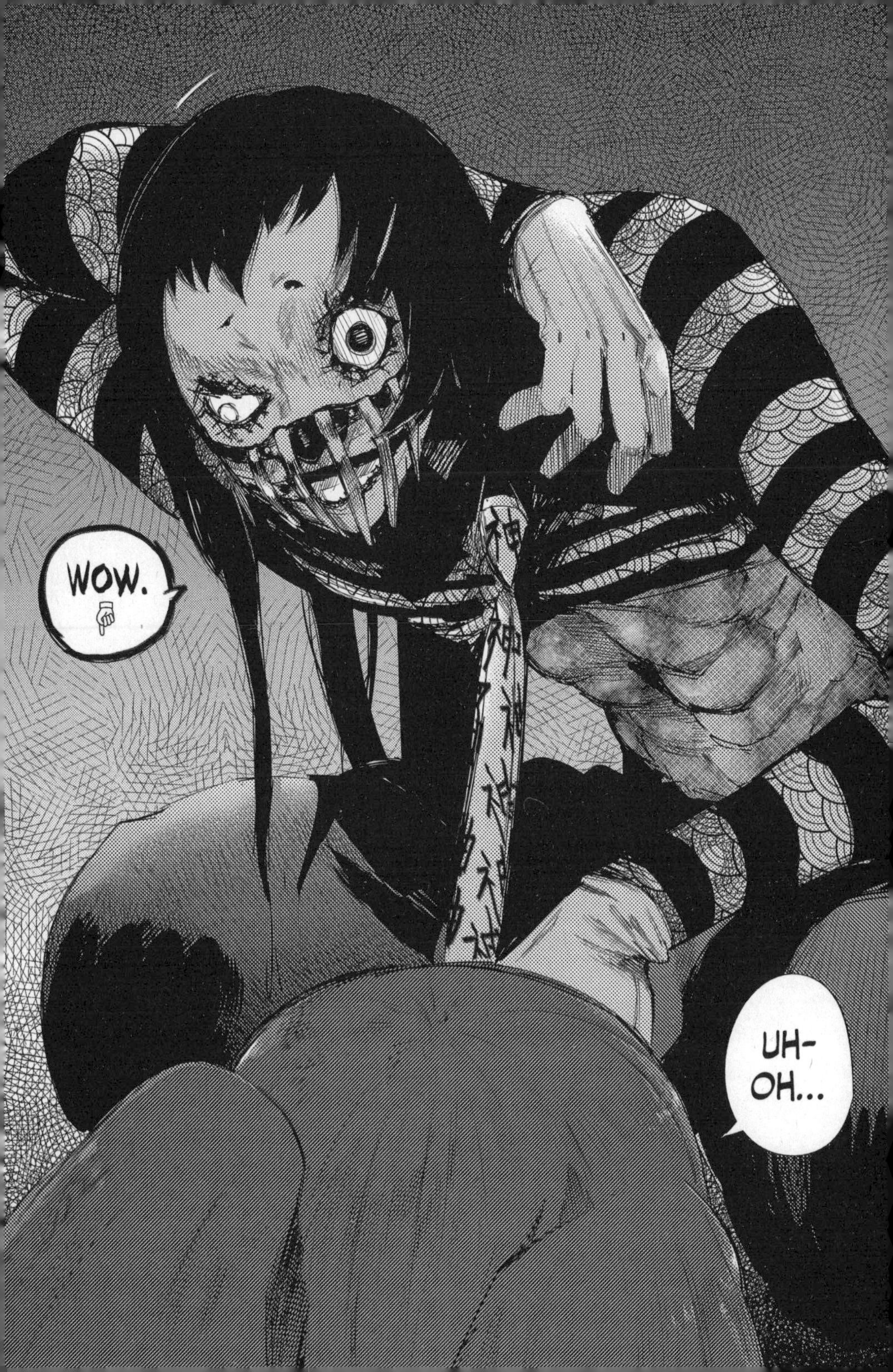
WOW.
UH-OH...

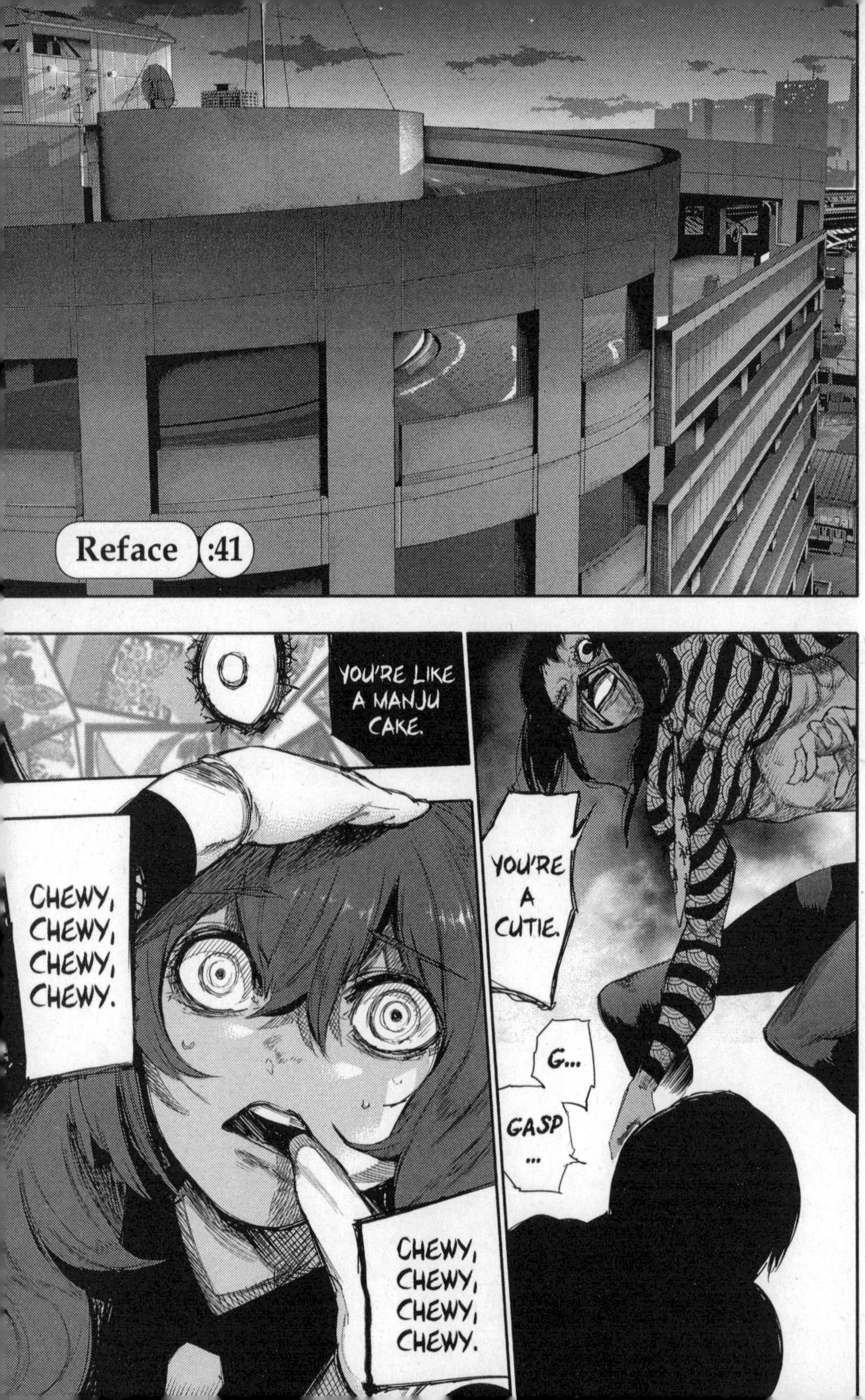
Reface :41
YOU'RE A CUTIE.
G...
GASP...
YOU'RE LIKE A MANJU CAKE.
CHEWY, CHEWY, CHEWY, CHEWY.
CHEWY, CHEWY, CHEWY, CHEWY.

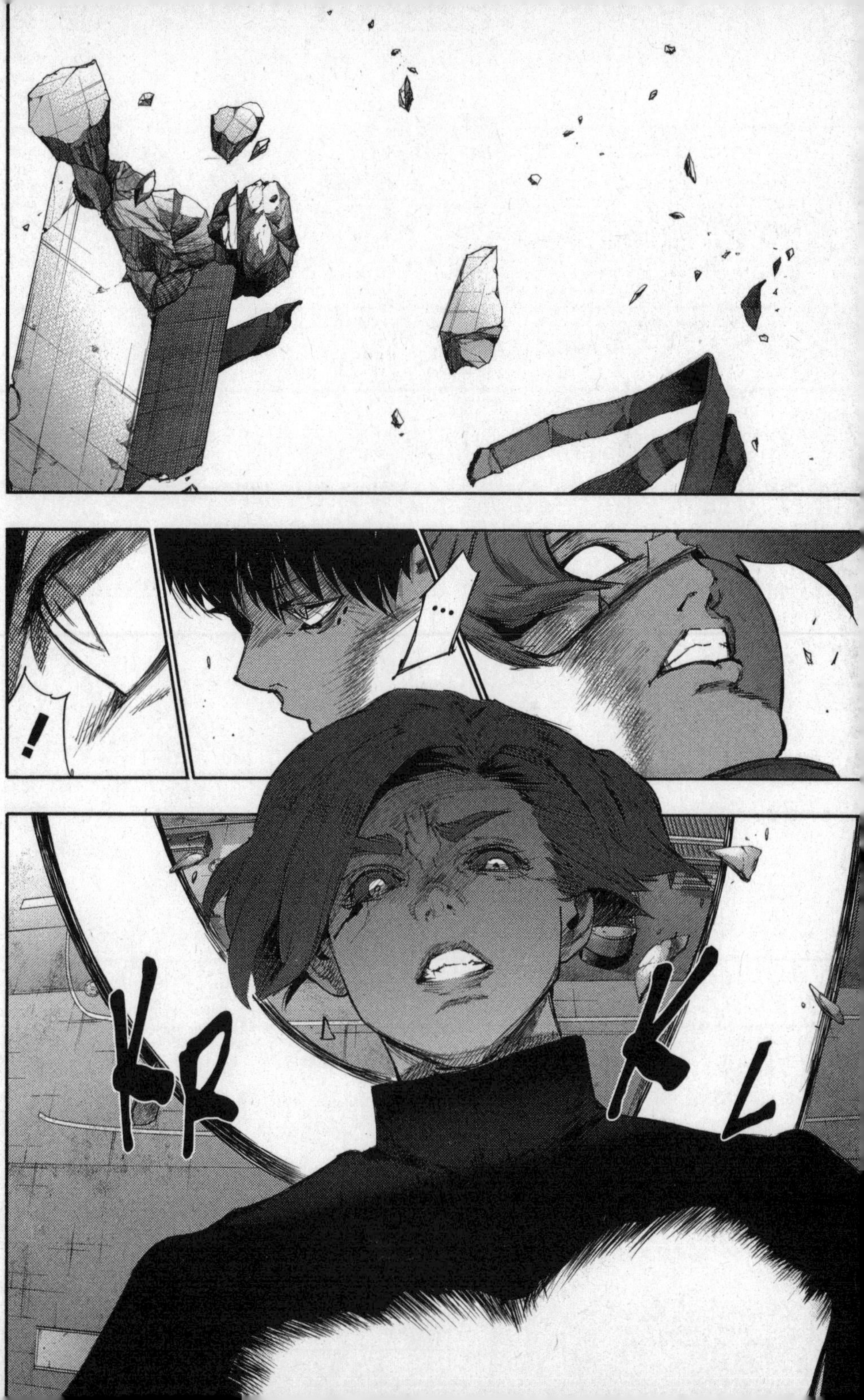
...
!
KRKL

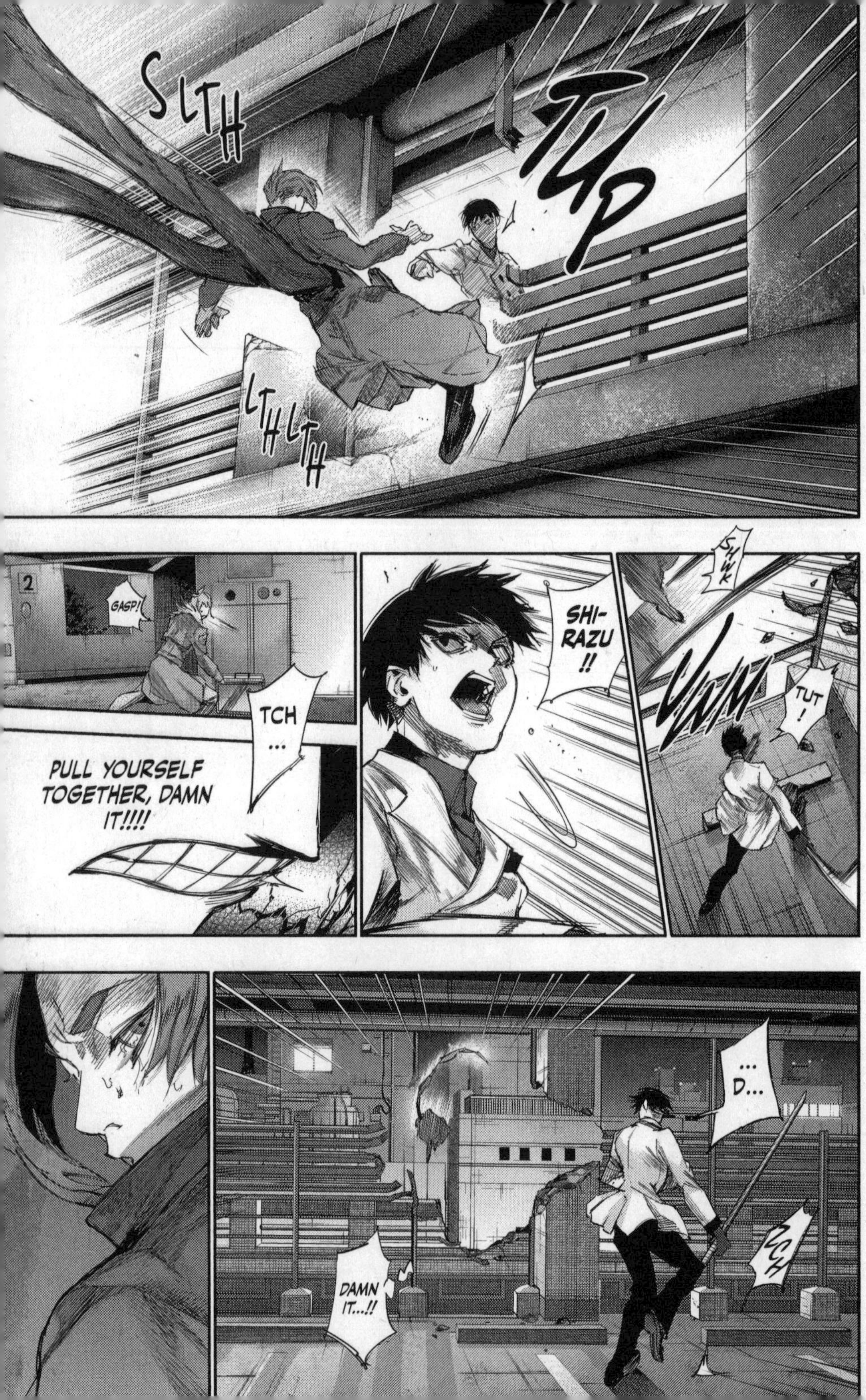
TUP
SLTH
LTHLTH
SHWK
VWM
TUT!
SHI-RAZU!!
GASP!
TCH...
PULL YOURSELF TOGETHER, DAMN IT!!!!
...D...
ZCH
DAMN IT...!!

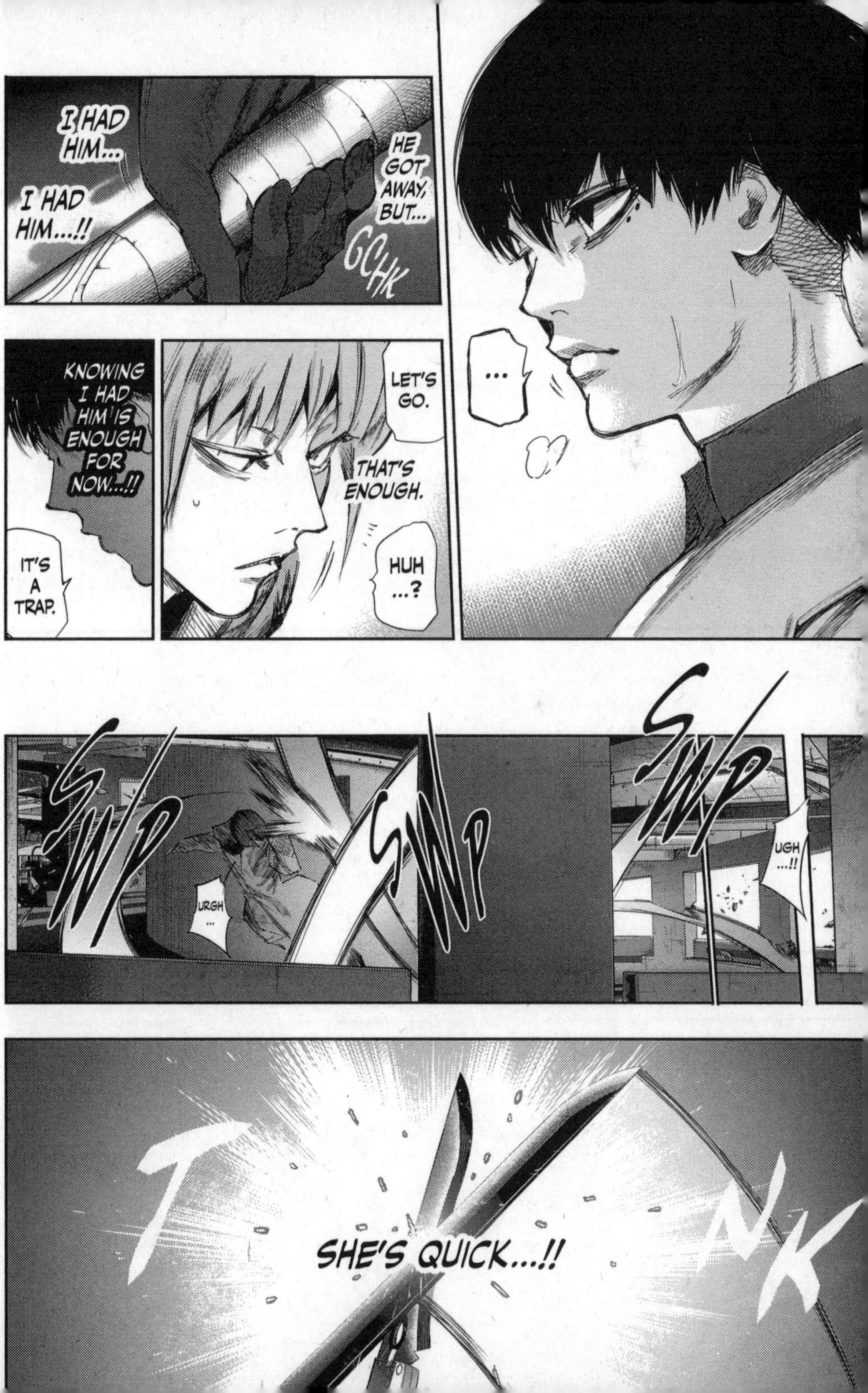
...
HE GOT AWAY, BUT...
I HAD HIM...
I HAD HIM...!!
GCHK
LET'S GO.
THAT'S ENOUGH.
HUH ...?
KNOWING I HAD HIM IS ENOUGH FOR NOW...!!
IT'S A TRAP.
SWP
UGH ...!!
SWP
SWP
URGH ...
TNK
SHE'S QUICK...!!

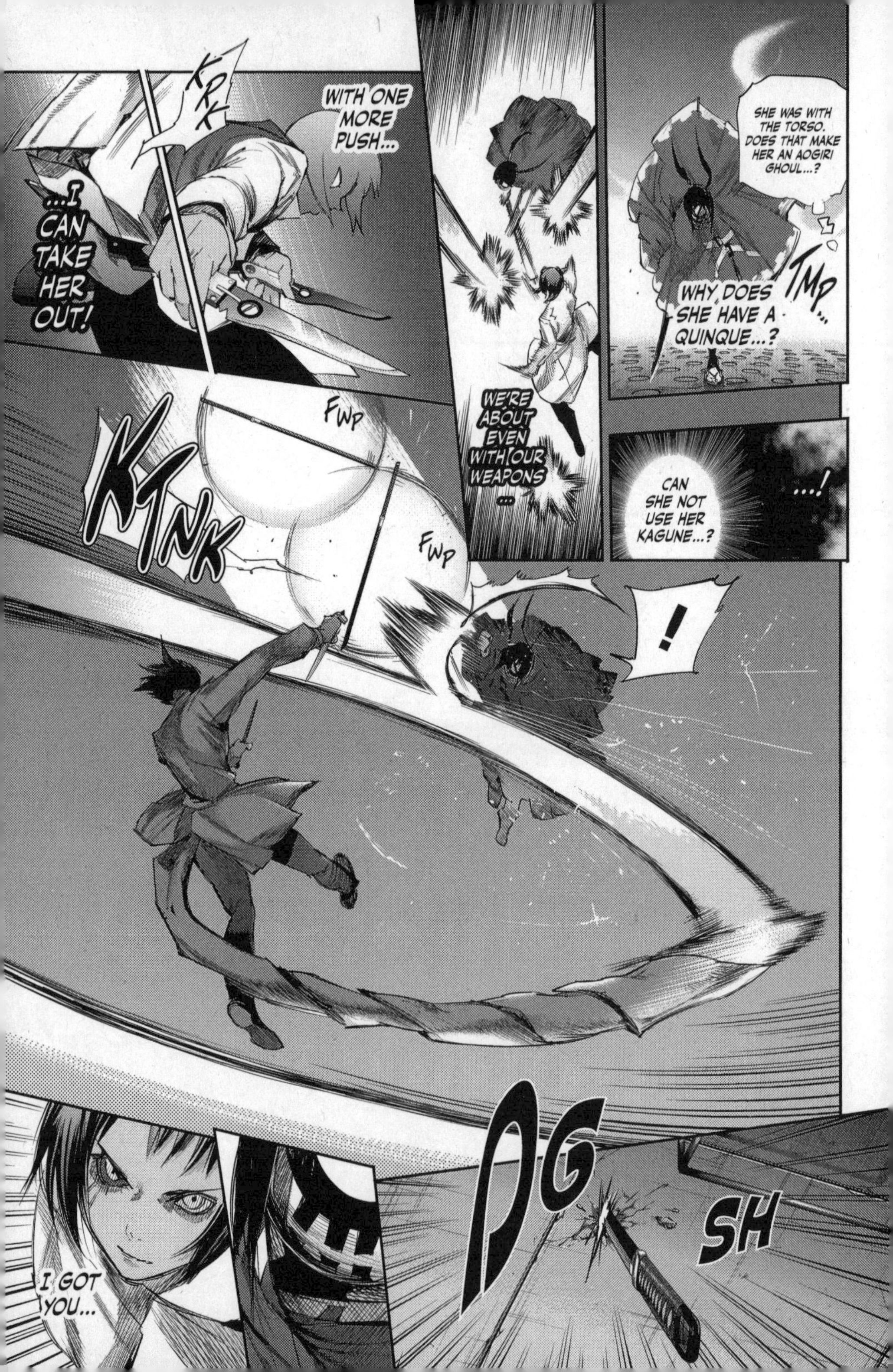
SHE WAS WITH THE TORSO. DOES THAT MAKE HER AN AOGIRI GHOUL...?
TMP...
WHY DOES SHE HAVE A QUINQUE...?
...!
CAN SHE NOT USE HER KAGUNE...?
WE'RE ABOUT EVEN WITH OUR WEAPONS...
WITH ONE MORE PUSH...
KRK
...I CAN TAKE HER OUT!
!
FWP
FWP
KANK
SH
DG
I GOT YOU...

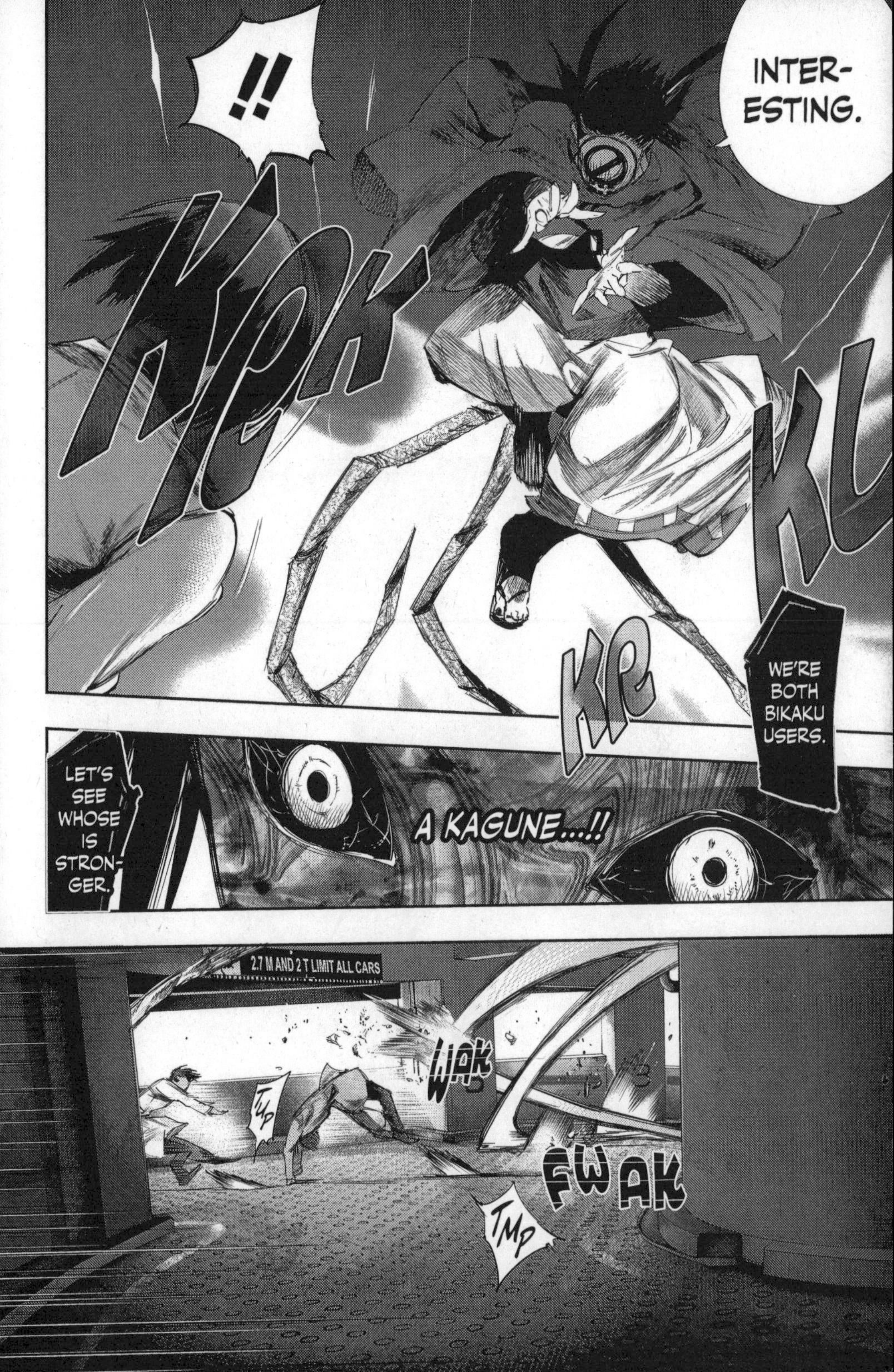
INTER-ESTING.
!!
KRAK
KR
WE'RE BOTH BIKAKU USERS.
A KAGUNE...!!
LET'S SEE WHOSE IS STRONGER.
2.7 M AND 2 T LIMIT ALL CARS
WAK
TUP
FWAK
TMP

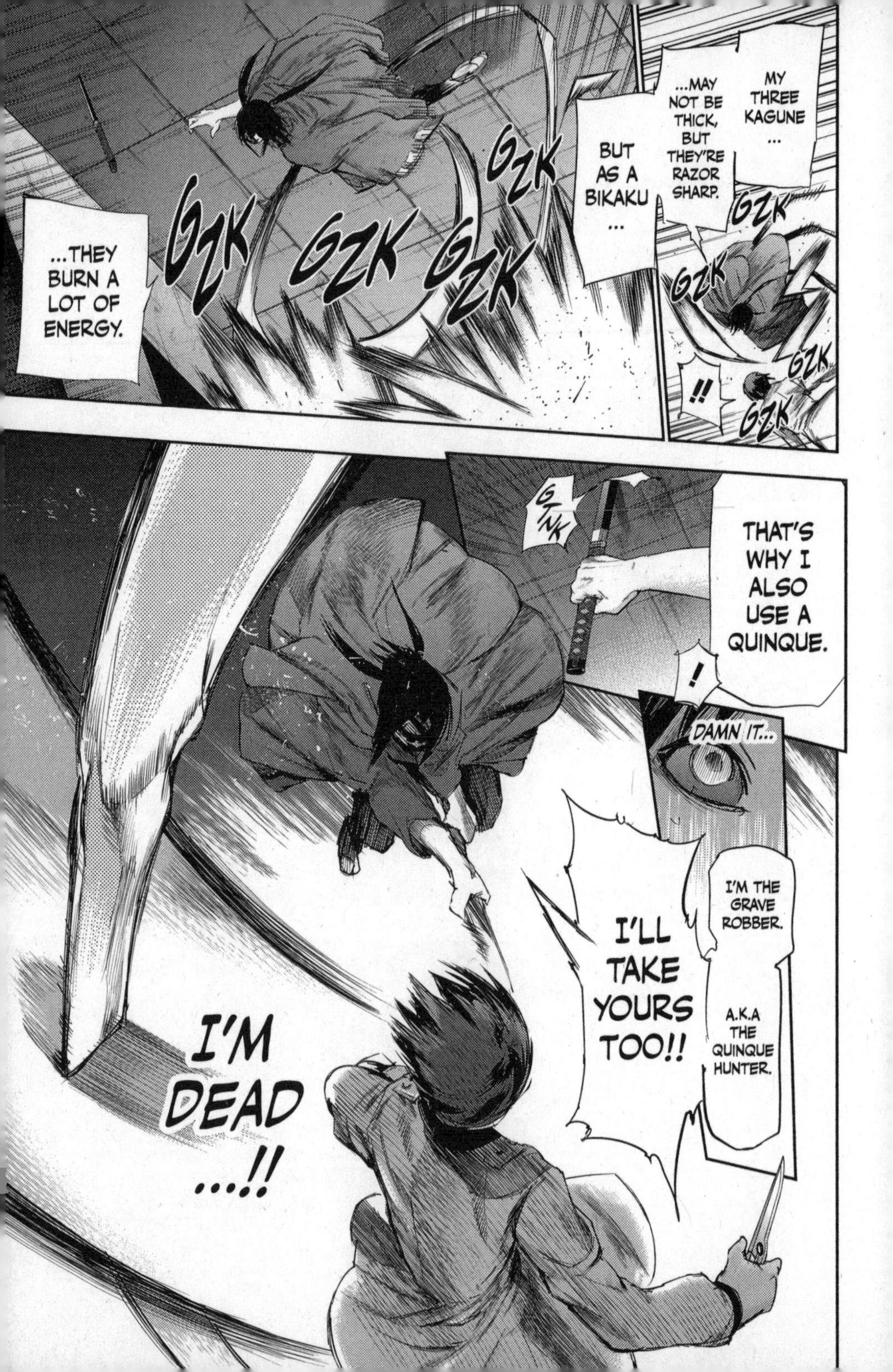
MY THREE KAGUNE ...
...MAY NOT BE THICK, BUT THEY'RE RAZOR SHARP.
GZK
GZK
!!
GZK
GZK
BUT AS A BIKAKU ...
GZK
GZK
GZK
GZK
GZK
...THEY BURN A LOT OF ENERGY.
THAT'S WHY I ALSO USE A QUINQUE.
GTINK
!
DAMN IT...
I'M THE GRAVE ROBBER.
A.K.A THE QUINQUE HUNTER.
I'LL TAKE YOURS TOO!!
I'M DEAD ...!!

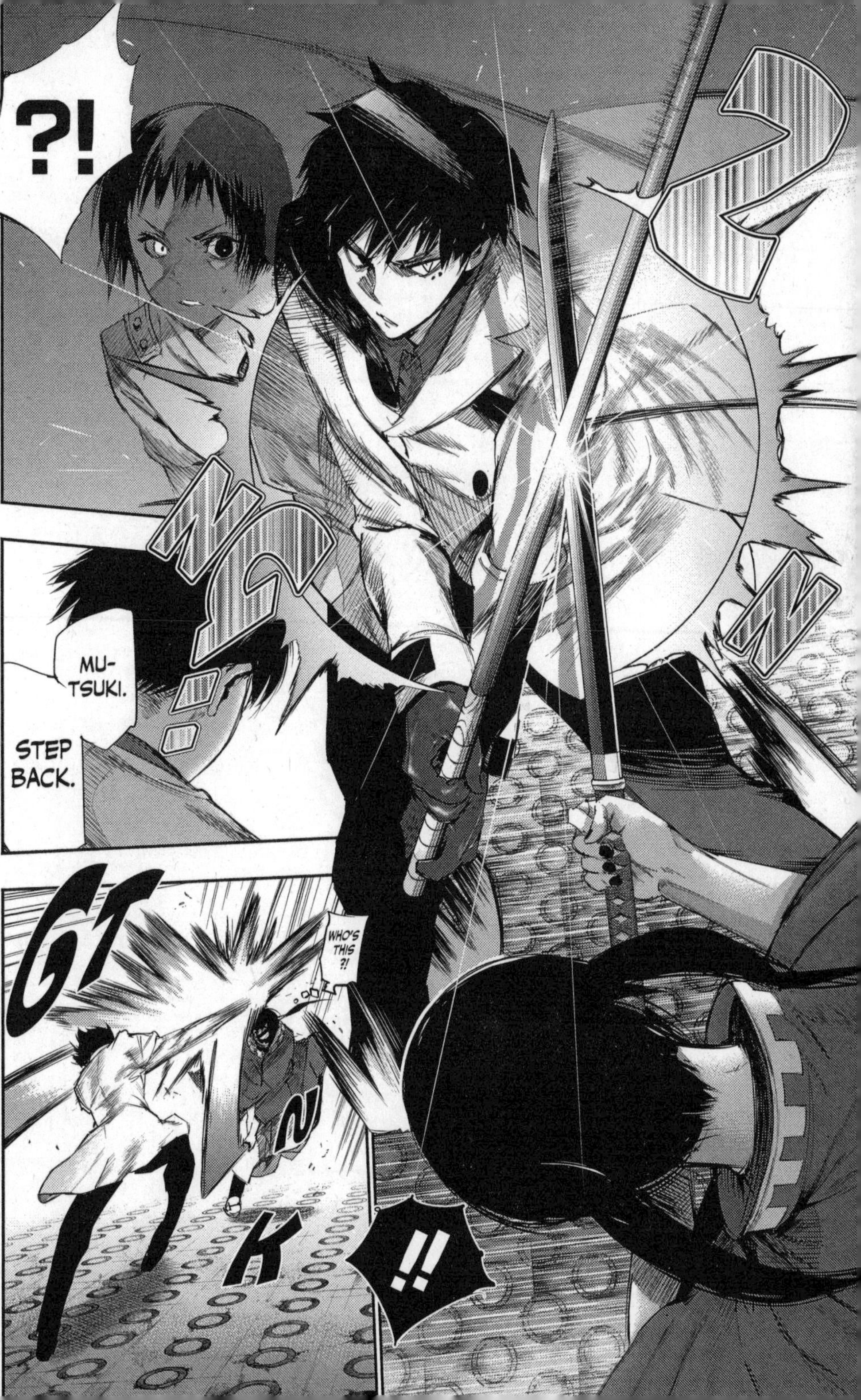
?!
MU-TSUKI.
STEP BACK.
WHO'S THIS ?!
!!

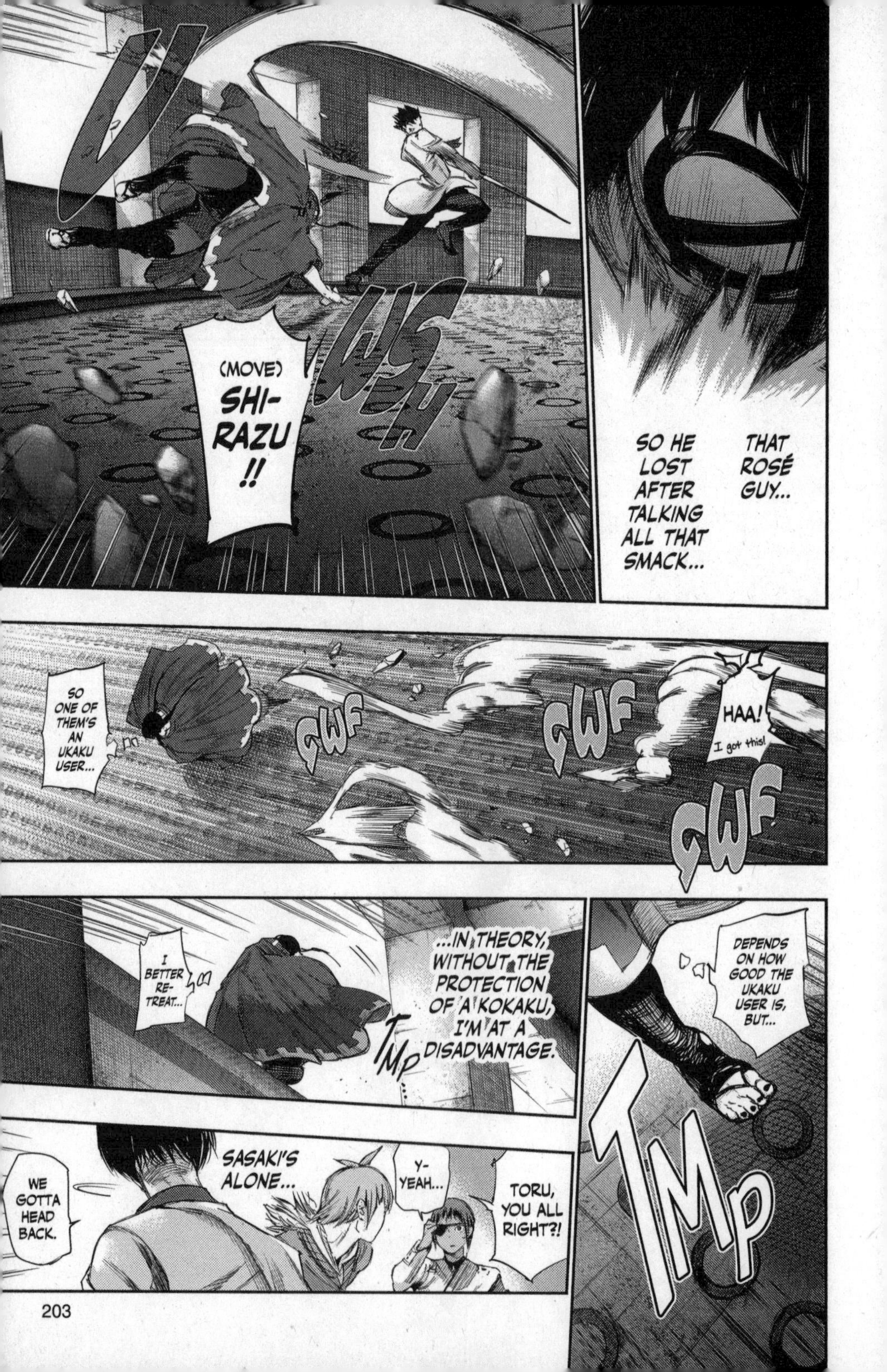

THAT ROSÉ GUY...
SO HE LOST AFTER TALKING ALL THAT SMACK...
(MOVE) SHI-RAZU!!
HAA! I got this!
GWF
GWF
GWF
SO ONE OF THEM'S AN UKAKU USER...
DEPENDS ON HOW GOOD THE UKAKU USER IS, BUT...
TMP
...IN THEORY, WITHOUT THE PROTECTION OF A KOKAKU, I'M AT A DISADVANTAGE.
TMP
I BETTER RE-TREAT...
TORU, YOU ALL RIGHT?!
Y-YEAH...
SASAKI'S ALONE...
WE GOTTA HEAD BACK.

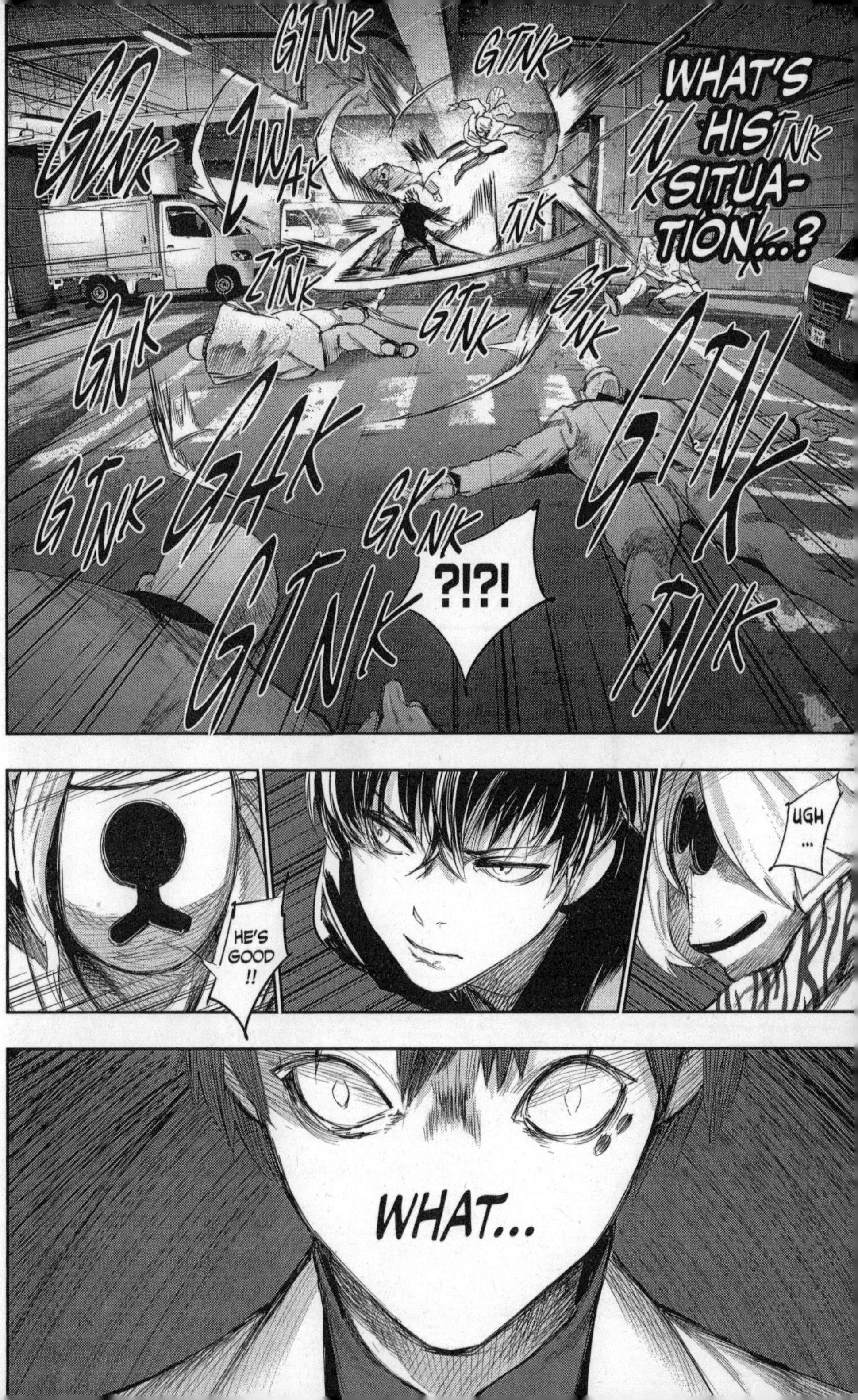
WHAT'S HIS SITUATION...?
GTNK
GTNK
ZWAK
GTNK
GTNK
GAK
GTNK
?!?!
UGH ...
HE'S GOOD !!
WHAT...

...THE?!

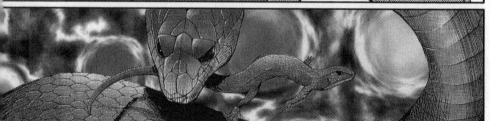

WHAT A SHAME !!!

HE'LL EAT US ALIVE!!

FOR- GET THIS!

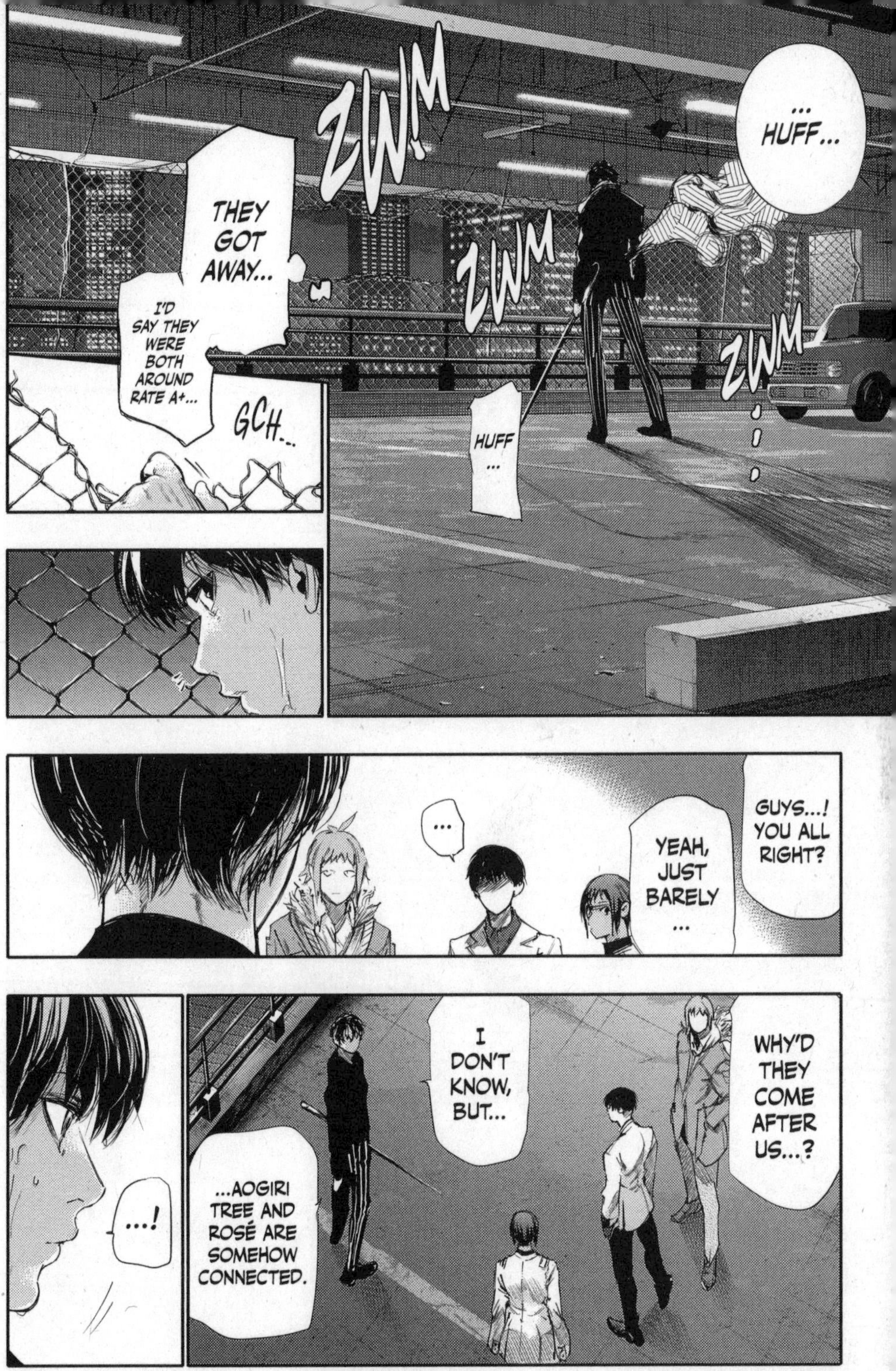
... HUFF...
ZWM
ZWM
ZWM
HUFF ...
THEY GOT AWAY...
I'D SAY THEY WERE BOTH AROUND RATE A+...
GCH...
GUYS...! YOU ALL RIGHT?
YEAH, JUST BARELY ...
...
WHY'D THEY COME AFTER US...?
I DON'T KNOW, BUT...
...AOGIRI TREE AND ROSÉ ARE SOMEHOW CONNECTED.
...!

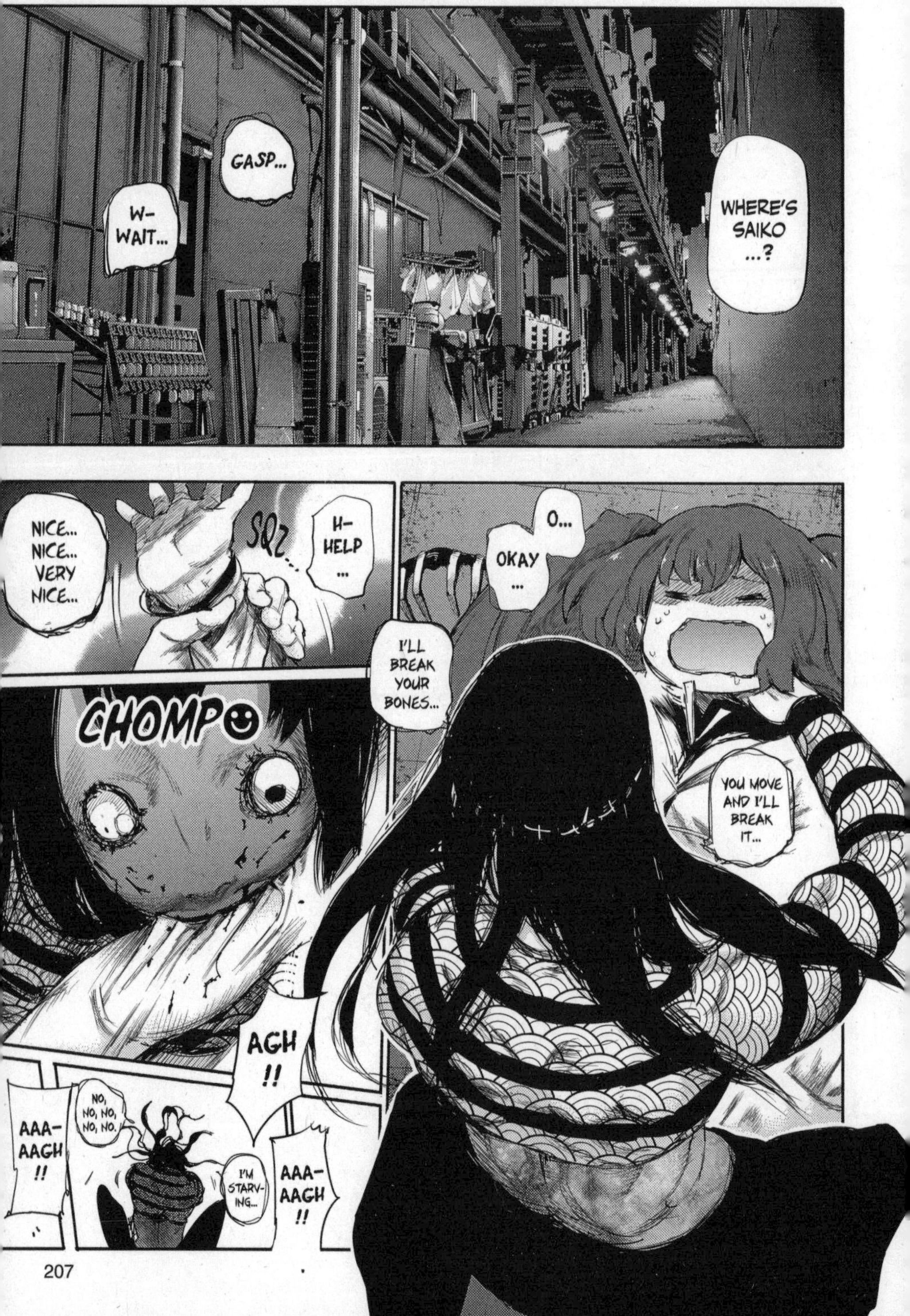
WHERE'S SAIKO ...?
GASP...
W- WAIT...
O... OKAY ...
I'LL BREAK YOUR BONES...
YOU MOVE AND I'LL BREAK IT...
H- HELP ...
SQZ...
NICE... NICE... VERY NICE...
CHOMP
AGH !!
AAA- AAGH !!
I'M STARV- ING...
NO, NO, NO, NO, NO.
AAA- AAGH !!

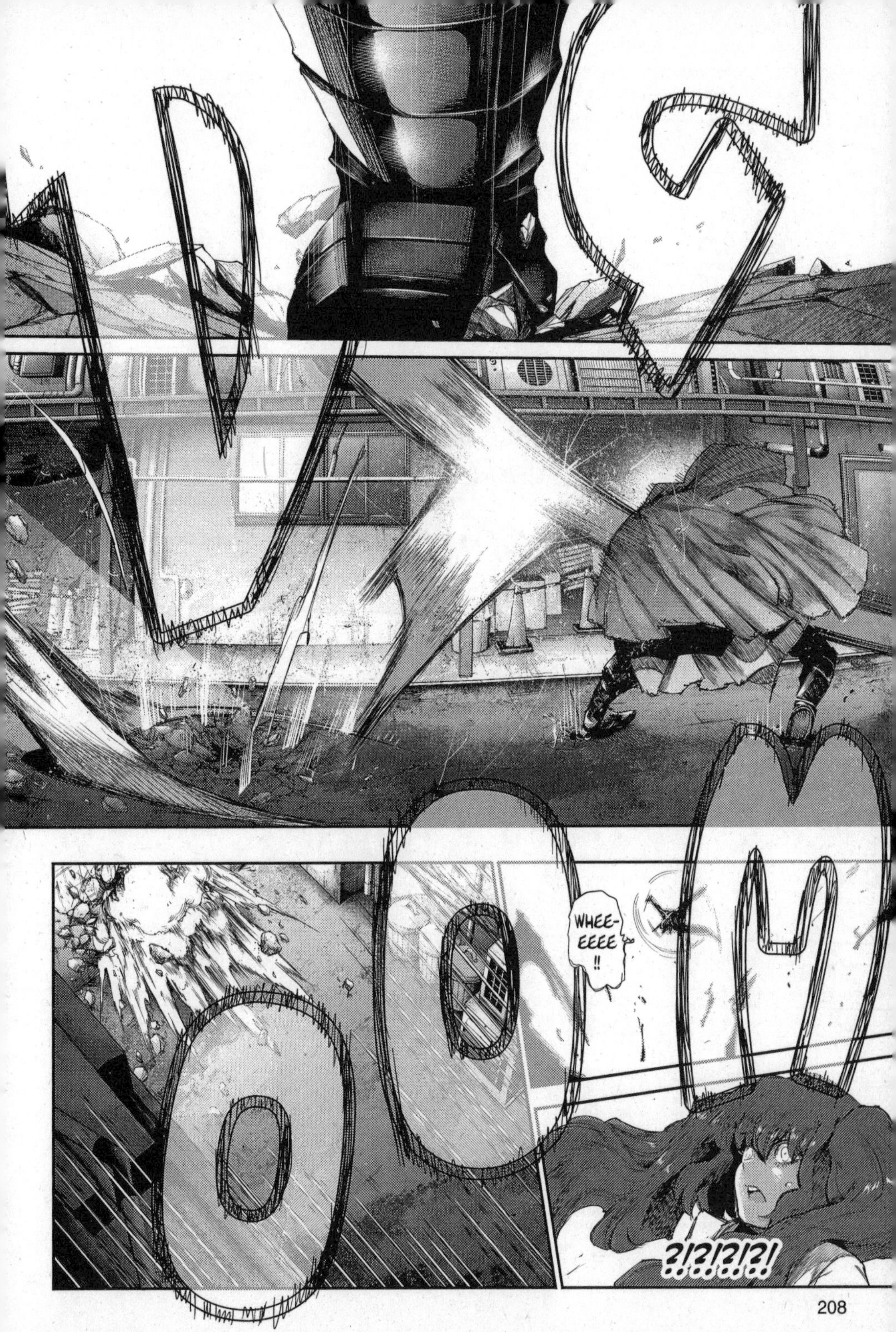
WHEEE-EEEE !!
!?!?!?!?

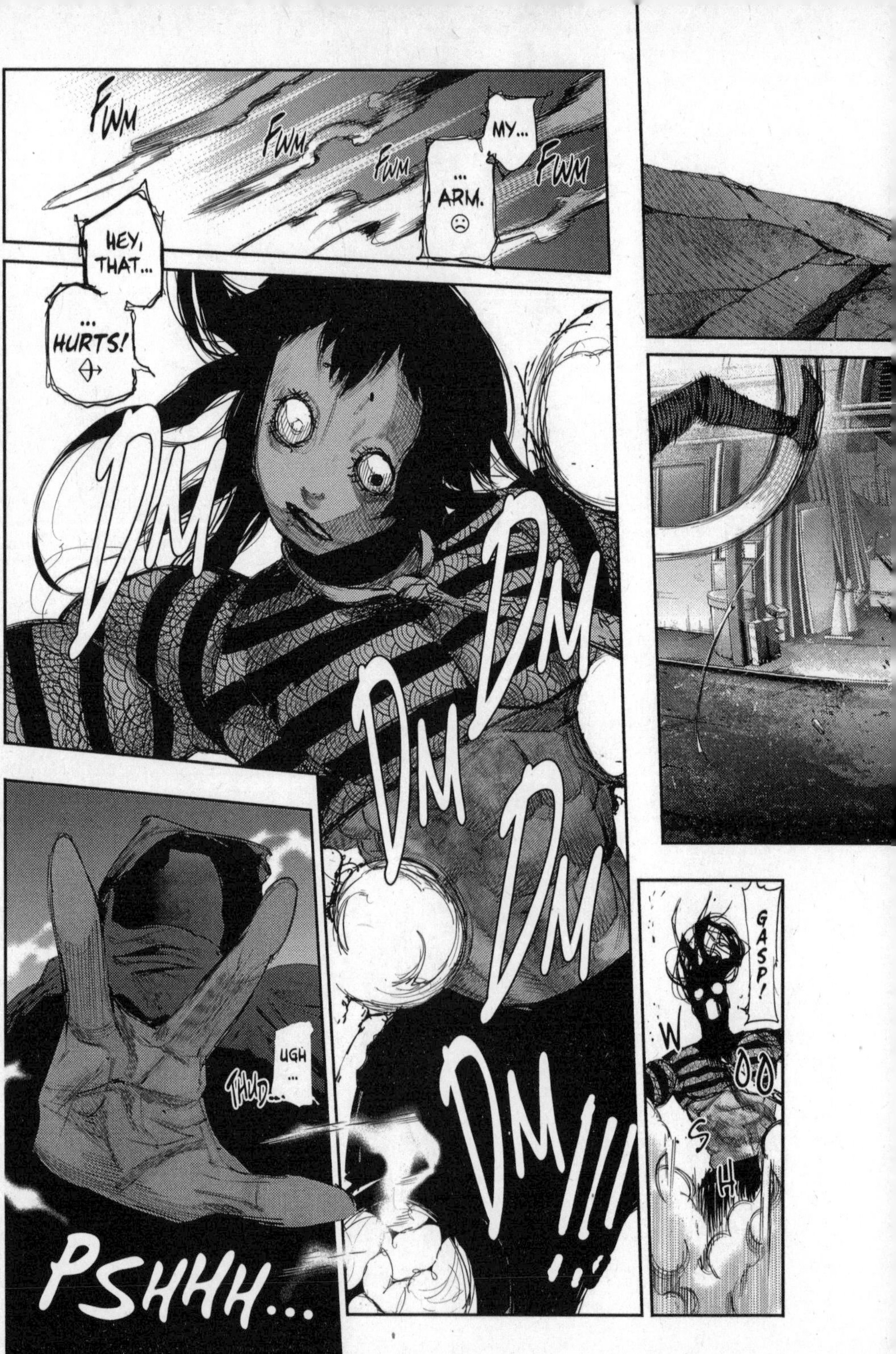
MY...
FWM
... ARM.
FWM
FWM
FWM
HEY, THAT...
... HURTS!
DM
DM
DM
DM
DM
DM!!!
GASP!
WOOSH
UGH...
THUD...
PSHHH...

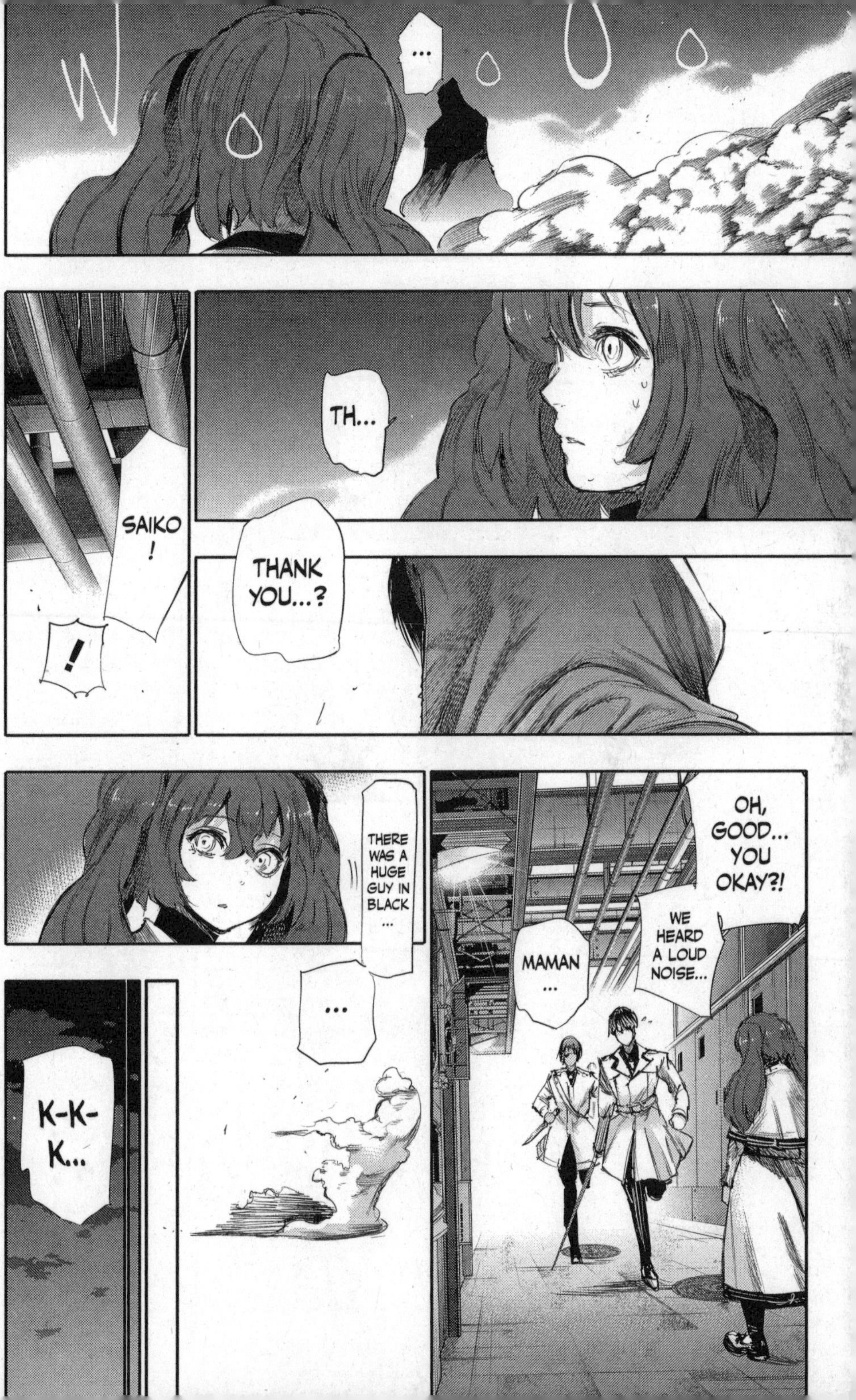
...
TH...
THANK YOU...?
SAIKO !
!
OH, GOOD... YOU OKAY?!
WE HEARD A LOUD NOISE...
MAMAN ...
THERE WAS A HUGE GUY IN BLACK ...
...
K-K-K...

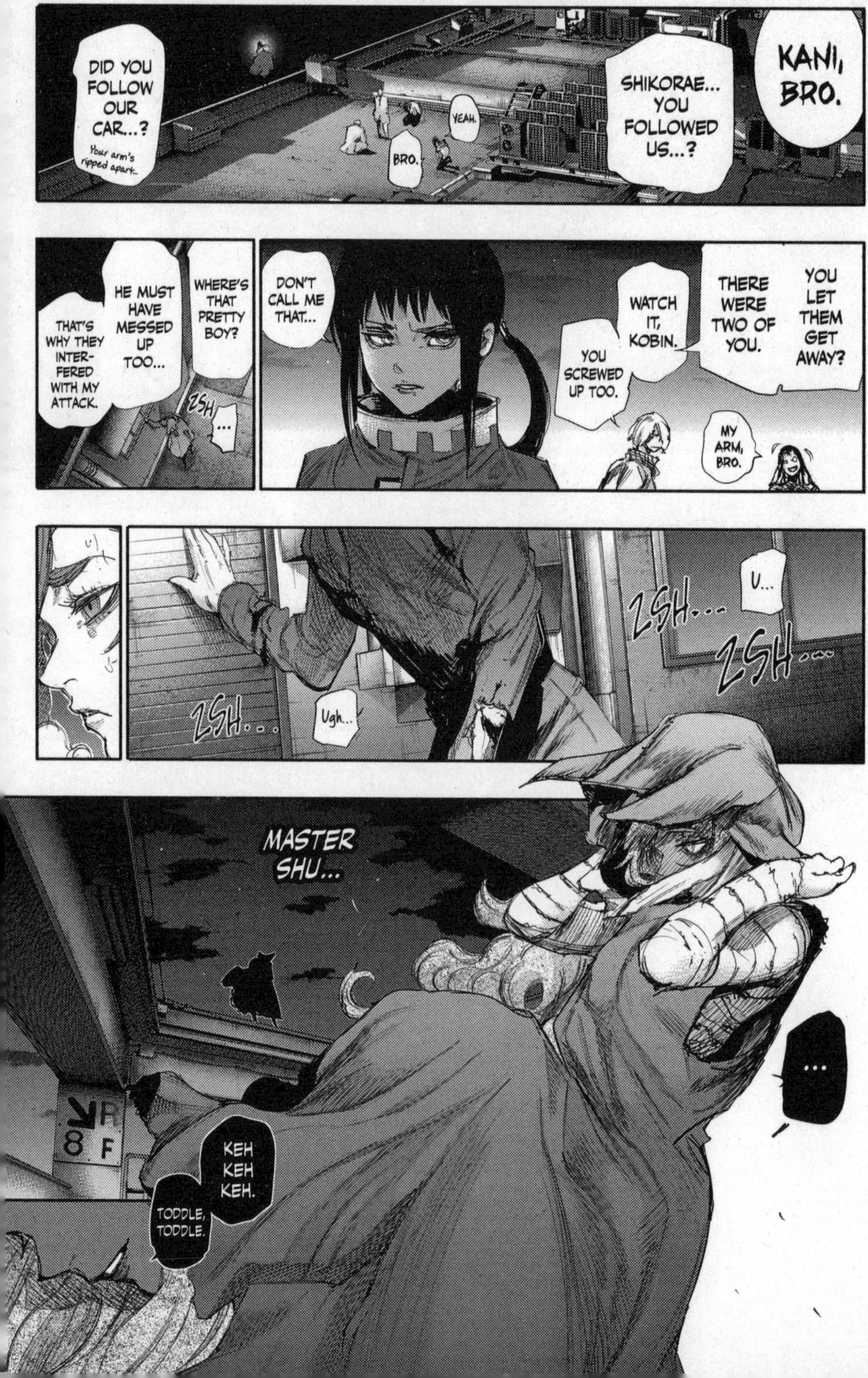
KANI, BRO.
SHIKORAE... YOU FOLLOWED US...?
YEAH.
BRO.
DID YOU FOLLOW OUR CAR...?
Your arm's ripped apart..
YOU LET THEM GET AWAY?
THERE WERE TWO OF YOU.
WATCH IT, KOBIN.
DON'T CALL ME THAT...
YOU SCREWED UP TOO.
MY ARM, BRO.
WHERE'S THAT PRETTY BOY?
HE MUST HAVE MESSED UP TOO...
THAT'S WHY THEY INTER-FERED WITH MY ATTACK.
ZSH
...
U...
ZSH...
ZSH...
Ugh...
ZSH...
...
MASTER SHU...
KEH KEH KEH.
TODDLE, TODDLE.

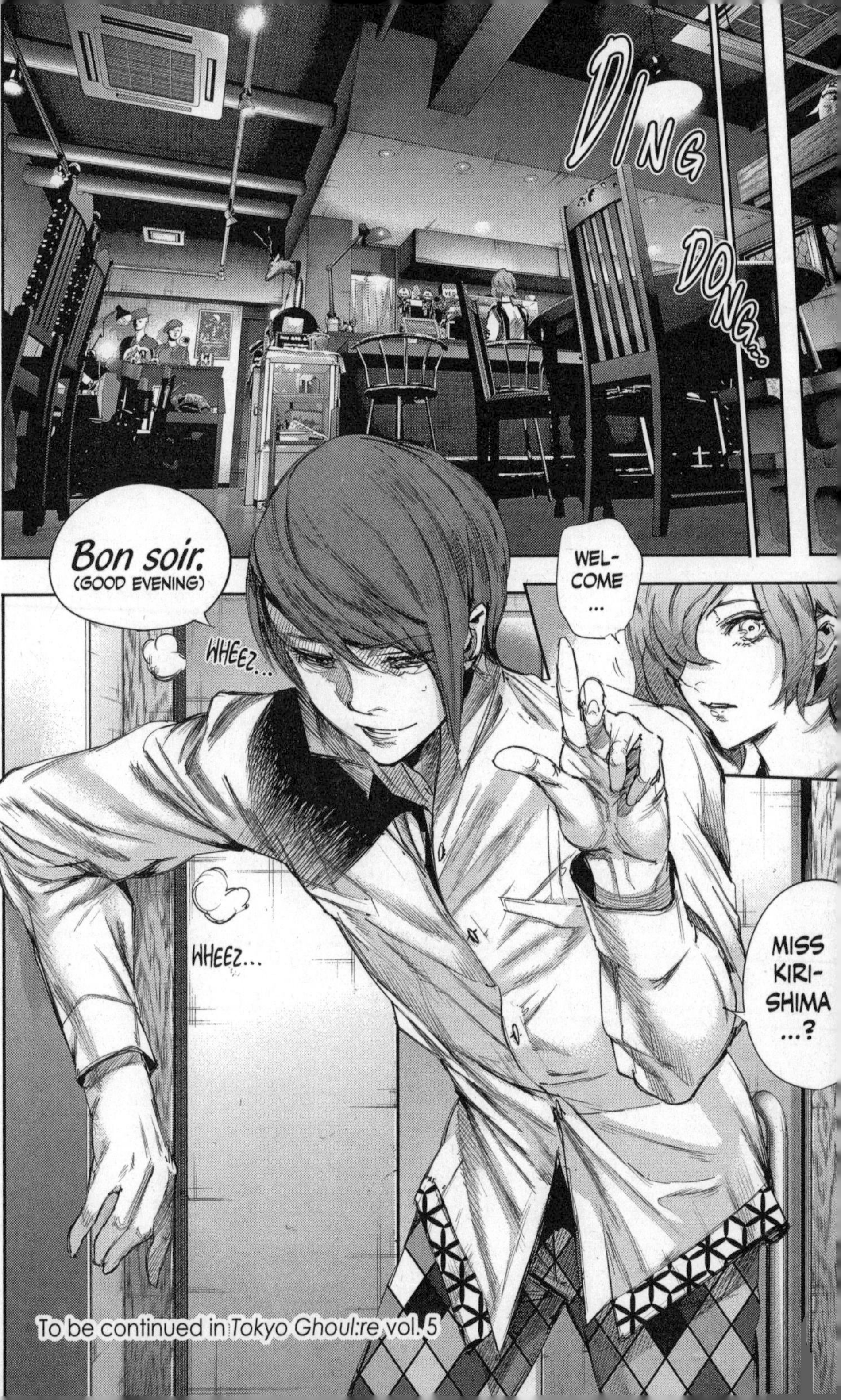
DING DONG...
WEL-COME ...
MISS KIRI-SHIMA ...?
Bon soir.
(GOOD EVENING)
WHEEZ...
WHEEZ...

To be continued in *Tokyo Ghoul:re* vol. 5

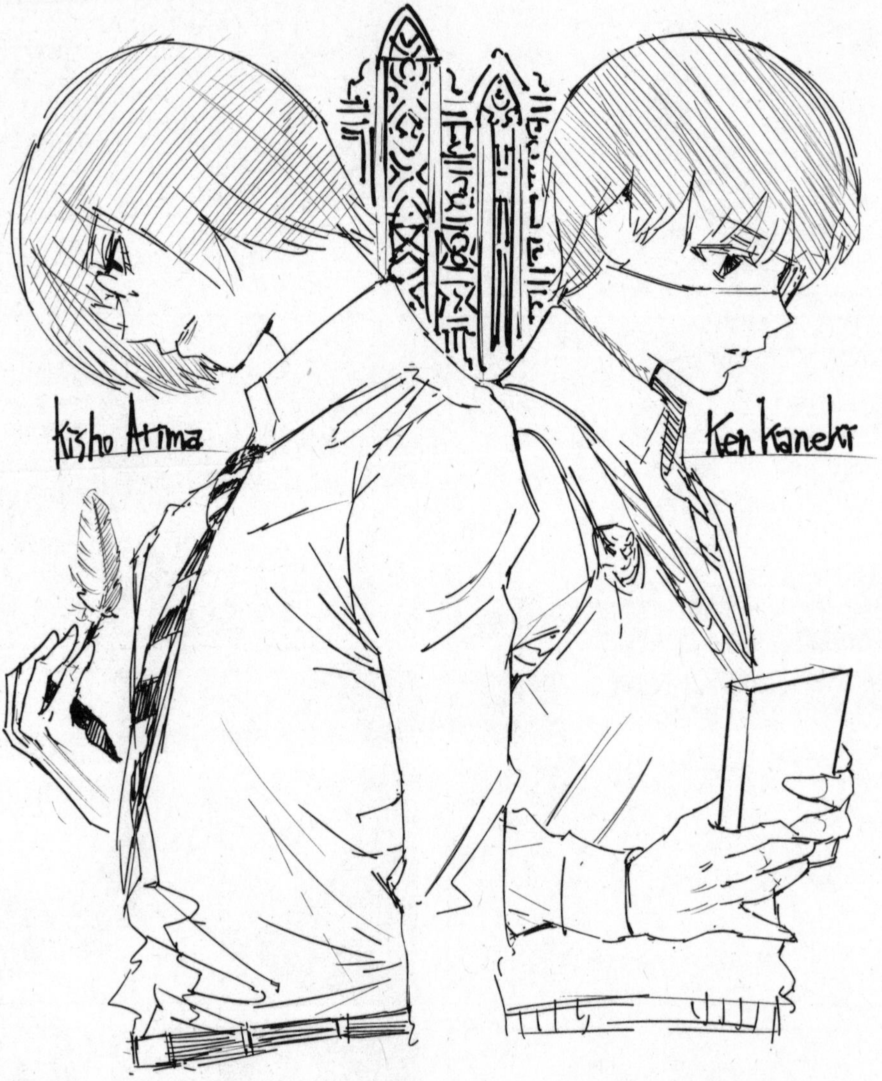
Kisho Arima
Ken Kaneki

Staff
Mizuki Ide
Kota Shugyo
Hashimoto
Kiyotaka Aihara
Rikako Miura

Comic design Hideaki Shimada (L.S.D.)
Magazine design Akie Demachi (POCKET)
Photography Wataru Tanaka
Editor Junpei Matsuo

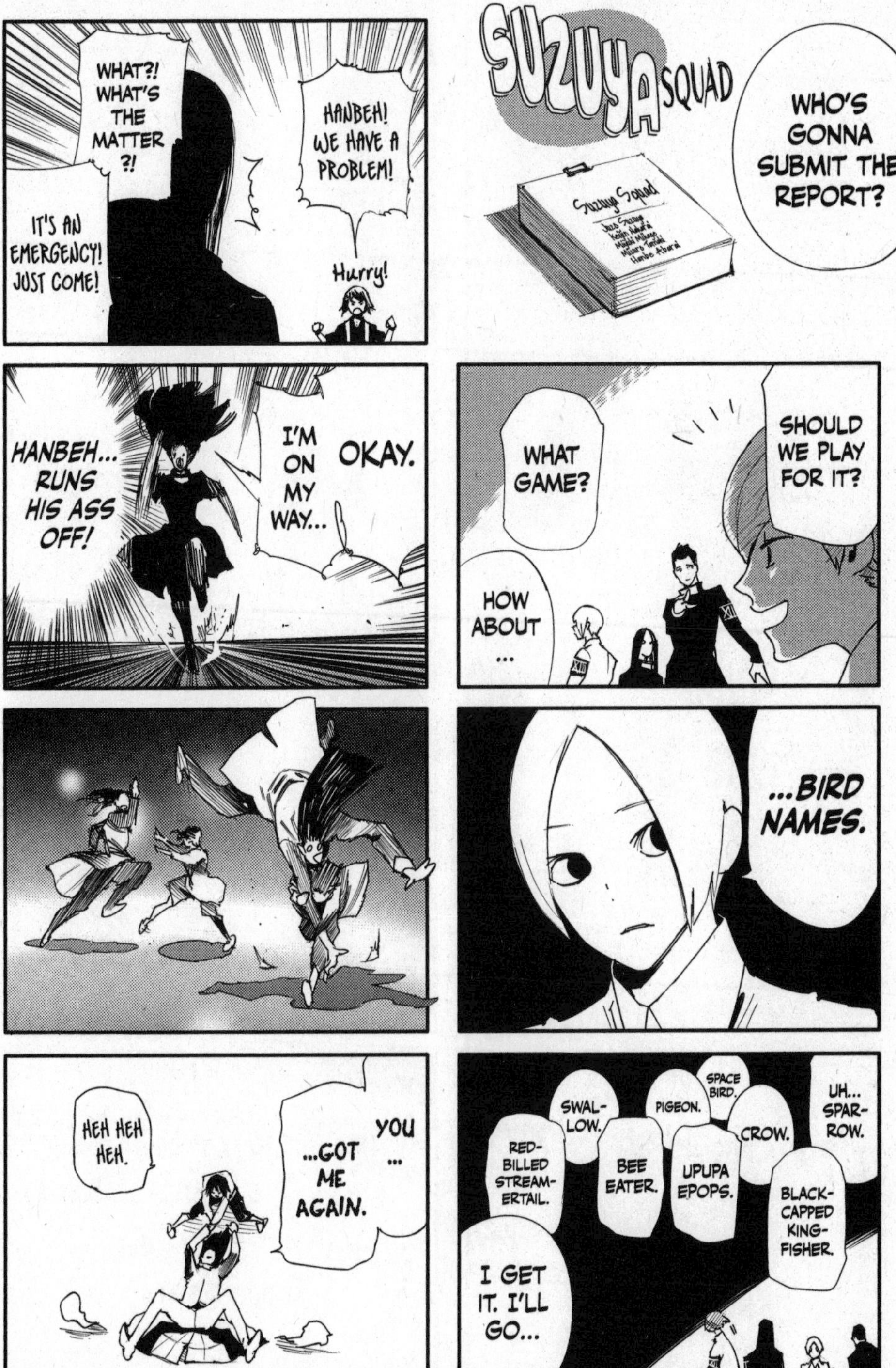
SUZUYA SQUAD
Suzuya Squad Juzo Suzuya Keijin Aekata Mizuki Mikage Mizuro Tamaki Hanbe Abara
WHO'S GONNA SUBMIT THE REPORT?
SHOULD WE PLAY FOR IT?
WHAT GAME?
HOW ABOUT ...
...BIRD NAMES.
UH... SPAR-ROW.
SPACE BIRD.
CROW.
PIGEON.
SWAL-LOW.
BLACK-CAPPED KING-FISHER.
UPUPA EPOPS.
BEE EATER.
RED-BILLED STREAM-ERTAIL.
I GET IT. I'LL GO...
HANBEH! WE HAVE A PROBLEM!
WHAT?! WHAT'S THE MATTER?!
IT'S AN EMERGENCY! JUST COME!
Hurry!
OKAY.
I'M ON MY WAY...
HANBEH... RUNS HIS ASS OFF!
YOU ...
...GOT ME AGAIN.
HEH HEH HEH.

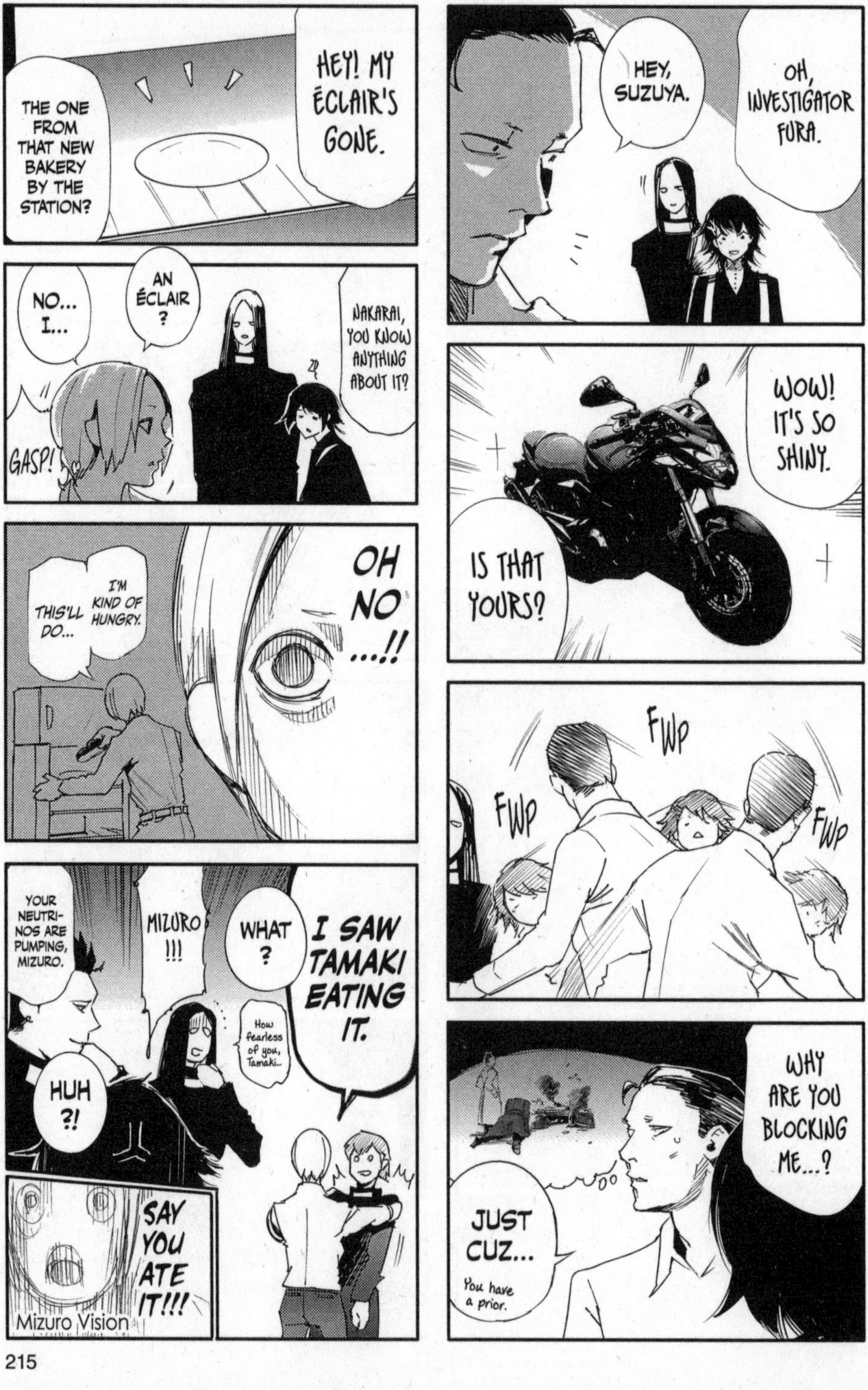
OH, INVESTIGATOR FURA.
HEY, SUZUYA.
WOW! IT'S SO SHINY.
IS THAT YOURS?
FWP
FWP
FWP
WHY ARE YOU BLOCKING ME...?
JUST CUZ...
You have a prior.
HEY! MY ÉCLAIR'S GONE.
THE ONE FROM THAT NEW BAKERY BY THE STATION?
NAKARAI, YOU KNOW ANYTHING ABOUT IT?
AN ÉCLAIR?
NO... I...
GASP!
OH NO ...!!
I'M KIND OF HUNGRY.
THIS'LL DO...
I SAW TAMAKI EATING IT.
WHAT?
MIZURO !!!
YOUR NEUTRINOS ARE PUMPING, MIZURO.
How fearless of you, Tamaki...
HUH?!
SAY YOU ATE IT!!!
Mizuro Vision

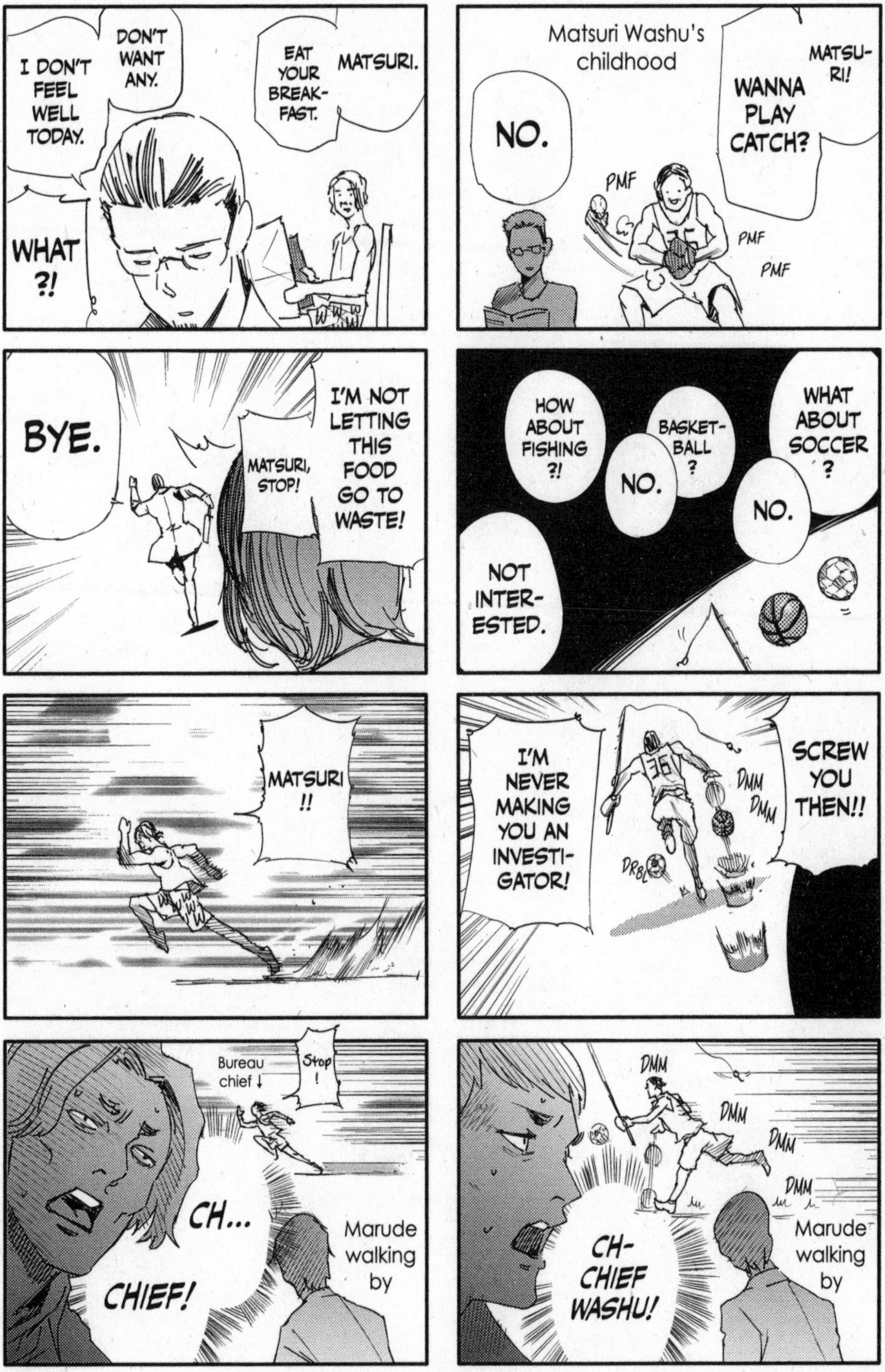
Matsuri Washu's childhood
MATSU-RI!
WANNA PLAY CATCH?
NO.
PMF
PMF
PMF
MATSURI.
EAT YOUR BREAK-FAST.
DON'T WANT ANY.
I DON'T FEEL WELL TODAY.
WHAT?!
WHAT ABOUT SOCCER?
NO.
BASKET-BALL?
NO.
HOW ABOUT FISHING?!
NOT INTER-ESTED.
I'M NOT LETTING THIS FOOD GO TO WASTE!
MATSURI, STOP!
BYE.
SCREW YOU THEN!!
DMM
DMM
I'M NEVER MAKING YOU AN INVESTI-GATOR!
DRBL
MATSURI!!
DMM
DMM
DMM
DMM
CH-CHIEF WASHU!
Marude walking by
Stop!
Bureau chief ↓
CH...
CHIEF!
Marude walking by

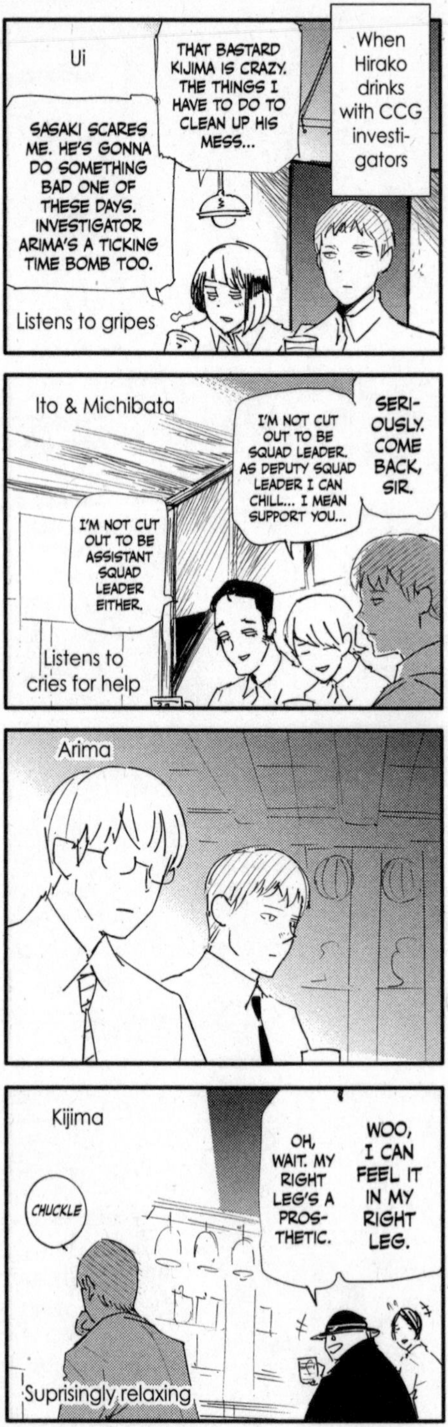
When Hirako drinks with CCG investigators
Ui
THAT BASTARD KIJIMA IS CRAZY. THE THINGS I HAVE TO DO TO CLEAN UP HIS MESS...
SASAKI SCARES ME. HE'S GONNA DO SOMETHING BAD ONE OF THESE DAYS. INVESTIGATOR ARIMA'S A TICKING TIME BOMB TOO.
Listens to gripes
Ito & Michibata
SERIOUSLY. COME BACK, SIR.
I'M NOT CUT OUT TO BE SQUAD LEADER. AS DEPUTY SQUAD LEADER I CAN CHILL... I MEAN SUPPORT YOU...
I'M NOT CUT OUT TO BE ASSISTANT SQUAD LEADER EITHER.
Listens to cries for help
Arima
Kijima
WOO, I CAN FEEL IT IN MY RIGHT LEG.
OH, WAIT. MY RIGHT LEG'S A PROSTHETIC.
CHUCKLE
Suprisingly relaxing

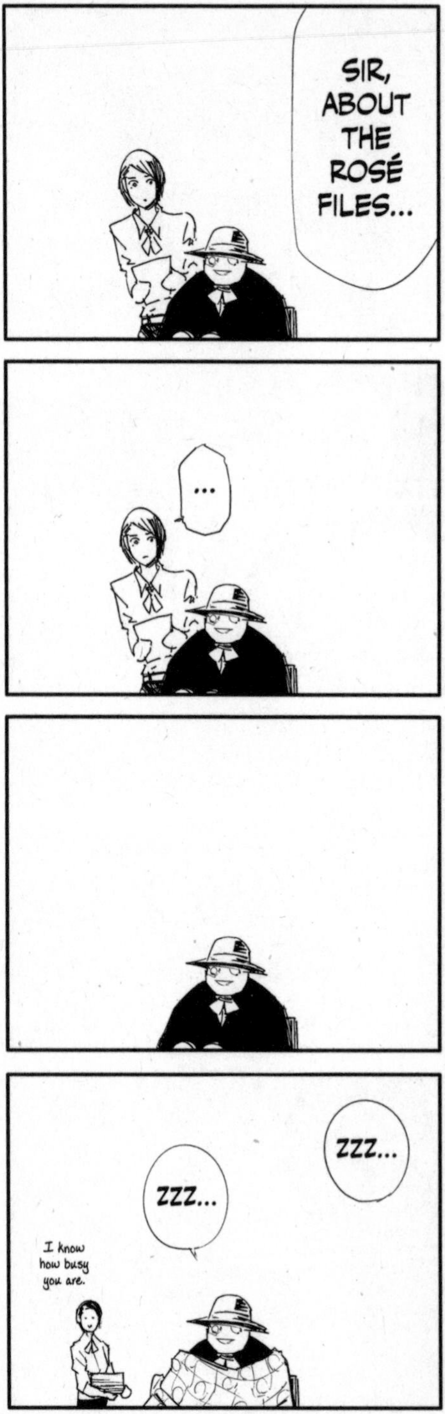
SIR, ABOUT THE ROSÉ FILES...
...
ZZZ...
ZZZ...
I know how busy you are.

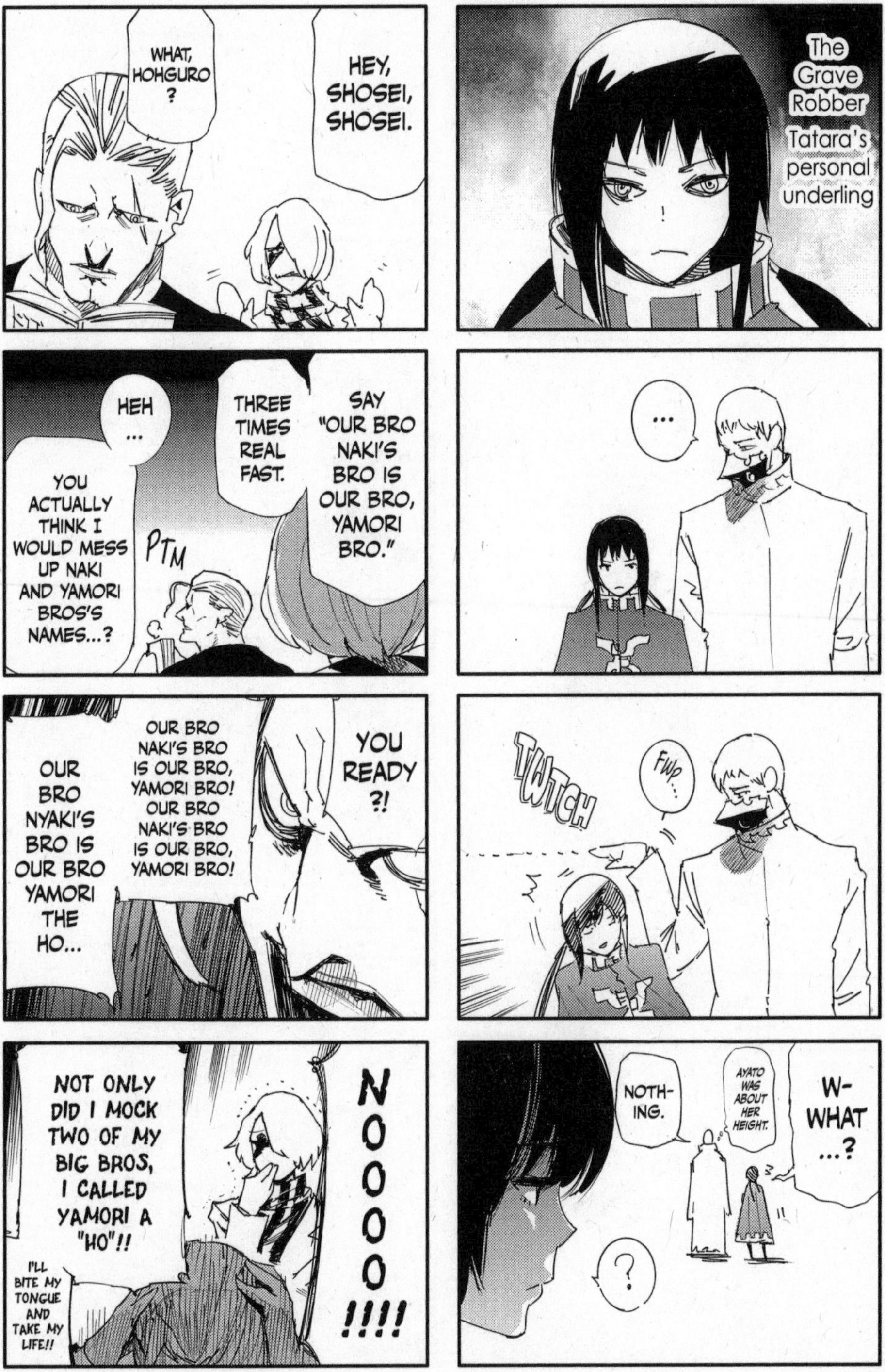
The Grave Robber Tatara's personal underling
...
TWITCH
FWP...
W-WHAT ...?
AYATO WAS ABOUT HER HEIGHT.
NOTH-ING.
?
HEY, SHOSEI, SHOSEI.
WHAT, HOHGURO ?
SAY "OUR BRO NAKI'S BRO IS OUR BRO, YAMORI BRO."
THREE TIMES REAL FAST.
HEH ...
YOU ACTUALLY THINK I WOULD MESS UP NAKI AND YAMORI BROS'S NAMES...?
PTM
YOU READY ?!
OUR BRO NAKI'S BRO IS OUR BRO, YAMORI BRO! OUR BRO NAKI'S BRO IS OUR BRO, YAMORI BRO!
OUR BRO NYAKI'S BRO IS OUR BRO YAMORI THE HO...
NOOOO !!!!
NOT ONLY DID I MOCK TWO OF MY BIG BROS, I CALLED YAMORI A "HO"!!
I'LL BITE MY TONGUE AND TAKE MY LIFE!!

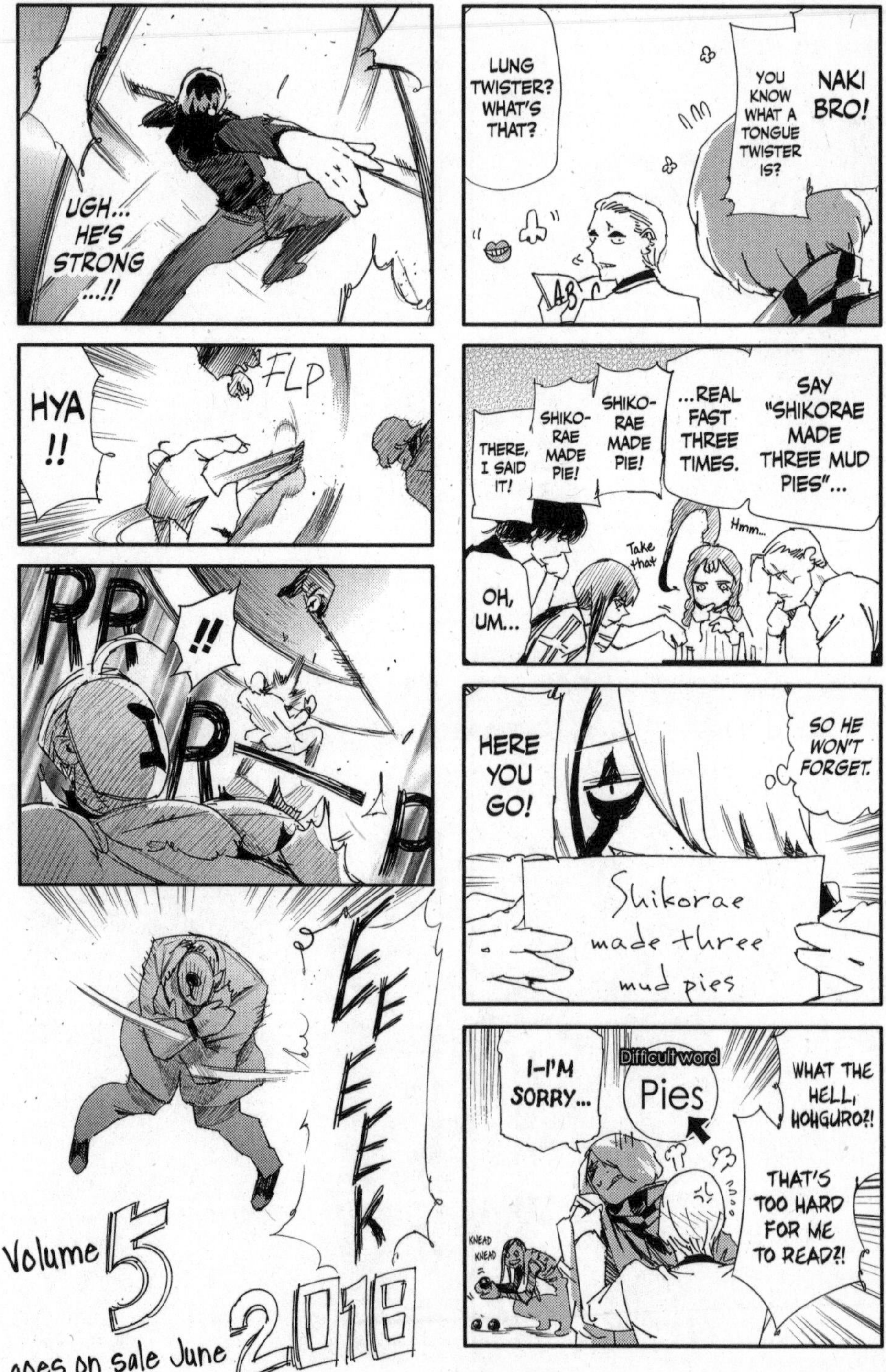
NAKI BRO!
YOU KNOW WHAT A TONGUE TWISTER IS?
LUNG TWISTER? WHAT'S THAT?
SAY "SHIKORAE MADE THREE MUD PIES"...
...REAL FAST THREE TIMES.
Hmm...
SHIKO-RAE MADE PIE!
SHIKO-RAE MADE PIE!
Take that
THERE, I SAID IT!
OH, UM...
SO HE WON'T FORGET.
HERE YOU GO!
Shikorae made three mud pies
WHAT THE HELL, HOHGURO?!
THAT'S TOO HARD FOR ME TO READ?!
Difficult word
Pies
I-I'M SORRY...
KNEAD KNEAD
UGH... HE'S STRONG ...!!
FLP
HYA !!
RRRP
!!
EEEEEK
Volume 5 goes on sale June 2018

UL:re

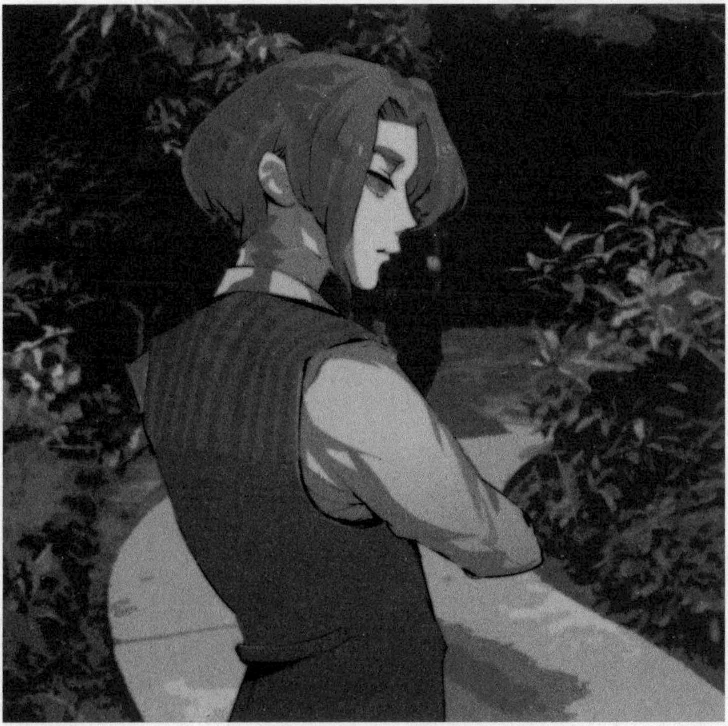

Kanae von Rosewald
カナエ＝フォンロゼヴァルト

- Age: 19 (DOB 4/23) ♂ • Blood type: B • Height/weight: 168cm/57kg
- RC type: Rinkaku • Life: Watering flowers, taking care of Shu
- Skills: Violin, tailoring, shoe repair

The youngest of the Rosewalds, a German branch of the Tsukiyama family. Tsukuru Tsukiyama's grandson and Shu Tsukiyama's cousin.

The Rosewald family was wiped out by Matsuri Washu, then a rank 2 investigator for the German CCG, and his team. Kanae, then ten years old, was the only survivor.

Kanae later moved to Japan and was hired by the Tsukiyama family.

JL:re

S1 Squad

- **Kori Ui** (Squad Leader)　　　　Special Investigator (Class 69)
  宇井 郡 (うい こうり)　　　　　　　　　　　　　　　1st Academy Junior

  - Age: 27 (DOB 10/3) ♂ • Blood type: O • Height/weight: 169cm/64kg
  - Quinque: Taruhi (Kokaku – Rate/A+) Ajite (Kokaku – Rate/SS)
  - Honors: Double White Wing Badge, Gold Osmanthus Badge,
    4th Ward Special Commander, etc.
  - Hobbies: Photo scrapbooking, collages, horseback riding
  - R&R: Solo karaoke, solo Korean barbeque, griping to
    Investigator Hirako over drinks
  - Family: Wealthy

- **Hairu Ihei** (Deputy Squad Leader)　　Senior Investigator (Class 74)
  伊丙 入 (いへい はいる)　　　　　　　　　　　　　　Hakubi Garden

  - Age: 20 (DOB 9/29) ♀ • Blood type: B • Height/weight: 160cm/58kg
  - Quinque: Aus (Rinkaku – Rate/S+) T-human (Ukaku – Rate/S+)
  - Honors: White Wing Badge, Gold Osmanthus Badge
  - Hobbies: Combat training, drawing, speaking to herself, observing Arima
  - Wishlist: Arima's Ixa

Fura Squad

- **Taishi Fura** (Squad Leader)　　　Senior Investigator (Class 64)
  富良 太志 (ふら たいし)　　　　　　　　　　　　　　4th Academy

  - Age: 32 (DOB 8/1) ♂ • Blood type: O • Height/weight: 182cm/87kg
  - Quinque: Steiner (Kokaku – Rate/S) Lantern (Bikaku – Rate/A+)
  - Honors: Osmanthus Badge, CCG Baseball League champion
  - Hobbies: Baseball, watching baseball, fixing motorcycles,
    playing with his daughter
  - Family: Aki (wife, 32), Natsu (daughter, 4)
  - Recently: Feels smokers are being stigmatized

GHOUL:re

SUI ISHIDA is the author of the immensely popular *Tokyo Ghoul* and several *Tokyo Ghoul* one-shots, including one that won second place in the *Weekly Young Jump* 113th Grand Prix award in 2010. *Tokyo Ghoul:re* is the sequel to *Tokyo Ghoul*.

Story and art by
SUI ISHIDA

TOKYO GHOUL:RE © 2014 by Sui Ishida
All rights reserved.
First published in Japan in 2014 by SHUEISHA Inc., Tokyo.
English translation rights arranged by SHUEISHA Inc.

Translation Joe Yamazaki
Touch-Up Art & Lettering Vanessa Satone
Design Shawn Carrico
Editor Pancha Diaz

Printed in the U.S.A.

Published by VIZ Media, LLC
P.O. Box 77010
San Francisco, CA 94107

10 9 8 7 6 5 4 3 2 1
First printing, February 2018

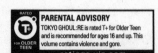

PARENTAL ADVISORY
TOKYO GHOUL:RE is rated T+ for Older Teen
and is recommended for ages 16 and up. This
volume contains violence and gore.
ratings.viz.com

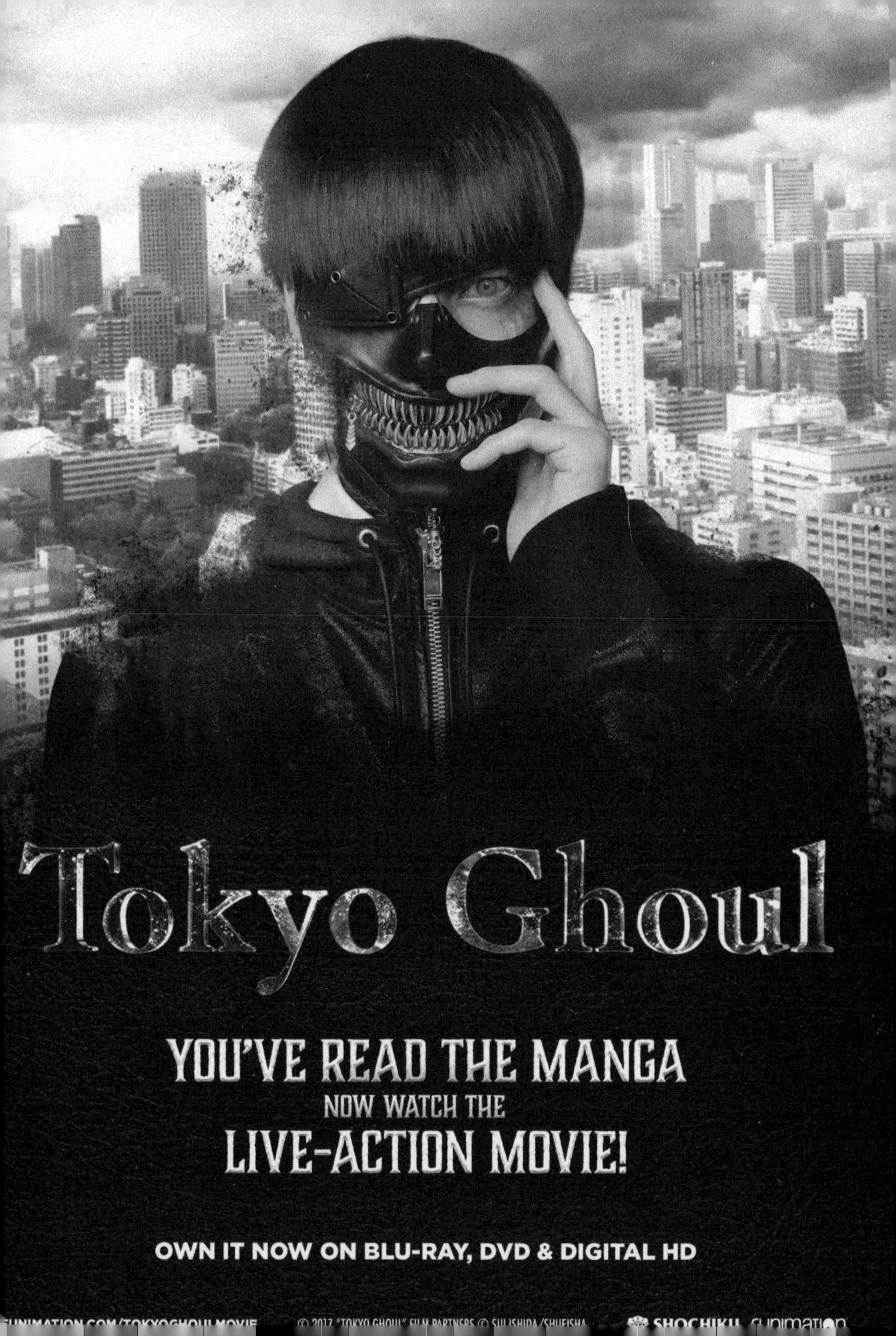
Tokyo Ghoul
YOU'VE READ THE MANGA
NOW WATCH THE
LIVE-ACTION MOVIE!
OWN IT NOW ON BLU-RAY, DVD & DIGITAL HD
FUNIMATION.COM/TOKYOGHOULMOVIE
© 2017 "TOKYO GHOUL" FILM PARTNERS © SUI ISHIDA/SHUEISHA

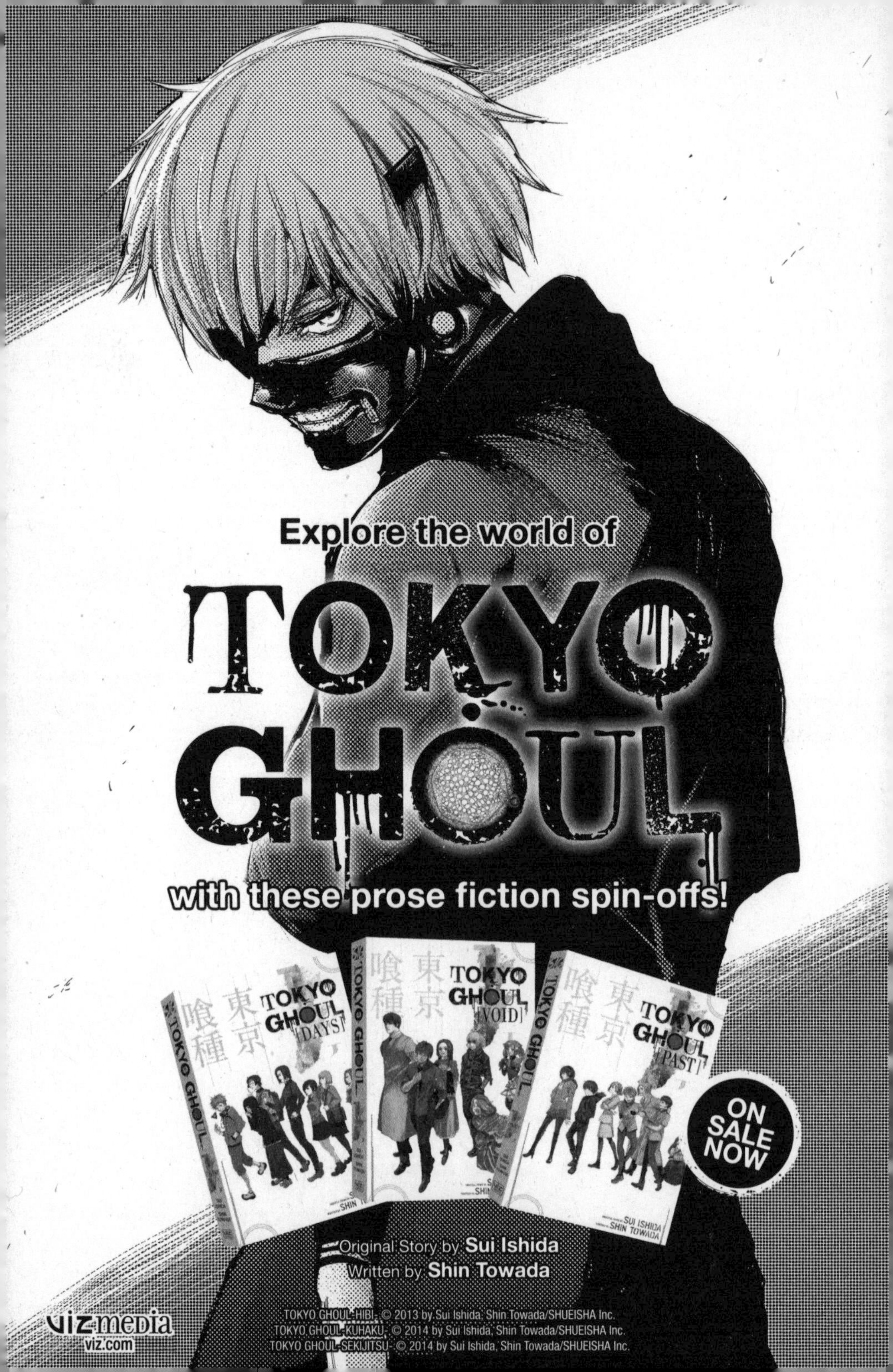

TOKYO GHOUL

This is the last page.
TOKYO GHOUL:re reads right to left.